Che's Travels

Duke University Press
Durham and London
2010

Paulo Drinot, editor

Che's Travels

The Making of a Revolutionary

in 1950s Latin America

© 2010 Duke University Press
All rights reserved
Printed in the United States of
America on acid-free paper ∞
Designed by C. H. Westmoreland
Typeset in Quadraat by
Keystone Typesetting, Inc.
Library of Congress Cataloging-in-
Publication Data appear on the last
printed page of this book.

Contents

Acknowledgments

This book started to take shape at a workshop held at the University of Manchester in September 2006. I am especially grateful to all those who participated as discussants or panelists, and particularly to Patrick Barr-Melej, Maggie Bolton, John Gledhill, Penny Harvey, Alan Knight, Fernanda Peñaloza, Patience Schell, and Peter Wade. Several institutions offered financial support that made the conference possible. I acknowledge gratefully the support of the research funds of the School of Arts, Histories and Cultures (SAHC), the School of Languages, Linguistics and Cultures, and the Centre for Latin American Cultural Studies (CLACS), all at the University of Manchester, as well as the Society for Latin American Studies and the Instituto Cervantes in Manchester. The Cartographic Unit at the University of Manchester helped with the production of the two maps of Che's travels. Special thanks go to Claudia Natteri, who, as CLACS administrator, was largely responsible for the logistics of the workshop, to the staff of the SAHC research office at the University of Manchester, and to Piotr Bienkowski and the staff of the Manchester Museum, where the meetings for the workshop took place. I am grateful to Valerie Millholland, Miriam Angress, and Neal McTighe of Duke University Press for their support in helping me bring this project to fruition. Special thanks go to the two anonymous reviewers chosen by the press. Their comments and suggestions have helped make this a better volume. Finally, in my capacity as the editor of the volume, I thank the contributors to this book for achieving a perfect balance of good humor and discipline throughout the publication process. I think Che would have approved.

Paulo Drinot

Introduction

For better or worse, justly or unjustly, Ernesto "Che" Guevara has
come to represent the history of twentieth-century Latin America in
a way that no other historical figure has done. There are good,
objective reasons for this, not least his participation in the Cuban
Revolution, arguably the single most important, and pivotal, process in twentieth-century Latin American history; a process that
radically redefined Latin America's role in the global political theatre. But there are also other, more subjective reasons, reasons that
historians and social scientists would be foolish to ignore. Che,
it must be said, was an attractive man. His allure derived partly from
his good looks but equally, and perhaps primarily, from the fact
that he appeared to lead the sort of life that many men, and some
women, secretly or avowedly wished to lead themselves. Either because they, too, believed passionately in revolution as the means of
achieving social justice or, more likely, because they associated the
man with adventure and a break from convention, many in Latin
America and throughout the world came to identify with Che, or the
idea of Che. Irrespective of the ways in which the Cuban Revolution
sought to claim Che as its primary symbol, in the half century that
saw the rise of the global media, Che quickly became a global political phenomenon and a cultural artifact that seemed to condense
both the very spirit of revolution (in both a social and an individual
sense) and the history and culture of Latin America and the way that
region came to be understood in a broader global context.

Che's enduring appeal was confirmed recently by the critical and
box office success of Walter Salles's film, The Motorcycle Diaries, released in 2004. Based on the diaries written by Guevara and his
traveling companion, Alberto Granado, during their journey across
South America in the early 1950s, the film revived general interest in

Guevara's life and, particularly, in his prerevolutionary experience.[1] Yet perhaps surprisingly`scholarship has largely ignored not only this period in Guevara's life but also the entire crucial decade for Latin America. The present volume seeks to address this gap in the literature by exploring the Latin America that Guevara encountered on his travels across the continent prior to boarding the *Granma* in late November 1956 on his way to Cuba and, more important, to the revolutionary pantheon. The contributors to this volume explore how Guevara's Latin American travels *produced* Che and how Che simultaneously *produced* Latin America through his travelogues. They do so by using Guevara's travels and, particularly, his travel writings as a window both into the societies that he encountered at that particular historical juncture and into the impact that the experience of those societies had on him. But the contributors also consider how Latin America has *reproduced* Che by examining the various roles assigned to him and the claims made on him by various actors. The chapters in this book thus focus on three interconnected themes: (1) the societies that Che encountered and experienced during his travels across the continent in the early 1950s; (2) Che's representations of those societies in his travelogues and other writings; and (3) Che's broader legacy for the societies he experienced. Each contributor places different weight on each of these themes, reflecting both individual interests and the nature of the documentary material engaged (Che, as we will see, had a lot more to say about Guatemala or Peru than about Colombia or Venezuela).

As various contributors to this volume remark, in some ways the man of the period covered by his early travel writings was little more than a young, petulant, and not very insightful Argentine of no great historical interest other than that he was to turn from the moth of Ernesto Guevara into the butterfly of Che. Yet as a number of historians have shown, relatively "unimportant" or "ordinary" historical figures may prove to be "extraordinary" conduits through which to understand complex historical processes.[2] Of course, unlike Carlo Ginzburg's late medieval peasant miller Menocchio or Miguel Barnet's runaway slave Esteban Montejo, it is not necessary to rescue Guevara from, pace E. P. Thompson, the enormous condescension of posterity.[3] But even during its unimportant and ordinary phase, Guevara's life story presents a unique opportunity to reflect on Latin

America in the 1950s and beyond, as well as on Che as political phenomenon and cultural artifact. It is the relative uniqueness of Guevara's diaries of his travels from Argentina to Mexico, and more generally his "self-musealization," that makes them and him so compelling.[4] There may certainly exist many more such diaries telling of the incredible regional mobility of Latin Americans in the middle decades of the twentieth century. But so far few if any historians have sought to uncover them, let alone make them centerpieces of historical study. Given Guevara's subsequent historical trajectory, a closer examination of his youthful experience that moves beyond the purely biographical seems eminently worthwhile.

By approaching Guevara's early travels as a conduit to historical study, the current volume provides a critical perspective and a fresh interpretative framework on a broad range of themes central to the history of Latin America and the region's global relations. In particular, the volume makes an original incursion into the recent and ongoing scholarly reassessment of Latin America's experience of the Cold War. Various historians, political scientists, and literary theorists have sought to complicate our understanding of this key period by considering how the Cold War was not experienced merely at the level of "high" politics, international relations, or diplomacy but also as "the politicization and internationalization of everyday life and familiar encounters."[5] As the chapters in this volume illustrate, Guevara experienced the Cold War *from below*, as part of everyday life and of familiar encounters (in Chile and Guatemala most notably), before he became one of its principal actors *from above*. Through the conduit of his travels and his travelogues, and through the counterpoint between the travelogues and a number of other historical sources, this volume provides a fresh and provocative perspective on Latin America's experience of the Cold War and the interplay of nationalism and anti-imperialism in a crucial but largely underresearched decade. It does so from the unusual perspective offered by the writings of a young and at times juvenile Argentine man who was transformed by his experience of Latin America and who, although he could not have imagined it when he first kick-started his travel companion's Norton 500 motorcycle in 1951, would in time transform Latin America.

While this volume seeks to contribute to a broader reassessment of how global processes shaped Latin America in the 1950s as a region, it also pays careful attention to the distinct national realities of Latin America and considers how Guevara experienced and understood them. What emerges is a more complex, less heroic, but perhaps more interesting picture of a young Guevara, one that overcomes simplistic hagiographic or demonizing narratives. The young man traveled through a number of countries undergoing profound change as a consequence of the interplay of local and global forces. In Argentina, he encountered the "populist" corporatism of the Perón years; in Peru and Venezuela, the authoritarian regimes of Manuel Odría and Marcos Pérez Jiménez; in Bolivia and Guatemala, social revolutions. With the notable exception of Guatemala, Guevara showed little concern with the politics of the countries he visited. He viewed the wildly diverse Latin America of his travels through young, inquisitive, but ultimately provincial Argentine eyes. His travels awakened in him noble sentiments of pan-Americanism, but he also traded on being Argentine to sponge off the police and the locals (particularly the women). His indignation at the racism and discrimination suffered by Peru's Indians provoked paternalistic and essentializing sentiments. His poorly articulated but strong sense of social justice sat alongside a predilection for scatological schoolboy humor. His penchant for improvisation was continuously checked by the discipline that his asthma imposed on his life.

Che Guevara as a Subject of Historical Inquiry

Despite Che's global iconic status and singular importance to twentieth-century Latin American and global history, there is surprisingly little scholarship on him, as opposed to publications, of which there are plenty. We can broadly divide the literature on Guevara into three categories: the hagiographical, the biographical, and the autobiographical (which includes Guevara's two diaries from his youth, published in English as the *Motorcycle Diaries* and *Back on the Road*, as well as his *Reminiscences of the Cuban Revolutionary War*, *The Diaries of the Revolutionary War in the Congo*, and the *Bolivian Diary*, and a number of speeches and writings collected in various compilations).[6] There are also several banal myth-busters that seek to present Guevara, and by extension the Latin American "new" Left, as the source of all Latin America's ills.[7] In addition, there are some journalistic reconstructions of Che's early travels and even a graphic "biography" of his life.[8] Relatively few scholarly studies exist that seek to analyze Guevara as a historical subject. The three major biographies by Jon Lee Anderson, Jorge Castañeda, and Paco Ignacio Taibo 11, all published in 1997, provide useful and insightful overviews of Guevara's life on which the studies in this volume draw a fair amount. Most scholarly analyses, however, focus on Guevara's revolutionary thought and strategy, including his supposedly anti-dogmatic Marxism and his contributions to revolutionary theory and strategy (and, in some cases, economics).[9] More recently, the image or iconography of Che and its use and manipulation have received considerable attention.[10] The growing interest in Che's image, perhaps a reflection of the ways in which Che, like many other topics of scholarly inquiry, has been subjected to a cultural turn, is reflected in the success of a major exhibition on Che's iconography, held at London's Victoria and Albert Museum.[11]

Through the exploration of the volume's three central themes, the present volume seeks to make a timely and significant contribution to both the historiography of Latin America and the literature on Guevara. As regards the first theme, the societies that Guevara encountered and experienced during travels in the early 1950s, there is very uneven coverage of this decade in the historiography of Latin America. Countries like Argentina (Peronism), Bolivia (the revolution of 1952), and Guatemala (the coup of 1954) are well served because of the important social and political events and processes that occurred in the period, but others, such as Chile, Peru, and Mexico, have received only sporadic coverage. There exist, moreover, no multicountry studies of this period to match those published in the past few decades on the 1930s and 1940s.[12] This book therefore proves unique in providing a multicountry perspective on a decade that, certainly in the cases of Peru or Mexico, historians have only recently begun to examine. Bringing together specialists from across Latin America, each leg of Guevara's journey is analyzed in new depth to explore the distinctive societies, histories, politics, and cultures he encountered.

As regards the second theme, how Guevara represented the societies he experienced in the early 1950s in his travelogues and other writings, most analyses of Guevara's writings have focused on his Cuban and Bolivian diaries. When not depressingly hagiographical, these studies have tended to emphasize the lessons that can be drawn from Guevara's guerrilla campaigns and personality in terms of either the pursuit of guerrilla warfare in other contexts (such as in the case of the work of Régis Debray and his *Revolution in the Revolution*) or the emergence of a new (revolutionary) man for others to emulate (such as in the case of the pronouncements and writings on Che of philosopher Jean-Paul Sartre, Argentine author Julio Cortázar, and others).[13] Few scholars have examined seriously and critically what Guevara had to say about Latin America.[14] And yet, as the various chapters in this book clearly demonstrate, the travelogues he produced in the early 1950s contain a wealth of information that can be analyzed to get a sense of how Guevara understood and represented the societies he encountered and how his experience of these societies shaped his worldview. In its essays the present book moves beyond the traditional narratives on Guevara and offers an interpretation of his formative years based on a careful analysis of his ideas and impressions of Latin America, which challenges hagiographical accounts and complicates our understanding of the man. A broad range of factors (his social background, his pursuit of adventure, his intellectual interests) shaped his idea of Latin America, and they predisposed him to see certain things in a particular way and some things not at all.

Finally, as regards the third theme, Guevara's broader legacy for the societies he experienced in the early 1950s, it is surprising that given the ubiquity of Che's image in Latin America (on mudguards and T-shirts, for example), few scholars have sought to systematically study his legacy in the region.[15] Most available analyses of Guevara's legacy are uncritically celebratory in tone.[16] Few scholars, and particularly few historians, have given serious attention to how Che is remembered or memorialized and the uses to which his memory has been put, both by those who claim to follow his example and by those who see him as the source of Latin America's ills. And yet this living legacy is key to understanding how people relate to both the revolutionary and the counterrevolutionary projects that have shaped and continue to shape Latin America. The various guerrilla movements that arose in the region between the 1960s and the 1980s in various ways found inspiration in Guevara's revolutionary example and in his ideas about the revolutionary *foco*. Today, Che remains a key political referent for political projects in Venezuela and Bolivia but also for various groups involved in struggles for inclusionary citizenship and social justice, from indigenous activists in Guatemala to *piqueteros* in Argentina, from students in Mexico City to *cocaleros* in the Bolivian Yungas. But Che has also been "indigenized" as a cultural artifact throughout the region—appropriated as a cultural and, in some cases, religious symbol by myriad Latin Americans who associate Che with values and aspirations key to their self-definition. By examining seriously, and critically, Che's legacy in the various countries that he visited in the early 1950s, the contributors to this volume seek to further complicate our understanding of the various ways in which the man, as both political phenomenon and cultural artifact, has shaped and continues to shape Latin America.

A Word on Sources

All the contributors to this volume have to some degree based their essays on Guevara's writings. Two travelogues, *The Motorcycle Diaries* and *Back on the Road*, form a connecting thread that links all contributions. Additional texts are used: most important, the travelogue written by Granado, Guevara's travel companion during the first trip, but also the memoirs of those who knew Guevara intimately, such as his father, Ernesto Guevara Lynch, his first wife, Hilda Gadea, and his friends and traveling companions from the second trip, Calica Ferrer and Ricardo Rojo.[17] In some ways, Guevara's travelogues should be seen as part of a long tradition of travel writing in Latin America, to which historians and other scholars are increasingly paying attention.[18] The publishing success of Guevara's travelogues, and indeed the box office success of Salles's film, of course primarily derives from Che's iconic status. But the diaries, and the experience of travel they narrate, are in themselves compelling. As Casey Blanton notes, "the travel narrative is a compelling and seductive form of story telling. Its reader is swept along the surface of the text by the pure forward motion of the journey while being initiated into strange and often dangerous new territory."[19] But the diaries also compel because they appear to take us on a journey of discovery of their author, a journey "where the hero is seen as one who travels on a path of self-improvement and integration, doing battle with 'others' who are unresolved parts of himself or herself."[20] This seductive quality of travel writing, heightened in this case by the iconic nature of the travelogue's author, can help occlude that Guevara's prose, like "all travel writing, as a process of inscription and appropriation, spins webs of colonizing power."[21] Put more simply, travelogues are not only narratives about travel but also narratives about, and constitutive of, power. Like, say, the authorized version of Captain Cook's travels, Guevara's travel writing is "a composite, fractured and spatialized construction."[22]

The use of Guevara's travel diaries as historical sources thus presents a number of problems to the historian. Yet these problems do not differ significantly from the challenges that all sources present. True, both Guevara and others, including the Cuban authorities, have reworked these texts for reasons of either self-fashioning or political benefit. Guevara explicitly notes his own "doctoring" of the evidence in The Motorcycle Diaries: "The person who wrote these notes passed away the moment his feet touched Argentine soil. The person who reorganizes and polishes them, me, is no longer, at least I'm not the person I once was."[23] But historians are well aware that all texts are doctored in one way or another. That Guevara's travelogues have been "reorganized" and "polished" in no way undermines their utility as historical sources. Even if "original" versions of these travelogues existed, historians would still have to approach them in much the same way that the contributors to this volume explore the versions available to them (i.e., fully aware that they are textual constructions of truth rather than truth itself). Differences between versions could provide useful hooks on which to hang discussions about, say, what either Guevara or the Cuban authorities believed should and should not be included in the diaries and what such an inclusion or omission tells us, for example, about how the Cuban government sought to construct or control the image of its most important icon. But the current volume does not seek to engage in these discussions. Instead, the contributors approach the diaries as cultural artifacts, and Guevara's life story itself as a cultural production, that can be usefully studied to provide a scholarly evaluation of the ways in which Guevara "produced" the Latin America he encountered in the 1950s and, in turn, of the ways in which the Latin America of the 1950s, and of later decades, "produced" and "reproduced" Che.

Chapter Structure

The book's structure follows Guevara's itineraries during his two journeys as narrated in *The Motorcycle Diaries* (Argentina-Chile-Peru-Colombia-Venezuela) and *Back on the Road* (Argentina-Bolivia-Peru-Guatemala-Mexico). Of course, Guevara visited several other countries during these two journeys, including the United States in the first trip and Ecuador and all the other Central American countries in the second. Unfortunately, it was not possible to include chapters on these other countries. The choice of the countries that Guevara visited as the basis for each chapter is neither inevitable nor unproblematic. It has the advantage of revealing local nuances that only national-level case studies, which draw on the contributors' country-focused expertise, can provide. In addition to focusing to different degrees on each of the volume's central themes, the authors have drawn on various methods and theoretical perspectives. Several have chosen to examine Guevara's travel narratives in counterpoint to those of other contemporary travelers. Others have turned to testimony and oral histories to examine the ways in which Che is memorialized. These choices reflect each author's methodological preferences and theoretical proclivities, as well as the particular nature of their personal expertise. They point to, and demonstrate, the diverse and productive interpretative and analytical roads that different scholars have chosen to take as they follow Guevara on his travels from Argentina to Mexico.

We begin, then, in Argentina, where, as Eduardo Elena shows, Guevara's experience of travel, which had begun far earlier than 1951, needs to be understood in the broader context of two key developments in mid-twentieth-century Argentina: the emergence of mass tourism and the rise of nationalism. Both developments shaped and were shaped by the advent of Peronism. Guevara sought to distance himself from the tourist masses, consciously opting for a practice of travel that marked him as a nontourist. This option, Elena suggests, reflected a distinctive position vis-à-vis the nationalism that Peronism sought to champion. Like other Argentines of his social class, including members of his own family, Guevara was skeptical of Juan Perón. However, he recognized more readily than most that Peronism brought real material and symbolic benefits to

Legend:
——— Overland route
- - - - Sea passage
━━━ Air travel

U.S.A.

Atlantic Ocean

Venezuela

Colombia

Peru

Bolivia

Pacific Ocean

Chile

Argentina

1 Córdoba
2 Buenos Aires
3 Miramar
4 Bahia Blanca
5 San Martín de los Andes
6 Bariloche
7 Osorno
8 Valdivia
9 Temuco
10 Santiago
11 Valparaiso
12 Antofagasta
13 Chuquicamata
14 Iquique
15 Arica
16 Tarata
17 Puno
18 Cuzco
19 Machu Picchu
20 Cuzco
21 Abancay
22 Ayacucho
23 Huancayo
24 San Ramón
25 Lima
26 Pucallpa
27 Iquitos
28 San Pablo colony
29 Leticia
30 Bogotá
31 Caracas
32 Miami
33 Buenos Aires

Map 1. Ernesto Guevara's first journey as recounted in *The Motorcycle Diaries*.

Legend:
— Overland route
- - - Sea passage

Mexico
24 25
23
Cuba
26

Honduras
see inset
Guatemala
18
El Salvador
Nicaragua
16 17
Panama
Costa Rica
15 13 14

Atlantic Ocean

Colombia

Ecuador
12
9 11
10 8
Peru

7
6
5
4
3
Bolivia
2

Pacific Ocean

Chile
1
Argentina

Inset:
22
20
21
19

1 Buenos Aires
2 La Quiaca
3 La Paz
4 Puno
5 Cuzco
6 Machu Picchu
7 Lima
8 Piura
9 Tumbes
10 Talara
11 Huaquillas
12 Guayaquil
13 Balboa
14 Panama City
15 Golfito
16 Puntarenas
17 San José
18 Managua
19 San Salvador
20 Guatemala City
21 San Salvador
22 Guatemala City
23 Mitla
24 Mexico City
25 Tuxpan
26 Playa las Coloradas

Map 2. Ernesto Guevara's second journey as recounted in *Back on the Road*.

the Argentine poor. But in choosing to travel beyond the borders of his native country, Guevara tacitly rejected Perón's narrow nationalism in favor of a more expansive notion that reflected an embrace of pan-Americanism as the basis of his awakening anti-imperialism. In considering his legacy in the Argentine context, Elena suggestively argues that it is possible to discern in Guevara's favored approach to seeing the world elements of his political ideology and praxis, one marked by the gradual replacement of curiosity by increasingly fixed convictions as the impetus for travel.

Patience A. Schell examines Guevara's experience of travel in Chile in counterpoint to the experiences of a number of European and U.S. travelers. Schell shows how Guevara and Granado reproduced in their observations a series of tropes common in much of the travel writing on Chile. Themes such as the beauty of Chilean women, the generosity of Chile's inhabitants, and the bounty of the country's natural resources shaped the two Argentines' travel accounts much in the same way as those of a German tourist, a British car enthusiast, a *National Geographic* reporter, and a Maryknoll nun. But these tropes, which Chileans seem to have been generally proud of, Schell argues, obscured the changes that Chilean society was experiencing and that, for the most part, these travelers paid little attention to. Thus Chile's beautiful women were not only increasingly active in the workplace but also in the political sphere. The generosity of Chile's population was all the more remarkable given the acute difficulties faced by the Chilean economy in the 1950s, difficulties disproportionately affecting the country's poor. Indeed, the semblance of natural bounty that so many travelers commented on hid the highly unequal distribution of land that left an increasing number of Chileans trying to make a living in the slums of Santiago. Ironically, though Guevara seems to have at best glimpsed some of the developments, they were at the root of the tensions that would shape Chile's turn, first, to socialism and, then, to brutal dictatorship in the 1970s, processes in which Guevara played a key role as a source of inspiration for some and as a symbol of ungodly communism for others.

As Schell notes, Guevara differed from other travelers in one respect: he was greatly interested in Chile's indigenous peoples. This interest, as the essay by Paulo Drinot shows, also proves central to Guevara's observations on Peru, the only country that Guevara visited twice during his two journeys across the continent. Like Schell, Drinot examines Guevara's observations of the country in counterpoint to those of other travelers. Guevara had little to say about the political situation in the country, and his diaries do not tell us much about Odría's dictatorship or the situation faced by political parties such as the American Popular Revolutionary Alliance (APRA, a populist party) or the Peruvian Communist Party. In contrast, Guevara wrote extensively about Peru's indigenous peoples and what he perceived as their wretched existence. Drinot argues that although Guevara wrote sympathetically about the indigenous, he reproduced racist views that essentialized the Indian. Guevara's understanding of the indigenous, and indeed of Peruvian society more broadly, Drinot shows, was shaped by his reading of indigenista authors. This predisposed him to view Andean society in ways that made it difficult for him to perceive how the indigenous challenged the subordinate roles assigned to them by Peruvian society to make claims for citizenship. Like Guevara, Drinot argues, those Peruvians who sought to emulate his revolutionary example in the 1960s had a limited understanding of the various forces shaping Peruvian society. Not surprisingly, their attempts to apply Guevara's model of revolution proved costly failures. In some ways the revolutionary project of the Shining Path (Sendero Luminoso), although overtly non-Guevarist, was better able to exploit the tensions at the heart of Peruvian society. However, its brutality and the harsh reaction from the Peruvian armed forces that it engendered produced some seventy thousand victims and did nothing to address the exclusion and poverty that had stirred Guevara's empathy toward Peru's indigenous peoples.

In contrast to Chile and Peru, Guevara spent little time in Colombia, and he recorded few of his impressions of the country in his diaries. But as Malcolm Deas shows, Guevara had a deep impact on Colombia, an impact that in some ways remains in evidence today and to a greater extent than in any other Latin American country. Deas notes that Guevara arrived in Colombia during the country's most repressive phase of the twentieth century—the military government of General Gustavo Rojas Pinilla—and in a broader context of acute sectarian guerrilla violence with deep roots in Colombian history. Deas argues that the Colombian guerrillas of the 1950s were not of the Guevarist kind. Though in some ways agrarian by virtue of their composition, they pursued a political struggle mirroring the broader one at the heart of Colombian society, not a social struggle for land. The influence of the Cuban Revolution and of Guevara's own revolutionary example and thinking would change this, giving a new life to older guerrillas and bringing into existence a whole new group of revolutionaries. As a consequence, Guevara's legacy has endured far longer in Colombia than in most other countries he visited in the 1950s.

Guevara also spent little time in Venezuela. As various contributors to the volume remark, he was far more enthused by the rural than the urban Latin America he encountered, and this may account for the brevity of his commentary on the cities he visited. Guevara's narrative of the few days he spent in Caracas nevertheless prove revealing. As Judith Ewell notes, Guevara largely made disparaging comments about the city's urban poor, and here as in Peru, his impressions were shaped by racialized assumptions. Guevara seems to have largely misread or failed to see the changes afoot in Caracas, particularly those that, at least partially, resulted from the country's increasing "Americanization," itself a consequence of the country's oil wealth. Venezuela, the destination of his first trip, was also that of Guevara's second. He never made it there the second time, but he did meet Rómulo Betancourt, deposed by Pérez Jiménez in 1948, in Costa Rica, along with a number of other political exiles. The two men differed greatly and seem to have thought little of each other, but the meeting, Ewell argues, proved important for Guevara's political development. It confirmed his negative views of a group of reformist political leaders, including Victor Raúl Haya de la Torre, José Figueres, and Víctor Paz Estenssoro, and of the political projects he associated with them, particularly with regard to the role that those projects gave to the United States in Latin America. Finally, Ewell considers Guevara's impact on Venezuela, both direct and indirect. He played an active role in the formation of Venezuelan guerrilla movements in the 1960s, although these, like many others, proved unsuccessful. Che's indirect influence has proved more enduring. He remains a powerful spiritual and political symbol in Venezuela, as evidenced by his incorporation into the pantheon of spirits in the religion of María Lionza and into the pantheon of heroes that constitute the genealogy of Hugo Chávez's Bolivarian revolution.

Bolivia was the first country that Guevara visited during his second journey. It was also, of course, the country to which he returned in a fatal mission to ignite a continental *foco* in the late 1960s. Ann Zulawski discusses the genealogy of the revolutionary situation that Guevara encountered during the few weeks he spent in the country in 1953. By the time of his arrival in La Paz, Guevara appears to have acquired a greater interest in the politics of the countries he visited (although his main motivation for travel remained a thirst for adventure). As Zulawski discusses, Guevara made a series of perceptive comments about the tensions at the heart of the revolutionary project that had brought the Revolutionary Nationalist Movement (MNR) to power. These tensions resulted from the uneasy alliance of peasants, miners, and middle-class reformists who had come together to end the oligarchic order but who pursued different and in some cases antagonistic interests. Zulawski contrasts Guevara's pithy observations on the MNR leadership to his limited engagement with the miners and particularly the indigenous peasantry, which he continued to view in largely simplistic and essentializing terms. In contrast to other contemporary travelers studied by Zulawski, such as Lilo Linke, a German woman who lived in Ecuador and traveled in the region, and Alicia Ortiz, an Argentine literary essayist and travel writer, Guevara seems to have found little time to discuss the changes in Bolivia with those people that his emergent social conscience made him identify with. Had he done so, Zulawski suggests, he might well have gained a better understanding of the revolutionary and, indeed, counterrevolutionary forces that were beginning to shape the country and that would shape the outcome of his revolutionary venture in the late 1960s. Still, despite or, rather, because of his death there, Che has acquired a powerful presence in Bolivia, where some revere him as a folk saint, while others, including President Evo Morales, embrace him as a symbol of social justice.

As in Bolivia, Guevara encountered a social revolution in Guatemala, though the latter was in the process of unraveling. Cindy Forster discusses the ways in which Guevara's experience of the last few months of Guatemala's "time of freedom" shaped his understanding, and later his practice and theorization, of revolution. Central to this development was Guevara's interaction in Guatemala with a broad group of political exiles, including his first wife, the Peruvian Hilda Gadea, and people attracted to Guatemala by the revolutionary changes that the government of Jacobo Arbenz had initiated, such as the U.S. academic Harold White. These connections exposed Guevara to Marxism. But equally, and perhaps more central to his political development, was the experience of the CIA-backed coup of 1954. As Forster shows, Guevara drew a number of conclusions from this experience regarding the reasons for the demise of the Guatemalan revolution, and these conclusions would shape the ways in which he would approach revolution in Cuba and elsewhere. Forster argues that although Guevara, much as in Peru and Bolivia, reproduced racist views of Guatemala's indigenous peoples, he nevertheless expressed respect for Indian culture; by the 1960s his views on race had begun to change, making the concept play a key role in his thinking on the revolutionary context in Guatemala. This explains, Forster suggests, the extent to which the Guatemalan guerrillas of the 1970s and 1980s, and particularly the Guerrilla Army of the Poor, embraced Che as a chief source of inspiration. It also explains the Argentine's enduring relevance to the struggles of the country's indigenous population to resist and reverse their historical marginalization.

Mexico was, in a sense, where Guevara's travel adventure ended and where Che's journey began. As is well known, Guevara's meeting with Fidel and Raúl Castro in Mexico set in motion the series of events that would result in the Cuban Revolution, which in turn radically altered Latin America's role in the Cold War and in the broader global political theatre. Eric Zolov frames Guevara's transformative experience in Mexico in the context of dramatic postwar changes in Mexico's revolutionary process but also in that of Mexico's place in the cultural revolution of the 1950s. Miguel Alemán's so-called counterrevolution had moved Mexico away from *cardenista* revolutionary policy and into the sphere of U.S. economic and political influence and the logic of the Cold War. But at the same time, 1950s Mexico was a key site of an emerging counterculture to which bohemians such as Jack Kerouac and Allen Ginsberg came to escape their own society's restrictions. In many ways, Zolov suggests, Guevara, like Kerouac and Ginsberg, was a bohemian guided in his travels by a spirit of adventure and a desire to engage the Other. His encounter with the Castro brothers, Zolov shows, gave a new direction to his spirit of adventure and transformed the carefree bohemian into a heroic revolutionary. During the early 1960s, when Mexico's own revolutionary heroes were discredited by association with an increasingly authoritarian regime, Che symbolized an emergent new Left in the country. Yet the experience of Tlatelolco (the student massacre of 1968) and a desire among the young to reclaim Mexico's revolutionary heroes led to the revaluation of national figures such as Miguel Hidalgo, José María Morelos, and especially Emiliano Zapata. Still, Che remains for many Mexicans and, indeed, for many Latin Americans, a powerful symbol of international solidarity and of the struggle for social justice.

We thus begin in late 1951, as Ernesto Guevara is preparing to set off on his voyage of adventure and self-discovery. This first journey from Argentina to Venezuela and (via Miami) back to Argentina, and the later journey of 1953, from Argentina to Mexico and then Cuba, were experiences of travel that shaped in profound ways not only Guevara's life but, eventually and indirectly, the lives of all Latin Americans and the very course of world history in the second half of the twentieth century. Guevara's legacy is examined in this book largely in its Latin American context. But it is clearly a global legacy, one at once banal and profound: it is at once a T-shirt practically devoid of meaning and a radical political vision polarizing the world and resonating on every continent in particular ways. Guevara's revolutionary ideals and goals may no longer have the purchase they once had, but the man and his legacy continue to influence in multiple ways how people across the world understand and imagine their self-fashioning as individuals and their collective past and future. This book demonstrates the important role that Guevara's travels in the 1950s had in determining his view of the world and his later revolutionary trajectory and practice. But it also, and perhaps primarily, draws our attention to and begins to answer how and why Che's travels in Latin America shaped the history of the world.

Notes

I am grateful to Jelke Boesten, Laurence Brown, Patience Schell, Eric Zolov, and two anonymous reviewers for their comments on earlier versions of this introduction.
1 It remains to be seen whether the release in 2008 of Steven Soderbergh's two films, *Che Part 1* and *Che Part 2*, or *The Argentine* and *Guerrilla*, based on Guevara's Cuban and Bolivian diaries, will create a similar

revival of interest in Guevara's life and revolutionary experience in the 1960s.

2 See Natalie Zemon Davis, *The Return of Martin Guerre* (Cambridge: Harvard University Press, 1983); Carlo Ginzburg, *The Cheese and the Worms: The Cosmos of a Sixteenth-Century Miller* (Baltimore: Johns Hopkins University Press, 1992); Natalie Zemon Davis, *Trickster Travels: A Sixteenth-Century Muslim between Worlds* (New York: Hill and Wang, 2006); Linda Colley, *The Ordeal of Elizabeth Marsh: A Woman in World History* (London: Harper Collins, 2007).

3 See Esteban Montejo, *The Autobiography of a Runaway Slave*, ed. Miguel Barnet, trans. Jocasta Innes (New York: Pantheon, 1968).

4 On "self-musealization," see Andreas Huyssen, "Present Pasts: Media, Politics, Amnesia," *Public Culture* 12:1 (2000), 21–38.

5 Greg Grandin, *The Last Colonial Massacre: Latin America in the Cold War* (Chicago: University of Chicago Press, 2004), 17; see also Jean Franco, *The Decline and Fall of the Lettered City: Latin America in the Cold War* (Cambridge: Harvard University Press, 2002); Marcos Cueto, *Cold War, Deadly Fevers: Malaria Eradication in Mexico, 1955–1975* (Baltimore: Johns Hopkins University Press, 2007); and, especially, Gilbert Joseph and Daniela Spenser, eds., *In from the Cold: Latin America's New Encounter with the Cold War* (Durham: Duke University Press, 2008).

6 Several biographies, of differing quality, were published to coincide with the thirtieth anniversary of Guevara's death. See, in particular, Jon Lee Anderson, *Che: A Revolutionary Life* (New York: Grove, 1997); Jorge G. Castañeda, *Compañero: The Life and Death of Che Guevara*, trans. Marina Castañeda (New York: Alfred Knopf, 1997); Paco Ignacio Taibo II, *Guevara, Also Known as Che*, trans. Martin Roberts (New York: St Martin's Press, 1997). A recent addition to the biographical corpus is Horacio López Das Eiras, *Ernestito Guevara: Antes de ser el Che* (Córdoba, Argentina: Ediciones del Boulevard, 2006).

7 Alvaro Vargas Llosa, *The Che Guevara Myth and the Future of Liberty* (Oakland, Calif.: Independent Institute, 2006); Humberto Fontova, *Exposing the Real Che Guevara and the Useful Idiots Who Idealize Him* (New York: Sentinel, 2007).

8 Patrick Symmes, *Chasing Che: A Freewheeling Adventure through the Wide Open Spaces of South America on the Trail of Che Guevara* (London: Robinson, 2000); Spain Rodriguez, *Che: A Graphic Biography*, ed. Paul Buhle (London: Verso, 2008).

9 The most interesting study in this vein is Paul Dosal, *Comandante Che: Guerrilla Soldier, Commander, and Strategist, 1956–1967* (University Park: Pennsylvania State University Press, 2003), but see also Michael Lowy, *La pensée de Che Guevara* (Paris: François Maspero, 1970); Che Guevara,

Guerrilla Warfare: With an Introduction and Case Studies by Brian Loveman and Thomas Davies Jr. (Manchester: Manchester University Press, 1986); Carlos Tablada Pérez, Che Guevara: Economics and Politics in the Transition to Socialism (New York: Pathfinder, 1989); Matt D. Childs, "An Historical Critique of the Emergence and Evolution of Ernesto Che Guevara's Foco Theory," Journal of Latin American Studies 27:3 (1995), 593–624. See, also, Peter McLaren, Che Guevara, Paulo Freire, and the Pedagogy of Revolution (Lanham, Md.: Rowman and Littlefield, 2000); and Mike Gonzalez, Che Guevara and the Cuban Revolution (London: Bookmark Books, 2004). For a recent study that considers Che's role in Cuba's economic restructuring following the revolution, see Helen Yaffe, Che Guevara: The Economics of Revolution, (Basingstoke, UK: Palgrave Macmillan, 2009).

10 David Kunzle, Che Guevara: Icon, Myth, and Message (Los Angeles: UCLA Fowler Museum of Cultural History in collaboration with the Center for the Study of Political Graphics, 1997); Paulo Drinot, "La imagen del Che," Márgenes (Peru), no. 16 (1998), 281–85; Paul Dosal, "San Ernesto de la Higuera; The Resurrection of Che Guevara," Death, Dismemberment, and Memory: Body Politics in Latin America, ed. Lyman L. Johnson (Albuquerque: University of New Mexico Press, 2004), 317–340. Ariana Hernández-Regnant, "Copyrighting Che: Art and Authorship under Cuban Late Socialism," Public Culture 16:1 (2004), 1–29; Phyllis Passariello, "Desperately Seeking Something: Che Guevara as Secular Saint," The Making of Saints: Contesting Sacred Ground, ed. James F. Hopgood (Tuscaloosa: University of Alabama Press, 2005), 75–89. See also the chapter on Guevara, which includes a discussion of the Motorcycle Diaries in its textual and filmed versions, in Erik Kristofer Ching, Christina Buckley, and Angélica Lozano-Alonso, Reframing Latin America: A Cultural Theory Reading of the Nineteenth and Twentieth Centuries (Austin: University of Texas Press, 2007), 237–68.

11 Tricia Ziff, Che Guevara: Revolutionary and Icon (London: V&A Publications, 2006).

12 See, for example, Rosemary Thorp, ed., Latin America in the 1930s: The Role of the Periphery in World Crisis (New York: St Martin's Press, 1984); Leslie Bethell and Ian Roxborough, eds., Latin America between the Second World War and the Cold War, 1944–1948 (New York: Cambridge University Press, 1992).

13 Régis Debray, Revolution in the Revolution, trans. Bobbye Ortiz (New York: MR Press, 1967). On Sartre and Cortazar's views on Che, see Paulo Drinot, "La imagen del Che," Márgenes (Peru), no. 16 (1998), 281–85.

14 An important exception is Ricardo Piglia's brilliant essay, "Ernesto Guevara: The Last Reader," Journal of Latin American Cultural Studies 17:3 (2008), 261–77.

15 A notable exception is Juan Ignacio Siles del Valle's *La guerrilla del Che y la narrativa boliviana* (1996) quoted in Richard Harris, "Reflections on Che Guevara's Legacy," *Latin American Perspectives* 25:4 (1998), 19–32.

16 See James Petras, "Latin America: Thirty Years after Che," *Monthly Review* 49:5 (1997), 8–21; Gordon H. McCormick, "Che Guevara: The Legacy of a Revolutionary Man," *World Policy Journal* 14:4 (1997–98), 63–79.

17 Alberto Granado, *Traveling with Che Guevara: The Making of a Revolutionary*, trans. Lucía Álvarez de Toledo (New York: Newmarket Press, 2004); Ernesto Guevara Lynch, *Mi hijo el Che* (Buenos Aires: Planeta, 1984); Hilda Gadea, *Ernesto: A Memoir of Che Guevara*, trans. Carmen Molina and Walter I. Bradbury (London: W. H. Allen, 1973); Carlos "Calica" Ferrer, *De Ernesto al Che: El segundo viaje de Guevara por Latinoamérica* (Buenos Aires: Marea Editorial, 2005); Ricardo Rojo, *My Friend Che*, trans. Julian Casart (New York: Grove, 1968).

18 See, for example, Ingrid E. Fey and Karen Racine, eds., *Strange Pilgrimages: Exile, Travel, and National Identity in Latin America, 1800–1900s* (Wilmington, Del.: Scholarly Resources, 2000); and Jürgen Buchenau, ed. and trans., *Mexico Otherwise: Modern Mexico in the Eyes of Foreign Observers* (Albuquerque: University of New Mexico Press, 2005).

19 Casey Blanton, *Travel Writing: The Self and the World* (London: Routledge, 2002), 2.

20 Ibid., 3.

21 James S. Duncan and Derek Gregory, eds., *Writes of Passage: Reading Travel Writing* (London, Routledge, 1999), 3.

22 Ibid., 3.

23 Ernesto Guevara, *The Motorcycle Diaries: A Journey Around South America*, trans. Alexandra Keeble (London: Harper Perennial, 1995), 32; emphasis added.

Eduardo Elena

Point of Departure
Travel and Nationalism in
Ernesto Guevara's Argentina

The story of Che Guevara is one of a series of personal transformations—from asthmatic youth to medical student, and then to wanderer, *guerrillero*, revolutionary leader, and, finally, martyr. The fundamental role played by travel throughout these changes is widely
acknowledged.[1] In fact, the one constant in Guevara's short life was
its unsettled nature: he never remained long in one place during his
youth, and he moved from country to country as an adult, embark-
ing on one voyage or mission after another. In the standard account
of his life story, it is the 1951–52 journey across South America that
marked Guevara's political awakening as he was pulled away from
his familiar life in Argentina and exposed to a continent of brutal extremes. This trip—recounted in Guevara's private journal and
published after his death (and more recently in English as *The Motorcycle Diaries*)—has thus attracted great attention from biographers,
commentators, and filmmakers. For all the insights provided by
these works, however, they usually consider this voyage in isolation, as an assertion of willful independence. Such an interpretation
hardly seems surprising, given that Guevara's self-presentation en-
courages this view, and it would later feed into the cult of heroism of
El Che. But one is left with a distorted picture of an individual
moving freely through a static landscape, as if he were the only
historical actor in motion during this time and place. As a consequence, we fail to see Guevara's position within the broader social
field of his homeland Argentina and the rest of Latin America, a
region whose population was increasingly on the move in the post–
Second World War era.

This essay aims to situate Guevara the traveler in the historical context of 1950s Argentina. In particular, it examines his early journeys from the vantage of two major contemporary trends: mid-twentieth-century mass migration and tourism; and the nationalist politics of the Peronist era (1943–55). This approach is premised on the assumption that to understand this particular traveler, one must examine his point of departure—in other words, the possibilities open to him at this moment and the conditions that he reacted against. Guevara came of age in a time marked by the regular movement of people across Argentina, from rural residents relocating to urban areas to short-term leisure travel. His decision to traverse vast expanses of his home country and Latin America can be seen in sharper relief by investigating these social displacements and cultural trends that accompanied them. This essay considers these historical subjects primarily through Guevara's earliest travel writings. During the journeys of his youth in Argentina, Guevara formulated his travel method—as reflected in his choice of itinerary, modes of transportation, and contact with the physical landscape and its inhabitants. *Method* is perhaps too rigorous a term to describe these wanderings, but it serves the useful purpose of grouping together his habits and preferences as a traveler, all of which reveal much about postwar Argentina and Guevara's place within it.

This type of historical analysis runs the danger of being reductive, that is, of explaining individual thought and action as the automatic outcome of structural pressures, political forces, and abstract social categories. To be sure, a measure of "sociologizing" may be welcome in this case, if only to counteract the inevitable mythologizing of El Che. But as we shall see, one of the distinguishing features of Guevara's early travels was, in fact, their anticonformist character. His ambitious trek across South America, on a minimal budget and just shy of earning his medical degree, clearly bucked convention. At the most obvious level, he pursued a self-conscious goal to evade acceptable practices of tourism. Although Guevara's rebellion was not yet aimed at fomenting revolution, his travels offered a gesture of rejection against prevailing class norms, cultural expectations, and the political trends of the 1950s. In contesting certain features of this milieu, however, Guevara continued to cling to others, and his travel writings reflect earlier paradigms of exploration and affinities with contemporary nationalist perspectives.

In keeping with the objectives of this volume, the essay also departs from a purely biographical analysis by reconsidering the history of postwar Argentina from the vantage of Guevara's travel accounts. The pages that follow will consider which central historical developments in his homeland Guevara saw (and which ones he did not see). Principal among these was the eruption of Peronism as the nation's largest political force. Discussions of Guevara's youth have tended to revolve around his somewhat perplexing distance from the partisan convulsions of Peronist rule. Nevertheless, a closer look at Guevara's travel writings reveals the inroads made by Peronist politics into everyday life across the national territory. Juan and Eva Perón's government accelerated ongoing social trends, such as urbanization, rural migration, and popular tourism (partly through state-sponsored programs). Despite his best efforts the young Guevara found it impossible to extricate himself fully from Peronism, even after he left behind his country's borders.

The essay begins by considering Guevara's place in the history of migration and travel in mid-twentieth-century Argentina. It then probes Peronist-era trends that shaped the parameter of his travels (such as the nationalist fascination with rural spaces). It concludes with a brief discussion of Guevara's return to Argentina as El Che, the embodiment of revolutionary action. There are a number of obstacles to examining Guevara and his travels in this manner. One relies by necessity on a critical reading of Guevara's own writings, yet they reflect the priorities of a youth seeking adventure in foreign lands, rather than meditations on his homeland. While Guevara and his companion Alberto Granado devoted more than a month to crisscrossing southern Argentina, the journals that comprise *The Motorcycle Diaries* are devoted primarily to their experiences elsewhere. In addition, these travel writings have a complicated provenance, which makes it difficult to address the scope of subsequent revisions and editing.[2] With an awareness of these interpretive dilemmas, the current essay draws on the *Diaries* and a range of other materials: additional Guevara writings, Peronist-era political and cultural sources, and secondary biographical works. What emerges from this analysis is a better appreciation for the historical significance of Guevara's choices as a traveler, including how his earliest journeys within Argentina blazed the trail for encounters elsewhere in Latin America.

On the Road in Argentina

Contrary to conventional wisdom, the 1951–52 journey recounted in *The Motorcycle Diaries* did not constitute Guevara's first travel experience, nor even his first trip abroad. As his biographers have shown, Guevara traveled extensively in his teenage years and early twenties, covering thousands of kilometers across Argentina by hitchhiking, bicycling, and other means. Along the way he crossed paths with other Argentines circulating throughout their country in ever larger numbers. Such is the emphasis on Guevara's exceptionality, however, that few observers have stopped to consider his relationship to these travelers or to the phenomenon of postwar migration more generally. In fact, Guevara took pains to distinguish himself from his contemporaries and embraced a different paradigm of travel, shaped by readings of explorer accounts, conversations with political refugees, and youthful adventures on a shoestring budget. It is therefore hard to imagine Guevara in the shadow of mass migration, to see him surrounded by crowds at a train station or lingering with vacationers at a popular resort. Yet his writings reveal glimpses of encounters not only with rural migrants seeking work but also with other urban Argentines who had taken to the road in search of leisure. Guevara's reactions to these chance meetings suggest much about his own social position and effort to define an alternative approach to travel.

Migration was a way of life for Guevara and his family. Both of his parents came from privileged backgrounds and boasted distinguished family names, but they were the downwardly mobile black sheep of the fold. Financial pressures contributed to an unsettled upbringing for the family's children, albeit one still characterized by middle-class comforts and connections to wealthy relatives. As the household provider, Ernesto Guevara Lynch went from one failed business venture to the next, and the family moved frequently within Argentina. Born in the city of Rosario, the future Che grew up on a yerba mate plantation in Misiones, in the provincial hill town of Alta Gracia, and in the metropolises of Córdoba and Buenos Aires—in addition to living through shorter stays elsewhere in Argentina and through countless visits to relatives and friends. Guevara's vagabond tendencies later in life can be traced further back as well. On both sides of the family tree ancestors had journeyed far and wide across Argentina, Chile, and even the United States. Ernesto's favorite grandmother would entertain him for hours with stories of her father's experiences as an exile from the regime of the nineteenth-century Argentine dictator Juan Manuel de Rosas and of his time living in California during the 1840s gold rush. A string of visitors in the 1930s and 1940s brought more tales of adventure in foreign lands. In particular, the Guevara family hosted ex-combatants from the Spanish Civil War whose stories of the Republic's brave struggles against right-wing nationalists captivated the young Ernesto.[3]

Equally important, the written word proved integral to Guevara's formation as a traveler. The family library was stocked with scores of travel chronicles and related books.[4] Confined to the indoors for long periods of time due to asthma and other illnesses, Guevara became a devoted reader and spent hours poring over books by Jules Verne, adventure fiction, and more esoteric works on scientific expeditions and missions. (By his teenage years he had also familiarized himself with Karl Marx and other leftist authors, but his readings were extremely eclectic and his interests dispersed.) For the remainder of his life Guevara would keep journals of his voyages as a traveling routine, often revising them on his return. He rarely traveled without bringing books along. In a remarkable essay on Guevara the reader, Ricardo Piglia describes a photograph illustrating the centrality of the written word for Guevara later in life: close to his final days, while seeking to spark a guerrilla war in Bolivia and pursued by counterinsurgency forces, Guevara was pictured sitting in a tree reading a book. Even with the enemy closing in, suffering from exhaustion and wounds, he continued to carry books and diaries in a folder strapped to his body. Most incredibly, reading and writing were among Guevara's last recorded acts. After his capture and only hours prior to his execution, he was visited by a teacher, who offered him some food as he lay dying in the classroom of a rural school; Guevara asked her to correct a misspelling of a sentence on the blackboard: "I know how to read."[5]

The most famous of Guevara's writings—The Motorcycle Diaries, as well as the accounts of his Congo and Bolivian campaigns—can be added to the canon of Argentine travel writing, a tradition that includes essential works such as Domingo Faustino Sarmiento's Facundo and Lucio V. Mansilla's A Visit to the Ranquel Indians. At times Guevara's accounts suggest a conscious awareness of this literary tradition and precocious attempts to situate himself within it. The opening salvo of the Diaries declares, "The person who wrote these notes passed away the moment his feet touched Argentine soil again. The person who reorganizes and polishes them, me, is no longer, at least I am not the person I once was. All this wandering around 'Our America with a capital A' has changed me more than I thought"—an allusion perhaps to another celebrated writer-traveler-revolutionary, the Cuban nationalist José Martí and his classic work, Our America.[6] In any event, this passage captures the complex function of travel for Guevara, for whom the physical experience of the voyage remained inseparable from reading and writing about travel, each sphere of activity continually informing the others.

Like that of his celebrated literary precursors, Guevara's approach to travel was shaped by his relatively privileged social position. Gender factors into the equation here not only in the desire for sexual adventure evidenced clearly in The Motorcycle Diaries (Guevara and Granado appear concerned as much with unlocking the mysteries of the continent as adding to their conquests with foreign women). More important, the text highlights the supreme confidence that guided Guevara's travels, the freedom with which he transgressed both social norms and spatial boundaries, an ease facilitated by his position as a male in 1950s Argentine society. Guevara's recklessness and romanticism as a traveler follow in the tradition of nineteenth-century male voyagers of a similar class and educational background. Within Argentine letters Guevara's travels have more in common in tone with those of a figure like Mansilla (who journeyed across much of Europe and Asia in his youth, before being sent on his famed expedition into Argentina's Indian territories) than, say, those of Juana Manuela Gorriti (who ranged widely across South America in the nineteenth century but is best known for her keen observations of postindependence society).[7] Guevara's journals appear to echo, whether intentionally or not, Mansilla's combination of puffed-up arrogance and self-deprecating humor in the face of adversity.

Exposed to a range of travel experiences (physical and literary) during his upbringing, Guevara further established his preferences as a wanderer during his excursions across Argentina in the 1940s and 1950s. While in school he often hitchhiked hundreds of miles from Córdoba and Buenos Aires to visit friends and family. In his early twenties he took a part-time job as a medic on ships that sailed as far as northern Brazil and Jamaica (though little is known about these trips).[8] But Guevara's most ambitious experience before his Latin American journey with Granado was a solo trek on a motorized bicycle across Argentina in 1950. Descriptions of this trip survive in a short travel diary uncovered after Guevara's death. His father discovered these notes in a box of old notebooks in the family's Buenos Aires apartment. Although the paper was damaged and the young Ernesto's handwriting is difficult to decipher, Guevara Lynch transcribed the original document and published excerpts of it in his memoir, *Mi hijo El Che*.[9] As with *The Motorcycle Diaries*, there are unanswered questions as to how accurately this account reflects the original (in this case, at least, there appear to have been fewer possibilities for editing from Cuban authorities). Nevertheless, this earliest surviving travel diary can serve as a crucial source for understanding the characteristics of Guevara the traveler.

For those familiar with the *Diaries* the account of 1950 possesses basic similarities. Much of the travelogue recounts the difficulties encountered by the twenty-two-year-old: the mechanical troubles with his bike, the perils of traversing a huge geographic expanse, and his endurance of the natural elements. The text offers vignettes of the landscape, anecdotes about the characters Guevara meets, and descriptions of medical centers along the way (including the leprosarium where Granado worked).[10] In six weeks Guevara covered four thousand kilometers, passing through twelve provinces but spending the majority of his time in the northwestern region of Salta, Tucumán, and Santiago del Estero. What comes through in this text, as in his subsequent travel writings, is Guevara's desire to find far-flung corners of the countryside and to spend time among the "ordinary," impoverished residents. Through forays into remote areas, Guevara expected the revelation of hidden aspects of social reality.

It is thus noteworthy that Guevara did not fully "see" a major social trend (or at least comment on it in his writings) reshaping these provincial areas. The 1950s were a time of internal migration on a massive scale, and rural populations headed by the millions to the cities; their main destination was Buenos Aires and its suburbs, the hub for industrial, commercial, and government employment. Migration was nothing new in Argentina; the countryside's inhabitants covered vast distances seeking ranching and harvest labor in the nineteenth century, and large-scale European immigration at the turn of the century transformed social structures. But the pace of internal migration built steadily to reach new highs in the postwar era. According to official estimates the metropolitan region of Buenos Aires received annually about 8,000 migrants from the provinces in the mid-1930s; by the early 1940s this number had grown to 70,000, and by 1947 to more than 117,000 provincial migrants a year.[11] This trend continued well into the 1950s and 1960s, and technically speaking the Guevara family's relocation to Buenos Aires city from Córdoba made them part of this exodus.

In his decision to investigate the heartland of Argentina, Guevara went against the predominant demographic trend. Given his fondness for travel, it surprises that he had very little to say about migration in his writings. In part, Guevara's travel method may explain this lacuna. He preferred to avoid large cities and devoted little time in his journals to describing metropolitan spaces or their inhabitants. In searching for ever more distant areas, Guevara was guided by a desire for contact with rural folk, those Argentines living close to the land and far from the harried urban world familiar to him. That these people were headed in increasing numbers from the countryside and towns to the big cities went against Guevara's very purpose of seeking their places of origin.

In one episode in his journal of 1950 Guevara discusses an encounter with a working-class migrant, and it offers insight into his sense of himself as a traveler. Having stopped to inflate one of his bike tires, Guevara was approached by a man, described as a linyera (vagabond or wanderer). The man was on his way from the cotton harvest in El Chaco, heading most likely to the grape harvest in San Juan. According to the journal, the linyera could simply not understand why Guevara was covering thousands of kilometers in his expedition through the provinces. Grabbing his head, the man supposedly exclaimed with an exasperated tone, "Mama mía, you are spending all that effort uselessly?"[12] On the surface the anecdote reveals Guevara's modest attempt at humor, although his portrait of the migrant borders on the paternalistic. The linyera made for a familiar social stereotype, a stock-and-trade character of comedic theatre and popular stories, and Guevara's account presents this man in similarly one-dimensional terms. The episode points to the crucial difference between Guevara and the majority of those on the road in the Peronist era: his class background and relative privilege allowed him the leisure to travel "uselessly," at least from the linyera's perspective.

Guevara defended the value of traveling in a free manner, liberated from the responsibilities of work and the routines of everyday life, but at the same time he rejected the paradigm of tourism. He saw himself as something more, as someone dedicated to the serious business of investigating the inner workings of society. Guevara was not the only young man of his generation to seek new forms of discovery through travel; other middle-class Argentines probed the expanses of their country, using vacations from their studies to roam off the beaten path.[13] Nor can one overlook that elsewhere in the Americas young bohemians were also taking to the road. In the course of his trips across the region, Guevara came into contact with these individuals, as well as with those forced abroad by political exile, some of whom would influence his trajectory as a leftist revolutionary.

Yet even in his earliest accounts Guevara had already staked his claim as a different kind of traveler, one that followed an alternate path, literally and metaphorically, from the average tourist of the Peronist era. His initial voyages occurred during a time of mass tourism, evidence of which emerges from his diaries. More than ever before, Argentines during the 1940s and 1950s left their jobs and homes to go on vacation, heading toward the coast and to the mountains of the interior. The country already boasted distinguished seaside resorts like Mar del Plata, and Ernesto's boyhood home of Alta Gracia in Córdoba was renowned as a destination for invalids and vacationers. But postwar economic and political conditions fueled the transformation of tourism into a regular activity for the middle class and for fortunate sectors of the working class. As one measure of the surge in tourism during the postwar years, the number of vacationers in the premier resort of Mar del Plata jumped from 380,000 in 1940 to 1.4 million by 1955. The Peronist administration was both directly and indirectly responsible for accentuating tourism. The regime's economic program of the mid-1940s, centered on boosting the domestic economy by increasing aggregate demand, helped redistribute income to wage earners. The political prerogatives of forging an alliance with organized labor and consolidating popular support served as the impetus behind social reforms that widened leisure opportunities. New labor legislation shortened the workweek and extended for the first time benefits such as vacations to much of the industrial working class and to state employees. Additional national holidays added to the free time of popular-sector Argentines, many of whom now enjoyed for the first time ever uninterrupted weekends and ten to fifteen days of paid vacation a year. The private tourism industry sought to capitalize on these changes: hotel developers, railroad companies, and organizations such as the Automobile Club of Argentina all took steps to attract and cater to the tourist market.

Moreover, Peronist authorities adopted measures to organize leisure time, inspired by a mixture of populist politics and managerial concern for the productivity and health of the labor force. National and provincial governments opened resorts, expanded the network of rural parks across the country, and offered subsidized train fares to tourists. The Eva Perón Foundation built hotels and vacation complexes (colonias de vacaciones) designed to minister to the needs of poor and working-class children. Most famously, the largest pro-Peronist labor unions constructed facilities for their growing memberships, in some cases expanding on limited leisure programs of the past. The union-operated hotels that dotted hill towns and seaside resorts—including in former elite playgrounds like Mar del Plata—lent evidence to organized labor's growing power, as well as to what historian Juan Carlos Torre and others have dubbed the "democratization of well-being" in the Peronist era.[14]

We have only fleeting signs of what Guevara thought of the new opportunities for mass tourism in Argentina. While many Peronist-era tourists headed for the beaches, public and private leisure facilities were located in the interior provinces traversed by Guevara during his youthful travels. It would have been difficult for him not to have crossed paths with other tourists. In his diary of his trip through the interior in 1950, Guevara took pains to distinguish his approach to travel from that of the common tourist. When asked by a hospital staff member in Salta what he had seen on a recent side trip—and presumably critiqued for having missed all the major sites —Guevara reflected on his travel philosophy. He argued, "At least I do not feed myself with the same forms as the tourists, and it seems strange to me to see on the tour guides [mapas de propaganda] for

Jujuy, for example: the altar of the *patria*, the cathedral where the patria was blessed . . . the miraculous virgin of the Rio Blanco; the house in which Lavalle was killed." These grand patriotic and religious sites were precisely the types of destinations advertised by the Peronist state and the Eva Perón Foundation in their travel pamphlets (complete with titles like *Tourism for the People*). One of the ideological goals of official tourism programs was to inculcate Peronist nationalism and Catholic religiosity in the hearts of working people by exposing them to symbolically important places.[15] Guevara rejected this version of travel: "That's not how one sees a pueblo, a way and interpretation of life, that's just a luxurious facade [*lujosa cubierta*]." Instead he enumerated the sorts of things he searched for in his travels: the "soul" of the people reflected in the sick, prisoners in jail, and ordinary pedestrians.[16] In short, Guevara described tourists as superficial and concerned only with what guidebooks told them to see, and his grittier mode of voyaging offered him a means to probe beyond the mapped destinations—which, it bears remembering, had just become more accessible to working people. His rejection of tourist banality in this sense also constituted a negative reaction to the popularization of leisure travel.

Ironically, however, Guevara's most famous journey began with stops in numerous tourist destinations in Argentina—a sign perhaps of the difficulties a middle-class youth encountered in attempting to break out of social routines. During the initial stages of his motorcycle trip in 1952, he and Granado visited the houses of relatives and friends along the beach resorts of the southern coast of Buenos Aires Province: Villa Gesell, Miramar, and Necochea (near where the vacation home of Guevara's then girlfriend was located). They arrived during the first weeks of January in the Southern Hemisphere summer, the very peak of the tourist season. On their way west across the Andes, the travelers passed through Argentina's mountain resort towns and found shelter in the region's national parks (a focal point of the Peronist government's tourism programs). Other travelers were close at hand. In fact, Granado mentions in his memoirs the pair's astonishment at meeting near the resort of Bariloche a sixty-year-old couple from New Jersey, who were traversing the continent in their station wagon.[17] At this stage of the journey, it is unclear which pair represented the greater alternative to mainstream tourism: the pair of middle-class Argentines, fresh from their stay in resort towns, or the married couple from Jersey?

Guevara's attempts to distance himself from Peronist-era tourism intensified after he left behind his country's borders, and financial necessity and his own preferences forced him to rough it during his travels.[18] There seems to be more at stake here than just a longing to avoid being confused with Latin America's leisure travelers or a hint of youthful snobbism. Most tourists' class background would have annoyingly reminded Guevara of his own social status; and certainly the presence of mass tourism would have intruded on his project of uncovering an untrammeled *América*.[19] Guevara thus cultivated a self-conscious approach not as a tourist but as an explorer. This characteristic would later resurface in the mythic status of El Che. In commenting on his son's journals, Guevara Lynch claimed that travel was no mere "hobby" for Che. His father went so far as to compare him to the Spanish conquistadores, with the major difference that Che's voyages of discovery led to Latin American liberation rather than subjugation.[20] With slightly less hyperbole, he claimed that his son approached travel as a "social investigator," as a scientist who sought to understand and document humanity and, if possible, to alleviate suffering. There is something to this metaphor, as Guevara's itinerary was shaped by his medical interests and attention to matters of public health. He punctuated his voyage of 1951–52 with stops at hospitals, clinics, and leprosariums that were hardly standard sites for tourists but held special interest to a young man concerned with the socially marginal and the sick. There is little doubt that the risk-taking Guevara went farther than his peers to seek out people from different social worlds.

It is this side of Guevara's personality that The Motorcycle Diaries best captures. By omitting references to previous travel experiences, the text presents an image of the young Guevara as wide-eyed and inexperienced, which only accentuates the drama of his discoveries on the road. This trajectory has informed subsequent representations of his voyages, including the film version of the Diaries directed by Walter Salles in 2004. This thoughtful adaptation begins with a portrait of Guevara as an unseasoned youth at home in Buenos Aires city, which sets up his ventures into the rural heart of the Latin American continent. Early scenes focus on Argentina's urbanity (with scenes of Granado and Guevara saying their goodbyes in Buenos Aires) and the nation's famed wealth (exemplified by the visit to the imposing vacation estate of Guevara's girlfriend, Chichina Ferreyra). These passages of the film underscore Guevara's connections to a privileged social milieu, but also his personal disdain for its pretensions (conveyed through the actor Gael García Bernal's formidable frown). The depiction of a comfortable life in Argentina establishes a foil to the poverty encountered during his journey: for example, the Ferreyra mansion, seemingly isolated in its opulence from the rest of society, offers a contrasting visual parallel to the remote San Pablo leper colony in Amazonian Peru near the movie's end. This narrative arc proves effective within the structure of the film and further contributes to the consolidation of Guevara as Latin America's emblematic traveler.

In the process, however, *The Motorcycle Diaries* (in both its written and film versions) achieves an effect at a cost: namely, obscuring for the audience key features of the historical setting of migration in which Guevara's voyages took place. The social landscape of the 1950s has been partially erased. Missing are the migrants moving between rural areas or relocating permanently to cities like Buenos Aires, further swelling the neighborhoods and suburbs of the postwar Argentine metropolis. Absent as well are the clusters of tourists on their way to resorts and other sites, among them working-class families participating for the first time in Peronist programs. These practices represented a point of departure for Guevara's "rebellious" approach, which constituted a partial rejection of prevailing cultural norms and expectations related to travel in Argentina. That Guevara's journals contain passing references to wandering laborers, patriotic tourists, and his own visits to resorts illustrates the veiled presence of this wider social milieu. It also helps explain exactly what he was attempting to leave behind in his decision to journey outside his country's borders and pursue an unknown Latin America.

Peronism, Nationalism, and Discovery

If migration constituted a major social trend in the Argentine 1950s, it was politically and culturally an era dominated by new forms of nationalism. At the forefront was the Peronist movement, whose leaders deployed the power of the state and of partisan organizations to project their vision of a New Argentina—a country "politically sovereign, economically independent, and socially just," as the propaganda slogan went. The grandeur of the Argentine nation and of its *pueblo* (people) was extolled through the media, federal government institutions, and other means available to officials. Peronist initiatives built on nationalist trends gathering force since the early twentieth century and encompassing artistic circles and political sectors across the ideological spectrum. What, then, was Guevara's place within this society shaped by multiple nationalist currents? On the whole he attempted to distance himself from Peronist nationalism. We can view Guevara's decision to embark on a voyage outside Argentina as an attempt to break free from a nationalist political milieu, or at the very least, as the expression of a desire to immerse himself in a different reality. Yet in spite of his mistrust of official patriotism, Guevara's orientation toward travel bore the marks of broader nationalist cultural influences, above all in his constant attraction to remote, "authentic" rural spaces and their inhabitants. Although the motorcycle voyage of 1951–52 opened up a wider world, Guevara's writings reveal the ultimate difficulties of leaving behind Peronism and the nationalist trends of his youth.

Biographers have drawn attention to the young Guevara's seeming indifference toward Peronism—what one author has dubbed his "a-Peronism."[21] Guevara lived through a time of ardent partisan conflict, but he managed somehow to remain aloof. According to the recollections of friends and family, he raised the subject of Peronism only occasionally in conversation, and it appears rarely in letters or personal notebooks from his teenage years and early twenties. On the surface, this attitude seems improbable: how could the young man who would become the most famed revolutionary in Latin America have such little interest in the central political phenomenon of twentieth-century Argentina? A closer look, however, suggests that Guevara's silence derived, at least in part, from being caught up in the contradictions of Peronism, a mass movement that at once embraced elements of state authoritarianism and of working-class empowerment. Guevara responded to this dilemma by drawing back from political life, a reaction less uncommon than one might first assume in an era of mounting polarization.

On the one hand, Guevara shared the anti-Peronist sentiments of his family and circle of friends. If the base of the Peronist movement lay among the working class, then the core of anti-Peronism could be found among upper- and middle-class sectors—with exceptions, of course, as class never mapped perfectly onto political loyalties. Like the majority of their social peers, the members of the Guevara family viewed Perón as a demagogue who manipulated the populace with false promises of social justice, motivated only by a thirst for personal power. The Guevaras' involvement in leftist political causes and intellectual circles only strengthened this resolve. Guevara Lynch voted typically for Argentina's reformist Socialist Party, whose leaders staunchly opposed Peronist rule and many of whom were eventually forced into exile. Negative views of Peronism also derived from the entire family's support of the republican cause in the Spanish Civil War and from members' participation in anti-fascist organizations such as Acción Argentina.[22] These efforts no doubt inclined them to consider Peronism in a similar light; after all, Spain's Francisco Franco and Perón were both military men whose coalitions included conservative Catholics and the extreme Right. The point here is not that Peronism constituted a form of fascism, but merely that there was a logic behind the Guevaras' and others' understanding of Argentine politics along these lines.[23]

On the other hand, Guevara remained an ambivalent anti-Peronist compared to his family and friends. Granado took part in student protests against the revolution of 1943, from which Perón began his rapid rise to prominence. Decades later, in his own travel memoirs, Granado would continue to describe the politics of this period as "our own local Nazism . . . dressed up as nationalism."[24] Guevara felt scant enthusiasm for the formal political opposition. He had long disdained Argentina's traditional centrist party, the Radicals, and he viewed most leftist groups as ineffectual and mistaken in allying themselves with conservatives in defying Perón. This outlook may explain why he never participated in political organizations, even during his days at the University of Buenos Aires, a locus of student protest, where he studied medicine from 1947 to 1953. While Guevara considered Juan and Eva Perón little more than opportunists, he acknowledged the significance of Peronism for the working class. His biographer Jon Anderson recounts an anecdote in which Guevara advised his family's maids to vote for Perón, arguing that they would benefit from the government's policies (an example that illustrates both Guevara's social advantages and his tendency to view politics in class terms).[25] In this regard Guevara's attitude mirrored those of a minority on the Argentine Left, who felt unsure how to respond to this working-class movement. While most continued to view Peronism as a form of homegrown fascism, a few leftists explored the possibility of a rapprochement with this popular political force. Much as this problem perplexed Guevara in the early 1950s, the issue of whether socialism and Peronism were compatible would dominate the attention of progressives for decades after Perón's overthrow.[26]

For those like Guevara, opposition to Peronism was further complicated by the question of anti-imperialism. The Peronist regime had taken up the cause of asserting national sovereignty by railing against the interference of foreign powers. Its leaders adopted inward-oriented economic policies and limited nationalizations (most notably, the purchase of the British-owned railroads in 1947). Anti-imperialism was perhaps Guevara's strongest political interest during this period, and he often butted heads with his father over the influence of the United States in the hemisphere. The young Guevara may have been an anti-imperialist, but he was no narrow nationalist; this is a crucial distinction for understanding his later vision as a revolutionary, one based on international guerrilla struggle. He was aware of the dark side of nationalist politics in Perón's Argentina, especially the state's censorship of the media and its harassment of dissenters. As a young man Guevara preferred reading about nationalists from other countries over those closer to home, and one of his favorite books was, supposedly, Jawaharlal Nehru's The Discovery of India.[27] The cosmopolitan, educated, and ostensibly left-leaning Nehru appeared far more palatable to an individual of Guevara's intellectual tastes than his own country's ruler. As with the class characteristics of Peronism, the government's embrace of anti-imperialism did not suffice to convert Guevara into a supporter—that would have been too great a leap for someone from his background. But the pull between these opposing impulses helps to explain why he would stay on the political sidelines during this turbulent age.

Yet the task of isolating oneself from Peronism was none too easy in Argentina in the 1950s. Passages from The Motorcycle Diaries capture the ubiquity, even inescapability, of Peronism. Indeed, the very idea for Guevara's odyssey across Latin America was intertwined with a central Peronist ritual, for plans for the motorcycle trip were hatched on 17 October. Commemorating a worker-led protest against Perón's imprisonment in 1945, this date constituted the highpoint of the Peronist calendar, becoming by the 1950s a national holiday and an occasion for an outpouring of partisan enthusiasm.[28] Every year the government encouraged its supporters to make a pilgrimage to Buenos Aires, where they would gather in the Plaza de Mayo for a joyous rally. This particular 17 October had special significance, as Perón was up for reelection only a few weeks later in November 1951, and state and party authorities thus redoubled their efforts to stage a public celebration of devotion. Guevara, however, opted for another itinerary. As befitted his anti-Peronist leanings, he made use of the holiday to exit the capital and visit friends in Córdoba. (One wonders how many thousands of Perón supporters he must have crossed along the road heading in the opposite direction.) It seems hardly coincidental that on the most Peronist day of the year, Guevara and Granado began planning their trip across the continent—in essence, their flight from Perón's New Argentina.

Months later, while traveling through the country's southern reaches, Guevara found himself frequently reminded of Peronism. During a stop in Mar del Plata in January 1952, the duo met with a medical doctor, who Guevara noted had "joined the [Peronist] party, with all its consequent privileges." This reference points to the increasingly partisan nature of the state bureaucracy by the early 1950s. Like many professionals who worked in hospitals and other public institutions, this doctor was presumably under pressure to display loyalty to the regime as a condition of securing or maintaining employment—an often overlooked impact of Peronist rule on middle-class life. Certainly this issue would have been on the minds of two young men at the beginning of their medical careers; in Guevara's case, the Peronization of public institutions was no small matter, given that he was still eligible for mandatory military service. In the next town, however, the pair lunched with one of Granado's anti-Peronist friends, a doctor with ties to the Radical Party. But Guevara refused to identify with either doctor, noting that we "were as remote from one as the other. Support for the Radicals was never a tenable position for me and was also losing its significance for Alberto, who had been quite close at one time to some of the leaders he respected."[29] Crossing the Andes, near San Martín de los Andes, the pair stayed at the ranch of some acquaintances, one of whom Guevara described comically as a "Peronist, always drunk, the best of the three."[30] In this regard Guevara's texts complement the findings of recent historical studies. By the early 1950s the Peronization of society had come into full swing, and public institutions such as the educational and health systems were deployed to overt partisan ends.[31] Guevara's travel writings illustrate the penetration of Peronism on a national scale and into various aspects of quotidian life.

As Guevara would discover with some surprise, Peronism did not end at Argentina's borders. When traveling through the rural highland zones of Peru, the two travelers found themselves questioned by local residents on more than one occasion about life in Argentina. Near the town of Tarata, Guevara and Granado sought refuge among the popular inhabitants of two roadside huts, who are described simply as "cholos." The Peruvians peppered the duo with questions, and Guevara wrote the following description of the encounter: "We were like demigods to these simple people: Alberto brandished his doctor's certificate for them, and moreover, we had come from that wonderful country Argentina, where Perón lived with his wife Evita, where the poor have as much as the rich and the Indian isn't exploited or treated as severely as he is in this country."[32] A few days later the pair had a similar exchange with rural Peruvians: "At one of the many stops we made along the road, an Indian timidly approached us with his son who spoke good Spanish, and began to ask us all about the wonderful 'land of Perón.'" Once again, the duo offered embellished accounts of life in Peronist Argentina, condescendingly assuming this was what the "Indians" wanted to hear, mainly to secure some food and shelter from them. In this case the older man even asked the travelers to send him a copy of the Argentine constitution "with its declaration of the rights of the elderly."[33]

Guevara's description of these encounters is fascinating on many levels. Putting aside for the moment the issue of his ethnic stereotyping, these episodes shed light on a topic that has escaped much scholarly attention, namely, the impact of Peronism on other Latin American countries during the 1950s. Observers have commented on certain aspects, such as the humanitarian aid of the Eva Perón Foundation or the efforts of pro-Peronist unions to form ties with counterparts elsewhere in the region. Yet we can obtain some fresh insight from finding residents of rural Peru so interested in Argentina's domestic politics and possessing a detailed awareness of Peronist state policy. These passages in Guevara's travel writings encourage us to reconsider the resonance of Peronism among popular sectors in other countries.[34] The mechanisms through which information circulated remain a mystery, although they probably included multiple channels: Peronist propaganda disseminated abroad; reports in radio, newspapers, and film, both domestically produced and imported; word of mouth carried through migratory networks, partly through postwar immigrants from Peru and elsewhere to Argentina; and, of course, conversations with passing Argentine tourists and travelers. In *The Motorcycle Diaries* these encounters with Peronism abroad rupture temporarily the illusion of an undiscovered Latin America, the guiding idea that originally drove the two travelers onward.

That Guevara decided to embark on a long journey outside his country—precisely during a time when state authorities exalted the greatness of Argentina and encouraged the population to travel domestically as good patriots—constituted a tacit rejection of Peronist nationalism. Yet Guevara did not entertain an entirely negative relationship to the nationalism of the Peronist era. In fact, nationalist cultural elements are present in Guevara's writings and shaped his very approach to travel. Guevara was driven by an impulse of discovery to journey off the beaten path and test his physical limits. Most important, his travels represented a means to witness and uncover a hidden social reality located far from urban population centers. In viewing rural dwellers as repositories of folk authenticity and examples of collective exploitation, he resorted to racial and class stereotypes strikingly similar to those of contemporary nationalist writers. Indeed, Peronist authorities adopted similar tropes of national discovery in their propaganda and tourism policies. One must, however, be careful not to insist on a direct line of causality between Peronist initiatives and Guevara's outlook, for both were shaped by nationalist trends in mid-twentieth-century Argentina. Rather than pinpointing an exact set of influences, it makes more sense to situate Guevara the traveler within these broader cultural currents.

Although nationalism was tainted through its association with the xenophobic Right in the Argentina of Guevara's youth, a handful of progressive models may also have served as sources of inspiration.[35] During the 1930s and 1940s a growing number of Argentine leftists expanded their focus outside their traditional urban base. One such example is Alfredo Palacios's book of 1944, *Pueblos desamparados*, which analyzed the problems facing residents of Argentina's northwestern provinces. A longtime Socialist Party politician and member of congress representing Buenos Aires city, Palacios combined a social exposé of poverty with his own reflections on travel through the region. He recounted stories of rural families in arid La Rioja (a province visited by Guevara in 1950) who suffered extreme poverty due to drought and malnourishment. With indignation the author explained his shock at discovering how his compatriots lived: "My pride as an Argentine suffered a rude blow, confronted with the misery of this good *pueblo*, sad and resigned, whom we shamefully forget."[36] In response he advocated greater involvement of the national government in improving the education, health, and economic opportunities of this "forgotten" people. Palacios devoted much of his book to concrete legislative suggestions, thus limiting its readership. (It might, however, have been available in the Guevara household: Guevara Lynch supported Palacios and was known to collect books on such subjects.[37]) In any event, Guevara would set forth into the same regions traveled by Palacios during his motorbike journey, in search of his own experience of national discovery in the provincial interior. He would encounter the same devastating signs of deprivation along the roadsides of Argentina's backcountry.

The Peronist regime reworked the themes of earlier nationalist writers and political actors during the 1940s and 1950s, amplifying the discourse of discovery to an unprecedented level. Although Perón had his most reliable support base among the working-class populations of major cities and suburbs, his government also highlighted rural themes in outlining its vision of national progress. Propagandists applied the nationalist's favored contrast between the "visible" and "invisible" country, including the Argentina of urban abundance and its forgotten hinterland.[38] Newsreels and short films produced under the regime's auspices presented audiences with poignant views of rural poverty, allowing them to witness the living conditions of their fellow citizens in other regions, separated from them by thousands of miles. Pro-regime pamphlets, newspapers, and magazines—all of which allowed audiences to travel virtually to what for many was an unfamiliar side of their country—used similar strategies. "This is how working people lived in the incredibly rich Argentine Republic," proclaimed one newsreel of 1948 that showed images of poverty-stricken rural and urban communities. The rural poor in the northwestern provinces dwelled in "dark caves, almost ashamed to be alive" and "without water and without bread, a life of perpetual punishment." Footage showed dark-skinned men in tattered clothing gathering cane during the sugar harvest. The newsreel then cut to images of their children playing amid garbage in the open sewers running alongside shacks. To correct past injustices and usher in a modern age, Perón's government was "raising for the *pueblo* a house of equality, fraternity, and harmony."[39] Depictions of the discovery of social problems by Peronist propagandists contrasted the dire conditions of the very recent past with the dawn of another era in the New Argentina. This temporal frame sent the message that exploitation of the type suffered by workers in the northwest would soon be a thing of the past.[40] In a time of increasing state control of the mass media and propaganda on an unprecedented scale, nationalist representations of a hidden rural reality would have been impossible for members of Guevara's generation to avoid.[41]

Popular culture and the arts echoed similar themes. The Peronist regime counted on the support of nationalist intellectuals, many of whom embraced the notion that the true identity of the country resided in rural folk culture and a criollo heritage, by which they meant Hispanic traditions, originating in the colonial past.[42] At the same time the era saw a growing interest in folk music and dance— including among middle-class people who in other respects remained anti-Peronist. Domestic filmmakers also paid increasing attention from the 1930s onward to nationalist concerns and representations of rural life for mainly urban moviegoers. Social realist filmmaking mirrored propagandistic treatments of exploitation in the interior. For instance, the films *Los isleros* (dir. Lucas Demare, 1951) and *Las aguas bajan turbias* (dir. Hugo del Carril, 1952) dealt with the lives of working people in the northeastern regions. These films also offered a virtual voyage for audiences into little-traveled areas. *Las aguas bajan turbias*, in particular, probed the brutal world of laborers on yerba mate plantations near the Paraguayan border. Hugo del Carril's film (based on the novel *El río oscuro* by Alfredo

Varela) depicted a region far removed from most Argentines. It illustrated the misery of the largely indigenous workforce in the Alto Paraná, the violence meted out by bosses, and the entrapments of debt peonage. Del Carril carefully avoided upsetting Peronist authorities, and his film began with a voice-over noting that the social reality described in the film occurred "some years ago, only a few years ago," and not in the supposedly glorious present of the New Argentina.

We have no hard evidence of Guevara's reactions to Peronist propaganda or commercial entertainments. Given that the Guevara family once owned a yerba mate plantation, Ernesto might have been interested in del Carril's film, but he had already embarked on his trip when it was released in theatres. One can assume that he would have viewed with great skepticism suggestions that poverty was a thing of the past in Perón's Argentina. After all, he had seen social inequalities firsthand during his youth in small-town Córdoba, in his work in hospitals, and on early voyages around his country.

Yet one can identify a sensibility in Guevara's travel writings similar to the nationalist cultural expressions of the era. The Motorcycle Diaries echoes the language employed by Argentine nationalists in describing rural inhabitants. As seen in his encounters in Peru, Guevara often resorted to stock depictions of indigenous populations, replete with stereotypes about the innate, timeless characteristics of Indian psychology—even as he railed against the abuse of Indians as workers and against the racism they suffered. This was not simply a case of the arrogance of a foreigner abroad, as Guevara employed similar language in describing rural populations of indigenous ancestry in Argentina as well. While journeying across the southern Andean region of Argentina, Guevara and Granado crossed paths with a group of male farm laborers who made fun of the duo's preference for drinking their infusions of mate with sugar—"mate for girls," as they dubbed it. (Here is an example of Guevara's use of a confident self-deprecation that often accompanies his stereotyping; it reads almost like an updated passage from Mansilla.) Yet the conversation did not progress much further: "In general, they didn't try to communicate with us, as is typical of the subjugated Araucanian race who maintain a deep suspicion of the white man who in the past brought them so much misfortune and now continues to exploit them. They answered our questions about the land and their work by shrugging their shoulders and saying 'don't know' or 'maybe,' quickly ending the conversation."[43] In this case, Guevara's stereotype of the silent Indian is not entirely a negative one, even if its overt class analysis overlooks other reasons why these laboring men would have been reticent to answer the interrogation of curious outsiders. This passage's emphasis on Indian exploitation and racism mirrored the social realism of films such as *Las aguas bajan turbias*, popular fiction, and Peronist propaganda. Guevara would fall back repeatedly on these types of representations for understanding rural populations and indigenous people outside his own country.

The nationalist tendency to see rural areas and populations as repositories of cultural authenticity appears to have rubbed off on Guevara. Had he been born a generation earlier, the future Che might have selected a different itinerary for his tour of 1950 and later voyages. One can imagine him crossing the Atlantic like his social peers to visit Paris or London. (There are hints of this alternative itinerary in the Salles film version of *The Motorcycle Diaries* during the dinner scene at the lavish vacation home of Guevara's girlfriend: the travelers cross paths with a wealthy young Argentine, a law student who had just returned from studying in Cambridge.) To be precise, Guevara did not abandon completely earlier travel traditions of his social milieu; he envisioned Latin America as a first leg of a journey that would take him to North America, Europe, and India. Yet he and his companion set out on a voyage in tune with the nationalist sensibilities of their time, shaped in turn by their own cosmopolitan interests and outsized ambitions. They would seek to explore the enormity of the American continent, in particular the remnants of ancient indigenous civilizations and the supposedly untrammeled expanses of its countryside. In their fascination for rural spaces Guevara and his companion did not ignore Latin America's cities. In fact, the itinerary of their trip in 1952 suggests that they spent much time in cities such as Santiago, Lima, Bogotá, and Caracas. But Guevara had comparatively less to say about these areas in the diaries, and his observations about urban spaces and populations pale in comparison to his accounts of the countryside. The longest stop of the trip in 1951–52, eighteen days, took place in Lima, more time than the pair stayed at the leper colony of San Pablo in the Amazon region—even though the *Diaries* devotes seemingly greater attention to the later destination.

In traveling outside Argentina Guevara went against the grain of his times, leaving behind a country immersed in the politics of Peronism, whose contradictions he was unable to fully transcend. What was an anti-imperialist, progressive medical student to make of a regime that combined vast social programs and nationalizations with authoritarian controls of public expression, that staged mass rallies of partisan devotion in Buenos Aires but also enabled members of the working class to become tourists? In the course of his travels Guevara sought out the Latin American countryside where social injustice was seemingly in starker relief. Here, too, he would stumble across reminders of Peronist Argentina and signs of the interconnectedness among the countries of the region. Nevertheless, he continued to look farther afield, spending long periods of time in Bolivia and Guatemala, which as Jorge Castañeda has noted, were not coincidentally two of the continent's most rural and unequal societies, and among those with the largest concentrations of indigenous populations.[44] Driven by the impulse of discovery, Guevara's sensibility as a traveler would lead him back to those corners of Latin America that most contrasted with the politics and places of his youth.

Ernesto's Departure, Che's Return

At the end of his trip in 1952, Guevara returned to his family's home in Buenos Aires. He would not remain there long. Having completed his medical school examinations and obtained his title as doctor, he set forth on another continent-wide journey in July 1953, one that would eventually take him as far north as Mexico and would culminate in his decision to join Fidel Castro's band of insurgents. Guevara went back to Argentina once in 1961 for a momentary visit (the occasion for his secret meeting with President Arturo Frondizi). As part of his transformation into El Che, his travels as a representative of Cuba's government carried him elsewhere in the world— Europe, Africa, and India, the destinations that he had dreamed of reaching as a boy. Yet the idea of a return to Argentina remained on Guevara's mind: this time not as a young wanderer but as the head of an international revolutionary movement. It was in Bolivia, the geographical heart of South America, that Guevara arrived in 1966 to start a guerrilla war, with the ultimate objective of spreading revolution to surrounding nations. He would meet his demise less than a year later, hunted down and executed a few hundred miles from the border with Argentina.

Prior to his death, however, Guevara had in a sense already returned to Argentina as an emblem of the Cuban Revolution and its socialist New Man. By the mid-1960s Guevara's impact on his homeland's politics had become profound. His example inspired a new generation of activists on the Left, who rejected the gradualist approach of their predecessors like Palacios in favor of immediate, radical change. Guevara had great appeal among young people who shared his middle-class background and university training, not to mention others drawn to his anti-imperialism and vision of social justice. Within the numerous factions on the Left, a minority applied the Cuban model of guerrilla struggle to their own society. Guevara backed these efforts, indirectly at first through the publication in 1960 of his work *La guerra de guerrillas* (part memoir of the Sierra Maestra campaign, part primer for would-be revolutionaries). He also supported early experiments to start an Argentine guerrilla movement. The first such effort—a campaign led by Jorge Ricardo Masetti to create a guerrilla *foco* of Argentines and a few Cuban advisors on the Bolivian border—was soon discovered by intelligence forces and crushed. This failure dismayed Guevara, but it did not dissuade him from his own Bolivian misadventure two years later. Nor would it stop subsequent guerrilla movements like the Ejército Revolucionario del Pueblo (Revolutionary People's Army) from pursuing similar tactics in the 1960s and 1970s.

More unexpectedly, the impact of Guevara's involvement in the Cuban Revolution was felt in Peronist circles as well. In a twist of Argentine history, the former anti-Peronist critic became a hero to many of its partisans. Guevara himself reacted with disappointment to Perón's overthrow in 1955. As he wrote to his mother, in the midst of his second long trek across the continent: "I confess to you quite frankly that Perón's fall has greatly embittered me, not on his account but because of what it means for the Americas. For however much you hate the idea, and however much it has been forced to give way in the recent period, Argentina was the champion of all of us who think that the enemy is in the north."[45] This statement downplayed that by then Perón had moderated his economic nationalism and had even courted foreign investment from the United States. Guevara, however, retained his suspicions about Perón, especially as the former ruler continued to exert an influence over Argentine politics from exile in the 1950s and 1960s.

Some Peronist supporters had fewer doubts, and they looked for ways to combine the characteristics of Perón's popular nationalism with Cuban socialism. The drive to revolutionize Peronism can be best seen in the career of John William Cooke, an Argentine-born member of Congress in the 1940s, who would become a well-known figure in the Peronist resistance against military rule in the mid-1950s. Inspired by the Cuban Revolution, he later relocated to the island to take a place by Guevara's side. Cooke's correspondence with Perón records his efforts to imagine a Guevarist variation on Peronism, as well as his futile attempt to convince the former Argentine president to join him in Castro's Cuba. Despite his dalliance with figures like Cooke, Perón was unwilling to abandon his supporters on the ideological center and right or to forfeit his personal authority. Nevertheless, Cooke was among the first Peronists to advocate guerrilla tactics and a radical swing leftward.[46] In his wake, insurgents such as the *montoneros* would reach a similar conclusion and take up arms under the flag of Peronism and of revolution. Here, too, guerrilla warfare would fall short of its objectives, as Argentina descended further into a cycle of bloodletting and state terror during the 1970s.

Guevara's homecoming to Argentina, as the epitome of the committed *guerrillero*, represented the ultimate, if unexpected, return to his original point of departure. Of course one must resist the temptation of a neat closure to this biographical circle, to see El Che as the product of the traveler in 1950s Argentina. Yet signs of the traveler's method could be seen in the theory and practice of the revolutionary. The *guerrillero* was in a sense a type of traveler, and Guevara's variation on guerrilla warfare centered on the idea of constant, unfettered movement through remote areas.[47] It rested as well on the ability of the guerrilla vanguard to live in poverty among rural populations, thus displaying their willful physical sacrifice and solidarity. As a strategy, guerrilla warfare represented the polar opposite of the style of nationalist politics associated with Peronism, even if the two approaches often shared common ground ideologically around anti-imperialism. From this vantage Perón and Guevara can be thought of as personifying two dominant modes of postwar Argentine politics. The former was flexible enough to accommodate himself to changing historical conditions and actors of diverse convictions. Perón's politics relied on deal making and alliances, on public displays of support and other mass rituals. By contrast, Guevara's politics focused on a more restricted group of believers devoted entirely to their cause, purposefully isolated from the rest of society (hence the oft-mentioned comparison between the *foco* and a religious sect). In Guevara's eyes the guerrilla should always be in motion and his politics a conspiracy against the status quo rather than an accommodation to it.

Despite the erosion of faith in guerrilla warfare and declining enthusiasm for the Cuban Revolution over the past decades, Guevara's influence in Argentine culture shows few signs of waning. As in other parts of the globe, the commercialization of his beret-clad and bearded image advances steadily. His visage graces more than a few T-shirts on the streets of Buenos Aires, but Guevara's image can still be found performing other roles—including serving as a symbol of defiance, albeit one malleable enough to grace the banners of protestors, rock fans, and soccer supporters of every club. Few commentators, however, have probed past these surface manifestations to consider more substantively Guevara's contemporary cultural relevance. To hazard but one passing observation, it seems that Guevara has come to personify a paradigm of socially aware Pan-Americanism. He serves as a reminder to some Argentines of their nation's ties to a larger continent—"Our America with a capital 'A,'" as Guevara put it in his paraphrase of Martí in The Motorcycle Diaries. In a time of undeniable pressure in Argentina to embrace the globalized orthodoxy of the United States and Western Europe, Guevara's impulse of looking toward the interior of a vast, immiserated continent remains a potent one.

The recent spike in popularity of The Motorcycle Diaries (in book and film versions) will likely further this legacy among a new generation. But that Guevara has come to represent a guide for those seeking to better understand the lives of fellow Americans is not without its ironies. For Guevara's trajectory ran counter to the conventional wisdom about travel: the more he journeyed, the less he apparently saw and the more his outlook on the world became reduced. From the late 1950s onward Guevara's voyages reflected the increasing rigidity of his view of political action, coupled with a deepening inability to perceive the full complexity of social conditions, especially in rural areas that seemed so deceptively straightforward in their extremes of exploitation. Certainly, the narrowing of Guevara's worldview contributed to his final failure in Bolivia, as the guerrilla-traveler attempted to lead a revolution among a largely indigenous population about whom he knew almost nothing. Unlike the average tourist's ignorance, this blindness did not result from inexperience; rather, it was the outcome of years spent floating from one place to the next.

We are accustomed to thinking about the voyage recounted in *The Motorcycle Diaries* as a personal epiphany, an awakening to the reality of a continent. But what if in addition to this familiar story, the journey of 1951–52 also represented the beginning of another, less obvious process that accompanied Guevara on his travels: the settling of certain convictions as unmovable truths, the gradual extinguishing of curiosity? This side of Guevara's personality stands as a source of attraction for those who seek an unshakable model of perfection, that is, a hero. But from the vantage of a less idealistic (not to say cynical) time, there is something in this extreme fixity of mind that is difficult to truly comprehend, let alone emulate, at the level of personal conduct. With the passing of years, the older Guevara stands ever more distant and cold, a "harsh angel" (to borrow Alma Guillermoprieto's apt description), just as the younger self depicted in *The Motorcycle Diaries* becomes seemingly more human.[48] Beyond his established place in history as a protagonist of Latin American revolution, it is this contradiction—the disconnect between the inflexible discipline of El Che and the vagabond sensibility of the young Ernesto—that makes Guevara's life an enduring enigma for the future.

Notes

1 The novelist and literary critic Ricardo Piglia has called attention to the metamorphoses of Guevara's life. Ricardo Piglia, "Ernesto Guevara: Rastros de lectura," *El último lector* (Barcelona: Editorial Anagrama, 2005), 103–38. The present essay is indebted to Piglia's insights, as well

as to the numerous biographical accounts of Guevara's life, including Jon Lee Anderson, *Che 'Guevara: A Revolutionary Life* (New York: Grove, 1997); Jorge G. Castañeda, *Companero: The Life and Death of Che Guevara*, trans. Marina Castañeda (New York: Alfred Knopf, 1997); Paco Ignacio Taibo 11, *Guevara, Also Known as Che*, trans. Martin Michael Roberts (New York: St. Martin's Press, 1997).

2 Rather than offering its own translations from earlier published editions (such as *Notas de viaje*), this essay will, for the sake of simplicity, employ the recent English-language edition of Guevara's travel journals. Ernesto Guevara, *The Motorcycle Diaries: Notes on a Latin American Journey*, ed. and trans. Alexandra Keeble (Melbourne: Ocean Press, 2004).

3 Anderson, *Che Guevara*, 14–42. Castañeda, *Compañero*, 3–24.

4 Ernesto Guevara Lynch, *Mi hijo El Che* (Buenos Aires: Planeta, 1984), 99–119.

5 The phrase was "Yo sé leer," and Guevara noted the missing accent. The recollections of this school teacher, Julia Cortéz, have been challenged by others present in Guevara's final hours, including the military officers who killed him. Piglia, "Ernesto Guevara," 106–8, 136–37. Anderson, *Che Guevara*, 738.

6 Guevara, *The Motorcycle Diaries*, 32. According to Alberto Granado's later recollections of the journey in 1952—based on journals written during the trip, but first published in Cuba in 1978 (after the appearance of Guevara's account) and only recently translated into English—Guevara was familiar enough with Martí to quote lines of his poetry during one of their evening conversations in Chile. Alberto Granado, *Traveling with Che Guevara: The Making of a Revolutionary*, trans. Lucía Álvarez de Toledo (New York: Newmarket Press, 2004), 73.

7 For English-language versions, see Lucio V. Mansilla, *A Visit to the Ranquel Indians*, trans. Eva Gilles (Lincoln: University of Nebraska Press, 1997); Juana Manuela Gorriti, *Dreams and Realities: Selected Fiction of Juana Manuela Gorriti*, ed. Francine Masiello, trans. Sergio Waisman (Oxford: Oxford University Press, 2003). On travel literature, see Beatriz Colombi, *Viaje intellectual: Migraciones y desplazamientos en América Latina, 1880–1915* (Rosario, Argentina: Beatriz Viterbo Editora, 2004).

8 Guevara Lynch, *Mi hijo El Che*, 180; Luis Altamira, *La infancia del Che* (Barcelona: Taller de Mario Muchnik, 2003), 60.

9 Guevara Lynch, *Mi hijo El Che*, 257–59.

10 Ibid., 257–72.

11 Juan Carlos Torre and Eliza Pastoriza, "La democratización del bienestar," *Nueva historia Argentina: Los años peronistas (1943–1955)*, vol. 8, ed. Torre (Buenos Aires: Editorial Sudamericana, 2002), 262.

12 Guevara Lynch, *Mi hijo El Che*, 266.

13 To take but one example, Félix Luna (one of Argentina's most widely read historians) recalls how during the early 1950s he and his friends would use vacation time to set off for the provinces, taking long journeys on horseback, hitchhiking, and engaging in other adventures. Félix Luna, *Perón y su tiempo*, vol. 2 (Buenos Aires: Editorial Sudamericana, 1984), 285–86.

14 Torre and Pastoriza, "La democratización del bienestar," 301; Eugenia Scarzanella, "El ocio peronista: Vacaciones y 'turismo popular' en la Argentina (1943–1955)," *Entrepasados, Revista de Historia* 7:14 (1998), 65–86; and Elisa Pastoriza and Juan Carlos Torre, "Mar del Plata, un sueño de los argentinos," *Historia de la vida privada en la Argentina*, vol. 3, ed. Fernando Devoto and Marta Madero (Buenos Aires: Taurus, 1999), 49–78.

15 Dirección General de Relaciones Culturales y Difusión, *Turismo para el pueblo* (Buenos Aires: n.p., 1950), 1–48.

16 Guevara Lynch, *Mi hijo El Che*, 270.

17 Granado, *Traveling with Che Guevara*, 30.

18 For instance, Guevara lambasted U.S. visitors to Machu Picchu, who he felt were too ignorant to appreciate the ruins and their connections between the Inca and present-day indigenous people. This aversion to tacky U.S. tourists may also explain why he so detested Miami during his brief sojourn there. Ernesto Guevara, *Back on the Road: A Journey to Latin America*, trans. Patrick Camiller (New York: Grove, 2001), 131.

19 Ibid., 131.

20 Guevara Lynch, *Mi hijo El Che*, 273, 275.

21 Castañeda, *Compañero*, 30–6; see also Anderson, *Che Guevara*, 14–70, and Taibo, *Guevara, Also Known as Che*, 1–19.

22 Anderson, *Che Guevara*, 21–5; Castañeda, *Companero*, 14–5.

23 The literature analyzing the similarities and differences between Peronism and fascism is vast. Works include Gino Germani, *Authoritarianism, Fascism, and National Populism* (New Brunswick, N.J.: Transaction Books, 1978); Ernesto Laclau, *Politics and Ideology in Marxist Theory: Capitalism, Fascism, Populism* (London: NLB, 1977); and Marcela García Sebastiani, ed. *Fascismo y antifascismo, peronismo y antiperonismo: Conflictos políticos e ideológicos en la Argentina entre 1930 y 1955* (Madrid: Editorial Iberoamericana, 2006).

24 Granado, *Traveling with Che Guevara*, xviii.

25 One wonders if Guevara would have encouraged his family's maids to participate in official tourism programs as well. Anderson, *Che Guevara*, 54.

26 For analysis of Peronism's impact on the Left, see Oscar Terán, *Nuestros años sesentas: La formación de la nueva izquierda intelectual en la*

Argentina, 1956–1966 (Buenos Aires: Puntosur Editores, 1991); Carlos Altamirano, Peronismo y cultura de izquierda (Buenos Aires: Temas Grupo Editorial, 2001); and Fernando Martínez Heredia et al., Che, el argentino (Buenos Aires: Ediciones De Mano en Mano, 1997).

27 Anderson, Che Guevara, 51.

28 Guevara, The Motorcycle Diaries, 32–33.

29 Ibid., 38.

30 Ibid., 50–51. For works on Peronism's impact in the provinces, see Darío Macor and César Tcach, La invención del peronismo en el interior del país (Santa Fe, Argentina: University Nacional del Litoral, 2003); and James P. Brennan and Ofelia Pianetto, eds., Region and Nation: Politics, Economy, and Society in Twentieth-Century Argentina (New York: St Martin's Press, 2000).

31 Mariano Ben Plotkin, Mañana es San Perón: A Cultural History of Perón's Argentina, trans. Keith Zahniser (Wilmington, Del.: Scholarly Resources, 2002); Marcela Gené, Un mundo feliz: Imágenes de los trabajadores en el primer peronismo, 1946–1955 (Buenos Aires: Universidad de San Andres, 2005); and Alberto Ciria, Política y cultura popular: La Argentina peronista, 1946–1955 (Buenos Aires: Ediciones de la Flor, 1983).

32 Guevara, The Motorcycle Diaries, 91.

33 Ibid., 95–96.

34 According to Carlos "Calica" Ferrer, who traveled with Guevara in Bolivia, Peru, and Ecuador during his second trip across Latin America: "Ernesto and I, of antiperonist stock, were impressed by the admiration that Perón elicited outside Argentina. He was seen as a champion of anti-imperialism, who had beaten that son of a bitch Braden, the famous ambassador who had supported the anti-peronist opposition and had been a member of the most imperialist yanqui companies, such as the United Fruit. In the rest of Latin America, resentment towards the gringos was much stronger than in Argentina: 'Perón has real balls, just look at how he confronted the Americans,' we would be told." De Ernesto al Che: El segundo viaje de Guevara por Latinoamérica (Buenos Aires: Marea Editorial, 2005), 142.

35 The term nacionalista carried an implicit right-wing connotation in Argentina during the 1930s. Cristián Buchrucker, Nacionalismo y peronismo: La Argentina en la crisis ideológica mundial (1927–1955) (Buenos Aires: Editorial Sudamericana, 1987); and Richard J. Walter, "The Right and the Peronists, 1943–1955," The Argentine Right: Its History and Intellectual Origins, 1910 to the Present, ed. Sandra McGee Deutsch and Ronald Dolkart (Wilmington, Del.: Scholarly Resources, 1993), 99–118.

36 Alfredo Palacios, Pueblos desamparados: Solución de las problemas del noroeste argentinos (Buenos Aires: Editorial Guillermo Kraft, 1944), 80, 60.

37 Guevara Lynch, *Mi hijo El Che*, 104.

38 Carlos Altamirano sees this emphasis on the "two Argentinas" as part of an intellectual tradition that reaches at least as far back as the 1930s to works such as Eduardo Mallea's *Historia de una pasión argentina* (Buenos Aires: Sur, 1937). Altamirano, *Peronismo y cultura de izquierda*, 27.

39 Urban areas were not neglected; the film lamented that the "social embarrassment" of filthy tenements existed just blocks away from the presidential palace in Buenos Aires. Archivo General de la Nación (Buenos Aires), Departamento de Cine, Audio y Video, *Justica social*, film, 16mm, seven minutes, 1948.

40 On the politics of the "construction of the new," see Maria Helena Rolim Capelato, *Multidões em cena: Propaganda política no varguismo e no peronismo* (Campinas, Brazil: Papirus, 1998), 114; and Ciria, *Política y cultura popular*, 261–63.

41 With national literacy rates at nearly 90 percent, print media was widely accessible. Information about radio and film audiences is scant, but with more than half of all households owning a radio and a two-thirds increase in cinema attendance during Perón's first term, millions of Argentines came into contact with these forms of propaganda. Torre and Pastoriza, "La democratización del bienestar," 296–97.

42 Oscar Chamosa, "Archetypes of Nationhood: Folk Culture, the Sugar Industry, and the Birth of Cultural Nationalism in Argentina, 1895–1945" (PhD diss., University of North Carolina, Chapel Hill, 2003).

43 Guevara, *The Motorcycle Diaries*, 43.

44 Castañeda, *Compañero*, 71.

45 Guevara, *Back on the Road*, 92–93.

46 Richard Gillespie, *John William Cooke: El peronismo alternativo* (Buenos Aires: Cántaro Editores, 1989); and Richard Gillespie, *Soldiers of Perón: Argentina's Montoneros* (New York: Oxford University Press, 1982).

47 Ernesto "Che" Guevara, *La guerra de guerrillas* (Havana: Editorial de Ciencias Sociales, 1989). Piglia, "Ernesto Guevara," 123–26.

48 Alma Guillermoprieto, "The Harsh Angel," *Looking for History: Dispatches from Central America* (New York: Vintage, 2002), 72–86.

Patience A. Schell

Beauty and Bounty in Che's Chile

When in 1951 Ernesto "Che" Guevara began his now legendary journey through South America, Chile beckoned; it was foreign while familiar, exotic but manageable, and it had a reputation for welcoming strangers. Chile, with its diverse landscapes, folkloric *huasos* (cowboys), and German settlers was both neighbor and sibling culture. In his *Motorcycle Diaries*, Guevara filled passages with descriptions of Chileans' easy hospitality and the attractiveness of the women, also noting the bountiful landscape. But Guevara was not alone in remarking on generosity, Chilean women, and the country's natural bounty. In isolation, his observations tell us something about the young Che but less about Chile in the 1950s. Yet Guevara's reflections mirror those of other travelers of the period, alongside them offering a wider view of Chile in the mid-twentieth century. Complimentary travel narratives discussed here, written by French, U.S., German, and English authors, also focus on the nation's beauty and bounty. Authors include a Maryknoll nun who had been a prisoner of war in the Philippines, a latter-day German romantic, and a staid British couple obsessed with their car. Like Guevara, each of these authors visited Chile on a wider tour of South America. Also like this volume's subject, these other observers reproduced a Chilean national discourse in which women's accomplishments and racialized constructions of their beauty represented Chile's progressiveness and in which its bountiful landscape constituted the nation's essence. Juxtaposed with additional foreign and Chilean sources, including a woman's magazine and the classic *Chile o una loca geografía*, as well as secondary sources, the travelogues show how these twin discourses of bounty and beauty defined Chile. Yet as this essay also addresses, foreign observers and Chileans alike depicted and reproduced an ideal Chile that differed widely from the daily reality of millions of Chileans.

First Impressions

Guevara based his diary on notes he made during his South American journey, which he later revised into publication form.[1] This approach to documenting a journey is integral to the travel writing genre. Through this process of experience, note taking, and revision for publication, the genre allows for the invention of the self, the creation of a character, and the fashioning of a personality for the printed page.[2] As Mary Louise Pratt argues about the travels of Mungo Park in nineteenth-century Africa, "He made himself the protagonist and central figure of his own account, which takes the form of an epic series of trials, challenges, and encounters with the unpredictable."[3] Thus Guevara, the privileged, university-educated young man residing in Buenos Aires, became a trickster hero, an almost picaresque character, surviving through his wits and audacity. In Chile Guevara's account revolved around women, wine, and getting into scrapes. For Guevara, Chile, especially the country's south, constituted a space of conquest (often sexual) and a backdrop to his adventure. While we must consider the provenance and subsequent editing of the diary, a comparison between the accounts of Guevara and his traveling companion, Alberto Granado, still clearly indicate how Guevara shaped their experiences into humorous predicaments.[4]

Guevara and Granado entered Chile through the Lake District and began to travel north. Guevara had felt compelled to leave Argentina, drawn to the road and the unknown, even though the trip meant leaving his girlfriend, María del Carmen Ferreyra (Chichina), a wealthy young woman with a frivolous circle of friends. His attraction to Chichina was an attraction of opposites: his family was not wealthy and he was becoming increasingly serious and studious. Yet her letter ending the relationship, which reached Guevara in Bariloche, Argentina, broke his heart nonetheless.[5] With the end of the relationship, Guevara had lost one of his most important ties to home. His apparently cavalier attitude in southern Chile may in part have been a reaction to the breakup.

Arriving in Chile newly single, he sought after and delighted in the country's contrast to Argentina. For Guevara, Chile's indigenous community was one remarkable difference. He observed that southern Chile was authentically "American" in a way that Argentina, for him, was not. In Valdivia he noticed "the harbor, overflowing with goods that were completely foreign to us, the market where they sold different foods, the typical Chilean wooden houses, the special clothes of the guasos [sic, Chilean cowboys], were notably different from what we knew back home; there was something indigenously American, untouched by the exoticism invading our pampas. This may be because the Anglo-Saxon immigrants in Chile do not mix, so preserving the purity of the indigenous race, which in our country is practically nonexistent."[6] While Chileans and foreigners alike often commented on the German influence in southern Chile, because Guevara sought an American "authenticity," he paid less attention to European influences—or, as in the case of German-style wooden houses, ignored their origin—seeing instead evidence of indigenous influence. As Eduardo Elena argues in his contribution to this volume, Guevara sought to be a different kind of traveler, not a tourist but a researcher into the essence of America who used travel as a methodology.

While Guevara found Chile much more indigenous than Argentina, most of the other travelers and writers discussed in this essay noticed the European influence on Chile's ethnic and cultural mix. In a fictional account of two English children's life in Chile, the father explained to his son that "the chileno himself is a fine chap—intelligent, self-reliant, sincere, a good friend and what the Scots call a 'bonny fighter.' They're all of European descent, mostly Spanish but with a strong dash of German, British, and Italian, as well as other nationalities; but they are very proud of the fact that among their ancestors are the Araucanians."[7] André Maurois, a noted French novelist, biographer, and member of the Académie Française who was in his sixties during his tour of South America, was also impressed by the people, which he had not expected after reading "Subercaseaux's book," no doubt Chile, o una loca geografía. In that personal geography Benjamín Subercaseaux did not particularly flatter his compatriots, claiming Chileans had an "indolent and apathetic" character.[8] Yet like the English father, Maurois, who mostly paid attention to Chile's elites, also saw Chileans as a version of Europeans. "I discovered here an unfettered, lively intelligence, particularly among the women. The mixtures of races—Spanish, English, Nordic, sometimes Indian even—has produced an original and delicate type among the country's aristocracy. There are many red-blondes, with copper glints in their hair."[9]

But Europeans were not the only ones who found Chile impressive because of its familiarity. Kip Ross, a writer for *National Geographic*, felt comfortable in Chile in large part because of the recognition he experienced. "Chileans in temperament are much like North Americans [people of the United States]—industrious, bustling, sober. They are aptly called the Yankees of South America. Nowhere else below the border have I ever felt so much at home as in Chile." Moreover, according to Ross, "Indians" were seldom seen, either in Santiago or the rest of the country.[10] This lack of Indians was important because of heavily race-laden conceptions of progress that depicted indigenous and mixed-race people as a hindrance to national development. It was not only foreign observers but also Chilean elites who sought to erase or ignore evidence of indigenous and mestizo Chile. "Class uplift and economic advancement . . . were part of a process of racial whitening that would allow Chile to leave behind its degenerate mestizo past."[11] Unlike Guevara, who desired foreignness and difference, these travelers depicted Chile as a nation with the requisite European influence to ensure rapid advancement.

Thus Guevara's recognition of Chile as a country including a population of Indians proved unusual in travel accounts of the time. Two other visitors, however, also saw indigenous Chile. Although he denied that Chile had an indigenous population at one point in his *National Geographic* article, Ross later wrote about the indigenous people of the Temuco area. He found particularly frustrating that they did not permit him to take their picture. In the article, the only photograph of anyone indigenous was taken without permission, using a telephoto lens. When Ross tried to take a picture of an old woman in Mapuche dress, "she whirled, marched firmly up to me, and jabbed a stubby finger into my chest. 'How dare you take a picture behind my back?' she demanded in Indian-accented Spanish. 'I have a right to my own self.' She continued with surprising eloquence, emphasizing such words as *dignidad*, *reserva*, and *derechos* (rights)."[12] Ross clearly did not expect the "Indians," especially women, to talk back to him, much less have strong and well-expressed opinions about what was wrong with his behavior; perhaps he expected the woman to have the "primitive" fear that the camera would take her soul, not to remind him of her rights.

Ross's stolen photograph contrasts with the photograph of a Mapuche girl published in *In and Out the Andes*, the travel account of a Maryknoll nun, Sister Maria del Rey, engaged in missionary work in Latin America. Before becoming a nun, Sister del Rey had earned a bachelor of arts in journalism from the University of Pittsburgh and had worked as a reporter for the *Pittsburgh Press*. At this stage of her life she had already published two books drawing on approximately fifteen years of missionary work in Asia.[13] All her photographs of children tend to be taken from the child's level, allowing those portrayed the dignity of looking straight at the viewer. Sister del Rey's photograph of a Mapuche girl, about twelve, shows her in traditional dress, in front of a tree and a picket fence. The girl looks directly at the camera, smiling widely. Perhaps Sister del Rey's gender, her position as a nun, and her work in different communities helped her earn the trust of her subjects. Sister del Rey captioned this picture "Araucanians are a cheerful race in southern Chile,"[14] deliberately ignoring or unaware of their reputation as an "unconquerable" race of fierce warriors.

Diario de Aventuras Chilenas

While Guevara clearly had an interest in indigenous Chile, he focused much of his attention on Chilean women, regardless of their race. Moreover, his perception of southern Chile as authentically American and indigenous likely added to the allure of Chilean women. His attraction and subsequent marriage to the Peruvian Hilda Gadea (in 1955), who had both Chinese and indigenous ancestry, further indicates his desire for the "exotic."[15] Before his travels in Chile, Guevara already had a reputation among family and friends as being bold with women and having difficulties keeping his hands to himself.[16] This confidence with women and forward character was in evidence throughout southern Chile. Each town offered fresh opportunities for sexual conquest. In Los Angeles he and Granado "decided to move to the fire station lured by the charms of the caretaker's three daughters, exponents of the grace of Chilean women who, ugly or beautiful, have a certain spontaneity and freshness that captivates immediately."[17] Granado, who did not comment on Chilean women's particular charms or beauty, noted in his own account of the journey "the greater freedom of Chilean women. The prudishness of the Argentine middle class in keeping an eye on their daughters doesn't exist here." He also observed that Argentine and Chilean women had very different attitudes toward men (and, implicitly, toward sexual encounters). In Los Angeles a double date with two local women showed him that "things" were "more possible" in Chile than in Argentina.[18]

Their narratives evidence both men's desire for sexual encounters; yet Guevara also used thwarted desires to present himself as a comical rake. On their last night in Lautaro, Guevara described how, at a party, "one of the particularly friendly mechanics from the garage [which was fixing Granado's motorcycle] asked me to dance with his wife because he'd been mixing his drinks and was not feeling very well. His wife was hot and clearly in the mood and, full of Chilean wine, I took her by the hand and tried to steer her outside. She followed me meekly but then noticed her husband watching us and told me she would stay behind. I was in no state to listen to reason and . . . I started pulling her toward one of the doors, while everybody was watching, and then she tried to kick me, and as I was pulling her she lost her balance and fell crashing to the floor."[19] Granado's account confirms Guevara's, emphasizing how the wife "took a fancy to" Che and describing how Granado (and drunkenness) floored the aggrieved husband about to hit Guevara with a wine bottle. Needless to say, Guevara and Granado fled with an angry crowd close behind.[20] The clumsy failed seduction was clearly important to the travelers. As an old man Granado recounted how watching the filming of this scene for Walter Salles's film, *The Motorcycle Diaries* (2004) "moved [him] more than [he] could say."[21] What Guevara presents as drunken foolishness certainly suggests a selfishness in him, and perhaps recklessness as well. He neither respected the woman's wishes nor the husband's prerogative of sexual fidelity from his wife, nor even felt any debt for the help the mechanic had given the penniless travelers.

Although the women in mainland Chile appealed to Guevara and Granado, stories sent their imaginations further afield. Easter Island, ostensibly of interest because of the men's leprosy research, in fact attracted them for other reasons. Guevara mused: "Easter Island! The imagination . . . turn[s] somersaults at the very thought: 'Over there, having a white 'boyfriend' is an honor'; 'Work? Ha! the women do everything—you just eat, sleep and keep them content.' This marvelous place where the weather is perfect, the women are perfect, the food perfect, the work perfect (in its beatific nonexistence). What does it matter if we stay there a year; who cares about studying, work, family, etc."[22] While later in his travels Guevara began to see himself as engaged in research on societies and politics, and he described this journey as his "serious trip" in subsequent conversations with Ricardo Rojo, in these early days his main desires were ease, sex, and wine.[23]

Guevara principally wished to find young, lovely, and sexually available women, but the day-to-day difficulties that faced Chilean women also occasionally surfaced in his narrative, especially in central and northern Chile. This shift in how he depicted Chilean women coincided with more serious general reflections and a gradual move away from the larking in southern Chile. In a Valparaíso dive, La Gioncanda, Guevara and Granado settled into eating and drinking for free, thanks to the owner's generosity. Here Guevara heard the cook, "quite crazy" Rosita, who Granado described as looking like a "medieval witch" and being on the "very threshold of senile dementia," tell of domestic violence witnessed: the attempted murder of her neighbor. Rosita never sought to inform the police of the assault because they had laughed at her during a previous attempt to denounce a crime, accusing her of inventing stories.[24] Guevara offered no comment on the incident, but such brutality was part of daily life for many Chilean women, married to or in relationships with men who believed it their right to "discipline" their female partners. The violence, as long as it stayed reasonably private, was tolerated. In his work on El Teniente copper mine, in the Andes above Rancagua, Thomas Miller Klubock shows how relatives and neighbors sometimes defended women against domestic violence, but only when the violence caused a scene in public or could lead to serious physical consequences.[25]

Poverty and lack of health care were also day-to-day problems for many Chilean women. While in Valparaíso, Guevara tended to a sick woman, bedridden due to asthma and a heart condition. Recognizing her disease, smelling the poverty in her room, he acknowledged his own helplessness when faced with the structural causes of illness. As he traveled further in Latin America, however, the poverty and health problems he had witnessed in Chile were put into sad perspective. Looking back on his time in Chile, Guevara criticized the lack of free health care, yet he recognized that in comparison to other parts of Latin America, Chile was making good progress in improving national health.[26] In fact, in 1952 the government established the Servicio Nacional de Salud (National Health Service) to offer health care to all Chileans who required it. "Henceforth, women, men, and children, workers, indigents, and housewives, would all receive equivalent care in the same clinics and hospitals."[27] Prenatal care, antibiotics, and efforts to rid the country of tuberculosis, which was the single greatest killer at that time, also helped decrease mortality rates. As a result of these initiatives, life expectancy rose about fifteen years for both men and women, although infant mortality remained among the highest in Latin America.[28]

The last Chilean woman Guevara mentions was a communist living in internal exile. Guevara had encountered a communist couple looking for work in the mines of the northern desert. Amid domestic labor conflicts and increasing Cold War tensions, the Communist Party had been outlawed in 1948, its members persecuted. Guevara briefly saw himself through the eyes of the man, whose situation had become utterly precarious because of his political affiliation. Although they shared a fire that night, Guevara recognized that for this communist, their peregrinations had nothing in common. Guevara and Granado were poor, shabby, and wandering by choice. As a result of the repression of 1947 and 1948 under President Gabriel González Videla, this man's comrades were dead. The Chilean and his wife, having left their hungry children with a kind neighbor, lived exiled in their own country; they were headed toward the mines, where his politics would not matter but his health would quickly suffer.[29] In Guevara's account, the communist wife was a silent yet exemplary figure because of her loyalty during her husband's three months in prison.[30] Granado's account of the same meeting elaborated on her silence: "Unaware she was being observed, his wife watched him as he spoke, and she showed a kind of entranced admiration that touched a sentimental chord in me. I felt something warm inside that linked me fraternally to this woman, poor in money and in culture but rich in feeling, who had faced up to a long string of setbacks, persecution and disasters and was loyal to her companion even more in misfortune."[31] In this meeting Guevara and Granado proved acutely aware of their privilege, even while living as poor wanderers.

A National Resource

Other visitors and Chileans themselves shared Guevara's interest in Chilean women. Chile's middle-class and elite urban women were held as representative of and key to the nation's claim to modernity. Guevara, who had fashioned himself into a shabby vagabond, rarely had dealings with women like this in Chile—women who Chichina would have understood. His only recorded encounter of the sort was decidedly awkward. When the two travelers ran into Chilean women accompanying their acquaintances to see the view from Santa Lucia hill in Santiago, "the poor guys were embarrassed enough—unsure of whether to introduce us to these 'distinguished ladies of Chilean society,' as in the end they did, or play dumb and pretend not to know us (remember our unorthodox attire)."[32]

In his interactions with and depictions of women throughout Chilean society, Guevara was unusual: most travel writers focused on urban elite and middle-class women. In Santiago, Ross observed plenty of blue-eyed blondes who "bear witness to the heavy infusions of the same Anglo-Saxon and Teutonic blood that predominates in the United States." It was not only what these women looked like that he noticed but also what they were doing. "Particularly I was impressed by the number of young women in tailored suits or skirts and blouses who click along on spike heels to office or shop. Chile's women, unlike some of their Latin American sisters, have established their rights to work and to enter the professions, as well as to vote."[33]

Peter Schmid, a German touring South America, was fascinated by Chilean women. He begins his musings advising that "whoever observes Chile must never leave the women out of account." He then spends three pages addressing Chilean women's beauty, personality, and their contemporary situation.

> I could not help exclaiming as I walked along the streets for the first time. After an hour I took refuge in a dark café to be rid of the sight of women. . . . What shall I speak of first? Of their slim gazelle-like

figures, the soft oval faces, the dark eyes, or the natural complexion that gleams like a peach? Grace is to be found everywhere, of course, perhaps a softer and more sensitive grace than in this tropical paradise, but real beauty demands more than pretty forms. It demands a personality that flashes with the eyes, an ego that enchants you, and in my opinion the Chilean women possess this more than any of their sisters in South America. Whether it derives from the courage of the Araucanians or from English and German blood, whether. . . . [sic] But why bother to dig for the roots of beauty. We should merely rejoice its existence.[34]

In his lengthy reflection, Schmid depicts the characteristics of women in Chile as key to understanding the country. Still, his mention of Chile as a tropical paradise suggests that imagination and expectations were coloring his observations.

Even the fictional account of an English family's stance in Chile, written by Margaret Faraday, who had lived and traveled in South America for most of her life, addressed the subject of Chilean women's beauty and independence. In this novel for teenagers, the narrator observed about the family maid: "Carmen . . . was a cheerful soul, slim and attractive. The first time Harriet [the English daughter] saw her coming home after her afternoon off [Harriet] failed to recognize her and thought she must be a visitor, so smart did she look in her high-heeled shoes and well-cut linen suit; the lavish use of lipstick and eyebrow pencil still further altered her appearance. Harriet's mother explained to her, 'They're all like that . . . and after all, why not? Carmen's a pretty girl, and will be even prettier when she learns not to overdo her make-up. She tells me she's going to work in a shop when we leave. As long as she stays until then, I think it's a good idea. She's well educated—she went to the Liceo, and did quite well there.' "[35]

Another traveler who picked up on these discourses was Major W. T. Blake, whose previous publications included *The Royal Flying Corps in the War* and *Desert Adventures*. Blake and his wife toured the continent in a 1950 model Standard Vanguard car to prove that a British car was up to the challenge of South American roads and to strike a blow against the U.S. car industry. Thus much of his account describes in detail potholes, lack of paving, and the difficulty of finding indoor parking. Yet even Blake noticed the women of Chile when his wife, "R.," was confined to the hotel room ill: "During my wanderings in town . . . I came to the conclusion that the girls in Santiago have a much higher average of looks than in any other town that I had seen in South America, though perhaps they were not quite so smartly dressed as the women of Buenos Aires."[36]

The foreign observers addressing the beauty of Chilean women clearly keyed into a discourse of Chilean national identity. When Anne Merriman Peck, in South America during the late 1930s, traveled throughout Chile, local people often mentioned Chilean women's beauty. For example, before arriving in Santiago, Peck heard that the capital had a reputation for beautiful women.[37] She also learned the saying that Coquimbo was "famous for canaries and *las chicas bonitas*, pretty girls."[38] Once in Santiago, she observed the prosperous appearance of women on the street. A friend of hers advised her not to be fooled. " 'Don't think these women are prosperous because they have pretty clothes,' said an American friend who lives in Santiago. 'They spend everything they have on dress.' "[39] Other travelers also noticed this Chilean interest in the country's women. When Ross found himself stranded in the middle of the night at a small train station in central Chile, the ticket agent wanted to know, "What did I think of Chile? How did I like the wines? And then, inevitably, what did I think of Chilean women? I said I thought they were beautiful, which was polite—but also true."[40]

In 1954 the Chilean women's magazine *Eva* ran an article asking if Chilean woman really were as beautiful as Chilean men thought they were. The article noted that when famous foreign beauties arrived in Chile, it was common for Chilean men to say, " 'Geez . . . Chilean women are much prettier' . . . the men saying these proud and defiant comments . . . feel as knights [defending] this seemingly irrefutable truth." The magazine consulted three portrait photographers on the question. Javier Pérez, known as Rays, assured readers that 70 percent of Chilean women were beautiful, while the other 30 percent were "more than" acceptable. Their beauty came from their "intense" interior life, evident in their gestures and their provocative yet enchanting gazes. Like Guevara, Rays noticed Chilean women's indescribable appeal.

The next portrait photographer, Jorge Opazo, could not describe a "standard type" of Chilean woman; nonetheless he found the nation to have lovely women who were all tasteful in their clothing and makeup. For Opazo, Chilean women's beauty derived as much from their spirit as from their exterior. The Chilean woman's judgment and temperament "have made her emancipate herself before any other [woman] of the continent," yet once she had obtained her liberty, she used it sensibly. Opazo argued that "the Chilean woman is capable of performing very well in all types of technical, manual, professional, artistic, and cultural activities . . . and as a housewife, she knows how to manage her home very well." Chilean women's progress represented national progress, and Chile's women were a key resource and national trait. "If you'll allow me, I can confirm that the woman is the best that we have in Chile. Our country is the most special." Arguing that Chile's geography and isolation had fostered a nation of talented yet modest people, Opazo depicted these unique women as part of the nation's identity. "These characteristics of the Chilean people—a race that was forged between the experienced Spanish culture and the young, untutored Araucanian blood—are notoriously manifest in the women of this land: they are beautiful, distinguished, elegant, charming, refined, expressive, of good lines and great creative spirit." *Eva*'s staff argued that Opazo's opinion was conclusive because of his experience photographing so many lovely women.[41] Opazo explicitly articulated an undercurrent in much of the discussion about Chilean women: they constituted one of the nation's key resources and defined a part of Chilean national identity. This view of women as a national resource had been evident earlier in the century, too. For example, the Chilean contribution to the Pan-American Exhibition in Buffalo in 1901 included a photo album with portraits of lovely Chilean women, alongside photographs of steam locomotives built in Chile and naval warships.[42]

Evident in Opazo's discussion was a class-based and racialized view of female beauty. Maurois, enchanted by the elite women he met at social events, remarked that "the working women are not so lovely."[43] He concurred with Subercaseaux who contended that working women, even the young ones, had heavy gaits and lacked grace.[44] But Subercaseaux went further, fully acknowledging the class and racial elements of what he saw as a national myth: "The beauty of the 'Chilean woman' is a myth with which we are accustomed to duping the tourist. *She is very lovely in reality, but only in a certain middle class and in the aristocracy, where the European affiliation is* recent. The 'old' Chilean, and above all the one from the popular classes, is frankly ugly. She lacks daintiness, has wide hips and sagging breasts . . . [Chilean women] are extraordinarily uniform and lacking grace."[45] For Subercaseaux, Chilean women as a group lacked femininity, and this lack resulted from their essential passivity and their lack of spark or even maternal instincts. According to Subercaseaux the latter, rather than poor health care and poverty, was one the main reasons for the country's high infant mortality rate.[46]

Thus foreigners and Chileans alike saw in the discourse about women and beauty in Chile proof of the nation's European origin and an indication of its potential for future progress.[47] Chile is not unique in using women's beauty to define part of its national identity. Venezuela's national pride in producing so many Miss World and Miss Universe winners offers another example of female beauty representing the nation. Yet women's attractiveness in Chile also had other uses. Their beauty proved a useful tool to control male behavior. For example, at El Teniente copper mine, the company newspaper's *página feminina* promoted this useful beauty: to be a good wife and mother, a woman had to pay attention to her appearance. "According to the women's page, feminine attractiveness was necessary for maintaining a healthy marital relationship." Women's attractiveness would keep their husbands sexually interested and thus support stable marriages and lure men off the streets. Women had to have firm thighs, healthy teeth, and cared-for hands. One social worker quoted in the paper noted with disapproval and disgust that she had seen many women with dirty faces in the mining camps. But it was not only the U.S.-owned copper company that promoted this useful beauty. The national Welfare Department sponsored beauty contests for women who lived in the mining camp. In both cases, ideas about "female beauty reflected middle-class images of femininity that consisted of attributes to which only women devoted to domestic activity and with sufficient resources could aspire."[48] As Peck's friend knew, attractiveness had a high financial cost.

Chilean women's attractiveness also derived from their activities, not just their looks. The ideal woman was to be fit and physically active. In El Teniente, women's exercise was pushed as a means to develop "grace" and "elegance," while also promoting health and self-discipline. The mine newspaper "counseled women that to govern their bodies they should take cold showers and exercise regularly. Exercise and cosmetic care would promote modesty, restraint, and grace in women's behavior." Thus exercise, a middle-class activity, would inspire middle class–sanctioned lives.[49]

Organized sports further promoted women's physical activity. Chile had an internationally successful women's basketball team composed of players from different social classes and backgrounds. According to the women's magazine *Eva*, which ran many articles on women and sports, Chilean women's characteristics contributed to the basketball team's success. "Generally, the Chilean woman meets the basic requirements for the good cultivation of this sport. She is agile, perspicacious, quick in her reactions, and possesses a clear intelligence that allows her to organize her game well, confronting the adversary." The basketball team, which won the South American championship in the sixth international competition played in Quito, was described as made up of "simple young women," including factory workers, a teacher, a lawyer, and a mother. Although they all worked long hours and had other responsibilities, "they always have time to dedicate to the sport to make Chile's name stand out through basketball."[50] These women embodied ideal femininity while earning respect for Chile internationally and further proving what Chilean women could achieve.

As this description of the basketball team makes clear, it was not only a discourse about the singular beauty of Chilean women that foreigners, including Guevara, picked up on. Women in mid-twentieth-century Chile were doing things that women in other parts of Latin America were not—a fact that Guevara missed completely. Peck's interest was not just in women's appearance, but also in what they did. In Santiago she observed that attractive and well-dressed women—working, shopping, or heading to social activities—constantly filled the streets.[51] Peck concluded that "in all my associations with the people of Santiago I was most favorably impressed with the women. There are, of course, plenty of interesting men, but the women are outstanding. I had seen the pretty frivolous ones in tea shops and met some of them at parties. I had met the aristocrat who is the sympathetic *patrón*, and the aristocrat who combines interest in the arts with social service, and there were interesting contacts with other delightful women who are educators, teachers and writers."[52]

As these travelers noted, Chilean women did have many more professional opportunities than women in other countries, and they had a longer history in the professions. Women had first been admitted to the Universidad de Chile in 1877, from which the first few women doctors graduated in 1886.[53] Still, in the early twentieth century, women who sought learning were subjected to insults, social exclusion, and threats. Although more women were training as lawyers and doctors by the late 1920s,[54] clear gender divisions continued to exist among the professions. During the 1930s and 1940s, parents tried to keep their daughters from studying law or medicine for fear that they would become old maids. Other professions, like social work or pharmacology, were considered more appropriate for women.[55]

Regardless of these difficulties, the activities of Chilean women still served as proof of the nation's progressiveness. At a speech to the United Nations (UN) in 1946, the feminist Amanda Labarca noted the high number of women in paid labor: one-third of the working population. The nation, she argued, was proud of the "high culture and magnificent services of our [female] teachers, doctors, social workers, judges, engineers, and so on, in a word of the professional women." But Chile was also proud of women industrial workers, who increased the nation's production. All these women engaged in paid work while maintaining their social and maternal responsibilities. For Labarca, Gabriela Mistral's Nobel Prize was proof of the heights to which Chilean women could rise.[56]

In the 1950s, as earlier, women proved essential to the official and unofficial workforce. In 1952 an estimated 25 percent of the official workforce (2,155,243 workers) was female.[57] In the same year, 24 percent of women were classified as working in manufacturing (131,850) and 32 percent worked in domestic service (171,330).[58] Regardless of what Labarca argued in front of the UN, in some cases the appeal of hiring women workers resulted from gender inequalities. Management at the Yarur cotton mill, for example, preferred women "as machine operators because they earned 30 percent less than men for the same work, were more reliable, and were more receptive to . . . paternalistic charms." With the passage of effective equal-pay and maternity-leave legislation in the mid-1950s, women, who had made up 60 percent of that factory's labor force, began to be phased out as too expensive. This kind of decision was not unique to Yarur but formed part of a wider issue for women workers who had already found that improvements in their legal status could reduce their appeal to employers.[59] For many women, work meant finding informal opportunities that did not clash with their domestic responsibilities. Klubock describes the informal labor of many of the women living in the mining town of Sewell (home to the U.S. Braden Copper Company—which owned El Teniente mine); there, women sold homemade empanadas or candy door to door, took in boarders, washed clothing, and prepared meals for the men who worked in the mine.[60]

Regardless of their high participation in the labor force, women were seen both by the labor movement and by political leaders as having their proper place in the home; neither group valued female work in domestic service or the informal economy as real labor.[61] The company newspaper for El Teniente joined with Welfare Department social workers to argue that in a "modern" family, men earned the wages and women administered them, figuring out how to make these wages meet the family's needs.[62] Because women in paid labor were not seen as breadwinners, women workers continued to find themselves depicted as interlopers in a masculine realm.[63]

Seeking New Politics

Even though many travelers focused on women's activities, Schmid was the only foreign observer discussed here who addressed women's roles in contemporary politics, especially their roles in the recent presidential election. Women had gained the right to vote in municipal elections in 1934, but with separate polling stations and separate voter registries, making politics a highly gendered activity. Not until 1949 did women finally gain the right to vote in national elections.[64] In the years after women's suffrage became national law, strong, independent women's political parties made a clear (and potentially threatening) impact on political life, at a moment of crisis in Chilean party politics.[65] Women's parties and their vote proved particularly important in the election of Carlos Ibañez del Campo to the presidency in 1952. Ibañez brought together leftists and right-wing nationalists in an uneasy alliance. His appeal for both groups stemmed from a widespread dissatisfaction with the elitism and corruption of all politics. Ibañez's supporters saw him as an apolitical outsider, one therefore not beholden to party politics.[66] For his opponents, however, he was a Chilean version of Perón, like Ibañez a military leader "whose popular support threatened the interests of the oligarchy."[67] The opposition characterized Ibañez's previous presidency (1927–31) as a dictatorship that used illegal detention, torture, and the surveillance of telephone and postal communication to eliminate political and union opposition. Yet eight women's organizations endorsed the election of the populist general.[68]

Schmid did not talk about women's wide-ranging participation but, rather, noticed the showiest campaigner: María de la Cruz, the leader of the Partido Femenino Chileno. De la Cruz had a "raw sensual voice" and during her rallies "succumbed to passion, burst[ing] into uncontrollable sobbing and fl[inging] out her arms as though she were being pilloried." He was not impressed by her fervor and concluded that "Chile's soil and Chile's women are volcanic, and unfortunately so is Chile's social and political situation."[69] In her campaign to support Ibañez, de la Cruz became known for exactly the sort of performance that Schmid described. If Ibañez reminded voters of Perón, de la Cruz became an Evita figure. "As a senator with close ties to Ibañez, de la Cruz threatened conventional gender norms as well as standard practices in the economic and political realms." Members of her own party feared that she was acting more on her own behalf than representing them. De la Cruz's successful senatorial campaign increased the skepticism; Ibañez's belief that his strong polling among women (he won 43 percent of the women's vote) was down to de la Cruz proved their fears right.[70] But de la Cruz's career was cut short when she was accused of accepting a bribe. Although the charge proved unfounded, the story left her so discredited that she resigned.[71]

Another bribe accusation ended the period of successful, independent women's parties. In 1953, Ibañez, seeing the efficacy that organized women brought to his Argentine counterpart, planned a meeting between Perón himself and Chilean women's groups. After this meeting, at which Perón spoke of the importance that a unified women's movement had in Argentina, Chilean women's organizations met with two Argentine congresswomen. "The Argentines presented the Chilean women with a check, a gift that was to remain secret—ostensibly a bribe to get the women's groups to give up their independence and formally join Ibañez." When news of this bribe reached the media, the resulting scandal prompted the disbanding of all the women's groups that had participated in the Ibañez campaign. This revelation of corruption proved particularly damaging at a moment when women had only recently gained full participation in national politics, in part by claiming to stand above the everyday dirt of male politics. The Ibañez government and mainstream political parties, who feared that strong women's political parties and groups could threaten politics as usual, benefited from the scandal. Following the corruption incident politically active women joined traditional parties, doubting their ability to organize themselves independently. They had lost the moral superiority that had partially justified their political activity.

Thus the intense mobilization of women ceased shortly after women had finally gained the vote. As the Left gained strength in Chilean politics, women's issues were slowly displaced by class issues; left-wing women's groups lost their membership to political parties.[72] Meanwhile, as in Argentina, the unelected position of first lady came to have political significance. After women gained the vote in Chile, the first lady became an informal national leader of women's movements. She represented the voice of a conservative, Catholic, family-oriented anticommunist women's movement tied to the government.[73]

Traveling before the Ibañez elections, Guevara remained unaware of or uninterested in women's intense political mobilization, yet both he and Granado noticed many Chileans' expectation that life for working people would improve under Ibañez. In southern Chile, Granado took note of the common conviction that "only Ibañez can save the country. . . . People believe in him as if he were a godsend." Granado's one attempt to persuade a tenant farmer of the need for land reform failed because the farmer was convinced that Ibañez would ensure fair rural wages.[74] At the other end of the country, Ibañez was held in equal esteem. When Guevara and Granado showed up at the vast open-pit copper mine of Chuquicamata, owned and operated by the U.S. Anaconda Copper Company, they were grudgingly allowed to look around ahead of an expected strike. Their guide told them that the "imbecilic gringos" were foolishly "losing thousands of *pesos* every day in a strike so as not to give a poor worker a few more *centavos*. When my General Ibañez comes to power that'll all be over."[75] But Ibañez did not improve the lives of Chile's working people as they had hoped, leaving structural problems and economic inequalities intact.

Generous Hosts

One of the Chilean characteristics that most stood out to Guevara was the people's friendliness and quick hospitality. In Osorno he reported, "The Chileans, exceedingly friendly people, were warm and welcoming wherever we went."[76] In Valparaíso he mused, "To meet in Chile signifies a certain hospitality and neither of us was in a position to turn down this manna from heaven."[77] In Santiago the travelers finagled an invitation to "one of those Chilean-style meals that go something like, 'have some ham, try some cheese, drink a little more wine,' and that you stand up from—if you can—straining all the thorax muscles in your body."[78] According to Guevara's account, he and Granado accepted this consistent hospitality with a studied nonchalance that fit with his image of them as shrewd vagabonds.

They did not always adequately repay this hospitality. A German immigrant family in southern Chile gave Guevara and Granado a bed for the night and treated them "very well." In the night, awoken by his weak stomach, Guevara defecated out the window, rather than leave a mess in the bedpan, and (unintentionally) fouled peaches drying on the ground outside. In the morning, seeing the distasteful mess, he and Granado quickly departed, leaving the people who had taken care of them an unpleasant surprise.[79] Of another family who took them in, believing them to be internationally renowned leprosy experts, Guevara wrote, "basking in their admiration, we said goodbye to those people we remember nothing about, not even their names."[80] Perhaps age and bravado explain Guevara's self-depiction as a shameless con artist.

Guevara was not the only foreigner to find Chileans warm and hospitable. Perhaps Sister del Rey's own liveliness helped her see and bring out the cheerfulness in others. "There's such a vibrant life and gayety in Chile!"[81] she remarked, basing her observation on the pleasure and humor that people took from everyday situations. She described Galvarino, a town of fifteen hundred people between the coastal mountain range and Temuco as not having much in the way of modern infrastructure, adding, "But in a big way it goes in for friendliness, zest for living and bright-eyed children."[82] She was also amused and pleased at how much Chileans appeared to like Chile. "A great part of the charm of Chile, I've come to think, is that every Chilean thanks God from the bottom of his heart that he is a Chilean." In her experience of traveling, while most people from other countries were interested in information about the United States, Chileans wanted to talk about Chile. When the visitor suggested to a Chilean that the country was beautiful, " 'Yes!' he agrees. 'The mountains and the sea! Have you seen our national flower, the *copihue*? Everybody in Chile loves the *copihue*; we have it everywhere.' " At the suggestion that Chileans were "progressive," this imaginary Chilean would agree and argue that it was one of the country's unique characteristics.[83] She even titled one of her chapters, "Chile—The Chileans Like It!"

Ross agreed. In his *National Geographic* article, he reflected, "Everywhere I found the people a delight. The friendliness I have mentioned marked my contacts in every part of the country."[84] Ross opened his article describing how he stood on a street corner in Valdivia, feeling downhearted because of the rain. He was startled when a scooter-mounted student, Roberto González, told him to "get on" (in English). González wanted to give Ross a tour of the city. "This encounter was by no means my first experience with Chileans, but it symbolized adventures that marked my every step throughout their country. . . . Chile is without a doubt the friendliest land I know."[85] He concluded his article by reflecting, "I feel that Chile's real wealth lies in the breadth of her people and their capacity for friendship."[86]

Even bored Blake (motoring around South America in his British car) was struck by Chilean hospitality, which he often wished he could demur because of his own fastidiousness. Descending from the Portillo pass to Santiago, Blake and his wife found a picnic spot on the side of the road in Los Andes. "In a few minutes one man with an extremely dirty child came, with great hospitality, to ask us if we should not be more at our ease if we took our lunch in his house. . . . We made what we hoped were suitable excuses for not accepting his invitation [and] gave the child a bar of chocolate." Later in the day, when they stopped by a muddy stream to refill the radiator, a police officer appeared offering help, taking them back to the police station to fetch clean water.[87] Similarly, near La Serena, Blake and his wife stopped to watch men threshing grain on horseback. One of the men "invited us to come in and take some refreshment with them." The couple received a close-up view of the threshing, and then "one of the women of the household . . . came out and invited us to sit on the veranda where we were given plates heaped up with boiled wheat, with castor sugar and water to mix with the grain." Blake and his wife doubted the water's quality, as it came from a local well, but "courtesy demanded that we should eat it up and I think we did our duty rather nobly."[88] Despite his reservations about the hospitality, Blake reflected, "The more I see of other parts of the world the more I realize what a curiously inhospitable lot of people we are in England."[89]

Many of these travelers, although not Guevara, Granado, or Sister del Rey, remained unaware that the generosity and cheerfulness that so charmed them took place in the context of an increasingly difficult economic situation, especially for industrial and rural workers. Ibáñez's presidency did not bring improvements. Instead, the cost of living rose dramatically, as did inflation: in 1953 there was a 50 percent rise in the cost of living, which grew to 58 percent in 1954 and 88 percent in 1955. In 1955 inflation itself was at 86 percent. Unemployment also rose precipitously, almost doubling. Meanwhile, the peso lost two-thirds of its value; people with money bought dollars. The tax burden, moreover, was increasingly felt by those least able to afford it. Between 1946 and 1952 government revenues derived from direct taxes fell from 4.3 percent to 4 percent, while at the same time revenue from indirect taxes increased from 7.8 percent to 9.2 percent of the total. By 1956, estimates suggest, the rich were paying 14.7 percent of their income in taxes, while spending 64.3 percent of their income on consumer goods.[90] Chilean hospitality was costing poor and middle-class Chileans far more than these foreigners realized.

A Chilean Cornucopia

The admiration for people's friendliness was matched by wonder at the country's natural bounty. The depiction of Chile as blessed with fertile lands was a common one for Chileans and foreigners alike.

Subercaseaux titled one of the chapters in his geography of Chile, "Where the Agricultural Part Begins, Which Some Confuse with Chile."[91] Like other visitors, Guevara had noticed the fertile farmland, placing it in stark contrast to Argentine Patagonia, which he framed as a desert. "We arrived in Osorno, we scrounged around in Osorno, we left Osorno and continued ever northward through the delightful Chilean countryside, divided into plots, every bit farmed, in stark contrast to our own arid south."[92] Granado also reflected on the stunning and productive landscape: "The beauty of the Andes, the small farms golden with wheat, the rich orchards dripping with apples and pears," although he also noticed "the downtrodden huasos, poorly dressed in their unfailing ponchos and frayed, wide-brimmed hats, on small horses as famished as the riders themselves."[93]

Schmid was as lyrical about the land as he had been about the women. He asked himself, "Why is it that everyone in this country is not a poet?" He then reflected that "Chile is the most indolent of the South American lands. Her fields are a riot of flowers and the blossoms assail even the houses like a flood. . . . Vines grow in the plains with heavy bunches of grapes . . . nowhere does the wine turn out so nobly as here. . . . Wine is akin to poetry. It is no coincidence that this soil produced the finest lyrics in the Spanish tongue; Gabriela Mistral and Pablo Neruda are children of this land."[94] Hardly interested in Chile or its inhabitants, even Blake joined in the chorus depicting Chile as a natural garden, famed for its profusion of flowers.[95]

Sister del Rey, too, was captivated by Chile's bounty and beauty, which she understood through her religious vocation: "It does something to you to see broad fields, in which the curving lines the plow has made, stretch far off to a splendid line of poplar trees marking off one neighbor's farm from another. It does you good to see the two-wheeled carts piled high with big cabbages, carrots, radishes, and onions that make your mouth water; to talk to men riding majestic horses and wearing the manta [poncho] which might well be an emperor's uniform; to sink your teeth into beautiful apples and oranges. And then almost anywhere in Chile you can lift your eyes to a panorama of snow-covered mountains. It is as if God has put a fence around Chile and said, 'This much is My special property.' "[96]

Ross felt equally impressed with the farmland in central Chile. "From the Aconcagua south to the Bío-Bío, the land smiles bountifully on the farmer. There the brown of foothills and deserts yields to green. Rows of eucalyptus trees line fields of cereal grains, orchards, endless expanses of grapes, and pastures filled with Friesians [cows]."[97] The fertility of the Aconcagua Valley, one of Chile's most productive regions in the 1950s, was indeed remarkable: 36,600 hectares of land in cultivation yielded close to 10 percent of Chile's annual agricultural production. The crops of the Aconcagua Valley included fruit, wine grapes, wheat, hemp, alfalfa, vegetables, and flowers, cultivated during multiple growing seasons nurtured by the temperate climate. Subercaseaux wrote of it, "It is enough to look out the train window for the Biblical image of the land of plenty to come to mind." The image shifted at the various little stations, where vendors sold not "fruits of the Orient" but cherimoyas, avocados, grapes, and figs. He described it as a "fruity exuberance."[98]

Yet these travelers found bounty throughout Chile. In the far south, which no other traveler discussed in this chapter visited, Ross observed further fertility. Mario Habit, the chief agronomist for the Tierra del Fuego Development Society, had proudly told Ross that "we can grow almost anything here," the only impediment being the brush. That vegetation was being cleared as quickly as possible by burning or Caterpillar tractors hauling chains across the land.[99]

Schmid also observed this clearing of the land for cultivation in the Lake District, witnessing a process begun a hundred years before. Foreign immigration to that region had begun in the midnineteenth century when the Chilean government encouraged Germans to settle and farm the land, displacing the indigenous Mapuche. Visiting a German settler, who was burning vegetation to create fields for cultivation, Schmid observed, "Here and there a withered or burnt branch from some undestroyed tree seems to curse God and man that it had become a cripple. Each tree had become a kind of personality. They adorned the landscape as far as the town—memorials to the primeval forest which a few hundred years ago still knocked on its doors." Schmid described the landscape in the Lake District as "primeval . . . which offers itself with open arms to the bold colonist."[100] This discussion about the "primeval" land, of course, legitimized the clearing and colonization, erased its history, and put the place in a suspended state of timelessness, as if the land had remained trapped in amber until the European colonist came to free it from indigenous underuse. The "open arms" of the land also suggest a well-worn trope sexualizing the landscape and its conquest.

Once the land was clear of these withered and angry trees, Schmid observed the same fecundity that other travelers noted elsewhere: "Each seed here possessed a devastating fertility. All the flowers and fruits of the old country yield threefold on this young soil. Someone imported blackberries and soon they grew in profusion over all the fields. Had they been allowed to grow unhindered they would have turned Osorno into a sleeping beauty's castle."[101] Chile provided a clear lesson to these visitors in how productive subdued nature could be.

While these comments on fertility were based on observations of the Central Valley and the south, even the north shared in the miracle. In the Huasco Valley, a small family of English farmers marveled at the fertility of the irrigated desert. E. B. Herivel expressed amazement at the results her inexperienced hands could produce in her garden. When she began to make a flower garden, "It was then that the true miracle of soil and climate became apparent to me. There was nothing that would not grow. Cuttings of roses . . . surreptitiously and feloniously snicked off by me with a pair of embroidery scissors, not only struck at once but rapidly grew into huge bushes of flowering sweetness. . . . They grew with such an alarming speed and vigour that it was not unusual for them to make nine to ten metres of growth in the year."[102]

Not only foreign visitors tried to understand Chile through its landscape. Chileans also partially attributed their country's uniqueness to its geographic variety. Gabriela Mistral wrote to Subercaseaux that although other countries had variety, in the "reduced" section of the planet that was Chile, this diversity proved near miraculous, ranging from icebergs to rainforest to gardens.[103] Subercaseaux himself argued that this plurality turned into unity in Chile. Chile's geography made it "eternal and immutable."[104] His musing on Chilean nationality and geography, *Chile o una loca geografía*, clearly resonated with Chileans. The book went into a second edition in only six months and into a third edition within two years, a remarkable success in Chile's publishing history.[105]

The discussion of geographic variety and fertility so common in travel accounts ignored a structural problem in the Chilean economy and dramatic inequalities, to which most of these visitors seem blind. The problem lay with the inequality of land ownership and the system of unpaid labor, *inquilinaje*, to work that land. Although Guevara does not reflect on the concentration of land ownership in his account, Granado noted the problem and attempted to convince at least one (unreceptive) tenant farmer of the need for land redistribution, as I mentioned earlier.[106] The concentration of land in the hands of a few Chileans was indeed striking. Fewer than 9 percent of property owners controlled 82 percent of land under irrigation in 1955. Workers labored on the big farms and in return received rights to small plots, pasture, fuel, housing, and food. Workers also had to donate a portion of their produce to the estates they worked on. Indicating the extent of the problem, a law of 1954 stipulated that landowners must provide cash for at least 20 percent of their workers' salaries. Yet these same rural workers were legally prohibited from organizing, and protests were disbanded. During seasonal highs additional labor was provided by waged workers who might also receive in-kind payments, but no rights to land. These landless rural laborers and subsistence farmers, who made up the majority of the population, began work very young and only had a life expectancy of forty-five, while suffering from some of the "nation's highest rates of illiteracy, malnutrition, and infant mortality."[107] Moreover, low food prices and the inefficiency of the *fundos* (large farms), as well as low rural salaries, combined to reduce agricultural output compared to the population, so that Chile had to import food. By the end of the 1950s agricultural imports were greater than 45 million dollars per year.[108] And while the population in the same period was growing at a rate of 2 percent, agricultural production only rose by 1.4 percent.[109] The lyrical descriptions of natural cornucopias ignored that in the 1950s Chile could not feed itself.

Visits to the Capital

While the accounts considered here agreed that some essence of Chile could be captured in rural scenes, Santiago represented Chile's claim to modernity. Guevara had little to say about the Chilean capital, hurrying on to Valparaíso and its promise of a lift to the tropical paradise of Easter Island. To him the city resembled

Argentina's Córdoba, except for having a faster pace and more traffic.[110] Santiago also reminded Granado of Córdoba, although it was bigger, more modern, and closer to the Andes than his home city.[111] Subercaseaux noted the existence of more than one Santiago: "There is a Santiago that only the tourist sees. (It is very important.) There is a Santiago for the person who lives there. There is a Santiago for those who visit its fields and hills. There is a Santiago for those who arrive from the south; another, for those who arrive from the north. Finally, there is our own Santiago according to the neighborhood in which we live."[112] Subercaseaux suspected that tourists would find the city surprisingly uncolonial, lively, and its population white.[113] He was right. Maurois described Santiago as "alive and up to date." Its regular streets pleased the French traveler, as did the arcades and newspaper kiosks that reminded him of home. The flowers in suburban gardens particularly enchanted him: "Yellow and pink trees, outlined against the distant snowclad heights, have the airy grace of some Chinese paintings."[114] Subercaseaux agreed that a combination of factors gave the capital its charm, including its views of the snowcapped Andes, fronted by little one-storey homes and the tall buildings and churches of the center.[115]

Ross liked the city because he recognized its energy. One intersection reminded him of the "corner of State and Madison in Chicago." Santiago "defies the popular conception of a Latin American city. No romantic guitar-playing caballeros lounge about her streets. No languid-eyed señoritas wait behind barred windows for serenades." Ross's expectations about what he would find in a Latin American city appear to be based on some loose "Latin" combination of Andalusia and Mexico. Finding nothing languid about Santiago, Ross described the capital's modern and bustling atmosphere, which he believed derived from its (northern) European origins.[116] Subercaseaux agreed that this bustle would appeal to the tourist: "At mid-day and in the afternoon, when the offices close, the city presents an unusual aspect with that avalanche of people who return home."[117]

The national capital would clearly attract the attention of most international tourists, but more important, by the 1950s Chile was already a predominantly urban country, and it was the capital that realized remarkable population growth. That urban population included the fastest growing among the social groups: the middle class and the urban working class. Depending on the precise definition of class, the middle class made up between 15 and 33 percent of the population. The lower figure is based only on income, the higher one on education and self-description. In the difficult economic times of the 1950s, aspirations and education did not necessarily equate financial stability. Moreover, even though high migration to urban areas was a feature of the 1950s, city life did not necessarily improve a migrant's standard of living. Urban and rural workers (approximately 74 percent of the economically active population) faced similar economic difficulties: although the urban worker earned three times the wages of a farm worker, the higher cost of city living kept the benefits of that income down.

Regardless of the cost of living, people kept moving to the city. In 1952, 30 percent of Chile's total population resided in the capital, and fully 60 percent of the population was urban.[118] By the early 1960s Santiago had more than 2 million inhabitants, up from only five hundred thousand in the 1930s. The growth of the city stratified its spaces socially, as the better off moved out of the center to the new, eastern suburbs of the *barrio alto*, while the south became predominantly working class. The observers discussed in the present article based their comments on the city center or the *barrio alto*. What these foreigners, with one exception, did not see were the shantytowns, called *callampas* (mushrooms), growing around the city. These neighborhoods lacked adequate infrastructure (such as drinking water, electricity, paved streets, schools, and health care), and most of the inhabitants struggled to survive in a situation of under- or unemployment. By the mid-1960s an estimated five hundred thousand people lived in these communities.[119]

The exceptional foreigner who not only saw but also worked in the shantytowns was Sister del Rey. She lived in Santiago's Buzeta neighborhood, for several months working in the Maryknoll parish school there, founded in March 1953, as well as acting as a de facto visiting nurse and social worker with some of the other nuns. When she observed that "Chile has deep social problems," she knew of them firsthand. Her introduction to Buzeta's reputation came when a taxi driver refused to take the missionaries there: he was not worried about getting stuck in the muddy streets but about what the local residents might do to him. He warned the nuns that "a lot of tough characters live in Buzeta." Even after her many years of missionary work in Asia and Hawaii, the nun remarked that the neighborhood "could not be surpassed for utter destitution." Sister del Rey described the area as "just a collection of huts and shacks and tumble-down lean-to's that people put up until they can afford something better." She recounted shivering children standing in mud, a derelict car, a horse surrounded by its own manure, and women trying to cook in tin cans over wood fires: "It made one sick at heart to know that human beings have to live thus." A photograph she included of the area shows a barefoot little girl, in a white pinafore, grinning up at a nun in her full habit, while a little boy looks carefully at his bare foot. Wooden shacks, laundry, and piles of sticks—perhaps for weaving into baskets and barriers—can be seen in the background.[120] The modern hustle and bustle of Santiago that so impressed Ross was built, in part, on the labor force of neighborhoods like Buzeta.

Che's Chilean Legacy

As this essay has shown, Guevara was just one among many travelers and Chileans seeking to understand the essence of the country in the 1950s. While stealing wine and being chased by angry husbands, Guevara also observed and reproduced interlinking discourses of Chilean national identity: friendly people, a fruitful landscape, and lovely women. In his account of his few weeks in Chile, Guevara depicted himself as a young man with a sense of fairness coming face to face with structural injustice, yet one still more interested his own sensual experiences. Yet regardless of his limited observations, he still recognized that Chile was a country with a significant indigenous population, and he experienced, albeit superficially, the country's deep social problems. Although Guevara clearly held a view of Chile that was partial and incomplete, he, unlike other travel writers of the period, had experiences and encounters with poor and working Chileans. The bustling facade of Santiago or the stylish women there did not blind Guevara. Yet as much as he imagined himself engaged in "scientific inquiry,"[121] his diary lacked real insight into the situations he witnessed. At times his compassion was aroused, but he remained fundamentally untouched by the people and places he visited. His account was, he admitted, "perhaps a little flashy and somewhat removed from the intended spirit of scientific inquiry." Although he reflected on Chile in a subsequent chapter of his published journal, "Chile, a Vision from Afar,"[122] the country seemingly did not influence his later development and thinking. The trip through Chile washed over Guevara without changing him.

Yet Guevara would fundamentally alter Chile, not because of this trip but because of his participation in the Cuban Revolution and his legacy as the quintessential romantic revolutionary. We see his most direct legacy in the Movimiento de Izquierda Revolucionaria (MIR); Guevara provided part of the inspiration for this Marxist-Leninist coalition of urban student groups founded in Santiago in August 1965. Determined to radicalize the Chilean Left and foment a Cuban-style popular revolution, the group sought recruits and supporters among the peasants in Chile's agricultural regions and those same *callampas* that so shocked Sister del Rey. Guevara's influence came not only through his ideology and experience but also through his image. Che's handsome face, bearded and framed by long hair, projected the romantic ideal of the masculine revolutionary hero, and his appeal "crossed class, ethnic, and political lines."[123]

Although both the MIR and Guevara sought to create revolutionary fervor at the grass-roots level in Chilean and Cuban societies respectively, as with others at the vanguard of revolutions, their socioeconomic backgrounds were markedly opposed to those they sought to liberate. Guevara hailed from Argentina's professional educated classes and the leadership of the MIR was more bourgeois elite than Chilean proletariat. The radical group of privileged origin, whose activities included land invasions and bank robberies, never had its roots among Chile's working people.

Seeking to create violent revolution from below, the MIR viewed Salvador Allende's election as a false promise of radical change. Nonetheless, Allende's Unidad Popular (UP) government felt reluctant to repress them; they were the idealistic and misguided younger generation with whom the president shared his goals. But in not taking stronger measures against them, the UP government ended up confronting enemies and critics on both the Left and the Right. The Pinochet dictatorship had no qualms about repressing the MIR once it seized power. By 1976 the organization had become significantly weakened by the exile of its leaders and the capture, torture, and murder of many of its militants. The MIR leadership, "after fomenting a climate of confrontation, revolutionary violence, and a hegemonic masculinity of long-haired, daring youth . . . simply pulled out. The peasants at the local level did not have that same option. Arrested, imprisoned, and tortured, they would have engraved on their bodies the consequences of this short-lived revolutionary romance."[124]

But Guevara's legacy in Chile can also be understood well beyond the MIR. Cuba's successful revolutionary example and the model for revolutionary action that Guevara promoted in *Guerrilla Warfare*, among his other writings, not only inspired left-wing radical movements but also prompted the United States to fund a variety of counterinsurgency programs through military, political, and civic means. In Chile, the overt repercussions of this policy included Alliance for Progress funding under President Jorge Alessandri toward educational, housing, and land-reform projects, while President Eduardo Frei's government welcomed the first Peace Corps volunteers to Chile.[125] Covertly, the Kennedy administration (and later the Johnson administration), recognizing that previous U.S. support for conservative oligarchies only strengthened the radical Left, sought to make conditions right for a middle-class revolution, rather than a socialist one. Four million dollars to ensure Frei's election victory in 1964 and 3 million to ensure Allende's defeat in the same election were to create the conditions for these reformist politics. Additionally, Chile received 1.2 billion dollars in grants and loans, 91 million as military aid, between 1962 and 1970.

Allende's election in 1970 meant the failure of a decade-long U.S. policy to keep him from La Moneda, the Chilean presidential palace. At the same time, the previous decade of overt and covert intervention had made U.S. policymakers and politicians believe in their entitlement to overrule Chile's democratic institutions.[126] Meanwhile, within Chile, military elites drew the conclusion that "only a military regime could confront the dual challenges of modernization and the threat to national security posed by Communist insurgency."[127] The very success of the Cuban Revolution amid the tensions of the Cold War had polarized domestic and international politics in Latin America, diminishing the possibility of another Cuba.

Notes

My thanks to Paulo Drinot, Stuart Durkin, Fernanda Peñaloza, Natalie Zacek, the Nottingham University Hispanic Studies Research Seminar participants, and two anonymous reviewers for their helpful comments on earlier versions of this essay. My research was partially funded by the School of Languages, Linguistics, and Cultures at the University of Manchester.

1 Jorge G. Casteñada, *Compañero: The Life and Death of Che Guevara*, trans. Marina Casteñada (London: Bloomsbury Publishing, 1997), 46.

2 Susan Bassnett, "Travel Writing and Gender," *The Cambridge Companion to Travel Writing*, ed. Peter Hulme and Tim Youngs (Cambridge: Cambridge University Press, 2002), 234.

3 Mary Louise Pratt, *Imperial Eyes: Travel Writing and Transculturation* (London: Routledge, 1992), 75.

4 See, for example, Ernesto "Che" Guevara, *The Motorcycle Diaries: Notes on a Latin American Journey* (London: Harper Perennial, 2004), 56, 57, 62–63, 65, 76–77; and Alberto Granado, *Traveling with Che Guevara: The Making of a Revolutionary*, trans. Lucía Alvarez de Toledo (New York: Newmarket Press, 2004), 34, 41–42, 45–46, 54–55.

5 Casteñada, *Compañero*, 38–43. See also Ernesto Guevara Lynch, *The Young Che: Memories of Che Guevara*, trans. Lúcia Alvarez de Toledo (London: Vintage, 2007), 140–41.

6 Guevara, *The Motorcycle Diaries*, 57.

7 Margaret Faraday, *The Young Traveller in South America* (London: Phoenix House, 1957), 59.

8 Benjamín Subercaseaux, *Chile, o una loca geografía*, 3rd edn. (Santiago de Chile: Editorial Ercilla, 1940), 47.

9 André Maurois, *My Latin-American Diary*, trans. Frank Jackson (London: Falcon Press, 1953), 58–59.

10 Kip Ross, "Chile: The Long and Narrow Land," *National Geographic*, February 1960, 187.

11 Karin Alejandra Rosemblatt, *Gendered Compromises: Political Cultures and the State in Chile, 1920–1950* (Chapel Hill: University of North Carolina Press, 2000), 38.

12 Ross, "Chile," 213–14.

13 "Sister Maria del Rey Danforth, O.P.," CatholicAuthors.com (accessed 20 December 2007).

14 Sister Maria del Rey, *In and Out the Andes: Mission Trails from Yucatan to Chile* (New York: Charles Scribner, 1955), photographs between 186–87.

15 Casteñada, *Compañero*, 65–67.

16 Ibid., 36.

17 Guevara, *The Motorcycle Diaries*, 64.

18 Granado, *Traveling with Che Guevara*, 41, 44–45.
19 Guevara, *The Motorcycle Diaries*, 61–62.
20 Granado, *Traveling with Che Guevara*, 40.
21 Ibid., xiv.
22 Guevara, *The Motorcycle Diaries*, 69.
23 Ricardo Rojo, *My Friend Ché*, trans. Julian Casart (New York: Grove, 1969), 16–17.
24 Guevara, *The Motorcycle Diaries*, 71; and Granado, *Traveling with Che Guevara*, 50.
25 Thomas Miller Klubock, *Contested Communities: Class, Gender, and Politics in Chile's El Teniente Copper Mine, 1904–1951* (Durham: Duke University Press, 1998), 214.
26 Guevara, *The Motorcycle Diaries*, 70–71, 87.
27 Rosemblatt, *Gendered Compromises*, 147.
28 Simon Collier and William F. Sater, *A History of Chile, 1808–1994* (Cambridge: Cambridge University Press, 1996), 289. On child mortality in an earlier period, see Asunción Lavrin, *Women, Feminism, and Social Change in Argentina, Chile, and Uruguay, 1890–1940* (Lincoln: University of Nebraska Press, 1995), 100–101.
29 Klubock, *Contested Communities*, 13.
30 Guevara, *The Motorcycle Diaries*, 77–78.
31 Granado, *Traveling with Che Guevara*, 58.
32 Guevara, *The Motorcycle Diaries*, 67.
33 Ross, "Chile," 188.
34 Peter Schmid, *Beggars on Golden Stools: A Journey through Latin America*, trans. Mervyn Savill (London: Weidenfeld and Nicholson, 1956), 293–94.
35 Faraday, *The Young Traveller in South America*, 60.
36 W. T. Blake, *The Pampas and the Andes* (London: Travel Book Club, 1950), 51.
37 Anne Merriman Peck, *Roundabout South America* (New York: Harper, 1940), 147.
38 Ibid., 138.
39 Ibid., 145.
40 Ross, "Chile," 235.
41 "¿Es realmente hermosa la mujer chilena"? *Eva*, 3 December 1954, 6–7.
42 Chile: Comisión para la Exposición Pan-Americana, Buffalo, *Chile at the Pan-American Exposition: Brief Notes on Chile and General Catalogue of Chile Exhibitions* (Buffalo, n.p., 1901).
43 Maurois, *My Latin-American Diary*, 59.
44 Subercaseaux, *Chile*, 187.

45 Ibid., 191–92; emphasis original.

46 Ibid., 192–93.

47 Rosemblatt, *Gendered Compromises*, 110.

48 Klubock, *Contested Communities*, 65.

49 Ibid., 65–66.

50 Marlore Anwandter and Graciela Romero, "Las doce Chilenas invictas," *Eva*, 31 August 1956, 30, 31.

51 Peck, *Roundabout South America*, 145.

52 Ibid., 156–57.

53 Amanda Labarca H., *Feminismo contemporáneo* (Santiago de Chile: Editorial Zig-Zag, 1947), 125.

54 Julieta Kirkwood, *Ser política en Chile: Las feministas y los partidos* (Santiago de Chile: Facultad Latinoamericana de Ciencias Sociales, 1986), 87–88.

55 Rosemblatt, *Gendered Compromises*, 137.

56 Labarca, *Feminismo contemporáneo*, 126–27.

57 Karin Alejandra Rosemblatt, "Charity, Rights, and Entitlement: Gender, Labor, and Welfare in Early-Twentieth-Century Chile," *Hispanic American Historical Review* 81:3–4 (2001), 565. On women in the official workforce earlier in the twentieth century, see Lavrin, *Women, Feminism, and Social Change*, 62–65.

58 Rosemblatt, "Charity, Rights, and Entitlement," 569.

59 Kirkwood, *Ser política en Chile*, 139; and Peter Winn, *Weavers of Revolution: The Yarur Workers and Chile's Road to Socialism* (Oxford: Oxford University Press, 1986), 43–44, quote on 43. On earlier legislation to protect women workers, see Lavrin, *Women, Feminism, and Social Change*, 78–85.

60 Klubock, *Contested Communities*, 204–5.

61 Rosemblatt, *Gendered Compromises*, 51, 276.

62 Klubock, *Contested Communities*, 63.

63 Rosemblatt, *Gendered Compromises*, 76–79.

64 Lisa Baldez, *Why Women Protest: Women's Movements in Chile* (Cambridge: Cambridge University Press, 2002), 24–26.

65 Jean Grugel, "Populism and the Political System in Chile: Ibañismo (1952–1958)," *Bulletin of Latin American Research* 11:2 (1992), 175; and Kirkwood, *Ser política en Chile*, 56, 81.

66 Grugel, "Populism and the Political System in Chile," 175–77.

67 Baldez, *Why Women Protest*, 28.

68 Ibid., 27; and Elizabeth Lira et al., *Historia, política y ética de la verdad en Chile, 1891–2001: Reflexiones sobre la paz social y la impunidad* (Santiago de Chile: LOM Ediciones, 2001), 48.

69 Schmid, *Beggars on Golden Stools*, 296.

70 Baldez, *Why Women Protest*, 28–29.

71 Ibid., 28; and Annie G. Dandavati, *The Women's Movement and the Transition to Democracy in Chile* (New York: Peter Lang, 1996), 19. See also Kirkwood, *Ser política en Chile*, 152–53.

72 Baldez, *Why Women Protest*, 30–31; and Kirkwood, *Ser política en Chile*, 153–55.

73 Kirkwood, *Ser política en Chile*, 56.

74 Granado, *Traveling with Che Guevara*, 35–36.

75 Guevara, *The Motorcycle Diaries*, 79.

76 Ibid., 56.

77 Ibid., 68.

78 Ibid., 67.

79 Ibid., 63. Granado omits this episode.

80 Ibid., 59.

81 Del Rey, *In and Out the Andes*, 140.

82 Ibid., 166.

83 Ibid., 141–42.

84 Ross, "Chile," 217–18.

85 Ibid., 185–87.

86 Ibid., 233.

87 Blake, *The Pampas and the Andes*, 46–47.

88 Ibid., 66.

89 Ibid., 67.

90 Collier and Sater, *A History of Chile*, 278; Mario Góngora, *Ensayo histórico sobre la noción de estado en Chile en los siglos XIX y XX* (Santiago de Chile: Ediciones de la Ciudad, 1981), 123; and Jay Kinsbruner, *Chile: A Historical Interpretation* (New York: Harper and Row, 1973), 139–41.

91 Subercaseaux, *Chile*, 170.

92 Guevara, *The Motorcycle Diaries*, 56.

93 Granado, *Traveling with Che Guevara*, 43.

94 Schmid, *Beggars on Golden Stools*, 276.

95 Blake, *The Pampas and the Andes*, 42.

96 Del Rey, *In and Out the Andes*, 141.

97 Ross, "Chile," 217.

98 Heidi Tinsman, *Partners in Conflict: The Politics of Gender, Sexuality, and Labor in the Chilean Agrarian Reform, 1950–1973* (Durham: Duke University Press, 2002), 19. The direct quote is taken from Subercaseaux, *Chile*, 139–40.

99 Ross, "Chile," 187, quote on 201.

100 Schmid, *Beggars on Golden Stools*, 280–81.

101 Ibid., 281.

102 E. B. Lambert Herivel, *We Farmed a Desert* (London: Faber and Faber, 1957), 107.

103 Gabriela Mistral, "Contadores de patrias," quoted in Subercaseaux, *Chile*, 16.

104 Subercaseaux, *Chile*, 24.

105 Ibid., 25, 28.

106 Granado, *Traveling with Che Guevara*, 35–36.

107 Arnold J. Bauer, "Industry and the Missing Bourgeoisie: Consumption and Development in Chile, 1850–1950," *Hispanic American Historical Review* 70:2 (1990), 238; and Tinsman, *Partners in Conflict*, 21–25.

108 John L. Rector, *The History of Chile* (Westport, Conn.: Greenwood, 2003), 141.

109 Jay Kinsbruner, *Chile: A Historical Interpretation* (New York: Harper and Row, 1973), 150.

110 Guevara, *The Motorcycle Diaries*, 66.

111 Granado, *Traveling with Che Guevara*, 46, 48.

112 Subercaseaux, *Chile*, 110.

113 Ibid., 116.

114 Maurois, *My Latin-American Diary*, 58.

115 Subercaseaux, *Chile*, 114.

116 Ross, "Chile," 187.

117 Subercaseaux, *Chile*, 114.

118 Rector, *The History of Chile*, 139. See also Góngora, *Ensayo histórico sobre la noción de estado en Chile*, 124.

119 Collier and Sater, *A History of Chile*, 291–92.

120 Del Rey, *In and Out the Andes*, 135–42, quotes on 135, 136–37, 142, photograph between 186–87.

121 Guevara, *The Motorcycle Diaries*, 86.

122 Ibid., 86.

123 Florencia E. Mallon, "*Barbudos*, Warriors, and *Rotos*: The MIR, Masculinity, and Power in the Chilean Agrarian Reform, 1965–74," in *Changing Men and Masculinities in Latin America*, ed. Matthew C. Gutmann (Durham: Duke University Press, 2003), 179–215, quote on 211.

124 Mallon, "*Barbudos*, Warriors, and *Rotos*", 202–3. See also Brian Loveman, *Chile: The Legacy of Hispanic Capitalism*, 2nd edn. (New York: Oxford University Press, 1988), 292, 315; Gabriel Smirnow, *The Revolution Disarmed: Chile, 1970–1973* (New York: Monthly Review Press, 1979), 30, 105, 149; Steve J. Stern, *Remembering Pinochet's Chile: On the Eve of London, 1998* (Durham: Duke University Press, 2006), 17, 24.

125 Rector, *The History of Chile*, 161, 165.

126 Peter Kornbluh, *The Pinochet File: A Declassified Dossier on Atrocity and Accountability* (New York: New Press, 2003), 3–6.

127 Che Guevara, *Guerrilla Warfare: With an Introduction and Case Studies by Brian Loveman and Thomas M. Davies, Jr.* (Manchester: Manchester University Press, 1986), 27–29, quote on 29.

Paulo Drinot

Awaiting the Blood of a
Truly Emancipating Revolution
Che Guevara in 1950s Peru

Ernesto Guevara de la Serna traveled through Peru twice in the
1950s, first between 24 March and 22 June 1952, corresponding to
the trip with Alberto Granado recounted in the *Motorcycle Diaries* and
in Granado's own diaries, published as *Traveling with Che Guevara*,
and later for much of August and September 1953, as recounted in
Back on the Road.[1] During the first trip, Guevara and Granado entered
Peru from Chile and spent most of April traveling in the southern
highlands, famously visiting Machu Picchu. In late April they arrived
in the central sierra, and from there they moved on to Lima on 1 May,
where they stayed three weeks and met Hugo Pesce, one of Peru's
most eminent physicians who in the late 1920s had helped José
Carlos Mariátegui found the Peruvian Socialist Party. Pesce took the
travelers under his wing, feeding them and even giving them clothes
(a white suit for Granado and a white jacket for Guevara). They then
retraced their steps back through the central sierra and down into
the selva, to the river port of Pucallpa, where they boarded the boat
that took them to Iquitos. From Iquitos they went downstream to
the San Pablo "leper" colony, and from there made their way, un-
knowingly via Brazil, to Leticia on the Colombian side of the border.

The second trip through Peru began on the Peru-Bolivia border
on 7 August 1953. Guevara undertook this trip with Carlos "Calica"
Ferrer, an old childhood friend.[2] After a few days in Cuzco, during
which Guevara visited Machu Picchu for a second time, Che and
Calica embarked on a grueling three-day journey to Lima. They
spent a few weeks in the capital, during which Guevara visited some
of the people he had met on his first trip, including Pesce, and

then headed north to the Ecuadorian border. Unfortunately, Guevara's diary includes very little information on this trip up the arid Peruvian coast, which the two friends appear to have covered in a great hurry, arriving in Piura after a single day. Although he passed through the cities of Piura, Talara, and Tumbes, Guevara had little to say about these places. It seems particularly surprising, not least in light of the anti-imperialist sentiment that his visit to Chuquicamata engendered (perhaps suggesting the formulation of those sentiments ex post facto), that he describes Talara, an oil enclave controlled by the International Petroleum Company, itself a subsidiary of Standard Oil, as a "rather picturesque oil port."[3] Guevara, who appears to have been suffering from particularly bad asthma attacks during much of the trip north, crossed into Ecuador on 27 September 1953.

The Peru that Guevara encountered in his travels and narrates in his diaries has received limited attention from historians. Peruvian historiography tends to end in the 1930s, when, typically, sociologists and political scientists take over, particularly for the period after 1968 and the so-called Peruvian Experiment of General Juan Velasco Alvarado.[4] It is undoubtedly through fiction that the decade has received its most profound analysis. Our understanding of the 1950s in Peru has been fashioned by the novels and short stories of Mario Vargas Llosa, José Maria Arguedas, and Julio Ramón Ribeyro to a far greater extent than any work of social science. Indeed, the dominant interpretation of that decade arguably remains encapsulated in the question that Santiago Zavala, "Zavalita," Vargas Llosa's main character in *Conversation in the Cathedral*, asks at the beginning of the novel: "At what precise moment had Peru fucked itself up"?[5] This phrase has become popular in Peru and has been interpreted in myriad ways.[6] It is, as several scholars have pointed out, a question that fits neatly into defeatist narratives of Peruvian history. Such narratives are clearly the product of particular readings of Peruvian history formulated, ironically, by historians of both the Left and the Right.[7] It is, as Gonzalo Portocarrero suggests, a particularly Creole (i.e., white/coastal) form of thinking about Peru's history.[8] However, the question arguably should be understood primarily in the context of the period in which the novel is set. According to Guillermo Nugent, the answer to Zavalita's question that the novel itself provides is that "Peru fucked itself up when the cholos arrived. To

Lima, it is assumed, since Lima is Peru."[9] Zavalita's question points to a highly racist hegemonic reading of Peru's history based on the idealization of, and the reduction of all Peruvian history to, a largely imagined past in which Lima was a white city untouched and yet dominant over an Indian and "cholo" national hinterland.

Zavalita's question thus expresses the racialized way in which elite Peruvians made sense of the beginnings of mass internal migration in the 1950s, but also, more generally, their understandings of the nature of Peruvian society and history. But the question also proves revealing from the perspective of historical analysis because it indicates a demographic, social, and cultural point of inflexion in Peruvian history, rather than a political or economic one. In fact, such a demographic and cultural periodization of Peru's twentieth-century history is finding acceptance in some of the more recent master narratives or "national histories" of Peru. As historians of Peru refocus their gaze on new subjects and adopt new theoretical perspectives, they—in contrast to older "national histories," which favored political and economic turning points (the 1930s, 1968)—give increasing importance to the 1950s.[10] In large measure this has to do with the fact that from today's perspective, the changes that fashioned that decade, particularly what we may call the "peruvianization of Lima," seem to explain the country's contemporary challenges more compellingly than, say, the displacement of British merchant capital by U.S. monopoly capital or the rise of military corporatism.

The present essay explores the Peru of the early 1950s through the perspective of Guevara's diaries. As his biographers agree, Guevara's travels through Latin America in the 1950s had a profound impact on his worldview. According to Paul Dosal, "the poverty and injustice that [Che Guevara] observed struck a sensitive chord" while he came "to identify United States imperialism as the source of the injustices and poverty that he observed in South America."[11] The experiences lived in those travels and, just as important, the diaries that served as the medium to order and give meaning to those experiences, helped produce Che Guevara, helped create Che from Ernesto Guevara. As I will suggest, Peru provided plenty of examples of injustice and poverty, and Guevara's experience of them, framed by the experiences of an unforgiving environment (roasting deserts, freezing mountains, and mosquito-infested jungles), hunger, and asthma attacks, undoubtedly contributed to his radicalization. At the same time, like the European travelers that Mary Louise Pratt and others have studied and whose "travel and exploration writing produced 'the rest of the world' for European readerships," Guevara, with his writings on Peru and Latin America more generally, also produced a Peru and a Latin America—initially for himself and later for others.[12] Through a close reading of Guevara's diaries in conjunction with and in counterpoint to other contemporary travelogues, including Granado's, I critically examine Guevara's production of early 1950s Peru.

Political Silences in the Land of Flourishing Barracks

Guevara traveled in Peru during the middle years of Manuel Odría's eight-year dictatorship (1948–56). Odría's coup in 1948 ended one of Peru's few periods of democratic rule in the twentieth century, but also, according to contemporary commentators, one of the most chaotic.[13] Historians have tended to view Odría's coup as part of a general and unfortunate return to military dictatorship throughout Latin America after the democratic spring of the immediate postwar period. However, contemporary opinions on the character of the dictatorship, although certainly divided, were for the most part relatively favorable. Peter Schmid, a German traveler who crossed the entire continent from Mexico to Brazil in the first half of the 1950s, presented a somber picture of the dictatorship: "The country is . . . one of the most 'reactionary' in South America. Not only in the amiable patriarchal sense that Ecuador is conservative, but in the evil sense of a conspiracy of the dark powers: feudal lords, church, army and foreign capitalist companies."[14] But Schmid nevertheless felt he had to concede that "Peru may have the atmosphere of a barracks parade ground, but paradoxically it is a flourishing barracks."[15] Although most foreign observers criticized the lack of political freedoms and the severe if selective repression that came to characterize the regime, most would have agreed with the *New York Times* journalist Tad Szulc's conclusion that "if Odría's political behavior may have left much to be desired, his administrative record was impressive."[16] *Time* magazine, for one, certainly agreed, and approvingly pointed out that "General Manuel Odría has ruled Peru as a fatherly, sometimes Big Brotherly dictator" and that "the country has moved forward economically under honest, efficient Dictator Odría."[17]

Odría based his regime on three basic pillars: (1) the ruthless but selective elimination of political opposition; (2) liberal economic policies that benefited from a favorable international economic context; and (3) social reform aimed at the working and middle classes. Odría justified the coup by pointing to President José Bustamante's failure "to deal firmly with the APRA [American Popular Revolutionary Alliance] menace [that] was leading the country towards disaster and ruin."[18] One of his first measures was to outlaw both APRA and the Peruvian Communist Party, while simultaneously increasing the army's pay by 20 percent. Political opponents found themselves summarily arrested and subjected to court martial without a right of appeal. The regime formalized repression through the passing of the Law of Interior Security on 21 July 1948, which, as British diplomats noted, "deprives Peruvian citizens of most of the elementary democratic rights to which, on paper at any rate, they are entitled under the Constitution."[19] Yet although repression could take extreme forms (as well as absurd ones, such as attempts to link the APRA leader, Víctor Raúl Haya de la Torre, with a gang of cocaine smugglers arrested in New York in mid-1949), it was for the most part selective.[20] For a time at least the regime even allowed newspapers deemed pro-communist, such as the satirical *Yá*, to continue operations, in part because they tended to be critical of the APRA but also because, "[Odría] realises that it is sound politics to allow people to let off steam and considers these small semi-Communist publications provide a harmless and even convenient medium for this purpose [sic]."[21] The British ambassador for one concluded that "it would be a mistake to picture Peru as being anything like a Police State of the Fascist variety. . . . The ordinary individual unless he is suspected of plotting against the regime is free to come and go as he likes (there is nothing in Peru equivalent to the Gestapo)."[22] But some would have been hard pressed to agree with this evaluation, not least *aprista* labor leaders such as Luis Negreiros, whose murder by the secret police brought about a formal letter of protest from the American Federation of Labor against "this latest crime committed by the Fascist-minded military dictatorship of Peru."[23]

Odría's economic policies stand out in the Latin American context of this period because Peru fulfilled, as Rosemary Thorp and Geoffrey Bertram suggest, "the dream of orthodox development economists" at a time when many neighboring countries were moving toward increasing state intervention in the economy.[24] The economic achievements of this period of free-market policies, which included the reduction of barriers to capital flows and the encouragement of foreign direct investment, are notable: between 1948 and 1951 exports rose 6 percent a year and then, buoyed by the effects of the Korean War, increased to 10 percent a year from 1951 to 1959. Gross national product, meanwhile, increased by 4.7 percent annually, although in per capita terms the increase proved more modest, at only 2.4 percent per annum, a consequence of considerable demographic growth.[25] No doubt mindful that political repression and economic growth alone would not undermine widespread support for APRA among Peru's middle and working classes, Odría also implemented highly visible if not necessarily highly effective social reforms. Whether purely political considerations or a higher ideal motivated him remains unclear, although he was certainly not the first dictator seeking relations with organized labor through statist social action.[26]

Like Augusto B. Leguía (1919–30) and Oscar Benavides (1933–39) before him, Odría introduced a series of social measures, described as an "avalanche" by the British ambassador, including a revamped social insurance scheme for employees, a substantial increase in indemnities paid to workers for accidents and professional illnesses, a controversial profit-sharing scheme for workers and employees, and improved pensions.[27] In addition, the government embarked on an extensive program of reform and expansion in housing, public health, and education. The extent to which these reforms succeeded in their objectives remains unclear. Early on, British diplomats, convinced that Peru was "economically . . . not ready for it," noted that Odría's "ambitious" social program had been met with apathy, "for the people would prefer cheap bread to the promise of social benefits to come, while General Odría, who is not really successful as a demagogue, has not managed, like Perón, to kindle the imagination of the masses."[28] Some of the infrastructural measures were certainly followed through. According to one source, the Odría government built 217 primary schools and created

691 new teaching positions in 1953 alone.[29] But whether the regime succeeded in co-opting labor and undermining the appeal of APRA remains less clear: Odría's progressive social program may have tamed militancy among the working classes, but the regime still occasionally had to turn to full-on repression to bring labor unrest under control, as happened during a general strike in Arequipa in early 1953, believed to have been instigated by Bolivian-influenced Trotskyites, during which some sixty "minor" labor leaders "were picked up."[30]

With the end of the Korean War, however, the economy started to weaken. Favorable trade balances became unfavorable ones and inflation, which had presented the Bustamante government with one of its biggest problems, resurfaced.[31] By early 1954, though they believed that the government remained in a strong position, British diplomats were forced to admit that "there is discontent in the country. The curtailment of the public works program (one of the measures designed to protect the currency) has led to unemployment; corruption is rampant; and the War Minister Noriega, is heartily disliked by many army officers."[32] In early 1955 the British ambassador explained to his superiors that critics of the regime, both inside and outside Peru, "are becoming bolder and more vocal." He pointed to growing discontent in the provinces, particularly in Arequipa, at the overcentralized character of the regime, and among "sections of the middle-classes—a class which is rapidly becoming more social and politically conscious—which believes that it would benefit from a policy of exchange controls, quotas, and increased import tariffs, in contrast to the Government's declared policy of interfering as little as possible with trade and finance." Yet he concluded that "as yet no party exists to serve as a focus for their interests. There is no sign at all of the development of party politics as we understand them."[33] But in the period leading up to the 1956 elections two fresh political forces emerged in representation of new, largely middle-class sectors; both had benefited from the political and economic stability of the Odría regime, but now they clamored for political representation. Fernando Belaúnde's National Front of Democratic Youth and the Christian Democratic Party (based in the provincial city of Arequipa) were unable to defeat Manuel Prado's National Coalition, which brought together the oligarchy and APRA in opposition to Odría. But we can locate the birth of a new form of expanded and more inclusive politics in the emergence of Belaúnde and the Christian Democrats and in the radicalization of younger sectors of APRA as a result of the party leaders' willingness to consort with the oligarchy.[34]

This, in broad strokes, was the political and economic context that Guevara encountered in Peru during his two visits in the early 1950s. Yet in contrast to his relatively extensive comments on, and keen interest in, political developments in Bolivia and Chile, Guevara left little of his impressions of Peru's regime or of the political situation in the country in his diaries. Despite spending time with Pesce, who had represented Mariátegui in Argentina during the meetings of the Comintern in 1928, Guevara's diaries remain silent on the Peruvian Communist Party that Pesce and Mariátegui established that same year (originally as the Peruvian Socialist Party). In Walter Salles's film, The Motorcycle Diaries (2004), Pesce gives Guevara a copy of Mariátegui's Seven Interpretative Essays on Peruvian Reality (first published in 1928), and Guevara is portrayed reading this book on several occasions, as if to suggest that his reading of Mariátegui hastened his political awakening. Yet Guevara makes no reference to the book or to Mariátegui in the diaries. According to the memoir of Hilda Gadea, Guevara's first wife and a former APRA militant, she, not Pesce, introduced Guevara to Mariátegui's writings, in Guatemala.[35] Guevara acknowledged Pesce's influence on him in the dedication he wrote into the copy of his first book, Guerrilla Warfare, which he sent to the Peruvian: "To Doctor Hugo Pesce: who without knowing it perhaps, provoked a great change in my attitude toward life and society, with the same adventurous spirit as always, but channeled toward goals more harmonious with the needs of America." Pesce may indeed have tutored Guevara and Granado in Marxist theory as Anderson suggests, but Guevara did not much remark on this in his diaries.[36] Guevara remained similarly silent on APRA. During his first trip he claimed to be ignorant of what the party stood for. When he and Granado met a schoolteacher from Puno, "whom the government had sacked for being a member of the APRA party," Guevara noted that the fact that the man was an aprista "meant nothing to us."[37] Similarly, while in Lima, Guevara alluded to Haya de la Torre's "exile" in the Colombian embassy, as if he did not really know what was going on: "An interesting fact was the number of police surrounding the Colombian embassy. There were no less than 50 uniformed and plainclothes doing permanent guard duty around the entire block."[38] According to Gadea, Guevara met several *aprista* leaders during his second trip, at the home of a "leftist nurse" in Lima.[39] But Guevara does not mention this meeting in his diary.

Yet during his second trip the politics of the country can be gleaned through Guevara's experience at the border with Bolivia, where the police confiscated some of his books: "On reaching Puno, I had two of my books confiscated at the last customs post: *El hombre en la Unión Soviética*, and a Ministry of Peasant Affairs publication, which they loudly accused of being 'Red, Red, Red.' After some banter with the main policeman, I agreed to look for a copy of the publication in Lima."[40] Ricardo Rojo, who traveled from Bolivia to Peru with Guevara, also discusses the altercation at the border post.[41] Rojo suggests that the Peruvian authorities worried that Bolivian agitators were seeking to export the revolution to Peru: "We lost a lot of time before we could convince the guards that our intentions were harmless and that we didn't plan to contaminate the Indians of Peru with the germs of the agrarian revolution. Actually, these crude border guards had learned to see the problem correctly, and inadvertently they gave us a free lesson in history: political frontiers never succeed in dividing human masses faced with the same problems; an agrarian revolution that flares up among the Indian masses of one country does not burn out at the political limits fixed by white men in faraway cities. The winds of Indian rebellions were blowing on the Peruvian border in 1953, and the customs men suspected that we were bringing more fuel in our shabby packs."[42] Perhaps Guevara viewed the incident in similar terms, but little in his diary indicates that he did. Apart from this episode, Guevara does not narrate much about police repression in Peru during the early 1950s. In fact, Guevara appears quite chummy with the police during both trips.[43]

Guevara's failure, or refusal, to discuss APRA is intriguing. Although it had been driven underground shortly after the 1948 coup, as contemporary travelers noted, the party still very much formed a part of the political landscape. According to Karl Eskelund, a Norwegian who traveled in Peru at the same time as Guevara, "In every town and hamlet, we saw large, red letters on the walls and fences: APRA—HAYA DE LA TORRE, TORRE, LIBERATOR OF PERU.

Sometimes the word 'liberator' had been crossed out and replaced by 'murderer' or 'bandit.' These unflattering terms had again been corrected to 'leader' or 'hope'."[44] Perhaps Guevara decided not to write about APRA for fear that his diary would fall into the wrong hands. Eskelund, for example, was told: "APRA has been outlawed . . . it's wiser not to talk politics."[45] It is equally possible that Guevara's silence on APRA owed to the fact that he saw in Haya de la Torre's party a Peruvian version of Juan Perón's Justicialista Party, about which he had serious misgivings. Certainly contemporary commentators often made the link between the two parties. Szulc, the New York Times journalist, for example, noted that had APRA reached power, "Peru would have been turned into something akin to a Justicialista state, with all its fascistoid and mob-rule characteristics."[46] But contemporary commentators also compared the Odría regime to Peronism, noting the strong parallels in both governments' claims to implant "another type of so-called democracy," although in the Peruvian case, "on a less spectacular scale and without the spirit of ultra-nationalism which pervades the Argentine experiment."[47]

According to Gadea, Guevara viewed Haya de la Torre and some other reformist leaders—Juan José Arévalo of Guatemala, Víctor Paz Estenssoro of Bolivia, and Rómulo Bétancourt of Venezuela—as traitors: "Ernesto said that these men were traitors to the Latin American revolution; they had sold out to Yankee imperialism, and that the road to follow was a different one: to fight directly against the imperialism that supported the oligarchies."[48] According to her narrative—which may not be fully reliable, given that she was a disaffected aprista—Guevara had a far more positive evaluation of Perón than of Haya de la Torre. Whereas he held that "Perón has done something; he has protected the workers; he has done something to take away economic power from the oligarchy and, to some extent, from the imperialists," Guevara believed that Haya de la Torre had turned his back on his initial program. According to Gadea, Guevara "did not believe that APRA was a revolutionary party, [he believed] that Haya de la Torre had gone against his first anti-imperialist platform of 1928, that he no longer spoke of fighting the Yankees or for the nationalization of the Panama Canal, and that if he ever took power he would not carry out the People's revolution."[49] It is unclear whether Guevara in fact reached this conclusion. It was certainly the conclusion reached by disaffected *apristas* such as Gadea and others who left the party to form more radical political movements, as I discuss below. Possibly Gadea therefore attributed it to Guevara for self-interested reasons. If it was Guevara's own view on Haya de la Torre, we do not know if it formed while he was still in Peru or once he had met several *aprista* exiles (including Andrés Townsend, Nicanor Mujica, Hipólito Alfaro, Jorge Raygada, Ricardo Temoche, and Carlos Malpica) in Guatemala.

If Guevara had little to say about APRA, his observations regarding the Odría dictatorship remained similarly limited, with the exception of one telling remark included in a letter sent to his friend Tita Infante shortly after arriving in Lima from Cuzco: "I think that for Peru Yankee domination has not even meant that fictitious economic prosperity which can be seen in Venezuela, for example."[50] Perhaps Guevara was unimpressed with the new hospitals and public buildings, such as the grandiose Ministry of Labor or the brand new national football stadium, erected in the capital. He certainly felt unimpressed with some aspects of the consumer culture emerging in Lima, such as films projected in 3D, of which he observed, curmudgeonly, "it doesn't seem at all revolutionary to me, and the films are the same as before."[51] Most likely, his observation reflected that few of the social reforms and infrastructural developments of the Odría dictatorship, or indeed of the gains from the commodity-driven export boom, had had much of an impact beyond Lima. As the British diplomats recognized, although urban workers were beginning to benefit from the social reforms, "it is as well to remember, in order to keep a sense of proportion about these things, that Peru's population is some seven million, of whom more than half are Indian, illiterate and voteless as well as gaining their living from the soil. These are not yet as extensively cared for in General Odría's legislation."[52]

The Indian

If Guevara had little inclination to write down his impressions of the political scene in Peru, the opposite holds true for his impressions of Peru's indigenous peoples. Guevara felt genuine empathy with the Indians he encountered, and he was clearly overwhelmed by what he understood to be a racist and violent social order that barely recognized the humanity of the indigenous. But Guevara's observations also point to his limited capacity to understand the society he encountered in Andean Peru. During his first trip Guevara claimed a moral and intellectual distance between himself and "tourists," suggesting that because of their comfortable travel arrangements, tourists "could only glean the vaguest idea of the conditions in which the Indians live."[53] At the same time, he seems to have believed that as a South American, he was better placed to understand Peru's indigenous population than other foreigners: "North American tourists, bound down by their practical word view, are able to place those members of the disintegrating tribes they have seen in their travels among these once living walls, unaware of the moral distance separating them, since only the semi-indigenous spirit of the South American can grasp the subtle differences."[54] But in reality Guevara reproduced most of prejudices about "the Indian" expressed by other travelers and by many nonindigenous Peruvians of the time. Moreover, he replicated an interpretation of the Andes as a static world in which nothing had changed since the colonial period just at a time when social and demographic forces were beginning radically to transform that world.

Guevara likely first encountered Andean Peru in the pages of Ciro Alegría's novels. As Jon Lee Anderson notes, Guevara spent much of his teenage years immersed in literature, and he read the works of Alegría but also Jorge Icaza, Rubén Darío, and Miguel Angel Asturias, whose "novels and poetry often dealt unprecedentedly with Latin American themes—including the unequal lives of marginalized Indians and mestizos—ignored in fashionable literature and Ernesto's social group."[55] That Guevara felt drawn to the work of Alegría seems unsurprising. Contemporary critics hailed Alegría's third novel, Broad and Alien Is the World, as "to date the finest and most full bodied example of the novela indianista."[56] Indeed, the impact of Alegría's novels in shaping contemporary views of Peru should not be underestimated. In 1945, Madaline W. Nichols of Duke University noted of the English translation of Broad and Alien Is the World that it was "most welcome as a general introduction to the field of Latin America's modern sociological novel" and recommended its use in the classroom, since it was "a novel which portrays American landscape and presents its appeal for justice for the Indian [but] which lacks the excessive stress on sexual depravity unfortunately present in many [similar] novels."[57] Scholars came to see the depiction of the Andean world in Alegría's novels in the same light as other more conventional sources. In an article published in 1952, for example, Robert J. Alexander, in footnoting a point about how in Peru and Bolivia "the ancient system of oppression [of the Indian] has hardly been cracked," draws the reader's attention to Alegría's Broad and Alien Is the World, "a very graphic source," which he places alongside more conventional ones, such as his conversations with Haya de la Torre.[58] Most famously, François Bourricaud based much of his sociological analysis of Peruvian society in the 1950s and 1960s in his Power and Society in Contemporary Peru (originally published in 1963) on Alegría's novels (as well as on those of Arguedas).[59]

However, though compelling and doubtless of great literary merit, Alegría's portrayal of rural society in northern Peru was far from accurate. As Lewis Taylor has suggested in a detailed study of the northern sierra that the novelist depicts in Broad and Alien Is the World, Alegría represented the region as characterized by conflict between great landowners and peasant communities, but such conflicts were rare both in the northern sierra and in the central highlands. Similarly, Alegría's idealized representation of the peasant community, in particular his idea of a highly developed peasant communal consciousness, is wide of the mark. By contrast, Taylor concedes, Alegría's representation of brigandage and sociopolitical change, particularly the rise of APRA, provides a much fairer reflection of the historical record.[60] Yet it was the idea of landowners exploiting indigenous peasants, coupled with the notion of a glorious Inca past whose source may have been Inca Garcilaso de la Vega's Comentarios reales de los Incas (1609), that seems to have stuck in Guevara's mind and that predisposed him to a particular interpretation of what he saw in Peru. Indeed, the direct influence of an earlier literary encounter with Peru on Guevara's and Granado's physical encounter with the country is clearly indicated by Granado in his diary entry of 30 March 1952: "I'm itching to get there and see the life of the exploited Quechua Indians at first hand, to really feel the wonders of the Inca civilization. To see for myself, not through the prose of Inca Garcilaso or the novels of Ciro Alegría, what remains of the Inca kingdom and its splendors, destroyed by the avarice of Pizarro and the Spanish Empire and exploited today by Peruvian landowners."[61] This passage proves revealing: although Granado explicitly states that he wants to see things for himself and "not through the novels of . . . Ciro Alegría," he already knows what he desires to see: on the one hand, the exploited Indians and, on the other, the wonders of the Inca civilization and "what remains of the Inca kingdom and its splendors." What Granado, and it is fair to assume, Guevara, expected to see in Peru is in fact what they had read in Alegría's novels.

That Guevara understood Peru in the dichotomous and somewhat Manichaean terms expressed by Granado, those of past wonders and present exploitation, is also palpable in Gadea's memoirs. Gadea claimed to be impressed by Guevara's knowledge of Peru's Indians, but the very language she uses to express that admiration points to the dominant dichotomous interpretation they shared: "[Ernesto's] love of archaeology had taken him into the indigenous cultures of America, and he already knew something about the Inca, Maya, and Aztec societies. Also, his travels had brought him into contact with the Indians."[62] According to Gadea, she and Guevara "talked widely about the Inca civilization and the present-day misery of the Indian. He surprised me with his knowledge and sensitivity. He knew about the exploited state in which our Indians lived, he understood the psychological barriers between Indians and mestizos and whites, who had been exploiting them for many centuries."[63] The dichotomy extended to a perception of the Indian as being outside the nation and the market: "These people retained their customs; as a whole they were not integrated into the economic system of the West but only suffered its repercussions."[64] Although Guevara and Gadea clearly sided with the Indians and sought to end the exploitation to which they believed them subject, in effect their vision of the Andean world differed little from that of the U.S. traveler Anne Merriman Peck who exclaimed in 1940: "How different was this mountain land of austere beauty, with its primitive Indians and apathetic cholo people from Lima and the coast! This land which bears a weight of history, whose people are gentle, slow-moving, steeped in tradition. There is a long way to go before Peru of the mountains and Peru of the coast become one country."[65]

In his travelogues, Guevara reproduced an essentialist vision of the Indian and his world: Guevara constructs a highly infantilized, superstitious Indian resigned to his fate. The indigenous, Guevara tells us, are "simple people."[66] Guevara speaks, for example, of "the timid kindness of the cholos" and of "the enigmatic soul of the true Andean peoples."[67] Similarly, after describing the terrible conditions of a hospital that he and Granado visited in the town of Huambo, Guevara suggests that those conditions "could have been borne only by the suffering, fatalistic spirit of the Peruvian mountain Indians."[68] Although he clearly feels empathy with the indigenous, Guevara nevertheless reproduces highly racist views, comparing some of their behavioral characteristics to those of animals: "The somewhat animal-like concept the indigenous people have of modesty and hygiene means that irrespective of gender or age they do their business by the roadside, the women cleaning themselves with their skirts, the men not bothering at all, and then carry on as before. The underskirts of Indian women who have kids are literally warehouses of excrement, a consequence of the way they wipe the rascals every time one of them passes wind."[69] Rojo's memoirs take the animalization of the indigenous further. The author recalls how, during the journey from Bolivia to Peru, he, Ferrer, and Guevara decided to sit in the back of a truck and not in the cabin, "the only possible place, the cholo [he is referring to a ticket clerk] insinuated, for three young white men, who could not be expected to mix with the Indians." However, the back of the truck is then described as a "hostile world" in which the three travelers are "trapped between bundles and people who looked like bundles." Although their decision to sit with the indigenous travelers signaled their rejection of racist conventions, Rojo reproduces a highly racialized view of the indigenous as barely human: "We discovered that it was impossible to try and show the sympathy we felt before those scrutinizing, metallic eyes, those lips clamped together forbiddingly, refusing to answer our questions. From time to time, a mouth would gape open and let out a foul breath of chewed coca, a breath it didn't seem possible could have fermented inside a human body."[70] The three young men held strongly to their views. Despite being asked "thousands of questions about our country and its way of life" by some "cholos," Guevara condescendingly concluded: "We were like demigods to these simple people: Alberto brandished his doctor's certificate for them, and moreover we had come from the wonderful country Argentina, where Perón lived with his wife Evita, where the poor have as much as the rich and the Indian isn't exploited or treated as severely as he is in this country."[71]

Guevara's failure to see in his "cholo" interlocutors' questions anything other than evidence of their simplicity resulted from more than just an essentialist view of Peru's indigenous people. Guevara also framed his interpretation of the indigenous population's present condition in a broader historical interpretation of Peruvian society. In describing the southern town of Tarata and its Aymara residents, Guevara noted: "The people before us are not the same proud race that repeatedly rose up against Inca rule, forcing them to maintain a permanent army on their borders; these people who watch us walk through the streets of the town are a defeated race. Their stares are tame, almost fearful, and completely indifferent to the outside world. Some give the impression that they go on living only because it's a habit they cannot shake."[72] Here, the population's negative traits, their tameness, their fearfulness, and their indifference appear not as innate characteristics but rather as the product of historical defeat. The proud race of old is the defeated race of today. The agent of transformation is colonialism. In Guevara's narrative the Spanish colonizers appear in an entirely negative light. In various discussions of Peru's colonial history, Guevara establishes a contrast between the Incas, a "sober race," and the "bestial," "unbridled," "abhorrent," and "sadistic" Spaniards, a "rabble" motivated by greed. He illustrates the Incas' superiority with reference to architecture: whereas colonial buildings crumble every time there is an earthquake, the Inca foundations on which these buildings are set remain unaffected: "Every so often, the heart of America, shuddering with indignation, sends a nervous spasm through the gentle back of the Andes, and tumultuous shock waves assault the surface of the land. Three times the cupola of proud Santo Domingo has collapsed from on high to the rhythm of broken bones and its worn walls have opened and fallen too. But the foundations they rest on are unmoved, the great blocks of the Temple of the Sun exhibit their gray stone indifferently; however colossal the disaster befalling its oppressor, not one of its huge rocks shifts from its place."[73] Yet, contradictorily, in trying to explain how such a clearly savage group of Spaniards could overcome the Inca Empire, Guevara also points to technology: "What use was the patient labor of the Indians, builders of the Inca Roca Palace, subtle sculptors of stone angles, when faced with the impetuous actions of the white conquistadores, and their knowledge of brick work, vaulting, and rounded arches?"[74]

Guevara held largely inconsistent ideas about the indigenous. In historicizing the present condition of the Indians, for example, he echoed some indigenista ideas about mestizaje as a source of racial degeneracy.[75] While describing a religious procession (in honor of the Lord of the Earthquakes) in Cuzco, Guevara established a hierarchy between what he considered "real" Indians and acculturated ones (he makes reference to the idea of "true" Indians or "the true Andean peoples" on more than one occasion).[76] On the one hand, Guevara approvingly pointed to "the many-colored clothes of the Indians, who wear for the occasion their best traditional costumes in expression of a culture or way of life which stills holds on to living values." At the same time, however, he equated acculturated Indians with treason and blamed them for the wretchedness of the Indian "race": "A cluster of Indians in European clothes march at the head of the procession, carrying banners. Their tired affected faces resemble an image of those Quechuas who refused to heed Manco II's call, pledging themselves to Pizarro and in the degradation of their defeat smothering the pride of an independent race."[77] Yet Guevara also appears to have sympathized with ideas of indigenous redemption through education (and therefore with their supposed acculturation). He approvingly narrates a meeting with the curator of Cuzco's archaeological museum: "He spoke to us of the splendid past and the present misery, of the urgent need to educate the Indians, as a first step toward total rehabilitation. He insisted that immediately raising the economic level of Indian families was the only way to mitigate the soporific effects of coca and drink and talked of fostering a fuller and more exact understanding of the Quechua people so that individuals of the race could look at their past and feel pride, rather than, looking at their present, feel only shame at belonging to the Indian or mestizo race."[78]

Guevara's attempt to explain the contradiction between the glorious Inca (and indeed, pre-Inca) past and the wretchedness of contemporary Indians echoes a common theme in other travelogues of the time.[79] George Sava, like Guevara a physician, traveled in Peru at more or less the same time. He expressed the conundrum in explicit terms: These very people, the descendants of that proud and accomplished race, are "perhaps the greatest mystery of all. On the one hand they destroy the legend of Inca greatness; on the other they raise new problems. For they are dull-eyed and lethargic, slow of speech and obtuse of understanding. Is it possible that these people were really those who constructed the Temple of the Sun or brought together the great fortress? Could men and women such as these be responsible for that brilliantly conceived pottery which is now the greatest treasure of many a museum? To watch them as they amble along beside their laden llamas, it seems incredible that the answer to these questions can be in the affirmative."[80] In seeking to resolve this problem, Sava concluded that those who "survived" the Spanish conquest were the slaves of the Incas, while the Incas themselves disappeared: "The engineers, the architects, the artists, who made these relics of civilization, were of a race of which no trace remains, an alien people, no more like those we call their descendants than those descendants are to the Spaniards who overcame them."[81] Like others, such as the Guatemalan historian Francisco de Paula García Peláez, who could not bring himself to accept that the Maya ruins had been built by the ancestors of his country's indigenous people and believed that they were the work of a mysterious people whose "very name is unknown," Sava could not admit that Peru's indigenous people were capable of great works of architecture or pottery. He felt such feats beyond their natural capabilities. It followed that other, superior beings had been responsible.[82]

Other interpretations also located the reasons for the decline of the indigenous in Peru's colonial past but arrived at very different conclusions. The Norwegian Eskelund, for example, in trying to understand why the Peru that he encountered in the early 1950s was, as he put it, so poor and backward, noted that the whites blamed the Indians: " "It's the fault of the Indians' say the whites. 'They are so lazy and unreliable—it would be best to castrate the lot of them or exterminate them in some other way. They're the ones who hold us back.' "[83] Yet Eskelund disagreed: he had visited Machu Picchu, "and here one can see what the useless Indians were capable of doing before the white man came."[84] For Eskelund, the explanation was historical and structural, rooted in the colonial system that the Spaniards had constructed: "It would be interesting to take an Indian, or a mestizo, or a white South American and bring him up in, say New

England. I believe that he would grow up to be an average American child, without any of the unfortunate characteristics such as unreliability and incompetence, which so many associate with the Latin Americans. These traits are not innate. They are the natural result of the Spanish colonial system, a system which destroyed master and slave alike. The pillars of this system still stand firmly established, and as long as they are permitted to remain, Latin America will continue to reap the bitter harvest which the Spanish conquerors sowed."[85] According to Eskelund, given the correct environment (preferably one devoid of unreliability and incompetence), Peruvian Indians could become just as advanced as New Englanders. Sava's and Eskelund's views, respectively, reflect what David Theo Goldberg has called naturalist and historicist interpretations of racial difference. One can trace these interpretations, Goldberg suggests, back to the early modern period.[86] They have resurfaced in various forms since then, not least in eugenics and in ideas of "hard" and "soft" inheritance.[87] Both interpretations are discernible in the ways in which Guevara sought to understand Peru's indigenous peoples.

Guevara's understanding of the indigenous experience provoked a desire for action. Reflecting on the Inca fortress of Sacsayhuamán that overlooks the city of Cuzco, Guevara remarked: "The vision of this Cuzco emerges mournfully from the fortress destroyed by the stupidity of illiterate Spanish conquistadores, from the violated ruins of the temples, from the sacked palaces, from the faces of a brutalized race. This is the Cuzco inviting you to become a warrior and to defend, club in hand, the freedom and the life of the Inca."[88] Guevara's vision of himself as a warrior defending the Inca against Spanish exploitation is consonant with an obvious feeling of indignation at the way in which Indians are treated by non-Indians. He perceived exploitation and injustice as something deeply ingrained in the belief systems of the rich and powerful: "In the mentality of the district's rich people it's perfectly natural that the servant, although travelling on foot should carry all the weight and discomfort."[89] Guevara understood that exploitation was based on non-Indians' capacity to deny the indigenous their full humanity. Thus he noted how Indians were treated like animals: "In these type of trains [to Machu Picchu] there are third class carriages 'reserved' for the local Indians: they are like the cattle transportation wagons they use in Argentina, except that the smell of cow shit is ever more pleasant than the human version."[90] But he also seems to have come to the conclusion that as far as non-Indians were concerned, the lives of Indians were worth very little. Recalling an incident in Andahuaylas during which Granado tried to defend an Indian woman insulted by some Civil Guard soldiers, Guevara noted: "His reaction must have seemed completely alien to people who considered the Indians were no more than objects, who deserve to live but only just."[91] However, Guevara's desire to "defend the life of the Inca" also suggests a less charitable reading of his understanding of Peru and of the Indians' exploitation.

Guevara's ideas about "the Indian" made it difficult for him to see anything other than a static world peopled by a "defeated race." In a particularly telling passage in Granado's travelogue, Guevara's travel companion narrates a meeting with an indigenous man who explains to them "in modest Spanish" how a landowner had pushed him off land that he had been cultivating for several years and how, faced with this situation, he had had no choice but to move his family further up the mountain. Granado and Guevara aim their reaction more at the Indian than at the landowner: "Pelao and I looked at each other, hardly knowing whether to be appalled or enraged in the face of such fatalistic submission. How meekly the man told the story of this immense, unpunished justice."[92] From this it is only a short step to Granado's revealingly juvenile pipe dream to marry a young girl he had recently met ("I am going to marry Maria Magdalena. Since she's a descendant of Manco Capac II, I'll become Manco Capac III") so as to lead the Indian masses to their emancipation: "Then I'll form a pro-Indian party, I'll take these people to the coast to vote, and that'll be the start of the new Tupac Amaru revolution, the American Indian revolution!"[93] Guevara's reaction to Granado's comment ridicules his travel companion's disingenuousness at believing a nonviolent revolution possible: "Revolution without firing a shot? You're crazy, Petiso." But Guevara seems to have shared Granado's belief that the Indians needed to be led to their freedom. Guevara's Peruvian Indians, as I have suggested above, were "timid," "fatalistic," "fearful," hardly capable of defending themselves. It followed that they could only be defended by others.

That Guevara reached such conclusions should not surprise us. They were shared by many, not least by the anthropologists who in the 1950s set out to find and study those "wretched" Indians that were "not integrated into the economic system of the West but only [suffering] its repercussions" and "that . . . go on living only because it's a habit they cannot shake." But even a cursory examination of the archives of the Ministry of the Interior, and of the thousands of letters and petitions from indigenous communities throughout the early twentieth century, reveals that "the Indian" was far from remaining nonintegrated. Thus in 1948, the same year that Odría took power, Antonio Contreras, Ramón Palomino, Heraclio Minaya, and Carlos Zamora made their way to Lima as representatives of the indigenous communities of Tintay and Lucre in Apurimac to denounce the abuses of the owners of the Pampatamba Baja Hacienda, who were encroaching on their communal lands and "contributing, through these acts, to the shortage and high prices of subsistence goods, which Peru needs in large numbers," thus demonstrating a rather clear understanding of the workings of Peru's internal market.[94] Similarly, far from being fearful, resigned to their fate, or unappreciative of the gift of life, Cupertino de la Cruz, Pablo Ayala, Benedicto Prado, Máximo Quispe, Leoncio Cárdenas, and Cristobal Cisneros wrote that same year to the minister of the Interior in representation of the 1500 *colonos* (peons) of the Hacienda Ccaccamarca in Cangallo, Ayacucho, to complain that the *arrendatarios* (tenants) of the hacienda treated them in a "cruel and inhuman manner."[95] In the southern department of Puno, Carlos F. Belón, a local hacendado and parliamentarian, noted already in the mid-1940s that Indians had undertaken a reconquest of the hacienda.[96] By the mid-1950s, the workers on the Hacienda Maco, in the central highlands, had successfully resisted attempts to proletarianize the workforce.[97] By the late 1950s most of Andean Peru was experiencing a de facto, if not yet de jure, agrarian reform as a result of pressure from below, which resulted in hundreds of thousands of peasants taking over land.[98]

Guevara saw little of these various forms of "insurgent citizenship," or if he did, he did not accord them any significance.[99] But some of his contemporaries were keenly aware of coming and in all likelihood irreversible change. Writing in 1951, the newly arrived British ambassador noted: "The members of the Peruvian oligarchy, although they hesitate to admit it, are worried. Peru is still essentially a colonial country. Overshadowing Lima and the other coastal cities, with their gracious, old-world way of life, are the slopes of the Andes beyond which lies a vast hinterland inhabited for the most part by the illiterate Indian peasants. At the moment no trouble threatens from this quarter; but in the cities whose population swells steadily with the influx of peasants from the Sierra the process of industrialization goes on and there is growing up a politically conscious proletariat which, under the leadership of APRA and to a lesser extent that of the Communist Party, constitutes a potential threat to the interests of the ruling class."[100] Two years later the ambassador reprised his warning, suggesting that "judged by European standards, nine-tenths of the 8 million inhabitants of Peru, mostly Indians and half-breeds, still live in conditions of medieval poverty, squalor and ignorance, finding some solace in the chewing of coca and bouts of drinking. . . . The Indian problem remains therefore constant and hard to solve and if at any moment control of the rate of progress slips from the hands of the Government trouble such as now characterizes life in Bolivia will ensue."[101]

A Colonial City in a Colonized Country

"Trouble" of the Bolivian kind never properly materialized in Peru. But social and demographic pressures in the Andean provinces (or *departamentos*) were leading to a radical transformation of the relationship between the coast and the highlands. If in 1940 the urban population stood at 35 percent of the total, by 1960 it had risen to 50 percent. In 1950 the population of the city of Lima reached 1 million, fed by large-scale migration from the highlands. As pressure on housing reached unbearable levels, the population spilled out of the city, first, onto the hillsides of the various hills that pepper the eastern tip of the city and, later, onto what was often private agricultural land. This is what happened, for example, on Christmas day 1954, when several thousand people left Lima and "set up overnight a shanty town of straw-matting huts in a desert area a few miles outside the city. After a day or two thousands more had joined them and the new township had been christened La Ciudad de Dios (The City of God)."[102] Although many of the initial "invaders" left after they realized that there was no water or sanitation, others remained, and the following year a study found that some nine hundred families were living there.[103] But Lima's City of God was only one of a rapidly expanding number of new settlements. A study from 1956 of Lima's population growth noted that already in 1949 some twenty-five thousand people lived in what were then still called *barriadas clandestinas* (clandestine neighborhoods) but would later be referred to as Lima's *pueblos jóvenes* (young towns). By 1955 that figure had risen to one hundred thousand and represented 10 percent of Lima's total population.[104] These were the changes that led Vargas Llosa's character Zavalita to ask when Peru had fucked itself up and Arguedas to proclaim: "We have arrived in the enormous town of the masters, and we are shaking it up. . . . We are squeezing this immense city that hated us, that despised us like the excrement of horses."[105]

Travelogues from the 1940s and 1960s neatly illustrate these changes. Until the 1940s travelers typically pointed to the stark differences between Lima and the Andes. In their narrative of travels through South America, Heath Bowman and Stirling Dickinson recall a priest in the port of Mollendo expressing the difference between Bolivia and Peru: "Geography is fact, and is more durable than politics. . . . Now take Bolivia. You and I have seen Indians not only in the mountains there, but in La Paz. Of course, no capital is a perfect expression of its country, but La Paz has the advantage of being in the mountains, with a large Indian population. In Peru the difference is that Lima is on the coast. You cannot show me a face there with even half pure Indian features. Lima is Spanish and its psychology is still colonial. It is as if Bolivia had chosen Trinidad in the Beni for its capital. Lima is that cut off."[106] Perhaps to further emphasize, or render intelligible to their readers, Lima's non-Andean character, travelers stressed its tropicality, even if the weather was often quite untropical. Christopher Morley, for example, noted: "It is odd to see a city evidently tropical in humor and construction set in a cold London gloom."[107] George Woodcock chose a Scottish comparison: "Lima lies in the tropics, nearer to the Equator than such sweltering cities as Aden, but the morning into which we stepped was as bleakly untropical as a Glasgow dawn."[108] Writing in the late 1940s, the anthropologist Frances Tor similarly painted a tropical portrait of Lima: "I stepped out of the celebrated Hotel Bolivar to find myself in a pleasant world of singing colors, of women in light summer dresses, of men in white suits, a world of warm noons and refreshing evenings."[109]

In describing her first impressions of the city she encountered in the late 1940s, Tor noted that "today one sees few Indians in the city."[110] Staying at the Hotel Crillon, not too distant from the Hotel Bolivar where Tor had stayed, W. Byford-Jones encountered a very different scene in the 1960s. The tranquil tropical and colonial atmosphere had been replaced by a chaotic juxtaposition of the modern and the traditional. As Byford-Jones noted, "surely there is nothing so revolting as a confusion of glass and steel skyscrapers, at times smothered with jarring colours, alongside proportionately built houses for one family which reveal the work of real craftsmen."[111] Even more strikingly, whereas "few Indians" could be seen in Tor's Lima, Indians were the only inhabitants of Byford-Jones's capital city: "When I looked down into the streets the only upturned faces I saw, and these covered with bewilderment, were those of the descendants of the Incas. These pathetic survivors of empire had been forced to walk from their remote smallholdings in the high Sierra, still barefoot and wearing pathetically picturesque garb, because drought had ruined their crops. They wandered about like ghosts, too proud to beg and not knowing where to turn for help."[112]

In fact, some of these changes had already become apparent to Tor in the late 1940s. She noted that "most of the inhabitants of Lima are whites, descendants of Spaniards, known as criollos or creoles." But she added, "it is also a melting pot with a large percentage of Mestizos or Cholos (mixed white and Indian), a few Indians, Negroes, mulattos, Zambos (Negro and Indian), and a mixture of Europeans and Orientals. It is a composite of rich and poor, palaces and hovels, but a community that has through the centuries blended into a harmonious whole, one of the most attractive, liveable cities of South America."[113] Tor saw increasing dynamism and the seeds of democratization in a growing integration between the capital and the Andean provinces: "During recent decades a great change has taken place. There is an ever-growing group of liberal intellectuals working in the interest of the Indians. With new means of transportation, more Limeños are travelling to the Sierra, more Indians and cholos coming to the capital. Lima is beginning to take on a friendlier, more human attitude. In spite of recent military events, it is becoming a more democratic Lima, a more truly Peruvian city, made up of all kinds of people of all Peru."[114] Painting a somewhat less idealized picture, Eskelund noted in the early 1950s: "Lima is one of the finest towns on the Pacific coast; the slums are not so pretty, but they lie on the outskirts and are seldom seen by tourists."[115]

Guevara seems to have been one of these tourists. Despite spending some time in Lima during both trips, he had little to say about the changes afoot. His main considerations of the city were aesthetic. He appears to have been rather disappointed by Peru's capital, noting that "Lima is quite unlike Córdoba, but it has the same look of a colonial, or rather provincial, city."[116] He found the colonial architecture unimpressive for the most part and seems to have been far more enthusiastic about the well-to-do suburbs: "Lima as a city does not live up to its long tradition as a viceregal seat, but its residential suburbs are very pretty and spacious and so are its new streets."[117] But, interestingly, he also found it difficult to come to terms with the city's ambiguous character. On the one hand, perhaps to rationalize his disappointment with Lima's aesthetics and architecture, he suggested that its colonial past was dead and buried: "Lima is a pretty city, which has already suppressed its colonial past (after seeing Cuzco it seems more so) beneath new houses."[118] But at the same time, he identified this very same colonial legacy, which of necessity remained very much alive, as the source of the injustice he had encountered in his travels through the Andean provinces. In what appears at first to be a merely descriptive passage on Lima's baroque cathedral and churches, Guevara suddenly changes register: "This wealth enabled the aristocracy to resist the liberating armies of America until the last moment. Lima is the perfect example of a Peru which has not developed beyond the feudal condition of a colony. It still waits for the blood of a truly emancipating revolution."[119]

The apparent contradiction in his characterization of Lima, both postcolonial and simultaneously epitomizing a colonial, even feudal, society, in fact points to Guevara's broader interpretation of Lima's relationship with the rest of Peru, and of Peruvian society more widely. Lima may no longer be the formal colony of a foreign power, but, Guevara seems to suggest, it operates, and relates to the rest of Peru, according to a colonial and feudal logic. In fact, in a passage on the history of Cuzco, Guevara makes explicit what he sees as the almost parasitic role played by Lima with respect to the rest of the country: following the Spanish conquest, Guevara explains, "slowly Cuzco languished, pushed to the margins, lost in the cordillera, while on the coast a new rival emerged, Lima, growing with the fruits of the taxes levied by clever intermediaries on the wealth flowing out of Peru."[120] Granado's travelogue makes the parasitic nature of all cities, not just of Lima, explicit: "Everywhere we saw how Indians are exploited by whites. We realized that the parasites living in the city are taking advantage of the hard-working Indians, forcing them to sow crops higher and higher in the sierras."[121] Thus Guevara's interpretation of Lima fits well with his broader reading of Peru: a dual society characterized by deep injustice and exploitation, in which the legacy of colonialism has produced a parasitic elite that feeds off a once proud but now defeated "race." Much of this interpretation may have held true, but it was an interpretation that made it difficult for Guevara to see the profound changes happening before his very eyes.

The Amazon

Guevara showed similarly little awareness or interest in the structural changes beginning to transform the Peruvian selva or Amazon region, which he and Granado crossed from Pucallpa all the way to the Colombian border between late May and late June 1952. Beginning in the 1940s, a sustained and, from the 1950s on, accelerating process of colonization by Andean settlers had profoundly reshaped the region demographically and economically.[122] Guevara notes in a letter to his father that "the great riverbanks are full of settlements."[123] But for the most part, the Amazon depicted in Guevara's and Granado's travelogues is marked by the "exotic," including sexually available women, copulating dolphins, irate homosexuals, and "savage tribes . . . deep in the interior."[124] Guevara and Granado seem to have found little of interest in the region save for the "Yagua tribe" that they visited and whose "way of living was fascinating," even if the men appear to have been disappointed that "the women had abandoned their traditional costume for ordinary clothes so you cannot admire their jugs." Their interest in the Yagua is rendered as a disturbing mix of adolescent sexual curiosity and a medicalized and sociologized gaze expressing a racialized understanding of culture: "The kids have distended bellies and are rather scrawny but the older people show no signs of vitamin deficiency, in contrast with its rate among *more developed people living in the jungle*. Their basic diet consists of yucca, bananas and palm fruit, mixed with the animals they hunt with rifles. Their teeth are totally rotten. They speak their own dialect but some of them understand Spanish."[125]

Much has been made, as in Salles's film, of the time Guevara and Granado spent at the San Pablo "leper" colony.[126] Much has been made, in particular, of the speech that Guevara made and recounted in his diary, in which he declared that "we believe, and after this journey more firmly than ever, that the division of [Latin] America into unstable and illusory nations is completely fictional. We constitute a single mestizo race, which from Mexico to the Magellan straits bears notable ethnographic similarities. And so, in an attempt to rid myself of the weight of a small-minded provincialism, I propose a toast to Peru and to a United Latin America."[127] But like many of his contemporaries, and despite his genuine empathy with the poor, the indigenous, and the marginalized, Guevara was unable to escape precisely the sort of small-minded provincialism that made it possible for him to claim a belief in a single mestizo Latin American race while still classifying peoples according to their level of "development." This contradiction appears all the more striking given the genuine empathy evident in Guevara and Granado's attitude toward the patients in the San Pablo colony, and, more generally, toward people affected by Hansen's disease, as their diaries reveal. As Guevara wrote to his father, his and Granado's willingness to play soccer and shake hands with the patients they had met in the Lima leprosarium "may seem like pointless bravado, but the psychological lift it gives this people—treating them as normal human beings instead of animals, as they are used to—is incalculable and the risk to us is extremely unlikely."[128] Salles's film uses this empathy as a melodramatic device (witness the scene with the young girl). Yet it feels genuine enough in Guevara's and Granado's diaries.

In San Pablo, as in the Lima leprosarium, Guevara and Granado as physicians in the making were more predisposed, and possibly prepared, than most to interact, through conversation or (an important part of their trip) through impromptu games of soccer, with those whose condition rendered them social outcasts par excellence. It is difficult to avoid reading this episode in exegetical terms. As in the Bible, in San Pablo the lepers could be seen as both literal and metaphorical. By treating the San Pablo patients as humans, Guevara "healed" them (as he could "heal" all other outcasts: the poor,

the indigenous, the marginalized) like Christ healed the lepers in
the Bible. Like Christ, this episode seems to suggest, Guevara held
the power to right wrongs. Perhaps this episode, like the photograph of a dead Guevara taken in Vallegrande, Bolivia, has contributed, more or less unconsciously, to the transformation of Che into
a Christ-like figure, if not into Jesus Christ himself, in the eyes of
many. Certainly Guevara demonstrated an unusual degree of empathy, as revealed by the extraordinary autobiographical testimony of a
patient at San Pablo.[129] Although toward the end of her stay at San
Pablo conditions improved and although, on occasion, the cama-
raderie between patients made life at the colony tolerable, the experience of this anonymous female patient was marked by the extreme
precariousness of the living conditions and the medical facilities, as
well as by the general fear of infection among relatives of patients
and even among doctors. It was a fear reproduced by Hank Kelly, the
U.S. vice-consul in Iquitos, and his wife Dot. In their memoir the
pair pointed to the conflicting reports on San Pablo. Some described
it "as a place of horror and death—a concentration camp where the
unfortunate wretches were doomed to die a lingering death from
their disease or a more rapid death from starvation and insufficient
care."[130] Others claimed it was characterized by "splendid" service
achieved with meager funds. But the Kellys were certainly concerned
by the prospect of infection from a "contagious leper" in Iquitos
who earned a living "[whittling] sticks for raspadillas, the frozen
sherbet suckers that Iquiteños devoured by the thousands every
day!" According to Hank, "after hearing of the leprous whittler, Dot
and I lost our stomach for raspadillas and squeezed what comfort
we could from the thought that leprosy is not easily transmitted."[131]

Conclusions

Peru, wrote Guevara in 1952, "still waits for the blood of a truly
emancipating revolution." As this quote and his comments to Granado suggest, Guevara had already concluded while in Peru that
effective political change could be brought about only through a
violent revolution led by people capable of emancipating those who
could not emancipate themselves. That belief strengthened, particularly in Bolivia and Guatemala, as Guevara made his way to
Mexico and eventually to Cuba. It continued to shape Guevara's

worldview and political action following the victory of the Cuban revolutionaries and until his death. It came to shape how others, inspired by Guevara and the Cuban Revolution, came to view political action for at least a couple of generations. It was a view, as I have tried to show in this essay, to some extent shaped by how Guevara interpreted the situation of Peru's indigenous peoples. It was a view ultimately derived from how Guevara sought to make sense of the complex demographic, economic, and cultural changes shaping Peruvian society at midcentury, changes he barely perceived, by enclosing them in a largely preestablished interpretative framework. The point, naturally, is not to blame Guevara for his simplistic interpretation of Peruvian reality. True, other perspectives, such as Eskelund's, were possible. But they were clearly not possible for Guevara. My intention is merely to provide further elements for understanding the ideas that came to shape Guevara's view of the world, a view that would have a decisive influence on the course of world history, and, of course, Peruvian history.

Since 1952 Peru has to some degree experienced "the blood of a truly emancipating revolution" three times. Two of the revolutions have been moderately bloody, one extremely so. None have proven truly emancipating. The first revolution came in the mid-1960s, but it was soon aborted. It was led by not one but two Guevarist groups eager to fulfill Fidel Castro's call to turn the Andes into a hemispheric Sierra Maestra and to build on the apparent success of Hugo Blanco, a Trotskyite, in mobilizing the peasantry of La Convención, Cuzco.[132] Luis de la Puente Uceda, the leader of the Movimiento de Izquierda Revolucionaria (MIR), a group that agglutinated young radicalized APRA cadres and members of the Peruvian Communist Party, came into contact with Guevarista ideals though Gadea during a visit to Cuba in the late 1950s. Javier Heraud, a young poet, joined the ranks of the Ejército de Liberación Nacional (ELN), a group that split from the Peruvian Communist Party and was equally inspired by the Cuban Revolution. The Peruvian armed forces in 1965 swiftly eliminated both guerilla groups (Heraud was killed in 1963). Three Peruvians, Juan Pablo Chang Navarro (codename "Chino"), Lucio Edilberto Galván ("Eustaquio"), both of the ELN, and Restituto José Cabrera Flores ("Negro"), a physician who studied in Buenos Aires and practiced medicine in Cuba, would join Guevara in his own doomed revolutionary venture in Bolivia. None survived. But the guerrilla experience had a deep impact on subsequent Peruvian politics. The military coup of 1968 led by Juan Velasco Alvarado was in many ways a direct response to the guerrillas of the mid-1960s. This second "revolution" *from above* was aimed at addressing the problems that Peru's reformist military officers believed had created the conditions for the guerrilla insurgencies. This revolution, too, although in some ways more successful than the revolutions of 1965, was aborted by 1975.

In the 1980s Peru experienced a third revolution. This one proved extremely bloody but hardly emancipating, led by a movement, the Shining Path, that drew its inspiration not from Guevara or the Cuban Revolution but rather from Mao Zedong and the Chinese Revolution.[133] By the late 1970s most of the Guevarist Left in Peru had opted for supposedly bourgeois politics. A few, however, feeling that the Shining Path had stolen a march on them, opted for revolutionary insurgency. In the event, the MRTA (Movimiento Revolucionario Túpac Amaru) would play a bit part in the internal war that brought Peruvian society to near collapse in the 1980s and 1990s. Unlike Guevara, or indeed de la Puente and Heraud, Abimael Guzmán, or "Presidente Gonzalo," Shining Path's leader and ideologue, was not a charismatic man. Yet this dour philosophy professor proved far more successful in mobilizing support for his revolutionary project. Prior to his capture in 1992 and the swift disarticulation of the insurgency, many in Peru believed the Shining Path to be on the verge of taking power. What Guevara would have thought of Shining Path's revolution is difficult to say. Guzmán, by all accounts, thinks little of Guevara. But like Guevara, Guzmán believed that revolutions could not be won "without firing a shot." For the Peruvian, the revolution would only be won once a "quota of blood" had been achieved. That quota, which Guzmán put at a million deaths, was mercifully never achieved, but the war that the Shining Path initiated, and to which the Peruvian armed forces responded with extreme violence in an often indiscriminate way, left a toll of some seventy thousand victims.

As elsewhere in Latin America, Guevara can be seen regularly on mudguards and T-shirts in Peru. But in a country in which revolutionary projects have delivered little and in which the most recent revolutionary experience took the form of a genocidal internal armed conflict, Guevara's revolutionary message has little resonance. And yet, despite all their shortcomings, Guevara's youthful writings on Peru maintain a tragic relevance. Guevara may have simplified the experiences of Peru's indigenous peoples and denied them agency through his characterizations, but the indignation contained in Guevara's remark about those Peruvians who "considered the Indians were no more than objects, who deserve to live but only just," perfectly condenses the Peruvian Truth and Reconciliation Commission's conclusions (published in 2003) about the structural causes of Peru's "time of fear" and about the deep racial prejudice that underpins the country's entrenched inequalities. This indignation plays a key role in Salles's film, where it becomes a somewhat melodramatic device to flag Guevara's awakening social consciousness and revolutionary commitment. Its continued relevance because of the continued existence of that which provoked it—the wretched existence of that half of the Peruvian population, mostly indigenous, that, by virtue of its manifold exclusions from full citizenship, is reduced to "bare life"—points to the failure of the political projects that Guevara inspired, but also of those that claim to have superseded them.[134] At the same time we should not lose sight, as Guevara did in the 1950s, of myriad "insurgent citizenships" that challenge and destabilize the exclusionary character of Peruvian society.

Notes

I am grateful to Carlos Aguirre, Jelke Boesten, Penny Harvey, Paul Gootenberg, David Nugent, David Parker, José Luis Rénique, and two anonymous reviewers for their helpful comments on earlier versions of this article. Translations from the Spanish are my own.
1 See Ernesto Guevara, *The Motorcycle Diaries: A Journey around South America*, trans. Alexandra Keeble (London: Harper Perennial, 2004); Ernesto Guevara, *Back on the Road: A Journey to Central America*, trans. Patrick Camiller (London: Vintage, 2002); Alberto Granado, *Traveling with Che Guevara: The Making of a Revolutionary*, trans. Lucía Álvarez de Toledo (New York: Newmarket Press, 2004).
2 This trip is also recounted in Ferrer's book, *De Ernesto al Che: El segundo viaje de Guevara por Latinoamérica* (Buenos Aires: Marea Editorial, 2005).
3 Guevara, *Back on the Road*, 19.
4 The 1950s have been particularly badly served by social scientists, although one should not overlook some key sociological and anthropo-

logical studies produced during that decade by scholars from Peru and beyond. See Ramón Pajuelo, "Imágenes de la comunidad: Indígenas, campesinos y antropólogos en el Perú," *No hay país más diverso: Compendio de antropología peruana*, ed. Carlos Iván Degregori (Lima: Red para el Desarrollo de las Ciencias Sociales en el Perú, 2000), 123–79. Yet few social scientists, including historians, have explicitly focused on a decade that, ironically, many increasingly see as a key point of inflexion in Peruvian history. There are exceptions, of course, such as David Collier's study of squatter settlements, which looks in some detail at the 1950s, or Baltazar Caravedo's dependency-inspired regional history of Arequipa during Odría's "ochenio." David Collier, *Squatters and Oligarchs: Authoritarian Rule and Policy Change in Peru* (Baltimore: Johns Hopkins University Press, 1976); Baltazar Caravedo Molinari, *Desarrollo desigual y lucha política en el Perú, 1948–1956: La burguesía arequipeña y el estado peruano* (Lima: Instituto de Estudios Peruanos, 1978).

5 See Yolanda Westphalen, "La mirada de Zavalita hoy: ¿En qué momento se jodió el Perú?," *Estudios culturales: Discursos, poderes, pulsiones*, ed. Santiago López Maguiña et al. (Lima: Red para el Desarrollo de las Ciencias Sociales en el Perú, 2001), 315–35, and, particularly, the "Comentarios" by Carlos Iván Degregori, 337–41, in the same book. See also Mario Vargas Llosa, *Conversación en La Catedral* (Barcelona: Seix Barral, 1969).

6 Some social scientists, such as the contributors to a book published in 1990 with the phrase as its title, have even tried to date Peru's "fuckup," most apparently choosing to date it to the colonial period. It is easy to see how the question could be seen as applicable to all of Peruvian history. Carlos Milla Batres and Luis Guillermo Lumbreras, *En qué momento se jodió el Perú* (Lima: Editorial Milla Batres, 1990).

7 On this point, see Magdalena Chocano, "Ucronía y frustración en la conciencia histórica peruana," *Márgenes*, no. 2 (1987), 43–60; Cecilia Méndez, "Incas Sí, Indios No: Notes on Peruvian Creole Nationalism and Its Contemporary Crisis," *Journal of Latin American Studies* 28:1 (1996), 197–225, esp. n. 3; Paulo Drinot, "Historiography, Historiographic Identity, and Historical Consciousness in Peru," *Estudios Interdisciplinarios de América Latina y el Caribe* 15:1 (2004), 65–88.

8 Gonzalo Portocarrero, "Las relaciones estado-sociedad en el Perú: Un examen bibliográfico," http://www.pucp.edu.pe/departamento/cien cias_sociales/, accessed 26 November 2009.

9 Quoted in Degregori, "Comentarios," 339.

10 See Carlos Contreras and Marcos Cueto, *Historia del Perú contemporáneo* (Lima: Red para el Desarrollo de las Ciencias Sociales en el Perú, 1999).

11 Paul Dosal, *Comandante Che: Guerrilla Soldier, Commander, and Strategist, 1956–1967* (University Park: Pennsylvania University Press, 2003), 28–29.

12 Mary Louise Pratt, *Imperial Eyes: Travel Writing and Transculturation* (New York: Routledge, 1992), 5.

13 Gonzalo Portocarrero, *De Bustamante a Odría: El fracaso del Frente Democrático Nacional, 1945–1950* (Lima: Mosca Azul Editores, 1983).

14 Peter Schmid, *Beggars on Golden Stools: A Journey through Latin America* (London: Weidenfeld and Nicolson, 1956), 209.

15 Ibid., 218.

16 Tad Szulc, *Twilight of the Tyrants* (New York: Henry Holt and Co., 1959), 189.

17 *Time*, 25 April 1955.

18 National Archives, UK, Foreign Office [FO], 371 68292A/AS6297, Roberts to Bevin, 5 November 1948. I draw on foreign diplomatic reports in part because, similar to Guevara's diaries, they provide an outsider's perspective.

19 FO 371 74802/AS4540, Chancery to South American Department, 29 August 1949.

20 FO 371 74802/AS4540, Chancery to South American Department, 31 August 1949. On this episode, see Paul Gootenberg, "The 'Pre-Colombian' Era of Drug Trafficking in the Americas: Cocaine, 1945–1965," *Americas* 64:2 (2007), 133–76.

21 FO 371 74802/AS4540, Chancery to South American Department, 29 August 1949.

22 FO 371 81372/AF 1011/1, Dodds to McNeil, 3 February 1950. Arriving in Peru 1951, his successor agreed with him, noting that "as dictatorships go in this Continent, that of General Odría does not strike one as being oppressive and though the smart looking police force is much in evidence there is no feeling of living in a police state." Yet Ambassador Scott went on to remark that "it needs something of an effort of the imagination to remember that the gaols are packed with political prisoners and that many Peruvians are in exile; yet this is, of course, the case. Of the 221 prominent persons listed in this embassy's 1951/52 Personalities Report no less than 56 live under a political cloud." FO 371 90684/AF 1015/8, Scott to Morrison, 17 October 1951.

23 *Inter-American Labor News*, monthly bulletin issued by the Inter-American Confederation of Workers, 3:6 (1950), quoted in FO 371 81397/AF 2181/2, Murder of Luis Negreiros by secret police.

24 Rosemary Thorp and Geoffrey Bertram, *Peru, 1890–1977: Growth and Policy in an Open Economy* (London: Palgrave, 1978), 205.

25 Ibid., 205.

26 British diplomats saw these measures as essentially political, describing them as "a determined attempt to replace the popular appeal of the APRA and Communist Parties by means of an ambitious programme of social and labour legislation which, conceived on more or less Peronista lines, is clearly designed to win over the working class and white-collar employees, from whose support both APRA and the Communists derive most of their strength." FO 371 74802/AS 1261, Marett to South American Department, 17 February 1949.

27 FO 371 74802/AS 187, Marett to Bevin, 1 January 1949.

28 FO 371 74802/AS 3681, "Peru: Political Review for 1947 and 1948" (Dodds to Bevin, 28 January 1949); FO 371 74802/AS3016, Dodds to Bevin, 27 May 1949.

29 Stuart A. Anderson and Chester W. Wood, "Public Elementary Education in Peru," *Elementary School Journal* 56:4 (1955), 164.

30 FO 371 103337/AF 2181/2, Scott to Eden, 6 February 1953.

31 Frederick Pike, *The Modern History of Peru* (New York: Frederick Praeger, 1967), 293.

32 FO 371 108909/AF 1015/3, Montagu-Pollock to Garvery, 3 May 1954.

33 FO 371 114158/AF 1011/1, Montagu-Pollock to Eden, 25 February 1955 (annual review for 1954).

34 Pike, *The Modern History of Peru*, 293–96.

35 Hilda Gadea, *Ernesto: A Memoir of Che Guevara*, trans. Carmen Molina and Walter I. Bradbury (London and New York: W. H. Allen, a division of Howard and Wyndham, 1973), 5.

36 Jon Lee Anderson, *Che Guevara: A Revolutionary Life* (New York: Grove, 1997), 85–86.

37 Guevara, *Motorcycle Diaries*, 96.

38 Ibid., 138. Following Manuel Odría's coup in 1948, APRA's leader was granted political asylum by Colombia. However, the Peruvian authorities refused him a safe conduct out of the country, so Haya de la Torre was forced to live in the embassy until 1955.

39 Gadea, *Ernesto*, 16.

40 Guevara, *Back on the Road*, 10.

41 This is disputed by Ferrer, who claims that Rojo met up with them in Peru, but that they did not undertake the trip together (*De Ernesto al Che*, 113).

42 Ricardo Rojo, *My Friend Ché*, trans. Julian Casart (New York: Dial Press, 1968), 33–34.

43 In his memoirs Ferrer notes that they were struck by the extent to which Peru was "militarized" and that even in the smaller towns they came across heavily armed soldiers (*De Ernesto al Che*, 151).

44 Karl Eskelund, *Vagabond Fever: A Gay Journey in the Land of the Andes* (Chicago: Rand McNally, 1954), 156–57.

45 Ibid., 157.

46 Szulc, *Twilight*, 161.

47 FO 371–74802/AS 3681, Dodds to Bevin, 28 January 1949.

48 Gadea, *Ernesto*, xv. Gadea repeats this point several times in her memoir: "The position of Betancourt, [Guevara] went on to say, was the same as that of Haya de la Torre, Figueres, and Paz Estenssoro. 'They all represent complete submission to imperialism; they are afraid to seek the support of the people to fight it' " (4); "Guevara, however, felt that [the Bolivian revolution] was not a true revolution, that the leadership was corrupt and consequently would end up surrendering to Yankee imperialism" (10); "The only way, said Ernesto, was a violent revolution; the struggle had to be against Yankee imperialism and any other solutions, such those offered by APRA, Acción Democrática, MNR (National Revolutionary Movement, of Bolivia), were betrayals" (12).

49 Ibid., 49–50.

50 Guevara, *Back on the Road*, 18.

51 Ibid., 15.

52 FO 371 74806/AS 5533, Dodds to Bevin, 28 October 1949.

53 Guevara, *Motorcycle Diaries*, 117.

54 Ibid., 111.

55 Anderson, *Che Guevara*, 38.

56 Bertram Wolfe, "The Novel in Latin America," *Antioch Review* 3:2 (1943), 195.

57 Madaline W. Nichols, "A Prize Novel," *South Atlantic Bulletin* 11:3 (1945), 13.

58 Robert J. Alexander, "The Indians of Latin America," *Phylon* 13:1 (1952), 41.

59 Surprisingly, at the time of its publication, some historians saw little wrong with such a clear reliance on fictional sources. Peter Klarén, for example, noted that Bourricaud's major contribution "is his incisive analysis of the political behavior and motivation of the middle classes which he draws from an imaginative and brilliant examination of the characters who populate the novels of Ciro Alegría and José María Arguedas." Klarén's review of Bourricaud's book appears in *Hispanic American Historical Review* 51:1 (1971), 164–66, quote on 165.

60 Lewis Taylor, "Literature as History: Ciro Alegría's View of Rural Society in the Northern Peruvian Andes," *Ibero-Amerikanisches Archiv*, 10:1 (1984), 349–78.

61 Granado, *Traveling with Che Guevara*, 75.

62 Gadea, *Ernesto*, 11.

63 Ibid., 33.

64 Ibid., 11.

65 Anne Merriman Peck, *Roundabout South America* (New York: Harper, 1940), 114.

66 Guevara, *Motorcycle Diaries*, 91.

67 Ibid., 114, 92.

68 Ibid., 122.

69 Ibid., 116–17.

70 Rojo, *My Friend Ché*, 32–33. Ferrer's account reproduces this trope. The indigenous are "simple people" who "very often were ignorant of who their leaders were, or had a clear idea of their nationality" (*De Ernesto al Che*, 130–31).

71 Guevara, *Motorcycle Diaries*, 91.

72 Ibid., 93.

73 Ibid., 106–7.

74 Ibid., 107.

75 See Marisol de la Cadena, "Silent Racism and Intellectual Superiority in Peru," *Bulletin of Latin American Research* 17:2 (1998), 143–64.

76 Guevara, *Motorcycle Diaries*, 114.

77 Ibid., 113. The idea that acculturated Indians or mestizos are somehow inferior to "real" Indians extends to seeing them as particularly cruel to the latter group. According to Granado, "we noticed that the half castes are the ones who treat the pure Indians with the greatest cruelty" Granado, *Traveling with Che Guevara*, 84.

78 Guevara, *Motorcycle Diaries*, 117.

79 This seems to have been one of Guevara's key preoccupations. According to Ferrer, "[Guevara] always talked to me about the impotence and anxiety that he experienced when he saw the contrast between the glorious indigenous past, as in Machu Picchu, and the modern reality of the indigenous descendants, the poverty, exclusion and oppression in which they lived" (*De Ernesto al Che*, 58).

80 George Sava, *Surgeon under Capricorn* (London: Faber and Faber, 1954), 230–31.

81 Ibid., 231.

82 On García Peláez, see Rebecca Earle, *The Return of the Native: Indians and Myth-Making in Spanish America* (Durham: Duke University Press, 2007), 133.

83 Eskelund, *Vagabond Fever*, 184.

84 However, the idea that Machu Picchu confirmed the Incas as a great civilization was not shared by all. As Eskelund noted, someone had written in the guest book of his hotel: "Machu Picchu is okay, but have you ever been to Texas?" Ibid., 184, 186.

85 Ibid., 194–95.
86 David Theo Goldberg, *The Racial State* (London: Blackwell, 2002).
87 On eugenics in Latin America, see Nancy Leys Stepan, *The Hour of Eugenics: Race, Gender, and Nation in Latin America* (Ithaca: Cornell University Press, 1991). On "hard" and "soft" inheritance, see Peter Wade, *Race, Nature, and Culture: An Anthropological Perspective* (London: Pluto, 2002), chap 3.
88 Guevara, *Motorcycle Diaries*, 104.
89 Ibid., 123.
90 Ibid., 116.
91 Ibid., 124.
92 Granado, *Traveling with Che Guevara*, 90.
93 Ibid., 94.
94 Archivo General de la Nación (AGN), Ministerio del Interior (MI), Prefecturas 513, Cp No 372, 15 July 1948.
95 AGN, MI, Prefecturas 513, Cp No 241, 11 May 1948.
96 José Luis Rénique, *La batalla por Puno: Conflicto agrario y nación en los Andes peruanos* (Lima: Instituto de Estudios Peruanos, 2004), 136.
97 Fiona Wilson, "Conflict on a Peruvian Hacienda," *Bulletin of Latin American Research* 5:1 (1986), 65–94.
98 E. J. Hobsbawm, "A Case of Neo-feudalism: La Convención," *Journal of Latin American Studies* 1:1 (1969), 31–50; José Matos Mar, ed., *Hacienda, comunidad, y campesinado en el Perú* (Lima: Instituto de Estudios Peruanos, 1976).
99 I draw here on James Holston's useful concept and his understanding of insurgence as "a process that is an acting counter, a counterpolitics, that destabilizes the present and renders it fragile, defamiliarizing the coherence with which it usually presents itself." James Holston, *Insurgent Citizenship: Disjunctions of Democracy and Modernity in Brazil* (Princeton: Princeton University Press, 2008), 32.
100 FO 371 90684/AF 1015/8, Scott to Morrison, 17 October 1951.
101 FO 371 103317/AF 1012/4, Scott to Marquess of Salisbury, 15 September 1953.
102 FO 371 114159/AF 1015/6, Montagu-Pollock to Macmillan, 1 June 1955.
103 Jean-Claude Driant, *Las barriadas de Lima: Historia e interpretación* (Lima: Instituto Francés de Estudios Andinos/DESCO, 1991), 53.
104 J. P. Cole, "Some Town Planning Problems of Greater Lima," *Town Planning Review* 26:4 (1956), 247.
105 Quoted in Orin Starn, Carlos Iván Degregori, and Robin Kirk, eds., *The Peru Reader: History, Culture, Politics* (Durham: Duke University Press, 1995), 255.

106   Heath Bownman and Stirling Dickinson, *Westward from Rio* (Chicago: Willett, Clark, 1936), 326–27.

107   Christopher Morley, *Hasta la vista; or, A Postcard from Peru* (Garden City, N.Y.: Doubleday, Doran, 1935), 181–82.

108   George Woodcock, *Incas and Other Men* (London: Travel Book Club, 1959), 17.

109   Frances Tor, *The Three Worlds of Peru* (New York: Crown Publishers, 1949), 21.

110   Ibid., 34.

111   W. Byford-Jones, *Four Faces of Peru* (London: Travel Book Club, 1967), 136.

112   Ibid.

113   Tor, *The Three Worlds of Peru*, 22–23.

114   Ibid., 40.

115   Eskelund, *Vagabond Fever*, 158.

116   Guevara, *Motorcycle Diaries*, 134.

117   Ibid., 138.

118   Ibid., 133.

119   Ibid., 134.

120   Ibid., 113.

121   Granado, *Traveling with Che Guevara*, 90.

122   See Fernando Santos and Frederica Barclay, *La frontera domesticada: Historia económica y social de Loreto, 1850–2000* (Lima: Pontificia Universidad Católica, 2002).

123   Guevara, *Motorcycle Diaries*, 145.

124   Ibid.

125   Ibid., 149; emphasis added.

126   On the San Pablo colony, see Marcos Cueto, "Social Medicine and 'Leprosy' in the Peruvian Amazon," *Americas* 61:1 (2004), 55–80.

127   Guevara, *Motorcycle Diaries*, 149.

128   Ibid., 146.

129   The testimony is reproduced in Marcos Cueto and José Carlos de la Puente, "Vida de Leprosa: The Testimony of a Woman Living with Hansen's Disease in the Peruvian Amazon, 1947," *História, Ciências, Saúde, Manguinhos*, no.10, supplement 1 (2003), 337–60.

130   Hank Kelly and Dot Kelly, *Dancing Diplomats* (Albuquerque: University of New Mexico Press, 1950), 146.

131   Ibid., 147.

132   A useful overview of the literature on the Peruvian guerrillas of the 1960s, albeit one that reproduces the idea of the Indian's "fatalistic outlook on life in general" (62), is Leon G. Campbell, "The Historiography of the Peruvian Guerrilla Movement, 1960–1965," *Latin American*

Research Review 8:1 (1973), 45–70. For a more recent analysis, see José Luis Rénique, "De la traición aprista al gesto heroico—Luis de la Puente y la guerrilla del MIR," *Estudios Interdisciplinarios de América Latina y el Caribe* 15:1 (2004), 89–114.

133 The literature on the Shining Path is vast. For an excellent introduction, see Steve J. Stern, ed., *Shining and Other Paths: War and Society in Peru, 1980–1995* (Durham: Duke University Press, 1998).

134 See Giorgio Agamben, *Homo Sacer: Sovereign Power and Bare Life*, trans. Daniel Heller-Roazen (Stanford: Stanford University Press, 1998).

Malcolm Deas

"Putting Up" with Violence
Ernesto Guevara, Guevarismo, and Colombia

Ernesto Guevara's motorcycle did not reach Colombia. He and his
companion entered the country in June 1952 at the Amazon river
port of Leticia, and from there they flew to Bogotá. They stayed a few
days and then departed overland for Venezuela. The *Motorcycle Diaries*
have little to say about Colombia, and that little is of no exceptional
interest. What there is, occurs in Che's letter to his mother from
Bogotá, dated 6 July 1952: "There is more repression of individual
freedom here than in any country we've been to, the police patrol the
streets carrying rifles and demand your papers every few minutes,
which some of them read upside down. The atmosphere is tense and
it seems a revolution may be brewing. The countryside is in open
revolt and the army is powerless to suppress it. The conservatives
battle among themselves and cannot agree, and the memory of April
9, 1948, still weighs heavily on everyone's minds. In summary, it's
suffocating here. If the Colombians want to put up with it, good
luck to them, but we're getting out of here as soon as we can."[1]
Perhaps what is interesting in the diaries is precisely the little curiosity about politics that the author shows. If the entries are meant to
show signs of a political awakening, it is one of unusual torpor. A
text subsequently revised by Guevara himself, by his widow, and
probably by the Cuban government—not usually careless in this sort
of editing—contains little that foreshadows Guevara's later revolutionary career: a poor old lady dying in Valparaiso, an encounter
with a cold and disgruntled copper miner, a passing verdict that
Chile would be better off without the United States, and the defeated
mien of the Indians of the Peruvian sierra. A proper political awakening had to await his experiences in Guatemala.[2]
    Be that as it may, this brief intersection of Guevara and Colom-

bian history is a hook on which one can hang a number of reflections. There are many reasons for resisting a title akin to "Colombia in the Era of Che," but the man still had an undeniable impact on Colombia.[3] The country that he glimpsed was indeed a repressed one awaiting a revolution, though not the one he would later have in mind, and it is worthwhile analyzing why. The Cuban Revolution and Guevara's writings about it affected Colombia—that "countryside in open revolt" through which he rapidly passed in 1952 was to be the scene a decade or so later of one of the early *guevarista* experiments in South America, the ELN, the Ejército de Liberación Nacional (National Liberation Army). Colombia already had guerrillas then—and it has subsequently had more guerrillas than any other country in Latin America—who have repeatedly failed to achieve any revolutionary ends. Camilo Torres, who was killed when a novice member of the ELN a year and a half before Guevara's death, stands as another comparable guerrilla icon or martyr. Why did he die? What has this persistent fighting, and persistent failure, meant?

The Colombia Glimpsed by Che

Let us begin by filling out Guevara's sketch of July 1952. Colombia was indeed passing through one of the most violent and repressive stages of its twentieth-century history. The year 1946 saw the end of the domination of the Liberal Party, which had begun with the election of Enrique Olaya Herrera in 1930. His election on a minority vote was made possible by a split in the Conservative Party, whose various factions had ruled the country since 1885, and it was followed by some violence, as the Conservatives resisted the Liberal incomers with campaigns of civil and less civil disobedience. The comparative peacefulness of the previous three decades and of the transition itself—the violence was much less than that in store after 1946—largely resulted from the provisions for minority representation put into place after the previous disastrous formal civil war, the War of a Thousand Days (1899–1902), and the secession of Panama. Those guarantees of at least a slice of the cake, though somewhat simple and crude, and the traumatic memory of the worst of all the civil wars and the national disgrace that had followed it, kept the Liberal Party from resorting to arms, despite the provocation of some notoriously fraudulent elections. At several junctures in the early twentieth century it seemed possible that the Liberals might once again return to armed rebellion, most acutely in the aftermath of their defeat in the manifestly fraudulent presidential elections of 1922. The party leader General Benjamín Herrera, one of the most prominent Liberal generals of the War of a Thousand Days, famously resisted the temptation and instead founded the Universidad Libre. Between 1902 and 1946 prominent politicians lost the habit of taking to the field themselves.

The politics of the country nonetheless became increasingly polarized in the late 1930s and 1940s.[4] Simple minority guarantees were replaced by more sophisticated arrangements—proportional representation and the *cedula*, the voting identity card. Nobody really knew in 1930, or even considerably later, whether the majority of Colombian citizens were Liberals or Conservatives. While in office, the Conservatives habitually inflated the number of their votes in the areas they traditionally dominated, but Colombia was still a heavily rural country, and much of the peasant population of the highlands was indeed likely to vote Conservative. The Liberals had a greater hold in the cities, as well as in areas with a weak Church presence, some areas of more recent colonization, and those inhabited by blacks. Mestizos often tended to be Liberals—they were seen as anticlerical even in the days of the colony—and Colombia was and is a very mestizo country. Conservatives nonetheless would accuse the Liberal governments of fraud on the issue of the *cedulas*, which replaced the old voting lists. Against the new hegemony they resorted to electoral abstention. At the time, Colombia was governed by the centralist Constitution of 1886, under which departmental governors and municipal mayors, alcaldes, were nominated, not elected, creating the instruments for a winner-takes-all spoils system.

Given the depth of party loyalties in Colombia, this situation had always meant possible violence. The likelihood increased in the fifteen years of Liberal rule, during which the electorate expanded. Never overly deferential even in the nineteenth century, it was becoming increasingly undeferential. The 1930s constituted a period of mobilization and countermobilization, of political excitement. Both parties produced leaders of exceptional stature, great speakers and crowd-pullers: to name only the most prominent, the Liberals had Alfonso López Pumarejo and Jorge Eliécer Gaitán and the Conservatives Laureano Gómez.[5] López was a cosmopolitan modernizer, somewhat in the mold of Franklin Delano Roosevelt, who governed to open up his isolated and obscurantist country to all sorts of change. But he was also a Liberal prepared to wave the *trapo rojo*, the Liberal red flag, and shout his *vivas* to the *gran* Partido Liberal when it served him. Gaitán had a gift for attracting followers from across the party divide, and he engaged in a class rhetoric that reached large numbers of those previously unmobilized, but he was never able to escape the Liberal Party and his support remained predominantly Liberal. Gómez proved an ideologically complex Conservative —some have found the nearest parallel to him in the Spanish conservative Antonio Maura—but nobody wishing to understand Colombia at this time should make the mistake of doubting his popularity with the rank and file of his party, which had always viewed itself as a party of the people. Colombian Conservatives frequently attacked the Liberals as elitist: rich men, city dwellers, freethinkers, rootless bourgeois—the Conservative Party therefore seemed the natural home of the rural Catholic poor. Gómez could be as demagogic as Gaitán, and as a speaker in Congress, the coliseum of Colombia's gladiatorial politics, he proved Gaitán's superior.

When the Liberal Party split in the elections of 1946 and the Conservatives returned to power under Mariano Ospina Pérez, elected on a minority vote, the rising political temperature resulted in sectarian violence, intensified by the assassination of Gaitán on 9 April 1948.[6] This situation formed the background to the "suffocating atmosphere" Guevara refers to in July 1952.[7]

It was a prerevolutionary situation of sorts, but not one to appeal to Guevara, even if his revolutionary convictions had been formed by then, which they probably were not: "If the Colombians want to put up with it, good luck to them, but we're getting out of here as soon as we can." The immediate revolution was the ousting, to vast public relief, of Gómez on 13 June 1953 in a civil-military coup and the installation of General Gustavo Rojas Pinilla's military government.[8] Rojas Pinilla ruled for a mere four years. He had some initial success in pacifying the country, but his early popularity rapidly evaporated, and he proved no match for the bipartisan civilian maneuvers that removed him from office in 1957. A Conservative himself in his loyalties, he had little political imagination, and his occasional attempts to emulate Juan Perón or Marcos Pérez Jiménez were halfhearted. His government nonetheless left an outstanding legacy of public works, and when the game was up, he had the grace to go without resorting to repression.

The coming to power of Fidel Castro in Cuba coincided with the installation in Colombia of the power-sharing arrangement known as the Frente Nacional (National Front). The agreement between the two traditional parties, Liberals and Conservatives, to alternate in the presidency and to divide congressional seats and other spoils 50–50, had been made with the dual aim of ending sectarian conflict and removing the military government. The largest Liberal guerrilla group, that in the *llanos orientales*, the eastern plains, had already accepted an amnesty at the beginning of Rojas Pinilla's rule, but there were still guerrillas active in other parts of the country, mostly Liberals but also some of a vaguely communist orientation; the latter had deep roots in some localized agrarian conflicts of the 1930s. Some of these guerrillas accepted offers of amnesty, but for complex local reasons others did not, and it is here that Cuban and *guevarista* influences entered Colombia.[9]

Guevarismo in Colombia

I would argue that without the Cuban Revolution, all Colombian guerrillas would have died out in the early 1960s. Given historians' fascination with the local origins of both the Revolutionary Armed Forces of Colombia (Fuerzas Armadas Revolucionarias de Colombia, FARC) and the ELN, their nationalist sentiments and sympathy with the guerrillas, this hypothesis has not received the attention I think it deserves. The Cuban Revolution certainly had a great impact, and its success and the mode of its success, at least the sierra-guerrilla version of that mode, posed a challenge to the revolutionary credentials of Communist Parties throughout the region, including, of course, the Cuban Communist Party.

The Colombian Communist Party (CP) was not a very revolutionary organization. It was weak in numbers, and its main strength lay in the cities and in certain *sindicatos* (trade unions). It had always been close to the Liberal Party, many of whose leaders had been Marxists in their youth, and its leaders were indistinguishable in their social origins from many of the politicians of the traditional parties. Gilberto Viera White, for example, the eternal general secretary of the party, was what Colombians would call *de buena familia*, from a well-to-do and respectable family.[10] The Colombian CP had never been enthusiastic about Gaitán, whom it tended to regard as a self-seeking opportunist, ignorant of the true dialectic. Eduardo Santos, the Liberal president from 1938 to 1942 and the owner of the country's leading newspaper, El Tiempo, looked on the communists with a tolerant and paternal eye. When it was pointed out to him that the Frente Nacional was perhaps too exclusive, that it left no space for the communists, he supposedly responded that he would make sure that the Liberals looked after their interests. At the time this response was not as absurd as it now seems.

Faced with the necessity of responding to the Cuban Revolution, the communist leadership in Colombia found itself in what appeared at the time to be the fortunate position of having some guerrillas ready to hand. Not very aggressive ones—the line was still very much one of autodefensa campesina, of peasant self-defense—but guerrillas nonetheless. A closer look would have revealed that some, perhaps most, of the existing autodefensas campesinas were sincerely just that, peasant organizations intent on their local security and autonomy and on holding onto their gains in land, with no national revolutionary perspective at all. The leader of the Sumapaz movement, Juan de la Cruz Varela, always held to that line, and he was then at least as well known as Manuel Marulanda, the eventual leader of the FARC. Cruz Varela warily came to terms with the Frente Nacional. Had it not been for Cuba, the others would have done so too, or they would have shared the fate of Sangre Negra, Chispas, Desquite, and Efraín González, bandits whose careers were ended in the early 1960s.

Colombian circumstances alone would not have produced a sustained guerrilla, even on the small scale that for many years characterized the FARC. In its early years the FARC owed a lot to the party: material help, some of it from Cuba;[11] political guidance and sober instruction; and discipline—the FARC to this day largely maintains a Leninist heritage of "democratic centralism." Without the pressure exerted by the Cuban Revolution, in these years when the Andes were going to be the Sierra Maestra of South America, it is hard to imagine that the Colombian party would have supported a guerrilla line to the degree that it did, or that it would have adopted the fatal formula of "the combination of all forms of struggle." Nevertheless, it had to do so if it was to sustain its claim as the country's vanguard party. For there were rivals. Unlike the FARC, whose origins clearly antecede Castro's and Guevara's victory, the ELN was of pure Cuban inspiration. It followed the theory elaborated by Guevara and later by Régis Debray in his *Revolución en la revolución?*, the theory of the *foco*, the small motor of local rebellion that would start the large motor of national dissent, which in turn would lead to the fall of the government.[12] It had a clear starting date. Its leaders were trained in Cuba, and their conduct soon rather resembled Guevara's, one marked by many executions of informers, deserters, and suspects. Colombians found this shocking.[13]

The early 1960s in Colombia saw the formal creation of the FARC after the government had sent the army into the *repúblicas independientes* (independent republics), a term coined by Álvaro Gomez for the areas under the control of communist *autodefensas campesinas* (peasant self-defence organizations), embryo guerrillas. The most famous of these was Marquetalia in Tolima, where an embryonic FARC had been practicing, sometimes aggressively, *autodefensa campesina*, a strategy later denounced by Debray as unviable.[14] They also saw the arrival of the Alliance for Progress: the U.S. government at the time regarded Colombia as the leading and most successful recipient of aid, as well as of some military aid. In mid-1965 Torres left the priesthood and, after a brief political campaign with the naïve aim of "uniting the Colombian Left," joined the ELN.[15] But he did not survive long and soon after Guevara himself was killed in Bolivia.[16] The FARC did survive, yet without presenting any great threat to anyone—their numbers were in the low hundreds and they were located in distant and unimportant parts of the country. The numerous experts of the Alliance for Progress, having completed their quota of articles for peer-reviewed journals, returned home disillusioned, with the knowledge that a few billion dollars do not much alter the course of a country's development, and with some resentment at the Colombian government having managed to have the United States finance its deficits. The latter country soon turned its attention to Vietnam, its military observers having concluded that the Colombian army was capable of containing the low-level threat posed by the guerrillas.[17]

Yet some people still thought that they could discern a prerevolutionary situation in Colombia. One was Eric Hobsbawm, who argued in 1963: "That Colombia, in common with most Latin American countries with the possible exception of Argentina and Uruguay, contains the raw material for a social revolution both of the peasantry and of the urban poor is palpably obvious. As in other Latin American countries, the problem is not to discover inflammatory material but to explain why it has not yet burst into flames or—as in the Colombian case—why having spontaneously flared up, it has settled back into a smoky mass showing only an occasional glimmer." Though his succinct account itself hints at a number of explanations, he nonetheless concluded that "any observer who believes that Colombia is living through anything but a pause of exhaustion is likely to have a very sharp awakening."[18] Were observers like Hobsbawm right? Did Colombia offer a field where revolution could be made according to the Guevara recipe: the guerrilla vanguard or *foco* even in seemingly unripe time, the rural context, agrarian reform? Clearly not. In the early 1970s Jaime Arenas published a devastating and detailed critique in his account of the ELN, *La guerrilla por dentro*, an essential source that deserves to be better known outside Colombia—it went through at least six legitimate Bogotá editions in the 1970s, and a number of pirated ones. A lot of the criticisms concern tactical errors, but the mistakes ran deeper than that.

When first asked to write this essay, my mind turned to the rural Colombia I had first seen in 1964 and to the photographs of peasants taken by the photographer Luis B. Ramos in the two previous decades.[19] I thought then that I was seeing people representing the last of the European Middle Ages. The upland peasants of Cundinamarca and Boyacá still all dressed traditionally. The men wore hats, gray, black, or mud-colored *ruanas*, and the rest of their clothes were dark too. Many men wore *alpargatas*, fique sandals, and children went barefoot. The women wore straw hats, black shawls, and multiple skirts, outfits that derived not from the indigenous Chibchas but from the Spain of the sixteenth or seventeenth century. In these parts the church still had a strong influence, and these people went to Mass. Ramos's photographs are the work of an artist, but nothing in them is posed or invented. What they show is a peasantry maybe ready for a jacquerie but not for a revolution.

The *violencia* that many rural Colombians had suffered and participated in from 1946 until the Frente Nacional was essentially sectarian. The conflict certainly involved a sectarian government, and it would be wrong to picture the state as above the fray. It is also true that there were some agrarian elements in the conflict, dating back to the 1930s, and apologists for the FARC make much of these. Yet notwithstanding the persistent efforts of radical and Marxist historians to highlight these elements, the conflict cannot be characterized as an agrarian one: peasants were not fighting for land, and rebels not seeking to overthrow a class regime, either in the countryside or in the country as a whole.[20] The agreement of the Frente Nacional restored comparative peace, and one of the accord's achievements was to blunt for good the previously sharp sectarian divide that had dominated the country's political life.

The previous decade and a half of violence made most people unwilling to engage in renewed violence for revolutionary ends. The dominant desire was one for peace—plebiscites with high turnouts, especially in rural areas, overwhelmingly endorsed the power-sharing arrangements. Colombian peasants had voted for a long time, so there are no good reasons to doubt the sincerity of this endorsement. This phase of *violencia* ended in a painful truce, with an end to fighting but no end to distrust—a distrust of neighbors, bandits, the army and police, institutions, and of politics generally—and politics included guerrillas promising salvation through more guerrilla warfare. This explains the revolutionary Left's early emphasis on *autodefensa campesina*, as peasants still had to defend themselves against threats from a variety of quarters and had a strong desire to be left alone.

The theory of the *foco* proved a doubtful one for many reasons: if making revolution that way was so simple, why in human history had so few such revolutions occurred? The stimulating "small motor" seemed even less likely to initiate much in a country already inured to rural violence, where more of it could hardly be seen as a novelty. In Cuba, Castro's guerrilla, though not without antecedents in Cuba's independence wars and even in Cuban banditry, was a novelty: it was the first of its kind in a long time, and it could produce the Pancho Villa–Sandino effect on foreign journalists, the heirs of John Reed and Carleton Beals.[21] Colombian guerrillas were not usually news, either inside or outside Colombia. The ELN did manage to attract one rather unknown Mexican journalist, and perhaps inspired by Villa's example, the group robbed a train (quite a feat in a country with so few trains), so that he could get a story. Yet he and his photographs were then seized by the Colombian police on his way out.[22] Torres for a short time made the ELN news again, but he is generally remembered more outside Colombia than in the country, in some Catholic circles in Europe and by some *montoneros* in Argentina, a country particularly unsuited to guerrilla warfare in the twentieth century.[23]

The ELN also chose its area of operations badly. The young urban leadership—there was not much of a rank and file to start with—chose to start operations with an attack on Simacota, in a part of Santander previously famous as the territory of the Liberal guerrilla Rafael Rangel. A guerrilla emerging in the territory of a recently evaporated guerrilla—this only compounded the problem of a lack of novelty. Even in the 1920s the Colombian government, then Conservative, had had trouble distinguishing *bolcheviques* from what one of its loyal informants called "la misma liberalada de siempre" (the same old liberal mob) and though now the ELN was clearly *castrista*, its location in this Liberal region would be likely to circumscribe its appeal. For the Colombian countryside was politicized, though, many would say, perversely so. It was no tabula rasa.[24] Though sectarian political loyalties were not now—in the early 1960s—producing violent confrontation, they had not disappeared. Party leaders and their networks of aspirant subordinates still had a strong hold: the continual strength of the Conservative Party can be measured by its ability to insist on a fifty-fifty division of power.

There was as yet little demand for agrarian reform from those who might have gained from it, though there was some: Cruz Varela, for example, was an authentic peasant leader intent on maintaining the gains he and his following had secured in the Sumapaz region of Cundinamarca. Yet most Colombians simply wanted an end to violence and a return to peaceful political life. The designers of the Alliance for Progress—who appear to have been better acquainted with Mexico than with South America and much influenced by the political success of the Mexican agrarian reform, when they were not thinking of remodeling the entire hemisphere along the lines of rural Wisconsin—made agrarian reform one of its main provisions. The Colombian government dutifully complied with the establishment of an agrarian reform institute, the Agrarian Reform Institute of Colombia (INCORA), and some rather lax legislation.[25]

In 1972 the reform was effectively halted by the Pacto de Chicoral, an agreement between the government of Misael Pastrana and the landowners ending the threat of expropriation in return for vague promises of productivity. Demand from below thereafter increased in some parts of the country, but the opportunity had been lost, in part because of the delicate partisan balance in the countryside after the violence of the 1940s and 1950s. A radical land reform that would not disturb that balance seemed hard to conceive. Besides, radical land reforms have nowhere been the product of benevolent paternalist planners unsupported by peasant demand, collapsing hegemonies, or the sort of competitive political bidding that later took place in Chile.[26]

Che's Legacy in Colombia

Back to *The Motorcycle Diaries*: one trait the mature Che shared with the young Guevara was a lack of political curiosity. José Pardo Llada found him incurious even about Cuba.[27] The advocate of creating "one, two, three, many Vietnams" seems to have shown little interest in the existing politics of the Andes or of his own country, Argentina. Local Communist Parties were simply meant to serve his personal definition of the needs of world revolution, their observations to be brushed aside and sacrificed, along with a lot of other people, if they stood in his way. His interest in rural conditions was likewise superficial, as can be seen from the Salta guerrilla in Argentina in the early 1960s and by the casual way in which his last theatre of operations in Bolivia was chosen. (One rash Colombian critic ran some risk at the time when, on the campus of the Universidad Nacional in Bogotá, he referred to Che as "ese idiota que pensaba revolucionar a Bolivia con un mapa de la ESSO" [that idiot who thought he could revolutionize Bolivia with an ESSO map]—a memorable verdict with much truth in it.)[28]

Guevara certainly had some influence in Colombia, and not only among university students: Colombian guerrillas have their authentic elements, and I would never deny that they form a real part of the country's history, but much more foreign inspiration went into their formation and development than most accounts acknowledge: Cuban, Maoist, Albanian. The Popular Liberation Army (EPL), for example, divided into pro-Chinese Maoists and a pro-Albanian line of purer Maoists, who formed the Enver Hoxha Front, some of whose members even managed pilgrimages to Tirana for orientation, rest, and recreation. Later inspiration came from Nicaragua and El Salvador, and doubtless the FARC currently gets some comfort from Hugo Chávez.

I believe this influence was not beneficial. Guerrillas have cost Colombia a great deal. Economists in *Planeación Nacional* and elsewhere have in recent years made sophisticated attempts to calculate the costs of insecurity, just as they have attempted to quantify the results of the drug trade. The perhaps quantifiable costs are certainly high: in deaths and wasted lives, in kidnappings and extortion, in the flight and nonarrival of capital, in sabotage and destruction, in displaced persons, and in additional costs of various sorts. Yet the bill in misery and suffering cannot, of course, be quantified, and the less well-off have borne most of these costs.[29] There has also been a high political cost. One will, I suspect, be invited to stand back from the ugliness of the conflict, the massacres, the executions, and the body counts to contemplate some possible progressive compensation for it all. Yet I fail to find it. It seems to me that the beneficiaries have resided on the right of the political spectrum, that the cause best served has been that of reaction. In contemplating Guevara and his career I become more Westphalian: there is a lot to be said for the old inhibitions against interfering in other peoples' countries.

The guerrillas had no role in ending the Frente Nacional, which came to its predetermined end in the 1970s—a long time ago, so it is not convincing to blame that arrangement, which was far less "exclusive" than its critics allege, for the continued activities of guerrillas since. Behind the Constitution of 1991, which replaced that of 1886, was the notion that a more obviously modern and participatory democracy would bring peace, but that hope was only partially fulfilled as the main guerrilla groups, the FARC and the ELN, showed their lack of interest. Whatever the merits of the new Constitution, the guerrillas have not aided its implementation.

Many on the Left now acknowledge the "combination of all forms of struggle" as a fatal strategy. In the 1980s it produced the massacre of those who joined the Unión Patriótica (UP), the FARC's civil arm that the group launched with less than sincerity.[30] It made the emergence of a stronger civil, peaceful Left vastly more difficult, as it fed local *macartismo*, which in recent years has taken the virulent form of paramilitarism. Leaders of the violent Left in many conjunctures have succumbed to the illusion that they will always be able to control the level of violence, that they can turn it on and off at their own convenience. And when it turns out that they cannot, they regularly fall back on the argument that they are "unmasking the innate violence of the state," or of the ruling class, or of capitalism, or of globalization . . . . In Colombia such control was always an illusion. If the state was too weak or too peacefully inclined to confront the guerrillas, then others, such as the paramilitaries, would emerge who would do so, and who would use much more violent methods than the government would.[31]

In spite of this situation, Colombia has changed a great deal since 1952. It is a much more urban country. Though its middle classes were not even then negligible, they now make up for more of the population, and they are more autonomous, less deferential. The Catholic Church has lost influence, while Protestants and Evangelicals have gained power. The position of women has changed radically for the better, universities have proliferated. The country is much less isolated, millions of Colombians have emigrated, millions more have traveled abroad, there is now at least one mobile telephone per two Colombians, and most Colombians are better off; modernities have certainly arrived in waves. There are now of course also drugs, drugs not encountered by the two easy riders of 1952, and with drugs, there are still guerrillas.

Notes

1 Ernesto "Che" Guevara, *The Motorcycle Diaries: A Journey around South America*, trans. Ann Wright (London: Verso, 1995), 157. Romanticism begins with the title, as most of the ground was covered after the bike broke down. The blurbs on this paperback edition surely represent the sentimental Left at its worst and are too awful to be passed over unremarked: "On this journey of journeys, solitude found solidarity. 'I' turned into 'we.' "—Eduardo Galeano; "By the end of the journey, a politicized Guevara has emerged to predict his own legendary future."—*Time*; "There is pathos in these pages—the pathos of Che himself, ever thoughtful, ever willing to sacrifice all, burning with guilt over his own privileges and never letting his sufferings impede him."—*New Yorker*; "A revolutionary bestseller. . . . It's true, Marxists just wanna have fun."—

Guardian; "*Das Kapital* meets *Easy Rider.*"—*Times.* Not one of these statements, not even the last one, appears to me at all true; it is as if their authors had all been reading some other book. And how distance lends to enchantment! The further one is away from guerrillas, the more likely one is to see that poster on the wall. The account of Colombia in the diary of Guevara's fellow traveler Alberto Granado, *Travelling with Che Guevara: The Making of a Revolutionary,* trans. Lucía Alvarez de Toledo (New York: Newmarket Press, 2004), hardly proves more informative: it says more on the heavy police presence in Bogotá, but most of it concerns soccer.

2 The "exhaustive" account of his stay in Guatemala occurs in Jon Lee Anderson, *Che Guevara: A Revolutionary Life* (London: Bantam, 1997), 122–59, which is likely to remain the most detailed biography. An early critical sketch of Guevara published by a prominent Cuban exile in Colombia is José Pardo Llada, *El "Che" que yo conocí* (Medellín: Editorial Bedout, 1969). Pardo Llada still gets up Castro's nose: see Fidel Castro *My Life,* ed. Ignacio Ramonet, trans. Andrew Hurley (London: Penguin, 2007), 86–87.

3 In the biography of the forgotten Colombian poet Hernando de Bengoechea, killed fighting with the French army in the First World War, by Dario Achury Valenzuela, *Cita en la trinchera de la muerte* (Bogotá: Instituto Colombiano de Cultura, 1973), there is a photograph with the title "*Los Champs Elysées* en tiempos de Bengoechea" (The Champs Elysées of Bengoechea's time); such designations run the risk of failing to show a correct sense of proportion.

4 The best guide to the politics of these years is now James Henderson's detailed narrative *La modernización en Colombia: Los años de Laureano Gómez, 1889–1965* (Medellín: Universidad de Antioquia), 2006. This edition is to be preferred to the shorter English version: James D. Henderson, *Modernization in Colombia: The Laureano Gómez Years, 1889–1965.* (Gainesville, Fla: University Press of Florida, 2001).

5 There is no full study of Alfonso López; for an introduction see A. Tirado Mejía, *Aspectos políticos del primer gobierno de Alfonso López Pumarejo, 1934–1938* (Bogotá: Procultura, 1981); for the atmosphere of the era, see Kathleen Romoli, *Colombia: Gateway to South America* (New York: Doubleday, 1941). For Gaitán, Antonio García's *Gaitán y el problema de la revolución colombiana* (Bogotá: n.p., 1955), should still be read, along with the more recent studies, which tend to be themselves *gaitanista:* J. Cordell Robinson, *El movimiento gaitanista en Colombia* (Bogotá: Tercer Mundo, 1976); Richard E. Sharpless, *Gaitán of Colombia: A Political Biography* (Pittsburgh, Penn.: University of Pittsburgh Press, 1978); Herbert Braun, *The Assassination of Gaitán: Public Life and Urban Violence in Colombia*

(Madison: University of Wisconsin Press, 1985); W. John Green, *Gaitanismo, Left Liberalism, and Popular Mobilization in Colombia* (Gainesville: University Press of Florida, 2003), which has a full bibliography. For Gómez, see Henderson, *La modernización en Colombia*, and Christopher Abel, *Política, iglesia y partidos en Colombia, 1886–1953* (Bogotá: Universidad Nacional de Colombia, 1987).

6 Here perhaps the Cuba-oriented reader will expect a note on Fidel Castro's presence in Bogotá at the time of the *Bogotazo*, 9 April 1948. The Cuban student delegation and its possible involvement was mentioned in a subsequent investigation carried out at Ospina's request by two detectives from Scotland Yard, which concluded that the delegation's presence was entirely accidental. Mythmaking persists, the latest contribution coming from Castro himself, with help from Gabriel García Márquez: Castro recounts how during the riot he met a man in the street destroying a typewriter, and to help him he seized the machine and threw it into the air, so that it crashed down and shattered on the pavement; García Márquez listens to Fidel, and then says, "That man with the typewriter was me!" See Fidel Castro, "La novela de sus recuerdos," *El Tiempo*, 19 August 2006. Can such a tale be true? There are two further texts on 9 April worth considering: Alfonso López Michelsen's essay on the sociology of the Bogotá riot in his *Cuestiones colombianas* (Mexico City: Impresiones Modernas, 1955); and Ignacio Gómez Dávila's somber novel, *Viernes 9*, (Mexico City: Impresiones Modernas, 1953).

7 The general Latin American context of the decade is vividly described in Germán Arciniegas's *Entre la libertad y el miedo* (Mexico City: Editorial Cultura, 1952).

8 For Rojas Pinilla, see Silvia Galvis and Alberto Donadio, *El jefe supremo: Rojas Pinilla, en la violencia y el poder* (Bogotá: Planeta, 1988); María Eugenia Rojas de Moreno, *Rojas Pinilla, mi padre*, (Bogotá: Panamericana, 2000). A graphic and contemporary pro-Rojas survey of the country is Vernon Lee Fluharty, *Dance of the Millions: Military Rule and Social Revolution in Colombia, 1930–1956* (Pittsburgh, Penn.: University of Pittsburgh Press, 1957).

9 For the guerrillas of the Eastern Plains, see E. Franco Isaza, *Las guerrillas del llano: Testimonio de una lucha de cuatro años por la libertad* (Caracas: Editorial Universo, 1955); though some of the leadership was certainly radical, and some accounts picture the guerrillas' *ley del llano* (law of the plains) as a social revolution, they were essentially liberal. For the amnesty, see María Bárbara Gómez Rincón, ed., *Tiempos de paz: Acuerdos en Colombia, 1902–1994* (Bogotá: Alcaldía Mayor de Bogotá, Instituto Distrital de Cultura y Turismo, 2003). In parts of Cundinamarca and

Tolima the guerrillas were divided by local circumstances and rivalries into *limpios*, liberals, and *comunes*, communists. When the *limpios* made local peace with the army, the *comunes* found themselves excluded and had to look to their own defense. That the *comunes* did not accede to an amnesty was a matter of local circumstances, not of ideology or strategy. Details in M. Medina, *Historia del Partido Comunista*, vol. 1 (Bogotá: Centro de Estudios e Investigaciones Sociales, 1980); Eduardo Pizarro Leongomez and Ricardo Peñaranda, *Las FARC (1949–1966): De la autodefensa a la combinación de todas las formas de lucha* (Bogotá: Tercer Mundo, 1991); Alfredo Molano, *Los años de tropel: Relatos de la Violencia* (Bogotá: Fondo Editorial CEREC, 1985). There is a large literature on the agrarian conflicts of the 1930s; for an introduction, see the relevant parts of Catherine LeGrand, *Frontier Expansion and Peasant Protest in Colombia, 1830–1936* (Albuquerque: University of New Mexico Press, 1986). The post-1946 violence to some extent subsumed earlier agrarian conflicts but cannot itself be defined as essentially agrarian.

10 A number of memoirs by figures of the Colombian Left reveal the social composition of the party leadership and its relations with the traditional parties, particularly with the Liberals. See particularly the invaluable works of Ignacio Torres Giraldo, *Los inconformes: Historia de la rebeldía de masas en Colombia*, 5 vols (Bogotá: Editorial Margen Izquierdo, 1972), and his account of his early years, *Anecdotario* (Cali: Universidad del Valle, 2005).

11 The details are in Alonso Moncada Abello, *Un aspecto de la violencia* (Bogotá: Promotora Colombiana de Ediciones y Revistas, 1963). For a recent revelation of past Cuban support for the ELN, see León Valencia, "Fidel y el ELN," *El Tiempo*, 12 August 2006. It is now apparently progressive to call attention to these links in welcoming Castro's role as a possible peacemaker between the ELN and the Colombian government; at the time they were of course played down.

12 Régis Debray, *Revolución en la revolución?* (Havana: Casa de las Américas, 1967). For Debray's subsequent evolution and his considered opinion of Guevara, see his *Praised Be Our Lords: A Political Education*, trans. John Howe (London: Verso, 2007). In his review of the work in the *London Review of Books*, 7 February 2008, Jeremy Harding quotes him on Guevara as follows: "Gentleness and kindness were not among his salient characteristics. . . . What a fertile misunderstanding it was, in 1968, turning that believer in no-holds-barred authoritarianism into an emblem of anti-authoritarian revolt from Paris to Berkeley."

13 The FARC have always maintained strong discipline, handing down the death penalty for some offences, and the movement's history includes splits and subsequent massacres, but its leadership rightly or

wrongly managed to avoid the reputation for paranoid purging that the early ELN leaders soon earned. For an account by a participant in the beginnings of the ELN, and for further details of Cuban support, see Jaime Arenas, *La guerrilla por dentro* (Bogotá: Tercer Mundo, 1971). Arenas was himself murdered by the ELN in Bogotá soon after the publication of his book. For Guevara's record of executing *chivatos* (informers, in Colombia known as *sapos*), deserters, and suspects in the Cuban guerrilla, see the relevant chapters in Anderson's *Che Guevara*. This practice must have formed part of any Cuban training course.

14 See the photograph of Guevara's notes on Debray, captured in Bolivia, in Anderson, *Che Guevara*.

15 On Camilo Torres, see Germán Guzmán Campos, *Camilo, el cura guerrillero* (Bogotá: Servicios Especiales de Prensa, 1967); Walter J. Broderick, *Camilo Torres: A biography of the Priest-Guerrillero* (New York: Doubleday, 1975). Torres was followed into the ELN by two or three other priests, the most prominent being Spanish, from the Spain of Franco. Nonetheless, revolutionary Catholicism has not been a prominent feature of the Colombian church, and though it is respected, it would be wrong to say that Torres's memory is widely revered in his own country.

16 For my views on guerrilla prospects at that time, see my article "Guerrillas in Latin America: A Perspective," *World Today* 24:2 (1968). They have not changed since.

17 James M. Daniel, "Rural Violence in Colombia since 1946," Special Operations Research Office, American University under contract with the Department of the Army, Task Revolt, 1965, mimeo. See also Dennis M. Rempe, "The Past as Prologue? A History of U.S. Counterinsurgency Policy in Colombia, 1958–66," Strategic Studies Institute, U.S. Army War College, 2002, also available at http://www.strategicstudies institute.army.mil.

18 Eric Hobsbawm, "The Revolutionary Situation in Colombia," *World Today* 19:6 (1963). Hobsbawm also cites RC Williamson, *El estudiante colombiano* (Bogotá: Universidad Nacional de Colombia, 1962), on figures admired by students in Bogotá universities: the easy overall winner is John F. Kennedy, and in three out of four faculties in the public Universidad Nacional, Rómulo Betancourt gets more votes than Fidel Castro.

19 Beatriz González, and Martha Segura, eds., *Luís B. Ramos, 1899–1955: Pionero de la fotografía moderna en Colombia* (Bogotá: Banco de la República, Biblioteca Luís Ángel Arango, 1997). The classic descriptions of the peasantry of Cundinamarca and Boyacá are those by Orlando Fals Borda, the pioneer of Colombian rural sociology. See his *Peasant Society in the Colombian Andes: A Sociological Study of Saucío* (Gainesville: University Press of Florida, 1955), and *El hombre y la tierra en Boyacá: Bases sociológicas e históricas para una reforma agraria* (Bogotá: Antares, 1957). Fals Borda had studied under T. Lynn Smith, whose *Tabio: Estudio de la organización social rural* (Bogotá: Editorial Minerva, 1944), was perhaps the earliest academic study of a Colombian community. For a remarkable work on another anfractuous village, this time in the Sierra Nevada of Santa Marta, see Gerardo and Alicia Reichel-Dolmatoff, *The People of Aritama: The Cultural Personality of a Colombian Mestizo Village* (London: Routledge and Kegan Paul, 1961). These works are unfortunately light on politics, perhaps because they were written in politically difficult times, but they will introduce the reader to the nature and complexities of rural society in the 1950s.

20 Comparatively few of the numerous works on *la violencia* focus clearly on its agrarian aspects. For an introduction to agrarian problems, see Darío Fajardo M., *Haciendas, campesinos y políticas agrarias en Colombia, 1920–1980* (Bogotá: Editorial Oveja Negra, 1984), and P. Gilhodes, *La question agraire en Colombie, 1958–1971: Politique et violence* (Paris: Armand Colin, 1974), as well as his *Las luchas agrarias en Colombia* (Bogotá: El Tigre de Papel, 1970). The most accessible general introductions to *la violencia* are the collections edited by Charles Bergquist, Ricardo Peñaranda, and Gonzalo Sánchez G., *Violence in Colombia: The Contemporary Crisis in Historical Perspective* (Wilmington, Del.: SR Books, 1992), and *Violence in Colombia, 1990–2000: Waging War and Negotiating Peace,* (Wilmington, Del.: SR Books, 2001).

21 For those who do not remember, John Reed, the author of the classic account of the October Revolution, *Ten Days That Shook the World* (New York: Boni and Liveright, 1919) previously "rode with Villa"—see his *Insurgent Mexico* (New York: n.p., 1914); Carleton Beals "discovered Sandino." On Beals, the prototype for so many later journalists, see John A. Britton, *Carleton Beals: A Radical Journalist in Latin America* (Albuquerque: University of New Mexico Press, 1987).

22 See Arenas, *La guerrilla por dentro.*

23 On the hideous farce of the Salta guerrilla led by Ricardo Masetti, of which Guevara appears to have been the principal inspiration and planner, see the account in Anderson, *Che Guevara,* 572–79; see also sequels and accounts of other Cuban subversions in the memoirs of Masetti's son Jorge Masetti, *El furor y el delirio: Itinerario de un hijo de la Revolución cubana,* ed. Elizabeth Burgos (Barcelona: Tusquets, 1999). In the 1970s a guerrilla was started in the wilder parts of Tucumán, and it resulted in a similarly disastrous failure. Quite apart from all sociopolitical considerations, these guerrillas were geographically absurd. They made no more sense than the Free Wales Army, another product of the 1960s. "Good guerrilla country" is in fact rather rare: it is not just a matter of topography, but also one of demography, climate, adjacent frontiers, communications, and so on. Unfortunately there is rather a lot of it in Colombia.

24 I have written on the nineteenth-century background to Colombian party loyalties in two essays in *Del poder y la gramática*, 3rd edn. (Bogotá: Taurus, 2006), "Algunas notas sobre la historia del caciquismo en Colombia," and "La presencia de la política nacional en la vida provinciana, pueblerina y rural de Colombia en el primer siglo de la República," 209–33 and 177–207 respectively. See also my *Intercambios violentos: Reflexiones sobre la violencia política en Colombia* (Bogotá: Taurus, 1999).

25 See the account in Albert Hirschman's *Journeys towards Progress* (New York: Twentieth Century Fund, 1963). Hirschman admired Colombian reformism, in that book exemplified by Carlos Lleras Restrepo, president from 1962 to 1966. However, his optimistic view of progressive Colombian logrolling was not borne out by the later frustration of the reform. Lleras's critics pointed to his lack of any personal agricultural experience: they pictured him, somewhat unfairly, as very much an urban man. For the contemporary debate, see Carlos Lleras Restrepo et al., *Tierra: Diez ensayos sobre la reforma agraria en Colombia* (Bogotá: Tercer Mundo, 1962). For a communist view, see Gilhodes, *Politique et violence*. The traditional approach of Colombian governments to rural discontent since the 1920s had been parcelization. Rural Colombia is not characterized by *latifundios*; rural property is widely distributed, with many small and medium-size holdings. This holds particularly true for the coffee zone, coffee being for most of the twentieth century the mainstay of the export economy, and agrarian reform was never proposed for these parts of the country. For coffee, the indispensable work is Marco Palacios, *El café en Colombia, 1850–1970: Una historia económica, social y política* (Mexico City: El Ancora, 1983). The existence of such a large landowning peasantry and middle class is recognized by a number of progressive historians, for example, by Charles Bergquist in his *Labor in Latin America: Comparative Essays on Chile, Argentina, Venezuela, and Colombia* (Stanford: Stanford University Press, 1986), as posing particular problems to class politics in Colombia, and it naturally did not favor the agrarian reformers.

26 After leaving the presidency, Lleras became the chief promoter of the campesino organization Asociación Nacional de Usuarios Campesinos (National Association of Peasant, ANUC), which campaigned for agrarian reform, with an emergent radical wing supporting land invasions. It is significant that the initiative here first came from above.

It can certainly be argued that neglect of the countryside and a failure to carry out significant agrarian reform proved costly. The rank and file of the FARC has been made up largely of ill-educated rural and small-town youth without prospects, though few of them now aspire to work on the land.

27 In Pardo Llada, El *"Che" que yo conocí*, 70, he cites a fellow journalist, Agustín Tamargo: "His ignorance of Cuban ways led him to collide with everything. He did not perceive, or he deliberately ignored, that despite everything his own role was a subordinate one in the larger context of Cuba's struggles. He pretended to know nothing about not only the noble history of those struggles for liberty but also about the wider history of revolutionary elements in the fight against Batista. For him there were no more than just a few good Cubans, those with beards, and some passable ones, those who had belonged to the Communist Party. The rest were a lost cause, corrupted by United States money, and there was nothing to be done with them, apart from keeping them at all costs tightly under control. The country that he had entered two years before, and whose history he either despised or did not know—he treated always with the insolence of a conquistador, and when he could do no more, he signed its banknotes with his nickname" (translation mine).

28 The campus of the Universidad Nacional has a Plaza Che Guevara, a favorite location for student meetings; a recent proposal to change its name caused a predictable ruckus. Guevara is otherwise not much commemorated in Colombia, though he can occasionally be seen on the backs of buses, alongside, years ago, the likes of Bugs Bunny and, now, Homer Simpson.

29 This has even been the case in recent years with kidnapping. The rich can afford better protection.

30 For the history of the Unión Patriótica, see Steven Dudley, *Walking Ghosts: Murder and Guerilla Politics in Colombia* (London: Routledge, 2004). The government failed to protect the members of the UP, who perished at the hands of paramilitaries and their *narco* directors, the chief of these being José Gonzalo Rodríguez Gacha, "El Mexicano," Pablo Escobar's ally in central Colombia. The FARC interfered with his business, not as opponents but as rivals. Likewise, the FARC continued while setting up the UP to assassinate rival Liberals and Conservatives, and its more militarist wing was not sorry to see the UP fail: that failure let it continue to argue that armed struggle constituted the only recourse.

31 On paramilitaries, see Carlos Medina Gallego, *Autodefensas, paramilitares y narcotráfico en Colombia: Origen, desarrollo y consolidación; El caso de "Puerto Boyacá"* (Bogotá: Editorial Documentos Periodísticos, 1990); Fernando Cubides, "Los paramilitares y su estrategia," *Reconocer la guerra* *para construir la paz*, ed. Malcolm Deas and María Victoria Llorente (Bogotá: Universidad de los Andes, 1999), 151–99. Some paramilitaries derive from *autodefensas*—that term again—legally organized by the army prior to a change in the law in 1988, but also gaining support from people exacerbated by excessive guerrilla demands. Others have more direct *narco* origins. It is a mistake to think that none of them are popular. There are a number of historical precedents for these organizations and for the methods they use, and their emergence should not have come as a surprise.

Judith Ewell

Che Guevara and Venezuela

Tourist, Guerrilla Mentor, and

Revolutionary Spirit

Che Guevara learned little from or about Venezuela in the years
between December 1951 and 1956, the time period covered by his
first two diaries.[1] Neither the dictator Marcos Pérez Jiménez nor the
exiled leader of the democratic Acción Democrática (AD), Rómulo
Betancourt, appealed to the young idealist. In July 1952 he spent a
scant twelve days in Venezuela, mostly in Caracas, and he briefly met
Betancourt in Costa Rica in December 1953. Guevara did not appear
aware of the young people of his own generation, communists and
AD members, who were active in the underground opposition to
Pérez Jiménez in the 1950s.

Guevara's own ideology between 1953 and 1956 was inchoate,
rather than sophisticated or consistent, but some constants existed:
anti-Americanism, a dislike of the oligarchy, skepticism about nationalism, and sympathy for simple people. Such attitudes may have
been especially thick in the air in 1940s Argentina, where Juan Perón
thumbed his nose at Washington and organized a South American
labor confederation to challenge the United States. Guevara further
distrusted armies, electoral politics, and political parties, admired
those who acted on principle, and preferred action to reflection.
In commenting on Bolivia, Argentina, and Guatemala, Guevara
stressed that the political leaders had erred in not arming the populace to resist the army. Guevara held his political views strongly, but
he often responded as much to an individual's personality as he did
to their politics.

Guevara's travel account focuses on rural areas and people, where
he and Alberto Granado more easily found lodging and assistance.

There is little description of South American cities except as places to meet people, solicit visas, or, in the case of Lima, enjoy the museums. Although ostensibly the destination of their travels, Caracas, too, was just a means to an end: a job for Granado and a plane ride home for Guevara. Perhaps the biggest social change of the decade escaped Guevara's notice. The 1950s saw unprecedented urbanization in Latin America, especially in Venezuela. Shantytowns blossomed in all the major cities, and in Caracas they were estimated to contain more than one third of the urban population. Guevara visited some shantytowns, or *ranchos*, as they are called in Caracas, but the urban poor engaged neither his sympathy nor his political imagination.

Guevara's Venezuelan experience did not obviously contribute to the evolution of his political thinking. His writings offer no comment on the dictatorship, although they do express an almost visceral dislike of Betancourt. Their politics differed, but both Pérez Jiménez and Betancourt proved strong anticommunist allies of Washington in the Cold War. Both rejected structural change in favor of political reforms or modernization within the global capitalist system and within the U.S. orbit. Betancourt and Pérez Jiménez remained enmeshed in the East-West dichotomy, while Guevara groped toward a North-South opposition. Venezuela provided only negative models for the Argentine—paths to be avoided as he considered the future of Latin America.

After the success of the Cuban Revolution in 1959, Guevara directly and indirectly had as great an effect on Venezuela as anywhere else in Latin America, aside from Cuba. From 1959 until Guevara's death in 1967, his example and his urging encouraged young Venezuelans to mount a guerrilla effort to overthrow the elected governments of Betancourt and Raúl Leoni. The route to power for the Left, he counseled, lay in rural conflict, not in the cities. After the defeat of the Venezuelan guerrillas and forty years after Guevara's own death, Che's legacy continues to leave its mark on Venezuelan politics. President Hugo Chávez employed Che's image in a number of ways, but especially as the self-sacrificing model of the "new man" for Chávez's twenty-first century socialism. Ironically, that image helped cement Chávez's popularity with the very people that Guevara himself had overlooked, the urban poor.

Che and Miguel Otero Silva

The Guevara who prepared to leave Argentina in December 1951 was not the political animal he would become. "I'm off to Venezuela, Dad," he allegedly announced without any explanation for his choice.[2] What did he know of Venezuela and why did he choose that nation as his destination? Earlier, as a medical crew member on an Argentine petroleum vessel, Guevara had touched on Venezuela, but we have no record of his impressions.[3] The booming oil economy obviously held the promise of well-paid jobs, but more simply, Venezuela's position at the opposite end of the South American continent may have provided a reason for Guevara and his friend Granado to travel the entire intervening space.

An admirer of poetry, Guevara began his journal with a quotation from a Venezuelan poet, Miguel Otero Silva.[4] The diary quotes the last ten lines emphasizing the romantic parting between the poet and his lover.[5] The complete poem (published in 1937) is more politically charged than anything else in the diary, as a passage taken from the fourth and fifth stanzas illustrates. The poet turns from the eyes of his beloved to glance out the window

> To watch them pass.
> They walked paddling in the mud
> With bare feet.
> They paraded with faces darkened by hunger
> And their hands calloused by misery
> And souls twisted by injustice
> And voices awakened to hatred.
>
> They went forward to face life
> Rebels in harmony.[6]

Alas (or perhaps fortunately), Guevara's lover, Chichina, did not share his sympathies, and the two male friends left together instead. Yet nothing else in the diary suggests that the two youths considered their marvelous adventure as a journey to throw their lot in with the poor. As Granado commented in 2004, "Before we left Argentina, we didn't know about Latin America, about the enormous gulf between rich and poor and the terrible exploitation of the people. It had a great effect on us."[7]

Guevara makes no further mention of Otero Silva, but the Venezuelan's writing and, perhaps, his career up to then had drawn Guevara's attention. Otero Silva's poetry expressed sympathy for workers and the poor, attacked Nelson Rockefeller and others who had benefited from Venezuelan petroleum, lauded the fallen heroes of the Spanish Civil War, and praised the rebels who had opposed the Cuban dictator Gerardo Machado in 1933. Otero Silva formed part of the generation of idealistic university students who had rebelled against the caudillo Juan Vicente Gómez in 1928. Jailed and then exiled in Curaçao, Otero Silva later participated in a failed effort to invade Venezuela to overthrow the dictator. In 1930 he joined the Communist Party, but he left it again in the late 1940s, declaring that he had no stomach for party discipline. After completing his interrupted university studies in 1949, he devoted himself to writing and the arts, as well as to editing the Caracas newspaper El Nacional, which his father had founded in 1943. He remained in Venezuela during the 1950s and continued to edit the daily, suffering only a few temporary suspensions of the paper for violating censorship rules. Otero Silva did not openly challenge the dictatorship until 1958, a few weeks before it fell.[8]

Otero Silva's unorthodox Marxist humanism and anti-Americanism no doubt resonated with the young Guevara as he set out on his travels. As Guevara turned more toward a preference for direct action, however, Otero Silva's path as an intellectual who chose not to join the barefooted parade no longer satisfied the young Argentine.

Venezuela before Che, 1945–1952

Venezuela's economic prosperity coupled with minimal political modernization was unique in the Americas by the 1950s. A major world exporter of petroleum since the 1920s, Venezuela relied on petroleum income to provide over 50 percent of ordinary government revenues, but the country spent little on health care, education, housing, infrastructure, or efforts to develop agriculture or industry. The U.S., British, and Dutch multinational oil companies enjoyed near free rein in the country and paid few taxes until the 1940s. After the Second World War, U.S. capitalists and entrepreneurs became increasingly visible in Caracas, where they invested in all areas of commerce, service, industry, and construction. New hotels, skyscrapers, social clubs, shopping malls, and elegant houses in new neighborhoods began to transform the city. The affluence also manifested in the street, now clogged with automobiles fueled by cheap gasoline.

This wealth contrasted sharply with the shantytowns that sprang up in the hills around the capital as rural Venezuelans and European immigrants arrived to compete for jobs in the booming city. In 1941 Caracas had a population of 380,099, just 9.87 percent of the national population, but by 1961 the city's 1,257,515 inhabitants had grown represent 16.71 percent of the population. Many of the rural migrants to Caracas were unskilled or semiskilled laborers often unemployed or underemployed as vendors, domestic servants, or construction workers. The population growth quickly strained city services and urban housing. In 1941 the government commissioned the country's most famous architect, the Paris-trained Carlos Raúl Villanueva, to design a new popular-class housing and government office project in the center. El Silencio, as the model new development was called, bespoke modernity, but the growing number of shanties that covered the hills and *quebradas* (ravines) around the city contradicted this image. A few barrios or slums predated the Second World War, but the majority of them arose between 1940 and 1960. By one estimate, in 1952 roughly 38.5 percent of the Caracas metropolitan population lived in these *ranchos*.[9]

A recent study of Caracas barrios notes that although their number has grown exponentially into the twenty-first century, city maps usually depict them as blank space. In the 1940s, even for the people who advocated more progressive and responsive government, the barrio dwellers also represented a blank political space, a new underclass that did not fit easily into either populist or communist plans. More difficult to organize than skilled labor or even rural communities, they symbolized danger and disorder with little political payoff. The barrios always had a reputation for being crime ridden and volatile, and most Venezuelans who did not live there remained ignorant of the degree of self-policing, self-government, and self-help that characterized many of these communities.[10]

In contrast to the growth in Caracas and the petroleum regions, agriculture and industry in the rest of the country languished. At the conclusion of the Second World War in 1945, the Venezuelan modernizers had their moment. Civilian reformers and young military officers, impatient at national backwardness, advocated investment in infrastructure, human resources, and industrialization. Far from being revolutionaries, they wanted to modernize Venezuelan politics and the country's economy without challenging the capitalist system or altering the hierarchies of social class. None of them could conceive of a major petroleum exporter outside the structure of the capitalist world. They did, however, recognize the need for a partnership with organized labor, a prosperous middle class, and a native industrial or entrepreneurial elite.

New times and ambitions required new political institutions. The populist party, Acción Democrática, founded in 1941 under the leadership of Betancourt, proved the best organized of the new groups and boasted the most coherent program. The AD joined young military officers like Pérez Jiménez and Carlos Delgado Chalbaud to overthrow the government in October 1945. Acting as provisional president from 1945 to 1947, Betancourt characterized his administration as a "democratic revolution," but his program differed little from those of other multiclass populist parties like Peru's Alianza Popular Revolucionaria Americana (APRA) or Mexico's Partido Revolucionario Institucional (PRI). The trienio, or three-year period from 1945 to 1948, saw considerable social and educational reform, anticorruption campaigns, labor organization and legislation, nationalism, and economic development projects. The Venezuelan government extracted more taxes from and exercised more control over the foreign oil companies, but it pragmatically concluded that it could not afford to nationalize the industry. Therefore the regime cultivated careful relations with the United States and the foreign oil companies. Rockefeller, of Standard Oil (the subsidiary Creole in Venezuela), became a particular friend and invested heavily in infrastructure, industry, and agribusiness, often in partnership with the AD government.

The AD presided over a strongly partisan administration that scorned cooperation with other parties, primarily with Rafael Caldera's Christian Democratic Comité de Organización Política Electoral Independiente (COPEI), Jóvito Villaba's Unión Republicana Democrática (URD), and the Partido Comunista de Venezuela (PCV). The government's enemies, who increased by the day, charged that Betancourt planned to replicate the PRI's monopoly on political power. Foreign policy also proved contentious. Betancourt perceived his democratic revolution as roughly parallel to the democratic struggles against the dictatorships of the Second World War, and he supported armed movements that opposed authoritarian regimes like that of Rafael Trujillo of the Dominican Republic. Betancourt shared Washington's dislike of Perón and made little distinction between the Argentine's rule and that of more traditional dictators like Trujillo. Betancourt himself had been associated with the Communist Party of Costa Rica in the 1930s during his time of exile, but he had become a fervent anticommunist by the 1940s, alleging that communist international allegiances made them unfit allies for nationalists. Betancourt's public anticommunist campaign won him more friends in Washington and among the Venezuelan elite than did his efforts to unseat Trujillo.

Trienio politics thus stirred up fear and unease in Venezuela without being radical. Abruptly, in November 1948, the military officers Delgado Chalbaud, Pérez Jiménez, and Luís Felipe Llovera Páez overthrew President Rómulo Gallegos (AD) and established a three-man military junta. They quickly outlawed the AD, a portion of the Communist Party, and most labor unions, imprisoning or exiling their leaders. The more compliant COPEI and URD continued to operate legally, if cautiously, hoping to gain political ground when the promised elections were held.

This new military dictatorship and the clandestine struggle that opposed it provided the immediate background for Guevara's trip to Venezuela. Pérez Jiménez and his colleagues asserted their anticommunist alliance with the West in the Cold War. Like Trujillo and Anastasio Somoza of Nicaragua, they exploited the situation to label their opponents either communists or fellow travelers, thus justifying repression and the curtailment of civil liberties.

The AD and Betancourt failed to resist the golpe (coup d'état) in 1948. Yet shortly thereafter they and the communists separately began a clandestine struggle against the military junta and, after 1950, against the dictator Pérez Jiménez. Betancourt chose not to participate personally in the underground in Venezuela and directed the AD rebels from Cuba (until the 1952 rise of Fulgencio Batista), Costa Rica, and Puerto Rico. Like Betancourt, most of the AD's old guard also went into exile, most of them in the Caribbean, Central America, or Mexico. A younger generation of activists, headed primarily by the lawyer and poet Leonardo Ruíz Pineda and the lawyer Alberto Carnevali, led the AD network in Venezuela until late 1952. Ruíz and Carnevali died in the effort, but others like Domingo Alberto Rangel, Moisés Moleiro, Américo Martín, and Simón Sáez Mérida cut their political teeth in the 1950s underground, in the process developing a more radical perspective than the old guard. Similarly, when senior PCV members went into exile, many to Mexico, a younger generation of men like Pompeyo Márquez, Guillermo García Ponce, and Teodoro Petkoff assumed the local leadership in fighting against the dictatorship.

Continuing the partisanship of the *trienio*, Betancourt forbade his followers to cooperate with the PCV or other parties in their fight against the junta. He feared the communists as internationalists and as anathema to his U.S. allies, and he dismissed COPEI and the URD as collaborationists with the dictator. As the clandestine network weakened, Betancourt's international lobbying acquired ever more importance.[11] The communist historian Juan Bautista Fuenmayor charged that the AD leader became "more reactionary and submissive to imperialism and the conservative classes."[12]

The fragmented resistance was no match for the dictatorship. Pérez Jiménez and his secret police, the Seguridad Nacional, had well-nigh eliminated the dissidents by 1953. After the assassination of the junta president, Delgado Chalbaud, in November 1950, Pérez Jimenez's influence increased, and the repression intensified. Student and faculty criticism of the repression led to the closing of Caracas's Universidad Central de Venezuela for most of the time between October 1951 and August 1953. As a modest concession to appearances, Pérez Jiménez scheduled elections for November 1952. The AD and the PCV remained outlawed, but the URD and COPEI could field candidates. The government cooked up a new "party," the Frente Electoral Independiente (FEI), which endorsed Pérez Jiménez.[13]

The restricted electoral rules, however, did not prevent Jóvito Villaba of the URD from attracting support for his candidacy. No one, including Villaba, thought he would be allowed to win, but he and other civilians nonetheless mildly criticized the Pérez Jiménez junta and called for a return to open, democratic government.

Che in Caracas, July 1952

On 14 July 1952 during the most repressive phase of the dictatorship and the limited electoral process, Guevara and Granado crossed the Colombian border to enter Venezuela. They tarried little in the Andes, taking an all-night bus to Caracas, where they stayed a scant ten days until 26 July. Although he had complained about the authoritarian nature of Laureano Gómez's Colombian government, deeming the country the most repressive place he had yet seen, Guevara barely alluded to Venezuelan conditions, remarking only on an officious military man at the border.[14] He thought the petroleum-rich country looked more prosperous than Colombia, but he found it expensive. A later journal comment pointed to Venezuela's "fictitious economic prosperity" that derived from "Yankee domination," but Guevara ventured no such judgments at the time.[15]

Guevara's diary and Granado's account differ with respect to the ten days spent in Caracas. Between 17 and 22 July, Granado chronicles several social gatherings and various meetings that "we" had until Guevara left on 26 July. By contrast, Guevara gives the impression that he was alone in Caracas, and he recounts only his visit to a Caracas slum.

Granado's brief comments perceptively capture some of the spirit of that July in Caracas. As they entered the city, he writes, they noticed the "long lines of cars of many makes and sizes fighting to overtake each other and creating an unbelievable chaos."[16] The oil-rich nation saw automobile registration leap from 46,000 in 1946 to 206,000 in 1955.[17] The noisy traffic jams in Caracas kept ahead of the government's ability to build freeways, although the Pérez Jiménez dictatorship advertised its progress in that respect. Another example of Caracas's modernity was the handsome new Universidad Central de Venezuela campus being constructed on an old hacienda outside the city center. Villanueva designed several buildings, and the library and medical school, along with the covered walkways and green spaces, became an outstanding example of tropical modernist architecture. Yet the campus's beauty did not of course prevent Pérez Jiménez from closing the university between October 1951 and August 1953 in response to student protests. Granado did not refer to the closure, but he did comment on high police presence and an "unpleasant atmosphere." He pronounced the university "attractive," though standing in great contrast "with the poverty of the huts that crown the little neighboring hills."[18]

The nasty-looking slums also bothered Pérez Jiménez, interfering with his ambition to put a modern face on the capital city. After 1952 he began to bulldoze many of them, engaging Villanueva to design modern workers' apartments to replace them. Between 1954 and 1958 a huge complex of *superbloques* began to rise west of the city center, designed to house one hundred thousand people. The complex was christened El 2 de Diciembre in honor of the fraudulent election that Pérez Jiménez won in December 1952. The residents of the massive development would acquire a reputation for volatility in the years that followed Pérez Jiménez's ouster in 1958.

If Granado captured some of the spirit around the university and in the streets, he also discerned why the city had become such a magnet for immigrants. During a social gathering he reflected that "everyone present . . . had come to Venezuela with the secret hope of becoming at least rich."[19] Alfred P. Jankus and Neil M. Malloy summed up the view that U.S. entrepreneurs had of the country in their book, *Venezuela: Land of Opportunity*, published in 1956.[20] The English-language newspaper, *Caracas Journal*, frequently displayed that same boosterism, and an editorial in 1951 exclaimed, "Why, anybody who came to Venezuela in 1950 and isn't a millionaire by 1970 ought to go to the Mayo Clinic and have his head examined, we're thinking."[21] Of course, Granado and Guevara may not have planned to become millionaires, but they, too, were attracted to Caracas because of its prosperity, unique in South America.

Guevara's own account of his time in Caracas referred only to his visit to a shantytown. He wandered somewhat aimlessly from the city center toward the eastern suburbs "where houses were further apart" and began to climb the hills. He may have entered Marín, one of the larger barrios near the center of Caracas; it dated from 1927 but expanded greatly after the Second World War. As in many barrios, as Guevara observed, the houses here became more makeshift and the population poorer as one ascended the hill.[22] Earlier Guevara had said that he got along better with simple people than with the middle class,[23] but he gave no evidence of such empathy here. Characterizing the city as heterogeneous, Guevara encountered Portuguese immigrants and Afro-Venezuelans among the *ranchos*. After the Second World War, thousands of Spaniards, Portuguese, and

Italians had come to Venezuela in search of jobs. The massive government building projects, along with private land speculation and development, provided construction jobs for the newcomers. Pérez Jiménez further stepped up the pace after 1952, usually requiring that government projects be completed by 2 December so they could be inaugurated on the anniversary of his election. Workers were then often dismissed in January, and the seasonal unemployment brought misery to the slums. The vulnerability of the immigrant workers, the tensions between Venezuelans and foreigners, and the lack of legal unions effectively precluded workers' protests at their mistreatment. Guevara portrayed the Portuguese as "a different kind of slave" who had suffered discrimination just as the Afro-Venezuelans had over the years. Now poverty forced the two "ancient races" to engage in a daily struggle for survival.[24]

The competition that Venezuelans faced against the immigrants fed resentment at the dictatorship, but Guevara showed remarkably little sympathy for either group. He described the blacks as indolent and filthy (a bit ironic considering his own faulty hygiene!) and as people who spent their money on "frivolity and drink." By contrast, Guevara portrayed the European as coming "from a tradition of working and saving which follows him to this corner of America and drives him to get ahead, even independently of his own individual aspirations."[25] Reminiscent of welfare Cadillac stories about the poor, Guevara recorded seeing new refrigerators and radios in the packing crate houses and new automobiles parked outside. Although he gave a nod to the rivalry for jobs, his views on the origin of urban poverty were simplistic. He attributed the squalor he saw to laziness, wasteful spending, or racial or cultural factors.[26]

Guevara described in some detail his encounter with an Afro-Venezuelan family. The mother had "frizzy hair and droopy breasts," and she and her children refused to allow Guevara to take their photograph if they could not immediately have a copy. He teased and insisted and finally took a shot of the young boy, causing him to fall off his "new bicycle" and burst into tears. The family then threw stones at the Argentine as he beat a hasty retreat. In this encounter Guevara played the role of the insensitive tourist who insisted on photographing the locals in spite of their objections.[27]

At the conclusion of this little adventure, Guevara spoke of planes flying overhead and of the modern construction he saw encroaching on the colonial buildings in the center of Caracas. In fact, Caracas boasted almost no colonial buildings in 1951. Most of what was "old" Caracas dated from the building sprees of President Antonio Guzmán Blanco in the late nineteenth century. Rather inexplicably, Guevara ended his account by remarking on the "spirit of Caracas, impervious to the way of life of the North and stubbornly rooted in its retrograde semi-pastoral colonial past."[28] Even a brief ten days in the city should have suggested a different conclusion.

By 1952 the dictatorship was already known for its ostentatious public works, especially in the capital: the Caracas–La Guaira highway, the Círculo Militar, the towers of Avenida Bolívar, the Centro Simón Bolívar. The U.S. community was not large but quite visible through the Centro Venezolano Americano, the American Club, the North American Association, the Venezuelan-American Chamber of Commerce and the English-language *Daily Journal* (known earlier as the *Caracas Journal*), which was not subject to censorship. U.S. films, music, automobiles, advertisements, and magazines were ubiquitous. Some Venezuelans complained bitterly of the erosion of old traditions, pointing out that Santa Claus and Christmas trees had become more popular than the Niño Jesús and traditional *nacimientos* (manger scenes) during the holidays. Guevara's Peruvian wife Hilda Gadea wrote later that Guevara had told her that in Venezuela "everything was imported from the United States—even lettuce, eggs, chickens: he had checked this at the market in Caracas."[29] It is puzzling that Guevara's diary for 1952 contained no references to the U.S. influence.

Guevara's dislike for the city surfaces clearly in his writings. In fact, he seldom visited or described major cities during the rest of his trip. It is less clear why his observations on Caracas are so obtuse or incomplete. He usually refrained from commenting on politics in other countries, so silence on the dictatorship, Ruíz Pineda and the resistance, and the electoral campaign may not have been unusual. Like many Marxists and liberal populists, Guevara may have dismissed the urban poor as a miserable lot who lacked the romantic appeal of the indigenous peoples or the class consciousness of the proletariat. They did not fit neatly into political models or respond well to discipline and organization. Or, perhaps we look too hard for political sophistication in the young Guevara, whose reactions were frequently more personal than political. In Caracas Guevara may simply have been ready to return home and disinclined to labor over his descriptions or his empathy.

After his trip to Miami, Guevara returned to Argentina to complete his medical studies within a year. He also increased his reading and discussion of Marxism. In spite of his apparent dislike of Venezuela, Guevara planned to travel there again in July 1953 to take a job with Granado at the Cabo Blanco leper hospital. The booming oil economy offered employment opportunities, if nothing of political or archaeological interest.

During Guevara's year in Argentina, the political situation in Venezuela worsened. The Seguridad Nacional killed Ruíz Pineda on 21 October 1952, and other AD resistance leaders had also been murdered or imprisoned. In spite of the repression, the URD's Villaba won the 30 November election, and the government had to scramble to claim an obviously fraudulent victory for Pérez Jiménez. Villaba and other URD leaders prudently went into exile. The U.S. ambassador to Venezuela, Fletcher Warren, recommended that the United States congratulate Pérez Jiménez on his electoral "victory," deeming Pérez Jiménez to be the figure who could usher in democracy.[30] Or, if the dictator did nothing to advance the cause of democracy, he at least proved a dependable ally in Washington's Cold War campaign against the leftist government of Jacobo Arbenz in Guatemala.

Betancourt, harassed in Cuba after Batista came to power in March 1952, moved to Costa Rica. From there he claimed that AD voters had given the URD victory in the November election and continued to assert AD's status as the democratic government in exile. Betancourt's long view of the importance of the party to Venezuelan history was summarized in *Venezuela: Política y petróleo*, published in Mexico in 1956.[31] Neither the URD nor the PCV conceded that the AD and Betancourt alone represented the opposition, but the dictatorship's ensconced power made the issue moot.

Che and Betancourt, December 1953

Guevara's second trip and journal in July 1953 began like the first one, with the intention of traveling to Venezuela. His observations were much more political than during the first trip, and he expressed more curiosity about leftist political experiments. In Ecuador he became interested in the Guatemalan government of Arbenz and, on a whim, decided to go there. Granado wrote of Guevara's "decision to leave the beaten track offered by Venezuela."[32]

On his way to Guatemala, Guevara stopped in San José, Costa Rica, in December and met with Betancourt, other *adecos* (as AD members were popularly called), and Juan Bosch of the Dominican Republic. Betancourt was out of town when Guevara arrived, so the Argentine first met with Bosch and the Costa Rican communist Manuel Mora Valverde. Guevara spoke approvingly of the "history lesson" he received from Mora Valverde, and he thought Bosch an interesting man with "leftist tendencies."[33]

Betancourt, on the other hand, proved a disappointment. Guevara characterized Betancourt as one "with firm social ideas in his head, but otherwise capable of swaying and bending for what promises the greatest advantage." Guevara especially deplored Betancourt's firm adherence to the United States and his "raging" about communists.[34] Guevara's friend Ricardo Rojo perceived an "invisible barrier between him [Guevara] and Betancourt" and an initial "spontaneous antagonism" even before they clashed intellectually or politically. Guevara rejected Betancourt's belief that the United States had both a good and an evil face and his confidence that Latin America could depend on the good side.[35] After his brief time in Costa Rica, Guevara left for Guatemala, where he arrived on Christmas Eve.

In Guevara's second journal (and in the accounts of Rojo and Gadea),[36] Guevara described reformists like Victor Paz Estenssoro, José Figueres, and Víctor Raúl Haya de la Torre as mistaken and doomed to failure. He was less critical of Bosch, Arbenz, and, of course ultimately, Fidel Castro, even though their ideologies in 1953–54 did not deviate too much from those of the *apristas* and *adecos*. Guevara appeared to respond to personalities, and to anti-Americanism, as much as or more than to ideological positions. The harshness of his judgment of Betancourt suggests that some of the animus may have been personal.

Betancourt and Guevara were, of course, of different generations and backgrounds. Guevara was born in 1928, the year in which Betancourt first took part in the student rebellion against the old caudillo Gómez. In his youth in the 1930s, Betancourt had endorsed violent revolution, had participated in the clandestine movement against Eleazar López Contreras (1936–41), and had joined the Communist Party in Costa Rica. When he returned to open political activity in Venezuela in the 1940s, however, he renounced his Marxist and "garibaldi" past (with the obvious exception of the *golpe* of 1945) and sought to convince the United States, the Venezuelan oligarchy, and the oil companies that they had nothing to fear from him or the AD.[37] In 1953 he continued to believe, perhaps against better evidence, that his American allies would appreciate the AD's moderate reformism and facilitate his return to power in Venezuela. Always a man with a strong ego, Betancourt considered himself a Venezuelan shadow government. There is no contemporary evidence that Guevara made any impression at all on Betancourt, but if he did, it would have been as an idealistic hothead or as a youth of no consequence.

For his part, the newly graduated Argentine doctor saw an older man who never completed his university studies and who had devoted his life to a political party. Guevara placed no faith in parties, refusing even to join the Guatemalan Communist Party to get a job.[38] In contrast, the Venezuelan communist Bautista Fuenmayor wrote that for Betancourt "bureaucratic concerns were, then, placed before any question of principle."[39] Pragmatism dominated Betancourt's actions. He had concluded that democratic and social reform in a major petroleum-producing country could only be achieved with Washington's consent. Even before he fully committed himself to Marxism, Guevara had valued political innovation, action, and suspicion of the United States. Betancourt, and thus the Venezuelan opposition, failed on all these counts. Younger AD militants of Guevara's generation shared much of his outlook, but in 1953 they did not hold very prominent positions in their party.

Betancourt and Guevara also differed in their evaluation of contemporary political leaders in Latin America. Betancourt wrote of a Madrid–Buenos Aires Axis and classified Perón as a neofascist; he also believed that Perón had aided the *golpe* against the AD government in 1948.[40] Guevara's family opposed Perón, and Guevara was no *peronista*, but he wrote that "Argentina was the champion of all of us who think that the enemy is in the North."[41] In 1955 Betancourt rejoiced at Perón's fall as the beginning of the end of the dictators, while Guevara regretted that his compatriot had not urged the masses to fight against the *golpe*.[42]

Moreover, Betancourt was a firm friend of Costa Rica's Figueres. But Guevara agreed with Mora Valverde that Figueres was too friendly to the United States. Finally, and perhaps most important as Guevara was on his way to view the Guatemalan experiment, Betancourt and Guevara viewed Arbenz's government quite differently. Betancourt's virulent anticommunism, and perhaps his efforts to woo Washington, led him to be cool to the Guatemalan reformers and to write about an "extracontinental dictatorship."[43] He also was angry that some Guatemalans had called Venezuelan exiles "Yankee agents."[44] When Arbenz was overthrown six months later, Betancourt initially refused to issue a statement condemning Carlos Castillo Armas's *golpe.* Only when Rangel, Gallegos, and other AD members in Mexico threatened to make a statement without him did Betancourt offer a half-hearted comment about the fall in which he condemned the "armed intervention of one country in another or others."[45] He made it clear that his statement did not necessarily reflect solidarity with Arbenz, whom he considered too leftist at worst and foolish at best. Betancourt viewed the Americas through a Venezuelan and a Cold War lens. In effect, Betancourt's internationalism echoed the Second World War alliance of democratic governments against fascist dictatorships. Guevara's contrasting view, even at this early stage, heralded the emerging paradigm that divided nations into dominant and dependent, rather than democratic and dictatorial.

In retrospect we see sharp differences between the two men's outlooks. It is not clear, however, whether Guevara even revealed his opinions to Betancourt. Several accounts refer to Guevara's silence in groups. Bosch wrote of Guevara's meeting with some Cubans in Costa Rica: "Guevara spoke very little. He would answer questions, but not volunteer information. He would sit to one side and listen. . . . He seemed dissatisfied with all solutions proposed up to that time, and when he was asked specific questions, he criticized all parties, but never defined his own position."[46] Lucila Velásquez, an AD member and Gadea's roommate in Mexico, wrote that other exiles were surprised to learn that Castro and Guevara were heading up a subversive movement. They only learned of the conspiracy after the two men had been arrested in Mexico.[47] Another AD exile in Mexico, Said Raydan, wrote, "Che Guevara was also in Mexico, a person rather timid and withdrawn; I never imagined that he would come to be the world figure that he was. He was not then a forceful, charismatic man like, for example, Fidel Castro, Rómulo Betancourt and other political leaders in exile."[48] Betancourt was known for his garrulousness, and he might well have dominated the Costa Rican meeting without Guevara's contributing much to the conversation.

At the very least we can say that the meeting was more important to Guevara's political development than it was to Betancourt's. To the Argentine, Betancourt would have confirmed all his negative opinions about reformist political parties and dependence on the United States. Neither AD militants nor Washington fought to prevent the 1948 coup or to return the party to power. Nothing engaged Guevara's imagination or his sympathy for the Venezuelan exiles or their cause. What did Guevara learn from them? Perhaps he tacitly referred to Venezuela when he later wrote that he had learned a great deal during his travels: "You learn more than anything else how to avoid error."[49]

By mid-1954 the U.S. sponsorship of the *golpe* in Guatemala had confirmed Guevara's anti-Americanism and his suspicion of regular armies. Arbenz's failure to urge the people to resist Castillo Armas showed again that moderates failed, especially if they did not call the people into the streets. From September 1954 in Mexico onward, Guevara mixed with Guatemalan, Cuban, and Venezuelan exiles, including Venezuelan communists. Guevara makes little mention of Venezuelan communists, perhaps because they accepted their exile relatively passively, suffered from divisions, and were as afflicted with bureaucratic and partisan concerns as the AD followers. As Granado commented in 2004, "In Argentina, the communists were supposed to be for the people, but they were liars. And the Radical Party were only for the rich. So we had no faith in political parties."[50] Rojo wrote that Guevara "enjoyed the company" of the AD old guard exiles Gonzalo Barrios and Andrés Eloy Blanco, and his journal and Gadea's suggest an active social life.[51] Still, Guevara wrote, "I haven't met anyone interesting these days, and it seems as if I never will if I keep this life up."[52]

Guevara's boredom ended with closer contact to Raúl Castro and other Cubans. Rojo recalled that he was "inspired by their youth and the fact that so many of them were university students."[53] The Cubans planned to act rather than waiting for a "fairy tale of a triumphant return."[54] Although Fidel's politics were less Marxist than his brother's, he disliked the United States, his principles seemed devoid of ambition and opportunism, and he was plotting to take action. According to Paco Ignacio Taibo II, Guevara was impressed by Fidel's confidence, which accorded with his own view that "you have to stop whining and fight."[55] Guevara wrote that the younger Castro was "a young, intelligent guy, very sure of himself and extraordinarily audacious; I think we hit it off well."[56] They both believed that the fight against Batista was also one against the imperialist United States. Fidel was only two years older than Che, and he needed the Argentine's medical skills. Guevara had found a soul mate and a revolutionary home. The route toward the future, at least toward Guevara's future, led through Castro and the popular front of Cubans who embraced action and anti-imperialism. Their success on 1 January 1959 would alter American history.

Che's Legacy to 1967: The Venezuelan Guerrillas

Venezuela and Betancourt may have contributed a negative example to Guevara's evolving ideological views in the 1950s, and the Argentine's brief visit to the country and his encounter with Betancourt proved little more than historical footnotes. From 1959 until his death in 1967, however, Guevara had considerable influence on the Venezuelan Left.

The clandestine struggle against Pérez Jiménez concluded with his flight to exile in January 1958. By 1957 Betancourt had become near-irrelevant to the action in Venezuela. A younger generation of AD activists joined with the youth of the PCV and with the broad-based Patriotic Junta that emerged in 1957 to spearhead the resistance. Thousands of slum dwellers in Caracas, many of them unemployed in the construction lull that came in January, also spontaneously joined the strikes and demonstrations that resulted in Pérez Jiménez's departure on 23 January. Giving heart and muscle to the civilians, military officers launched an abortive revolt on 1 January and the decisive one on 22 January. Yet ultimately many of the revolt's participants came to believe that the chaotic January days proved a lost opportunity for those dreaming of a more radical government than the familiar AD populism.

Admiral Wolfgang Larrazábal took control of the interim government and refereed the political struggles between the traditional parties, representatives of the Patriotic Junta, and the business elite.

With his ties to Washington and his long experience, Betancourt quickly seized the leadership he had lost during the clandestine conflict. He secured the cooperation of other party leaders like Caldera of COPEI and Villaba of the URD, as well as of business, labor, and military leaders to support elections in December 1958 that would establish a progressive democratic government in Venezuela. The Pact of Punto Fijo, as the agreement came to be called, pointedly excluded the PCV and defined the successful revolution against Pérez Jiménez as one of democratic forces against dictatorship. The communists and young clandestine AD fighters advocated more radical social change and resented Betancourt's role in shattering the broad-fronted unity that had prevailed in the struggle.

Betancourt was wary of the volatile barrios of urban poor, whom he could not control. One of the revolt leaders from the 2 de Diciembre housing development, soon to be rechristened El 23 de Enero (the 23 January), was Diógenes Caballero. He and many of his companions remained suspicious of the Patriotic Junta, the political parties, and, initially, the interim president Larrazábal. Caballero pointed out that the poor on their own had contributed to the general strike of 21 January, had seized and occupied the nearly completed workers' housing complex, and had launched campaigns to sack the houses of *perezjimenistas*. The community had elected its own representative junta and had maintained order in the housing project. They did not want to be subsumed under the leadership of either Larrazábal's governing junta or the Patriotic Junta.[57] Rather surprisingly, Larrazábal acknowledged both the misery and the power of the barrios by implementing an emergency plan to provide work and benefits for them. People from the 23 de Enero built on their revolutionary reputation and, with the inhabitants of the *ranchos*, played an active role throughout 1958 and 1959. They protested U.S. Vice President Richard Nixon's presence in Caracas in May 1958, and the barrios wholeheartedly supported Larrazábal as a presidential candidate in December 1958. Betancourt won the election on the strength of AD organization in the rural areas and smaller cities, although he lost the capital city. When the results were announced, the poor took to the streets to protest the AD leader's election. Police and the armed forces contained them, and Betancourt later demonstrated his intention to bring the urban masses to heel. After his inauguration in March 1959, he canceled the emergency plan and announced that he would maintain order in the streets at whatever cost. By that time the Cuban Revolution already offered a different model of progressive change, making the contrast with Betancourt's policies starker. In August 1959 the Caracas poor, encouraged by the PCV, staged street protests, drawing fire from the police. Several people were killed, and many of the poor and young leftists charged that Betancourt had shed the first blood. Soon Betancourt faced dissent within the ranks of his own party. Youth like Rangel, Martín, and Gumersindo Rodríguez had objected to Betancourt's presidential candidacy and tried to force the AD to move left. Especially after the triumph of their generational cohorts Castro and Guevara in the Cuban Revolution in January 1959, the youth were impatient with the old formulas. Betancourt had shunned and criticized Castro as undemocratic, and he allowed no one in his party to advocate a more radical strategy. In 1960 Betancourt and the party's old guard forced many of the young people out because of their views or their unwillingness to accept party discipline. The PCV experienced much of the same generational struggle. The older generation wanted to strengthen the party and to compete with the AD in organizing the workers, but younger leaders like Pompeyo Márquez and Petkoff increasingly advocated direct action to challenge and weaken the Betancourt government.

The AD youth, taking the name of Movimiento de Izquierda Revolucionaria (MIR), and young communists organized violent actions against the government in Caracas and the countryside between 1959 and 1962. Márquez (PCV) described the initial strategy as that of a multifaceted mass movement including some guerrilla action as an auxiliary.[58] The rebels also allied with radical young military men who sought to bring down the government in two unsuccessful armed rebellions in 1962 at Carúpano and Puerto Cabello.

In their frustration at their failures, the Venezuelan leftists by 1963 were ready to accept Guevara's tutelage and example. Guevara argued that a small guerrilla group, the *foco*, could win over the countryside and eventually create the conditions that would allow the revolution to triumph nationally. Taking this advice, Venezuelans abandoned their urban, broad-based resistance in favor of establishing guerrilla *focos* in rural areas. Still, they insisted that their struggle derived from their own experience and that they were not blindly following the Cuban model. As Alfredo Maneiro, a communist and the later founder of the party La Causa R, explained, "The violence in Venezuela is inexplicable, unimaginable, . . . without the magic of the Cuban Revolution, without the guerrilla magic. . . . Nevertheless, at least with respect to Venezuela . . . , the Cuban Revolution is not sufficient to explain it."[59]

Guevara personally influenced Venezuelans as they debated their options and strategies. Rafael Elino Martínez (PCV) recounted a conversation he had had in Havana with Guevara in 1963. Martínez argued that the Venezuelan Left could rely on some sympathetic military officers as allies. Moreover, Venezuelan urban actions like bank robberies and kidnappings had provided material support for the guerrillas. Guevara discounted both arguments. The army's culture and training, he said, had been influenced by the Yankees. Although some individuals might be progressive, in general the army could not be relied on. As for urban actions, one could not maintain discipline in the cities, leaving the rebels easy targets for the military and police. People always wanted urban assignments, Guevara noted, but the robberies and kidnappings too easily slid into a gangsterism that proved difficult to control. Martínez and his colleague ultimately bowed to Guevara's superior experience, without recognizing his weakness with respect to urban strategy.[60] On his 1952 visit to Caracas, Guevara found the barrios devoid of political interest, and his theories had no role for the urban poor. As one scholar wrote, "Che had absolutely no experience in or understanding of clandestine urban operations."[61]

The Venezuelan *focos* established by the MIR and the PCV had little success, in spite of Cuban encouragement, training, and financing. Cooperation among the groups was minimal, and individuals competed for leadership. As Jorge Dager of the MIR later commented, "We all wanted to be Fidel Castro. No one was content to be Che, let alone Raúl."[62] Later many ruefully acknowledged that the strategy had been doomed almost from the first because the Venezuelan guerrillas had little rural experience and the AD and COPEI had already won campesino loyalty. Moleiro (MIR) observed that the campesinos felt some sympathy for the rebels but that they would not risk their lives with them.[63] The United States, of course, had contributed money, arms, and training for counterinsurgency campaigns, so the Venezuelan guerrillas faced more difficult odds than the Cubans had. Moreover, the guerrilla conflict gave Betancourt an opportunity to secure the loyalty of the armed forces by providing them with a national mission and the budget and tools to implement it.

In spite of discouraging signs, in 1965 Guevara saw the relatively well-established Venezuelan rebels as a crucial part of his campaign to foment a continental revolution of "many Vietnams." In late 1965 or 1966 a proposal was even floated to have Guevara lead one of the PCV focos in Venezuela. The PCV leadership, however, refused, believing that Guevara's presence would confirm Betancourt's allegation that the Venezuelan armed conflict was entirely orchestrated from Cuba.[64] Moreover, by 1966 many of the PCV leaders had concluded that the guerrilla war had been a mistake. They began to abandon the guerrilla struggle to accept amnesty, leading to a break with the Cuban leadership. Some young communists like Luben Petkoff and Douglas Bravo continued to fight. Petkoff personally invited Guevara to join him in Venezuela, but the latter refused, arguing then that he could aid the continental struggle more in a country in which the armed conflict had not yet begun. Yet Petkoff believed that Guevara's response reflected his knowledge that the PCV leadership did not want him.[65] Later that year Guevara surfaced in Bolivia. His death in 1967 marked the effective end of the Cuban effort to spark a continental revolution. The rest of the Venezuelan guerrillas trickled out of the snake-filled jungles to accept amnesty, and by 1969 few remained in the field. Most refused to return to the PCV or AD fold, however, and the guerrilla experience spawned a number of new leftist parties like Movimiento al Socialismo (MAS), Bandera Roja, and La Causa R. Most remained small, with only modest electoral success.

In addition to his direct influence on the Venezuelan guerrillas, Guevara's romantic image as revolutionary, self-sacrificing hero and martyr wafted over Venezuela in the same way it did over much of the world. As the former guerrilla Lino Martínez (MIR) acknowledged, the importance of Che's link to foquismo was "not because he was the one who originated, systematized, and popularized this practice, but because he incarnated it."[66] By the 1980s many former Venezuelan guerrillas recognized that even the Cuban Revolution had not succeeded through the foco alone, and Guevara's own death further revealed the flaws in the strategy. Che's legend has remained strong in Venezuela, but his image as a humanitarian and martyr has supplanted that of the heroic guerrilla.

None of the Venezuelan guerrillas ever achieved Che's legendary status in their own country, perhaps because of the disastrous failure of their armed struggle. The bitterness that accompanied and followed the struggle also led to allegations that many of them were self-seeking, even corrupt. One military officer involved in the Carúpano rebellion of 1962 later joined the guerrillas. J. T. Molina Villegas felt disappointment at the competition among guerrillas, at their lack of respect for his own formal military training, and at some chicanery with finances and supplies. He said: "I saw certain things that I did not understand. Things in which one could see that the *guerrilleros* were just like everybody else. I thought that the revolutionary had to be loyal, fraternal, and united, and there were very ugly things going on."[67] As leaders of political parties after 1970, the former guerrillas kept alive old feuds and ideological arguments. Too few Venezuelans saw the new leftist parties and the former guerrillas as viable alternatives to the Punto Fijo traditional parties. In contrast, the martyred Che could still incarnate social justice, self-sacrifice, and a genuine commitment to the people. He was outside history and beyond criticism. To many who wanted real change in Venezuela, not just reform, Che was still "their" guerrilla.

Further strengthening the hold of his legend over Venezuelans was Guevara's presence in the popular spiritist religion of María Lionza. The three primary deities were María Lionza, the indigenous chief Guaicaipuro, and the Negro Felipe, but these three presided over a series of eight courts of lesser spirits. There was a medical court, an outlaw's court, and a political court, among others. In the political court, the Venezuelan independence hero Simón Bolívar dominated, but Guevara made for another popular spirit. An eclectic mix of African, Christian, and indigenous beliefs, the religion resembled the Cuban Santería and proved especially popular in the urban barrios. The poor looked to the spirits for the healing, advice, and protection that societal institutions generally did not provide them. Bolívar and Che, like María Lionza, were considered especially pure spirits who did not approve of the corruption and misery rife in Venezuela in the 1980s and 1990s. In these decades the purer spirits came down to the mediums less frequently than the spirits of executed criminals or drug lords. The spirits may have been critical

of the politicians, but politicians sought their approval. Pérez Jiménez began the tradition when he had Alejandro Colina's large statue
of María Lionza erected beside a Caracas freeway in 1953. Other
Venezuelan politicians have often made highly visible visits to the
sacred mountain of Sorte in Yaracuy State or have had photographs
taken with the mediums.[68]

Che's Legacy after 1967: Hugo Chávez

For much of the 1970s, the fault lines in the political nation remained hidden under a flood of oil wealth the likes of which Venezuelans had not seen before. The money funded magnificent gestures like the nationalization of the Guayana steel works (1975) and
of the foreign oil companies (1976), as well as much high living and
luxury among the insiders of the political elite. The A D president
Carlos Andrés Pérez (1973–79) emerged as the most prominent face
of this expansiveness and the concurrent corruption. The wealth
trickled down a bit to provide some work, benefits, and greater well-
being to the poor and middle classes. The party ended abruptly in
1982, however, with devaluation, crashing banks, corruption scan-
dals, and leadership by political technocrats obsessed, first, with the
creditors of the International Monetary Fund (I M F) and Wall Street
and, second, with enriching themselves. They ignored the increasing poverty and unemployment in the cities, which proved especially
distressing after the recent good times. The police and the military
made the cost of urban violence high enough to render the slums
politically quiescent, although the crime rate rose drastically. From
1970 to the 1990s, the slum dwellers—estimated as 60 percent of the
Caracas population in 2003—received no serious attention either
from the Punto Fijo parties or from the parties of the Left.[69]

In December 1988 hope for better times returned with the reelection of Carlos Andrés Pérez on a populist platform. Pérez, however,
unwittingly reawakened the political force of the barrios with a
series of neoliberal austerity measures. A sharp rise in the price of
gasoline in this petroleum-producing country made public transportation more expensive, outraging the population. On 27 February and for days afterward, the barrios responded as they had in
1958 by mounting mass protests and riots. Days of violence followed, resulting in hundreds or even thousands dead, most at the

hands of the police and military. Venezuelans were shocked and demoralized by the collapse of the economy and by the *caracazo*, as the February violence was called. The *caracazo*, added to the other problems, caused many Venezuelans to characterize the Punto Fijo political system as bankrupt. Some openly called on military officers to stage a coup and restore the integrity of the nation. Many Venezuelans saw the *caracazo* as evidence of the need for a strong hand, but others also acknowledged that the Punto Fijo parties had provided no benefits and no safety net for the urban poor. How could Venezuela wrench itself out of the mess?

The response came from a new generation of conspirators who rejected *foquismo* and Guevara's example as a soldier but invoked his commitment to social justice. One young officer who began to conspire in the 1970s, Lieutenant Hugo Chávez, said, "We're not going to join the guerrillas, that's over and done with."[70] In 1982, as the economic crisis took hold, Chávez and a small group of officers formalized their conspiracy to overthrow the Punto Fijo system in favor of a more nationalistic and more equal society. They established sporadic contacts with some former guerrillas like Bravo and Maneiro, as well as with other communists and leftists. Some of the leftists like Bravo later became disillusioned with Chávez and drifted away, but many others remained his firmest allies.[71] During the *caracazo* of 1989 Chávez had been ill, so the officers missed the opportunity to exploit the situation. They were shaken by the violence and deplored their own role in killing their compatriots.

On 4 February 1992 Chávez led a military movement whose goal was to capture and unseat President Pérez. The movement failed, "por ahora" (for now) as Chávez ominously said in a televised broadcast, and Chávez was jailed. Once freed in 1996, his charismatic personality contrasted sharply with the perceived irrelevance or incompetence of the AD, COPEI, and the leftist politicians. Chávez handily won the presidential election of 1998, had a referendum for a new constitution in 1999, won a six-year presidential term in 2000, weathered a coup in 2002, withstood a recall election in 2004, and was reelected to a second six-year term in 2006. His enemies characterize his rule as authoritarian, but Chávez has gained power through democratic elections in which his populist appeal transformed the urban masses into a potent, if unpredictable, political force.

Chávez's victories signaled the end of influence of the two traditional parties, the AD and COPEI. Much of the middle class and elite despises Chávez, but they have lacked the morale, unity, leadership, credibility, and programs to defeat him at the polls. The opposition has fallen back on demonstrations, work stoppages (especially in the national oil company), complaints to international organizations and allies, and pleas to military leaders to depose the Venezuelan leader. It achieved a brief victory in April 2002 when military officers removed Chávez from office and hid him away in a location outside Caracas. Massive street demonstrations by barrio inhabitants protested the action, and the civilian leaders who assumed power arrogantly overplayed their hand. The conspirators recognized their error and within a few days returned Chávez to the Miraflores presidential palace. The opposition lost even more credibility through its participation in or endorsement of the bungled coup.

As in the guerrilla struggle, the Left divided over support of Chávez, but many Marxists and former guerrillas joined him, including sections of the PCV, of La Causa R, and of MAS. The Marxist Luís Miquilena, the former MAS presidential candidate José Vicente Rangel, and the former guerrilla Ali Rodríguez Araque became trusted ministers and advisors. Others like Bravo objected to Chávez's personalism and hostility toward political parties, and Teodoro Petkoff preferred a Eurocommunist model over Chávez's idiosyncratic "twenty-first century socialism," as he calls it.

Since 1998 Chávez has stood in a different relationship to Guevara than had the guerrillas of the 1960s. He had no need for the military strategist to show him the way to seize power, but he could use the powerful iconology of the martyr to broaden his popularity and to legitimize his own revolutionary programs. In Venezuela as in much of the world, Che still stands for selflessness, revolutionary change, and social justice. Beyond his international image, the Argentine's standing in the María Lionza hierarchy of spirits has given him a special status as someone with a personal relationship to Venezuelans. As Chávez downplayed political parties in favor of appealing directly to the Caracas barrios for support, he invoked the names of Guevara, Bolívar, and other national heroes in the battle of good against evil. Programs in education, job training, and health care, for example, bore the names of Guevara, Bolívar, Bolívar's tutor Simón Rodríguez, and the 1850s rebel Ezequiel Zamora. Venezuela's urban poor responded enthusiastically to the programs, to the imagery, and to the first president who personally asked for their support. As they had in 1958 and 1989, the masses took control of the streets and proved instrumental in having Chávez restored to power after the short-lived coup in 2002.

Chávez has used at least three different aspects of Guevara's legacy: his association with a continental, and global, challenge to the United States and imperialism; his humanitarian and reformist initiatives to construct the "new man" in Cuba; and his status as an icon in the pantheon of historical revolutionary heroes. A few examples will illustrate.

Many of Chávez's international speeches contain references to Guevara. In November 2004 Chávez addressed a mass meeting of workers in Madrid and reflected on how he might have been killed when kidnapped during the coup attempt two years earlier. He mused, "There, facing the death squad, I thought of Che . . . how men die." In January 2005, dressed in a red T-shirt emblazoned with Che's image, Chávez addressed the World Social Forum in Porto Alegre, Brazil. He reminded the crowd that Guevara was "that Argentine doctor that traveled through the continent in a motorcycle and who was a witness of the U.S. invasion of Guatemala in 1955 [sic], one of the many invasions of the U.S. empire in this continent."[72]

Reminiscent of Guevara's arguments in "Man and Socialism in Cuba," Chávez has advocated a new morality to supplant the old individualistic ones, introducing workers' cooperatives and experiments with direct democracy, rather than representative democracy. Some of these initiatives have foundered, and some of Chávez's followers advocate a more traditional approach that depends more heavily on bureaucracy, the party, and the state. Yet many of the barrio inhabitants remain suspicious of political parties and insist on grass-roots governance.[73] Both the presidential office Miraflores and the barrios use Che's image. The armed members of the Alexis Viva collective in the 23 de Enero barrio wear bandannas with Guevara's image on them. A mural in the barrio displays Jesus with an assault rifle and Che with a cigar. Is it only a coincidence that Guevara appears more peaceful than Christ?[74] In August 2007 the Venezuelan government announced the creation of a Che Guevara Mission to undertake the sponsorship and funding of microenterprises while training the beneficiaries in collective and moral consciousness, placing Che in the grass-roots camp. The struggle for moral good can have either a religious or a secular cast. In 2003 a Caracas mural depicted Jesus, Guevara, and Bolívar, bearing the words: "Don't allow yourself to be tricked. With Chávez, you get the Bolivarian truth."[75] On the other hand, in August 2007 Chávez renamed a Maracaibo hospital when the state took it over. The former Hospital Virgin de Coromoto became the Hospital Ernesto Che Guevara. Che's statue, and not that of the Virgin, would henceforth greet the ill as they entered. The retired Air Force colonel William Farinas, the president of Venezuela's Fondo Unico Social, summed up Guevara's significance in the following terms: "Che is the one single figure who represents commitment and altruism, and complete dedication to the cause of the people—everywhere in the world. He is an icon for all revolutionaries, as he is for me."[76]

Finally, Chávez has employed Guevara's image as a way to inflate his own popularity and reputation. Fabian Wagmister of the University of California, Los Angeles, Film and Television Department points out that Guevara has been seen as part of a historical continuum that includes other revolutionary heroes like Túpac Amaru, Bolívar, José Martí, Augusto Sandino, and Emiliano Zapata. Thus "Che is not a historical exception but the realization of the historical aspirations of the continent and the world. In him are expressed the struggles of the past and the victories of the future."[77] What politician could resist associating himself with such a revered icon? In 2004 Guevara's daughter, Aleida Guevara, conducted an extended interview with Chávez that subsequently became a book, a DVD, and the subject of a documentary.[78] Caracas venders sold a T-shirt in 2006 with the slogan "the four fantastic revolutionaries"; it bore the images of Bolívar, Chávez, Guevara, and Fidel Castro. A subliminal message is that if one rejects Chávez one also rejects Bolívar, Guevara, and perhaps even Christ. Chávez has also pleased the followers of the María Lionza religion by ensuring that the famous Colina statue was restored after it collapsed beside the freeway in 2004. The original statue will now reside in the Plaza Bolívar of the Universidad Central, while a replica will suffer the noxious fumes of the highway. In the battle between good and evil, Chávez aligns himself with the moral, and revolutionary, spirits.

Many Venezuelans criticized Guevara's *foco* theory, but few have objected to his rather saintly mythological image. One who did was the former MAS presidential candidate José Vicente Rangel in an interview in 1978. Rangel has held various prominent positions in the Chávez governments including that of vice president and foreign minister, and he might express himself differently today. Thirty years ago, however, Rangel said that he had a profound respect for Guevara but that he considered the growth of the Che myth unhealthy.

> If we emphasize exclusively the heroic aspect of one who sacrifices his life, we gravely damage the revolutionary movement, because we teach the young to become accustomed to the idea that revolution is brilliance, heroism, audacious action. Revolution is, on the contrary, a process of participation, collaboration, silent and quiet work, a patient organization of the masses.
>
> Among the outstanding qualities of Dr. Ernesto Guevara are his sincerity, his authenticity, his capacity to sacrifice himself for an idea, but as a human being I resist the error of turning him into a myth. Guevara made mistakes.[79]

Chávez's Venezuela prompts a consideration of two ironies in the current use of Che's image. Guevara himself usually avoided the spotlight, leaving that role to others. And, of course, he had no program for how to form the urban poor into a disciplined political force.

Conclusion

Guevara's direct experience with Venezuela and Venezuelans was slight. His visit in 1952 and his meeting with Betancourt in 1953 may have played a small role in his conviction that liberal populism and alliance with the United States would block revolutionary change in Latin America. By contrast, Guevara's leadership and arguments had an enormous influence on his generation of the Venezuelan Left in the 1960s, convincing many of its members that the route to power lay in the rural *focos*. The old populist whom Guevara had so scorned, Betancourt, survived and strengthened the democratic government partially because of the guerrilla's errors. Like Guevara, however, Betancourt failed to see political potential in the large population of the urban poor. By 2008 the urban poor and Chávez had largely relegated Guevara the warrior to history, but they continue to turn to him as a moral example and even a religious spirit. They have flaunted his image as an icon to usher in a new socialism and perhaps a continental, or global, revolution. Yet as José Vicente Rangel noted in 1978, one of the problems with making men into myths is that the process denies the rich complexity of their lives as they lived them.[80] Guevara's image on a T-shirt is still just a T-shirt.

Notes

1 Ernesto Guevara, *The Motorcycle Diaries: A Journey around South America*, trans. Ann Wright (London: Verso, 1995); Ernesto "Che" Guevara, *Back on the Road: A Journey through Latin America*, trans. Patrick Camiller (New York: Grove, 2000).

2 Ernesto Guevara Lynch, prologue to Guevara, *The Motorcycle Diaries*, 1.

3 Jon Lee Anderson, *Che Guevara: A Revolutionary Life* (New York: Grove, 1997), 68; Rolando E. Bonachea and Nelson P. Valdés, introduction to *Che: Selected Works of Ernesto Guevara*, ed. Bonachea and Valdés (Cambridge: MIT Press, 1969), 4. Bonachea and Valdés say the job was in 1947, but Anderson places it between February and June of 1951.

4 The poem is not well translated in *The Motorcycle Diaries*, and the emphasis is on the parting with his lover rather than on empathy with the miserable people the poet sees through the window.

5 The English translation mistakenly renders "Yo escuchaba chapotear en el barro / Los pies descalzos" as "I heard on the boat / Wet feet splashing" (16).

6 Miguel Otero Silva, "Encrucijada," *Poesía completa* (Caracas: Monte Avila, 1972), 30.

7 Bob Flynn, "Age of Dissent," *Herald* [*Tribune*] *Magazine*, 17 July 2004, 8.

8 Otero Silva also ran afoul of censorship after the return of democracy in 1958. President Rómulo Betancourt considered the paper too sympathetic to the Marxist guerrillas and forced Otero to leave the editorship.

9 Federico Brito Figueroa, *Historia económica y social de Venezuela* (Caracas: Universidad Central de Venezuela, 1966), 2, 558; Chi-Yi Chen and Michel Picouet, *Dinámica de la población: Caso de Venezuela* (Caracas: Edición UCAB-ORSTOM, 1979), 81, 292.

10 Kenneth L. Karst, Murray L. Schwartz, and Audrey J. Schwartz, *The Evolution of Law in the Barrios of Caracas* (Los Angeles: Latin American Center, University of California, 1973); Alfredo Brillembourg, Kristin

Feireiss, and Hubert Klumpner, eds., *Informal City: Caracas Case* (Munich: Kulturstiftung des Bundes and Caracas Urban Think Tank, 2005).

11 Robert J. Alexander, *Rómulo Betancourt and the Transformation of Venezuela* (New Brunswick, N.J.: Transaction Books, 1982), 350.

12 Juan Bautista Fuenmayor, *Historia de la Venezuela política contemporánea, 1899–1969*, 15 vols. (Caracas: n.p., 1975–1989), 10:63.

13 Technically, the election chose delegates to a constitutional convention, but those delegates named the next president.

14 Guevara, *The Motorcycle Diaries*, 144.

15 Guevara, *Back on Road*, 18.

16 Alberto Granado, *Traveling with Che Guevara: The Making of a Revolutionary*, trans. Lucía Álvarez de Toledo (New York: Newmarket Press, 1978), 194.

17 *Hispanic American Report*, November 1955, 471.

18 Granado, *Traveling with Che Guevara*, 197.

19 Ibid., 198.

20 Alfred P. Jankus and Neil M. Malloy, *Venezuela: Land of Opportunity* (New York: Pageant Press, 1956).

21 *Caracas Journal*, 23 July 1951.

22 Karst, Schwartz, and Schwartz, *The Evolution of Law in the Barrios of Caracas*, 13.

23 Guevara, *The Motorcycle Diaries*, 127.

24 Ibid., 148.

25 Ibid., 149.

26 Ibid., 149–50.

27 Ibid., 149.

28 Ibid., 150.

29 Hilda Gadea, *Ernesto: A Memoir of Che Guevara*, trans. Carmen Molina and Walter I. Bradbury (Garden City, N.Y.: Doubleday, 1972), 4.

30 Judith Ewell, *Venezuela and the United States: From Monroe's Hemisphere to Petroleum's Empire* (Athens: University of Georgia Press, 1996), 160.

31 Rómulo Betancourt, *Venezuela: Política y petróleo*, 3rd edn. (Caracas: Editorial Senderos, 1969). Originally published in Mexico in 1956.

32 Foreword to Guevara, *Back on the Road*, vii.

33 Guevara, *Back on the Road*, 30, 34–35.

34 Ibid., 35.

35 Ricardo Rojo, *My Friend Ché*, trans. Julian Casart (New York: Dial Press, 1968), 51.

36 Ibid., 74; Gadea, *Ernesto*, 55.

37 Rómulo Betancourt, *Rómulo Betancourt: Memoria del último destierro, 1948–1958* (Caracas: Ediciones Centauro, 1982), 78.

38 Bonachea and Valdés, *Che*, 377.

39 Fuenmayor, *Historia de la Venezuela política contemporánea, 1899–1969*, 9:160.

40 Rómulo Betancourt, *Rómulo Betancourt: Pensamiento y acción (recopilado y editado por miembros de Acción Democrático en el exilio)* (Mexico City: n.p., 1951), 127; Alexander, *Rómulo Betancourt and the Transformation of Venezuela*, 378.

41 Guevara, *Back on Road*, 93.

42 Alexander, *Rómulo Betancourt and the Transformation of Venezuela*, 328, 368; Gadea, *Ernesto*, 115.

43 Moisés Moleiro, *El partido del pueblo*, 2nd edn. (Caracas: Vadell Hermanos, 1979), 170.

44 Alexander, *Rómulo Betancourt and the Transformation of Venezuela*, 366.

45 Ibid., 367.

46 John Gerassi, ed., *Venceremos! The Speeches and Writings of Ernesto Che Guevara* (New York: Macmillan, 1968), 10.

47 Gadea, *Ernesto*, 219–20.

48 *El exilio venezolano en Mexico, 1948–1958* (Caracas: n.p., 1988), 175.

49 Bonachea and Valdés, *Che*, 386.

50 Flynn, "Age of Dissent," 10.

51 Rojo, *My Friend Ché*, 65.

52 Guevara, *Back on Road*, 89.

53 Rojo, *My Friend Ché*, 65.

54 Paco Ignacio Taibo II, *Guevara, also Known as Che*, trans. Martin Michael Roberts (New York: St. Martin's Press, 1997), 54.

55 Ibid., 54.

56 Guevara, *Back on the Road*, 99.

57 Agustín Blanco Muñoz, ed., *El 23 de enero: Habla la conspiración* (Caracas: Universidad Central de Venezuela, 1980), 368–81.

58 Agustín Blanco Muñoz, ed., *La lucha armada: Hablan cinco jefes* (Caracas: Universidad Central de Venezuela, 1980), 116.

59 Agustín Blanco Muñoz, ed., *La lucha armada: Hablan seis comandantes* (Caracas: Universidad Central de Venezuela, 1981), 349.

60 Rafael Elino Martínez. *Aquí todo el mundo está alzao!* (Caracas: n.p., 1973), 272–75.

61 Paul Dosal, *Comandante Che: Guerrilla Soldier, Commander, and Strategist, 1956–1967* (University Park: Pennsylvania State University Press, 2003), 263.

62 Agustín Blanco Muñoz, ed., *La lucha armada: La izquierda revolucionaria insurge* (Caracas: Universidad Central de Venezuela, 1981), 234.

63 Agustín Blanco Muñoz, ed., *La lucha armada: Hablan tres comandantes de la izquierda revolucionaria* (Caracas: Universidad Central de Venezuela, 1982), 271.

64 Blanco Muñoz, *La lucha armada: Hablan cinco jefes*, 119, 229.

65 Blanco Muñoz, *La lucha armada: Hablan seis comandantes*, 149.

66 Blanco Muñoz, *La lucha armada: Hablan tres comandantes de la izquierda revolucionaria*, 160.

67 Agustín Blanco Muñoz, ed., *La conspiración cívico-militar: Guairazo, barcelonazo, carupanazo, y porteñazo* (Caracas: Universidad Central de Venezuela, 1981), 123–24.

68 Francisco José Ferrandiz, "The Body in Its Senses: The Spirit Possession Cult of María Lionza in Contemporary Venezuela" (PhD diss., University of California, Berkeley, 1996); Daniel Flynn, "Venezuelans Turn to Magic in Difficult Times," *WorldWide Religious News*, 15 February 2001, http://www.wwrn.org.

69 Brillembourg, Feireiss, and Klumpner, *Informal City*, 180.

70 Quoted in Richard Gott, *In the Shadow of the Liberator: Hugo Chávez and the Transformation of Venezuela* (London: Verso, 2000), 39.

71 Ibid., 45.

72 Both quotations in Stuart Munckton, "Che Lives!" *Green Left Weekly*, 23 February 2005, http://www.greenleft.org.au.

73 See Steve Ellner, *Rethinking Venezuelan Politics: Class, Conflict, and the Chávez Phenomenon* (Boulder, Colo.: Lynne Rienner Publishers, 2008), chap. 7.

74 Simon Romero, "Behind the Che Bandannas, Shades of Potential Militias," *New York Times*, 18 June 2007.

75 Tom Haines, "The Power of Art," *Boston Globe*, 28 December, 2003.

76 Quoted in Gott, *In the Shadow of the Liberator*, 177.

77 David Kunzle, *Che Guevara: Icon, Myth, and Message* (Los Angeles: UCLA Fowler Museum of Cultural History, 1997), 47.

78 Ocean Press published the book (2004) and the DVD (2006).

79 Alfredo Peña, ed., *Conversaciones con José Vicente Rangel* (Caracas: Editorial Ateneo, 1978), 181.

80 Ibid.

Ann Zulawski

The National Revolution
and Bolivia in the 1950s
What Did Che See?

To read Che Guevara's diaries of his Latin American trips in the early
1950s is to witness his transition from a middle-class student traveling on the cheap to a serious supporter of revolutionary movements
by the time he reaches Mexico in 1954. It seems logical that in this
traveling education Bolivia would have had special significance
since, when Guevara arrived, the country was in the throes of a
revolutionary transformation, and it was to Bolivia that he returned
in 1966 to set up a guerrilla base. Yet although Guevara clearly drew
some conclusions about the nature of revolutionary processes from
what he saw in Bolivia, it is striking how little time he actually spent
in the country during his road trip, and how little the country's
social reality and political history influenced him when he went back
thirteen years later.

Guevara and his traveling companion Carlos "Calica" Ferrer arrived in Bolivia in July 1953. A little more than a year before, in April
1952, a nationalist revolution led by a reformist sector of the middle
class had overthrown the political elite that represented the country's major mining interests and landowners. In October of 1952 the
revolutionary government of President Víctor Paz Estenssoro had
nationalized Bolivia's biggest tin mines. While Guevara and Ferrer
were in the country, in August of 1953, the government took action
in the countryside and declared a sweeping agrarian reform. These
two actions certainly represented the most radical steps of the Bolivian government of the Movimiento Nacionalista Revolucionario
(MNR), yet Che apparently was not impressed. In his diary he
expressed rather detached criticism of the government and spent

much of his time in La Paz visiting members of the Argentine expatriate community.[1]

In this article I review the political and social history that created both a revolutionary situation in Bolivia and the conditions for that revolution to be undermined. I conclude that Guevara's ignorance of, or willful disregard for, the country's situation in the 1950s ultimately contributed to his defeat there in 1967. This conclusion does not simply result from hindsight more than half a century after the fact. While some of what is now known about Bolivia in the 1950s derives from recent scholarship, other foreign travelers who visited the country at about the same time as Guevara left remarkably insightful accounts of the reality of Bolivian life. I compare some of these descriptions to Guevara's and will speculate about his seeming myopia or lack of interest in the country. Why did he "see" less than other visitors in the same period? A postscript briefly discusses Guevara's legacy in Bolivia today.

Revolution or Reformism?

The general impression one has reading the relatively little that Guevara wrote about Bolivia during his visit in 1953 is that for the short amount of time he put in, he managed to draw quite accurate conclusions about the political sentiments of the middle and upper classes, as well as about the nature of the MNR government. He importantly observed that a populist, multiclass coalition like the MNR was unlikely to produce revolutionary change and that controlling armed force would prove key to controlling the state. As he wrote to his friend Tita Infante: "The MNR is a conglomerate with three more or less clear tendencies: the Right represented by Siles Suazo, the vice president and a hero of the revolution; the Centre represented by Paz Estenssoro, more slippery but probably as right wing as the first; and the Left represented by Lechín, the visible head of a serious protest movement but personally an upstart much given to partying and chasing women. The power will probably remain in the hands of the Lechín group, who can count on the support of the armed miners, but the resistance of other people in the government may prove serious, especially as the army is now going to be reorganized."[2] Guevara probably had a sharp eye for the situation because of his experience with Peronism in Argentina. He had seen Juan Perón build his power base in the working class (à la Lechín) and was critical of Perón's attempt to form a coalition between workers and sectors of the capitalist class. It was not farfetched to imagine that the leaders of the MNR wanted to emulate many aspects of Peronism, including taking power through a military coup. In 1945 the party briefly governed in alliance with the military, and many MNR leaders continued to see the army as a more reliable ally than workers or peasants. However, the comparison with the Argentine experience may have caused Guevara to underestimate the Bolivian situation's radical potential. Rather than coming to power through a military coup and then cultivating working-class support, the MNR had to first cultivate that support for an armed insurrection and then try to control it.

With respect to Bolivia's white minority Guevara wrote in his diary:

> The "well-to-do," refined people are shocked by what is happening and complain bitterly about the new importance conferred on Indians and mestizos, but in all of them I thought I could detect a spark of nationalist enthusiasm for some of what the government has done.
>
> No one denies that it is necessary to end the state of affairs symbolized by the power of the three tin-mine bosses, and young people think this has been a step forward in the struggle to make people and wealth more equal.[3]

Here Guevara reflects the middle- and upper middle-class opposition to the monopoly of the biggest tin miners and the sense that Bolivia's resources should in some way be nationalized. In the early 1950s many people also believed that for Bolivia to become a respected, modern nation, a greater degree of social and economic equality was inevitable, perhaps even desirable. Young people, who were very well represented in the MNR government, sometimes proved enthusiastic supporters of expanded political rights and economic opportunities for indigenous peasants, and a number of them worked actively in government ministries to bring abusive landlords and employers to account.[4] On the other hand, complaints and fears about the new importance of Indians and mestizos were widespread. Even today, many of the twenty-first-century counterparts of the "refined people" Guevara refers to feel deeply ambivalent about living in a country in which the indigenous majority has its rightful share of political power.

Although he makes many acute observations, Guevara seems to be just passing through Bolivia as an educated tourist. He and Calica visit the semitropical Yungas valleys near La Paz and Lake Titicaca and the Isla del Sol (both common side trips from the capital). They hang out in cafés on La Paz's central boulevard, enjoy the hospitality of the Argentine exile Isaías Nogués, and have amorous relationships with young women. The two do not even particularly seem to be roughing it: the account lacks the details of daily struggles so common in other parts of Guevara's diary.[5]

In fact, the political situation that Guevara encountered in 1953 was shaped by the contention among the different groups forming the revolutionary coalition of the previous year. These included militant workers and peasants as well as the middle-class reformers who through co-optation and repression attempted to gain control of the revolutionary process.

Various aspects of the Bolivian social and political situation in the 1940s and early 1950s make it possible to argue that the country was moving toward a revolutionary situation. These included the political and social ferment in the country after the Chaco War with Paraguay (1932–35), the existence of a radical workers' movement, especially among the tin miners, and a long history of peasant struggle for land and citizenship rights.

The Chaco War proved a military and political disaster for Bolivia. Provoked by Bolivia,[6] the war with Paraguay sharpened the contradictions of a society divided by class and ethnicity, reproducing existing social hierarchies in the army. The majority of the front-line troops comprised Aymara- or Quechua-speaking peasants and workers who often walked most of the way to the front without sufficient food, water, or clothing.[7] Officers, generally young criollos from socially prominent families,[8] suffered fewer privations and often received assignments behind the lines. Of the approximately 50,000 Bolivian troops who died in the war (out of 250,000), the majority succumbed to disease, the most common illness being "avitaminosis," which actually meant severe malnutrition and dehydration.[9]

As the war dragged on and Bolivia lost most battles and ceded ever more ground to Paraguay, President Daniel Salamanca was forced to resign. The execrable conditions of front-line troops and the apparent incompetence of the general staff became a national scandal. Some outright troop mutinies occurred, while at other times officers had to watch powerlessly as their men deserted while looking for water or something to eat.[10]

In the aftermath of the war there was a repudiation of the traditional political class, and centrist parties adopted some of the rhetoric of the Left in an effort to remain relevant. Their experiences in the conflict had made even some middle- and upper middle-class men recognize the gross inequalities in their society as the poorest people had been asked to make the greatest sacrifices for the homeland. Furthermore, as Guevara reported, many people in Bolivia, including some of the prosperous and prominent, resented that three firms (Patiño, Hochschild, and Aramayo), all with close ties to the government, controlled 80 percent of the tin industry, in turn responsible for 80 percent of national exports.[11] The three major tin industrialists further faced resentment for investing abroad and denationalizing key sectors of their enterprises.[12]

In the post-Chaco ferment new radical working-class parties formed, especially the Trotskyist Partido Obrero Revolucionario (POR) and the more Moscow-oriented Partido de la Izquierda Revolucionaria (PIR). In 1941 the group that was to lead the revolution of 1952, the MNR, was organized by a group of middle-class university graduates who had fought in the war. They subscribed to a rather undefined nationalism opposing government collusion with the major tin producers and foreign control of the Bolivian economy.

If these parties formed and attracted popular support after 1936, they were not without antecedents or natural allies. Bolivia had a considerable tradition of worker organization. Historically the industrial union movement in Bolivia has been associated with the organized tin miners who worked in isolated areas of the country in extremely dangerous conditions for poor pay. Although always representing a small percentage of the population, organized mine workers potentially held great power because of the centrality of tin to the Bolivian economy. Such was the importance of tin that mine owners and the state rarely hesitated to use massive repression against the miners, who could literally shut down the economy. Yet despite suffering serious defeats, the miners' unions tended to recuperate, reorganize, and continue to press their demands for better wages and improved working conditions.[13]

While the MNR influenced and strongly encouraged the forma-tion of the national miners' confederation, the Federación Sindical de Trabajadores Mineros de Bolivia (FSTMB), in 1943, the union in 1946 adopted a radical program for struggle known as the "Tesis de Pulacayo." Influenced by the POR, the thesis was based on the Trotskyist conception of raising strategic transitional demands (na-tionalization of the mines, agrarian reform, control of the mines by the workers) that would educate the union rank and file about what they could realistically expect from their employers and the state. It is worth mentioning that while the drafters of the "Tesis" believed in the ultimate necessity of armed struggle to create a socialist Bolivia, their approach contrasted sharply with the *foco* theory later em-braced by Guevara, since it raised demands designed to win broad working-class support. On the theoretical level the thesis classified Bolivia as a backward capitalist country, not a feudal one, and there-fore maintained that the tasks usually associated with the bourgeois-democratic revolution would be accomplished by the working class (whose vanguard was the miners) in coalition with the peasantry and the petty bourgeoisie as "a phase" of a socialist revolution.[14]

Modern peasant political organization in Bolivia goes back to the late nineteenth century, when indigenous people organized to keep or regain communally held lands threatened by the liberal laws privatizing land. Initially Indian communities and expropriated *com-uneros* found ways to make alliances with opposition political groups to regain their lands.[15] While these alliances generally proved un-satisfactory for rural people in the long run,[16] they nonetheless demonstrate that from the late 1800s indigenous people thought strategically about how to advance their interests and did not, as an MNR minister of education claimed in the 1950s, "inhabit a herme-tic world, inaccessible to the white and the mestizo."[17]

In the first decades of the twentieth century a series of rebellions in peasant communities occurred in the high plateau area surround-ing La Paz. These revolts were often provoked by specific abuses (e.g., the death of a community member at the hands of a local official), but frequently they also focused on the issue of land. These rebellions also often raised demands for schools in rural areas, political representation for native people, and access to markets.[18]

During the Chaco War alarmed hacendados and townspeople reported protests and even uprisings by *colonos* and members of nearby Indian communities all over the countryside.[19] The reasons for the discontent were multiple: communities that had gladly contributed food to the war effort at its beginning later saw themselves well-nigh expropriated of animals and provisions by the authorities. The abusive military conscription of rural workers, who often were supposed to be exempt, and the usurping of lands by haciendas while community members were off at war provoked a wave of resistance that some political authorities attempted to blame on communist agitators or the Paraguayan government.[20]

In the post-Chaco period peasant organization became more coordinated as rural leaders now had contacts with students, union leaders, and members of the newly formed radical and reformist parties. In 1943 the MNR joined with a group of dissident army officers to overthrow the conservative president Enrique Peñaranda, putting the army major Gualberto Villarroel in office. During Villarroel's term a National Indigenous Congress was held in La Paz. Yet the conference's outcome was controlled by the government and fell far short of meeting the demands for agrarian reform raised by hacienda workers and community members. Still, it set important precedents. Its final document outlawed *pongueaje* (unpaid personal service demanded of hacienda *colonos*) and mandated the establishment of schools on all haciendas.[21]

Villarroel was overthrown in 1946 by an alliance of traditional politicians and the pro-Soviet Partido de la Izquierda Revolucionaria. After his assassination at the hands of a mob outside the presidential palace, Villarroel was turned into a martyr by many indigenous people, a fallen hero to be vindicated by the MNR. With the demise of Villarroel, hacendados, freed of his decrees, attempted to reestablish total control in the countryside. As a result a new cycle of rural protests commenced in 1947; President Enrique Hertzog characterized them as the most serious in the nation's history.[22]

Thus a number of factors made Bolivia ripe for some kind of revolutionary coalition: (1) nationalist discontent with the economic and political elite in many sectors of the population, including the military, the middle class, and even the upper middle class; (2) traditions of militancy and organization among peasants and workers; and (3) the formation of new political parties that represented these groups or sought to make alliances with them. If Guevara had known a little more about the nature of popular movements in the country he might have seen that the situation had more radical potential than he initially assumed and possibly reconsidered his strategy and alliances when returning in the 1960s. If he had known more about the means by which the MNR gradually undermined its more militant allies, and what that could mean for future revolutionary efforts, he might in fact have decided not to return at all.

Skillful maneuvering by the MNR and U.S. Cold War policies gradually put a brake on the radical wing of the revolutionary movement. Although the MNR initially favored alliances with the military and even the traditional parties, rather than the workers and peasants, sectors of their leadership eventually realized the importance of developing a mass base. To do this the party successfully undercut the Marxist parties by adopting strategic points of their programs (nationalization of the mines and agrarian reform). Once in power, the MNR managed to deliver on some of its promises to peasants and workers and then to neutralize these groups through clientelism, compromise, foot dragging—and repression when the other measures did not work. That Bolivia's main market for its tin was the United States further limited the country's possibilities for nationalist action.

A major MNR effort to cultivate a mass base took place with the miners' union (FSTMB), which the party had helped to create. As Guevara noticed, the mine union president Juan Lechín Oquendo was an extremely astute and charismatic leader, though frequently guilty of opportunism. His political savvy and personal appeal seem to have swayed even many of the most militant labor leaders. When pressed to do so by radicals in the union, Lechín sometimes showed independence from the centrist MNR leaders, but once the MNR held power, he also frequently took on the role of convincing the rank and file of the political and economic necessity of highly unfavorable agreements with the United States and former mine owners.[23]

In 1949 the MNR led an armed revolt against President Mamerto Urriolagoitia. The revolt failed but the party received tenacious support from the mine workers. In the year or so after the failure of the rebellion the MNR made efforts to broaden its base. When the party entered the presidential elections in 1951 with Paz Estenssoro as its candidate, the MNR presented a program that in effect undercut the appeal of its left-wing rivals. For the first time it called for the nationalization of the mines, an agrarian reform, and universal suffrage.[24] What the party meant by the first two, and how it would carry out these measures, were to be issues of major contention later, but finally the MNR had laid out a program addressing the country's key problems and able to attract a majority of the population.

Although the MNR won the presidential election in 1951, Paz Estenssoro did not have an absolute majority and the final outcome should have been decided in congress. However, the military, supported by the major mining interests, staged a coup and Urriolagoitia turned the government over to a military junta headed by General Hugo Ballivian.

In 1952 the MNR finally led a successful revolution. But even in this effort sectors of the party still hoped to receive significant military support. The party's right wing even envisioned a joint MNR-military government that would bypass Paz Estenssoro, who had just won the election. In the end the majority of the military remained loyal to the Ballivian government, and armed factory workers and miners were responsible for the revolt's success.[25] Unlike the military coup in Argentina in 1943 that marked the beginning of Perón's ascendancy, the shift to power for the MNR had occurred in a way that the center-right of the party had not anticipated and did not support: they had been pushed into office by the armed workers. This fact made it imperative for the new government to find ways to bring the working class and the peasantry under party control.

Shortly after Paz Estenssoro's inauguration, a national labor confederation was founded. The MNR supported the creation of the Confederación Obrera Boliviana (COB), probably hoping that it would be able to make clients of militant workers in a manner similar to the Mexican or Argentine government. Yet although the MNR leader Lechín was elected head of the new union confederation, members of other parties were also active in the COB, and the organization's leaders always had to contend with the militancy of the unions' rank and file. The MNR government had thus not entirely succeeded in co-opting the labor movement and had to find ways to maneuver to win on a number of issues. These included the nationalization of the mines, the role the working class would have in running them, and whether the country should have a traditional army or people's militias such as those that had put the MNR in power.

While Paz Estenssoro talked about studying the possibilities of nationalizing the mines, the COB called for expropriation without compensation and worker co-management of the new state-owned enterprises. The MNR undercut this radical challenge in a variety of ways, most importantly by stalling and making COB representatives (particularly Lechín) complicit in government decisions. During this period government officials stridently repudiated the radicalism of the COB as communist internationalism. In the end the MNR took over the mines and ultimately paid the companies 27 million dollars in compensation. Rather than with workers' control of the mines, the FSTMB ended up with two representatives on the Compañia Minera Boliviana (COMIBOL) board, but these representatives were neither elected by nor accountable to the workers.[26]

With respect to the army, while those on the Left pushed for people's militias, and the government symbolically closed the military academy, Paz Estenssoro actually invited U.S. military advisers into the country and opened a new air force academy in Santa Cruz. Military buildup with U.S. support proceeded apace, with several of the officers trained in the new facilities eventually becoming leaders of military coups that overthrew elected governments.[27]

Of course the MNR government had the United States to contend with, and Paz Estenssoro and Hernán Siles Suazo, his vice president, were at pains to convince the U.S. embassy that theirs was a nationalist, not a communist, movement. During the deliberations about nationalizing the tin mines the Bolivian ambassador to Washington, Víctor Andrade, repeatedly assured the U.S. government that the only nationalizations would be those of the major tin barons and that the MNR had no intention of touching other private property.[28] Perhaps because U.S. economic interests were less directly affected, Bolivia was further away from the United States, and the MNR leaders proved more conciliatory than the Arbenz government in Guatemala, the United States chose to co-opt the new government rather than overthrow it.[29] In fact, Paz Estenssoro, Siles Suazo, and the center-right of the MNR probably welcomed U.S. involvement as a counterweight to the demands of the domestic Left.

The U.S. secretary of state John Foster Dulles expressed worry that a lack of U.S. economic aid and a tin contract would create chaos in Bolivia and that the country "would become a focus of Communist infection in South America."[30] Once the Eisenhower administration was satisfied that the Paz Estenssoro government had entered into good-faith negotiations to compensate the "Big Three," the United States renewed its tin contract with Bolivia and sent the country food and other types of economic aid.[31] In 1956, during the administration of Siles Suazo, the United States made an economic stabilization plan a requirement for further assistance.[32] The reforms implemented proved so devastating for the working class that Lechín and his wing of the labor movement were eventually forced to move into opposition.[33] Nonetheless, the government managed to hold on to an alliance with peasants that was, from the government's point of view, more successful than that with labor.

The MNR had more success co-opting peasant groups than it did the working class, even though rural indigenous people had a long history of organizing to achieve their demands. Peasants' willingness to go along with the MNR probably derived from it being the party of Villarroel, a man revered by hacienda *colonos* and community members. The MNR also had moral capital with many peasants because it was through the party that they had received land. As Xavier Albó describes it, in the first years, "with greater or lesser radicalism, the mobilized peasants had no doubts about the legitimacy of taking over the land, nor about the good intentions of the MNR."[34] According to Albó, when the question of land was no longer an issue, the MNR, determined to maintain peasant support, had to find other means of tying rural leaders to the party. These included various types of clientelist blandishments, with those leaders most loyal to the MNR tending to receive the most for their unions and themselves. This kind of patronage in many places eventually developed into a passive dependency on the government.[35]

As the MNR moved steadily to the right throughout the 1950s, it sought ever more to use the peasant unions as allies against the working class.[36] In 1964 Paz Estenssoro, who had just been elected president again, was overthrown by General René Barrientos, an MNR military man. Barrientos made official the subordination of the peasantry to the government by proclaiming the Pacto Militar-Campesino. This alliance specifically joined the peasants (especially those from Cochabamba) to the military government in their conflict with supposedly communist mine workers. But as Albó points out, this "subordination of the peasantry to an authoritarian regime was in reality the culmination of a long populist process" that had begun with Villaroel and the MNR.[37]

Contrasting Views of the Bolivian Revolution

First of all a proviso: Guevara's commentaries on his travels come in the form of diaries and letters. Diaries are primarily written for their authors, and letters have a specific limited audience. They can provide good sources for historians, but Guevara's early writings were not designed as travel books or analytical articles, so some degree of caution is necessary when comparing his descriptions with works more explanatory and detailed.

One thing that clouded the vision of nearly all observers of Bolivia in the 1950s was racism. Almost all writers, whether Bolivian or foreign, succumbed to stereotypes about indigenous Bolivians' temperament, intelligence, physical fortitude, work capacity, emotional life, and integration into the nation. Guevara was no exception to this pattern. While critical of the attitudes of many of the leaders of the new Bolivian government toward the country's indigenous majority, he himself tended to see Indians as long suffering and impervious to contemporary political realities. For instance, on his trip to Peru in 1952 Guevara described the Aymara people he met in this way: "But the people are not the same proud race that time after time rose up against Inca rule and forced them to maintain a permanent army on their borders; these people who watch us walk through the town streets are a defeated race. They look at us meekly, almost fearfully, completely indifferent to the outside world."[38]

While most observers at this time made similar statements at various points, it is striking that some travel writers or journalists exhibited almost a dual vision with respect to Bolivia's native peoples. When speaking generally they repeated many stereotypes, ones probably fed to them by Bolivian contacts or culled from Bolivian classics such as Alcides Arguedas's *Pueblo enfermo*.[39] Yet when reporting on actual conditions in the country or on conversations with indigenous people, they sometimes provided a more complex and active picture, one that helps the reader understand the way indigenous people actually lived and the demands they were making of the new government. Guevara's descriptions very seldom reach this level of detailed reporting. While he had a more sophisticated analysis of the political situation in the country and the problems facing a populist coalition like the MNR than many journalists, other writers tell us more about what the country was like in the 1950s and why there was a revolution. Guevara actually might have benefited from reading some of the accounts written by his contemporaries.

Guevara expressed outrage at the abuse Indians suffered at the hands of the Bolivian elite, including the new revolutionary leadership. One of his more vivid descriptions is of a visit to the Ministry of Peasant Affairs. He wrote that "masses of Indians from various groups in the Altiplano wait their turn to be given an audience. Each group, dressed in typical costume, has a leader or indoctrinator who speaks to them in their own native language. When they go in, the employees sprinkle them with DDT."[40] According to Ricardo Rojo, an anti-Peronist exile whom Guevara befriended in La Paz, Guevara was incensed enough about this humiliating procedure that he demanded an explanation for it from Ñuflo Chávez, the minister of peasant affairs, who agreed that the practice was deplorable but that the Indian was ignorant of soap and water. According to Rojo, Guevara later ruminated about this incident: "This revolution is bound to fail if it doesn't manage to break down the spiritual isolation of the Indians, if it doesn't succeed in reaching deep inside them, stirring them right down to the bone, and giving them back their stature as human beings."[41] What Guevara apparently did not know was that in the aftermath of the revolution a wave of protest and violence had occurred in the countryside as indigenous people demanded land, schools, a labor code, and the end of abuse by local officials. In fact, the creation of the Ministry of Peasant Affairs marked an attempt to control this uprising.[42] This kind of massive mobilization can hardly be attributed to the passive creatures Guevara thought he saw and understood.

This idea of the degraded Indian who needs to be rehumanized by the revolutionaries also was not challenged by any conversations with actual Indians. The one minimal interaction with an indigenous person that Guevara mentions is with a porter he and Calica hired at Lake Titicaca. They rather cruelly nicknamed him Túpac Amaru after the great Andean revolutionary, and Guevara commented that "he looked a sorry sight: each time he sat down to rest, he was unable to get up again without our help."[43]

The account of another foreign traveler who visited Bolivia a few months after the revolution gives more information on what Indians hoped to accomplish when they lined up at the Ministry of Peasant Affairs. Lilo Linke, a German woman who lived in Ecuador and wrote extensively about her travels in Latin America and elsewhere, arrived in Bolivia in August 1952. Linke spent considerable time in the Ministry of Peasant Affairs listening to people's petitions and observing the actions of the staff. The complaints varied: physical abuse of *colonos* by hacendados, theft of peasant property by landowners or their employees, unpaid salaries to rural workers, and even a petition from Joaquín Ronquillo, *autoridad indígena* of the Hacienda Huancayo, demanding that the owner of the hacienda be forced to abolish servitude and all unpaid services.[44] In many cases the ministry employees dispatched orders to local authorities to force the landowners to return land or animals or to cease the abuse of which they were accused. Although the agrarian reform had not yet become law, peasants clearly believed the MNR on their side and were using the mechanisms newly available to them to redress grievances.[45] From the landowners' point of view the Indians Guevara and Calica met were nowhere close to passive. At the ministry one landowner who had been called in to discuss a complaint said condescendingly to an official, "If you think you are going to arrive at an understanding with these people, you are mistaken." When she was told by the official to go back to the hacienda and immediately return the property she had taken from the *colonos*, the woman retorted: "But I'm not going back and neither is my husband. The Indians have threatened to kill us."[46]

Linke was aware of the potential threat to the elite posed by an agrarian reform and full citizenship rights for Bolivia's indigenous majority. She wrote that it was in these demands that:

> the real revolution resided. The nationalization of the mines, after all, was something approved by the majority of Bolivians, even if only for reasons of national pride. As an economic measure it could be successful or not, but in any case it was not going to overthrow Bolivia's social structure. On the other hand, that was exactly what many people thought would happen if the Indians were considered as equals.

More than 60 percent of Bolivians were Indian. Once they considered themselves as good as the white minority, would anyone be able to contain them?[47]

Here Linke very perceptively captures the same ambivalence about the revolution on the part of white Bolivians that Guevara had observed. In fact, many in the upper class supported the conservatives in the MNR, assuming that they would promote a mild nationalism, which included nationalizing the biggest tin mines, while preventing more fundamental social change.

Several times in his account Guevara refers to the organized mine workers as the radical wing of the revolution who, as long as they were armed, posed a potential threat to this more conservative leadership. While they were in Bolivia a local doctor arranged for Guevara and Ferrer to work in the medical facility of a tin mining camp. Yet they ultimately decided they were not interested enough in staying in Bolivia to spend two months working there. Had he taken the job, Guevara might have had an understanding of the social and political processes underway in the country that could have served him well in his later career as a revolutionary. Instead of going to work in the mines he and Calica settled for an overnight trip to a Wolfram mine not in operation the day they visited because the miners were in La Paz for the inauguration of the agrarian reform.[48] So they visited a mine that was not functioning and also missed the official ceremonies for the second most important reform of the revolution.

Linke did not work in a mining camp either during her stay in Bolivia, but she did spend a lot of time in mines, seeing the underground work, talking to miners about their living conditions and health, and meeting with union delegates and company officials. During her time there the mines had not yet been nationalized, but the MNR and the union movement had enough power already that at each mine she was guided by a union leader as well as a representative of the company, who often told very different stories. In the mines Linke, far from being a revolutionary herself, received some of the education Guevara missed.

She says that to understand the situation in the mines a person has to have lived in them, going on to describe the bleakness of the landscape, since most of the camps were located at between twelve and fifteen thousand feet above sea level. The cold, the wind, the lack of natural vegetation, and the squalor of the workers' housing that lacked minimal amenities made mining communities for Linke among the least inviting places imaginable.[49]

As she walked around the company housing at Llallagua, the mine company representative pointed out that the company cleaned the unpaved streets every day. He commented that if it did not the streets would prove intolerable. "The people don't have any sense of hygiene. They are too lazy even to use the latrines."[50] A little later Linke entered a house that had originally been built for a single man. The young man living there told her of four of them actually using the house, which only had two beds, a wash basin, and a rope suspended from the ceiling from which they hung their clothes. He explained that "the latrine is 300 yards away. At night it is too terribly cold to go that far so we try to avoid it if at all possible."[51] She saw other workers and their families crowded into one room in which the company had only recently replaced a dirt floor with a wooden one. These hovels had no water, and people had to wait at the neighborhood spigot in the middle of the day because it was the only time the water pipes were not frozen.

Linke also saw underground working conditions firsthand in many mines, including at the Compañia Huanchaca de Bolivia at Pulacayo, reportedly the hottest mine in the world with temperatures sometimes reaching 140 degrees Fahrenheit. In Pulacayo she studied statistics on the number of injuries each month and, as in other mines, saw evidence of silicosis and tuberculosis (TB) that disabled most miners after short underground careers. At the time she was in Bolivia most of the workforce inside the mines was between twenty and thirty years of age. A mine administrator at Pulacayo told Linke that after eight years on the job miners could get an indemnity for voluntary retirement, further commenting that if they even lasted eight years, laborers certainly were in the first stages of TB or silicosis and could no longer keep up with the other workers. Linke also saw figures on the alarmingly high infant mortality rate in the mining camp (seventy deaths in the previous month). Most of the children and babies succumbed to whooping cough, intestinal ailments, and other infections in an epidemiological pattern that had not changed since the early twentieth century.[52]

Even though she visited shortly before the mines' nationalization, at the company hospital in Pulacayo Linke saw the kind of place that Guevara and Ferrer might have worked in had they accepted employment. The hospital's doctor reported that workers did not have periodic medical checkups nor wanted them because, if they were found to have *mal de minas* (mine sickness), the company discharged them with a tiny pension insufficient to live on. He also claimed that the hospital only treated the least serious cases of TB (TB was more common in Pulacayo than silicosis). More severely ill patients were, according to law, released from the hospital, but the doctor did not know what happened to them since no provision for their treatment was made and Bolivia had no tuberculosis hospitals.[53]

Pulacayo of course was the place where the famous working-class program, the "Tesís de Pulacayo," had been drafted in 1946. During her stay Linke attended union meetings and learned about working-class life. She reported that many of the miners there and in other mines had come from the countryside, where they had been hacienda *colonos* or had had access to small plots of land.[54] This information shows a connection between peasants and workers that Guevara did not recognize, seeing the miners as militant proletarians and the peasants as indigenous people unable to defend themselves. The MNR government likewise sought to deny or obscure the similarity of background and interests of peasants and workers.

At union meetings Linke heard a sampling of rank-and-file miners' grievances and their demands for nationalization. There were complaints about mine safety and the company's unwillingness to spend money on security measures. Workers felt particularly outraged that the mining administration always blamed supposedly inattentive or lazy workers for accidents. Linke also heard from union miners that no one who worked inside the mines kept his health for more than two years, far short of the eight needed for the indemnity. This seemed particularly alarming since some of the laborers were boys in their early teens who should have been in school. One worker pointed out that the mining capitalist Simón Patiño had let the French government use one of his mansions in France as a hospital during the First World War but neglected the health of his workers in Bolivia.[55]

The union workers were full of hope about the benefits to them and to the nation that the impending nationalization would bring.

One said: "Nationalization will bring progress to Bolivia, which has for so long been exploited by Yankee capitalists. . . . The companies weren't interested in anything except taking our riches out of the country. For us the mines are everything, they mean progress, fraternal cooperation, schools for our children."[56] The workers at the meeting uniformly opposed the compensation of mining companies for the nationalization. The common position was articulated by "an indigenous miner" who asked the group: "Do you think compensation is reasonable? The foreign companies have exploited our riches for many years. It's true that they brought the machinery, but now it's old and the companies have made so much money that the equipment has paid for itself at least three times over. So why is the Bolivian government going to compensate them? Bolivia is poor while the companies have gotten rich."[57]

Although Guevara was told about the militant miners by people he met in Bolivia, he had no personal experience with them. We cannot know if living in a mining camp would have changed his ideas about the possible strategy for a revolutionary movement in Bolivia or made him hesitate before planning a guerrilla movement that had no real contact with workers or working-class parties, but it might have. In any event, Guevara left Bolivia for Peru after he had traveled there for a little over a month. According to Rojo, he, Ferrer, and Guevara went to Peru by truck.[58] Turning down the more comfortable possibility of riding in the truck's cab with the driver (what the ticket agent called "Panagra class"),[59] they piled into the back with indigenous peasants. Rojo described the experience this way: "The trip was an indispensable step in our education about Indian America. We entered a hostile world and were trapped between bundles and people who looked like bundles. Silence. Bruising jolts and silence. We discovered that it was impossible to try and show the sympathy we felt before those scrutinizing, metallic eyes, those lips clamped together forbiddingly, refusing to answer our questions. From time to time, a mouth would gape and let out a foul breath of chewed coca, a breath it didn't seem possible could have fermented inside a human body."[60] Rojo's account has the merit of revealing something more complicated than Indian passivity. He and his companions had to confront the silent hostility that three young white men bumming around might have expected. As they jolted out of Bolivia they may have learned a lesson, as Rojo maintains, but the lesson was not followed up with further education.

Alicia Ortiz, another Argentine visitor to Bolivia after the revolution, was a literary essayist and travel writer. She came to the country in late 1952 with a lot more illusions than Guevara about the revolutionary potential of the MNR. In July 1953, when she finished her book, *Amanecer en Bolivia*, she still believed that Paz Estenssoro, Siles Suazo, and other leaders had "a clear notion of justice and patriotic enthusiasm [and] were proposing to end the backwardness of the exploited Indians and the country's situation as a semicolonial, monoproducer."[61] Like Guevara, Ortiz was not above repeating stereotypes about Indians or romanticizing them. On the fishermen at Lake Titicaca she rhapsodized: "How interesting it would be to see those fishermen up close! To observe the indigenous race in its ancient tasks . . . would be like a glimpse of the most elemental forms of life in the Inca empire."[62] Yet Ortiz also actually got out and talked to people, and when she did, she gave concrete information about workers' and peasants' lives and demands, the splits in the MNR, the compromises the government was making, and other political groups in the country.

At various times during her trip Ortiz and her accompanying daughter had experiences similar to Guevara's and Ricardo Rojo's in the back of the truck. She remarked on how everyone seemed to be on the move. "With children and innumerable packages they travel by train or by truck, where they risk falling off while balanced on top of their bundles. [They are] exposed to the cold and snow in the mountains, the burning sun, the lukewarm mist in tropical zones. [These travelers] are dedicated to commerce. They bring bananas from the Yungas [tropical valleys near the city of La Paz] to exchange for chuño [freeze-dried potatoes] from the high plateau."[63] Ortiz did not seem to know that the elaborate trade she saw in Bolivia was probably a modern-day version of the ancient Andean practice of maximizing resources by having access to products from different ecological niches. Nonetheless she seemed aware of its purpose and felt impressed by the risks facing the traveling petty merchants.

Arriving in La Paz, Ortiz visited the working-class neighborhoods of Chijini and Villa Victoria with another Argentine woman who remarked on how picturesque the people were. Ortiz asks if one can really "be dazzled by the multicolored hues of a strange race, be blinded by the *pollera* [multi-layered skirt worn by urban indigenous women], . . . the striped poncho, the *quena* [reed flute], or the *charango* [small guitar, sometimes made out of the shell of an armadillo] when confronted with the *q'epiri* [indigenous person who carries burdens for people on the streets of La Paz] who disappears underneath the weight and size of the load tied to his curved back. . . . Who can feel the pleasure and the color of the landscape in the presence of this woman who with effort ascends the steep alleyway with a three-year-old child on her back and who says to you in passing 'I get tired because I have heart problems'? And who can find it amusing and entertaining to learn that the child isn't walking only because his legs are not sufficiently calcified and the mother only still has three of the nine children she brought into the world?"[64]

During her stay in Bolivia there was much agitation for the agrarian reform, which was finally promulgated in August of 1953. Visiting rural Sorata, Ortiz had the opportunity to talk with an agricultural *colono* about the situation and his efforts for the reform. The man said "*Ojalá* [I hope] that it becomes reality, all of us *colonos* want it. God should enlighten our *tata Presidente* [father in Quechua, used affectionately]." When she asks what benefits he expects from the reform, the man answers: "Now we are in bad shape. I work with my family in the fields every day. But that doesn't do us much good because I have to hand over to the landowner a large part of the harvest. Besides, two days a week I have to work for the *patrón*, either in the countryside or in his house in La Paz. Is this fair? I scarcely am able to eat some potatoes and corn, everything else is taken by the landowner. . . . It's not fair that such beautiful fields are in the hands of an owner who doesn't love them, who only wants to benefit at the expense of other people's labor."[65]

This exchange with the *colono* sheds light on the grievances and desires of rural people who Guevara only saw as automatons shuffling through the agrarian reform offices. Ortiz also learned that they were not simply waiting passively for the *tata Presidente*'s enlightenment. A little way from Sorata she and her daughter encountered the brother of a policeman who was traveling with them. The brother reported, and other *colonos* confirmed his story, that the owner of the hacienda where he worked had stockpiled arms to be used in a failed coup against the government that had occurred on 6 January. His *colonos* had observed the hacendado's actions and had taken turns watching his house to report any attempts to distribute them. One of the *colonos* explained of the landowner, "What is hurting him the most is the agrarian reform. He's fighting against it and that's why he is our enemy."[66]

Ortiz was in La Paz when the attempted coup took place and joined the people who filled the plaza outside the presidential palace to defend the government. Truckloads of miners arrived from outside La Paz, and Ortiz and her daughter found themselves surrounded by armed workers. While they were standing cheek to jowl with thousands of people, leaflets were dropped on the crowd by the *golpistas* organizing the coup. The leaflets explained that those supporting the coup were "not against Paz Estenssoro but opposed to the communists in the government."[67] According to Ortiz, the mass of people turned furiously on the person who threw the leaflets, an elegant upper-class woman who Ortiz said would have been lynched had soldiers not protected her. The assembled multitude listened to speeches by Paz Estenssoro and Lechín, but when came the turn of Sergio Almaraz, a representative of the Communist Party, to speak, the microphone went dead and Paz Estenssoro disappeared from the balcony. Furthermore, Ortiz reported that elements of the MNR right wing who had been involved in the coup received a generous amnesty. She seemed to believe that this was a proper conciliatory gesture and that the rightists in the MNR were only disoriented and still in favor of "national liberation."[68] Nonetheless, she saw for herself and reported on the MNR's political opportunism that Guevara had learned about secondhand.

At the MNR's national convention in February 1953 there was more evidence that the party was moving to the right and trying to control more radical elements. According to Ortiz, at that event the president's address aimed at "calming the national bourgeoisie's fears of leftism and braking the leftwing deviations" of the proletariat and the peasantry. Paz Estenssoro further declared that the MNR was "profoundly revolutionary but not communist."[69] Another exchange at the convention displayed the leadership's attitude toward the peasantry and that indigenous leaders opposed it. It occurred when Ñuflo Chávez made what Ortiz called "an unfortunate intervention," saying that a commission on peasant affairs ought to be made up of intellectuals who understood the issues because the Indians, due to their backwardness, were unable to defend their own interests. The auditorium apparently erupted in protest, and Chávez was answered by one of only four indigenous delegates at the convention. This delegate said that Indians "might be ignorant and not know how to express themselves with beautiful words or make eloquent speeches, but that nobody was more qualified than one who suffered an unjust and painful situation to know what its remedies might be."[70]

Why?

Anyone who supports revolutionary, or even progressive, change in Latin America must view Guevara's failure in Bolivia in 1967 as a sad chapter in the region's history. It caused his death and the deaths of many of his supporters, was a pretext for the Bolivian government's repression of the Left, and amounted to a victory for the United States and its Latin American allies. Ironically, Guevara's tragic miscalculations can partially be attributed to the success of the Cuban Revolution, which revolutionaries sought to duplicate elsewhere although the particular conditions that made revolution in Cuba possible did not exist in other parts of the world. The success in Cuba led Guevara and many leftists of the period to embrace the *foco* theory as a politico-military shortcut to organizing a revolutionary movement.[71] Yet Guevara's near-fatal experience in the Congo should have disabused him of the universal applicability of that model.

Perhaps given Guevara's experience, temperament, and class background he would never have been capable of engaging in a different type of political work for an extended period. Yet one has to wonder how he could have so misread the situation in Bolivia and if more time spent there in the 1950s might have made him more circumspect about using it as a base from which to launch his South American revolution. Guevara underestimated (or chose to ignore) both the revolutionary *and* the counterrevolutionary potential in Bolivia in the 1950s. His lack of knowledge about working-class, peasant, and radical movements made him seemingly unaware of what alliances might have proven useful in the 1960s. At the same time, although he understood that a populist coalition controlled by a middle-class party was unlikely to be revolutionary unless pushed by the armed workers, his lack of attention to how the MNR won and co-opted the support of peasants and workers left him unprepared for the dangers awaiting him in 1966–67.

When Guevara was in Bolivia in 1953 he correctly recognized the power of the armed workers and saw how the MNR maneuvered to disarm them. He viewed the peasants as passive recipients of the revolution's benefits, although other writers of the period showed them to be more active in making demands of the government. In 1966, when Guevara returned to Bolivia, dismissing peasants as clients of the government was probably realistic. In the military campaign against Guevara there was even a Barrientos Regiment made up of Cochabamba peasants organized specifically to fight the guerrillas. Still, he could hardly have found a less politically auspicious place to set up his camp than in rural Santa Cruz. Peasants there generally had sufficient land and no history of autonomous organization or connections with radical politics. Furthermore, the area was very thinly populated and isolated from national political events.[72] It was a good location for looking toward the Southern Cone that was Guevara's ultimate objective, but for winning recruits it proved hopeless.

When he went to Bolivia in 1966 Guevara almost seemed intentionally to ignore both the history of working-class and radical politics stretching back at least to the 1930s and the situation of the country under military rule. He maintained strained relations with the Bolivian Communist Party, a grouping far from the most important working-class organization in Bolivia. Arguably the Trotskyists had more influence among workers, and Bolivian working-class politics had always had a decidedly syndicalist tendency; political demands were often channeled through the unions. Although a few followers of the former mine worker Moises Guevara (who had broken from the pro-Chinese Partido Comunista-Marxista Leninista, or CP-ML) joined up with Guevara, many politically active miners remained ignorant of the Argentine's presence in the country.[73]

The MNR had been working since even before the revolution to bring the miners and other radical workers under control, either by the co-optation of their leaders or through direct repression. In 1966–67 the party used direct repression, leaving the union movement fighting for its life, while the official peasant organizations stood firmly behind the government. Guevara was apparently so wedded to the *foco* theory, as opposed to other revolutionary strategies that relied on working-class and popular organization, that he thought it could succeed despite the extremely unfavorable conditions. In the case of Bolivia, unfortunately, underestimating the strength of the military government and ignoring the history of worker and peasant organization undid both him and his theory.

Postscript

Since Guevara's death his portrait has become ubiquitous in Bolivia as a memorial to the man and as a symbol of defying U.S. imperialism. It is almost as if the country is compensating for not knowing of his presence in 1967 by making him almost omnipresent now. Since his election in 2005 President Evo Morales and his MAS (Movimiento al Socialismo) party have openly embraced Guevara for his commitment to social justice, even while the president has carefully distanced himself from Guevara's strategy. In an interview in 2007 Morales said, "Che Guevara continues to be a symbol of someone who gave his life for the peoples, when in Bolivia and in other countries around the world military dictatorships reigned. So that's why it's amazing to see that all over the world Che Guevara is still there, forty years later. But now, we're living in other times. But to value and recognize that thinking, that struggle . . . doesn't mean to mechanically follow the steps that he took in terms of military uprising."[74]

So in Bolivia Guevara is revered as the youthful *guerrillero heroico* who fought for social justice and as a symbol of Cuba, a small country, like Bolivia, that stood up to the United States. But there is more. That Guevara died in Bolivia has produced mixed emotions and commemorations. Many feel shame or frustration that to some foreigners their country is exclusively known as the place where Guevara died. For others Guevara, particularly because of the Christ-like photograph taken of his cadaver, has become a folk saint referred to as San Ernesto de La Higuera (the village where he was killed) or El Cristo de Vallegrande (a larger town near La Higuera). It is said that after his death people who viewed the body tried to cut off strands of hair as relics. A recent report claimed that each of the thirty-five houses in La Higuera had some kind of a shrine or altar dedicated to Guevara.[75]

A Bolivian film from 2005, *Di buen día a papá* (*Say Good Morning to Papá*), focused on a family in Vallegrande in 1997 when Guevara's body was exhumed from a grave at the town's airport. With flashbacks to 1967 the film explores questions of guilt and the possible complicity of local people in the capture and assassination of Guevara. But the film also conceptualizes Guevara as a lost soul of Andean traditions who, having died before his time, wanders through the world acting as an intermediary between the living and the dead. The image of the wanderer seems particularly apt, and in death Guevara does serve as a connection for many people, in Bolivia and around the world, to an earlier generation of revolutionaries.

Notes

1 Ernesto "Che" Guevara, *Back on the Road: A Journey to Latin America*, trans. Patrick Camiller (New York: Grove, 2001).

2 Ibid., 17–18.

3 Ibid., 4–5.

4 Lilo Linke discusses the youth of the M N R ministerial staff and also the number of young, middle-class women employed in government offices. See her *Viaje por una revolución* (Quito: Casa de la Cultura Ecuatoriana, 1956), 24–31.

5 According to Calica Ferrer's memoir, during their stay in the Bolivian capital the two travelers "alternated somewhat schizophrenically between La Paz society parties and the discovery of an emerging social reality." Carlos "Calica" Ferrer, *De Ernesto al Che: El segundo viaje de Guevara por Latinoamérica* (Buenos Aires: Marea Editorial, 2005), 101.

6 The most plausible explanation for President Daniel Salamanca leading Bolivia into conflict with Paraguay is that he hoped to rally nationalist support at a time at which he came increasingly under attack due to the world economic depression and his repression of opposition groups. See Herbert S. Klein, *Bolivia: The Evolution of a Multi-ethnic Society*, 2nd edn. (New York: Oxford University Press, 1992), 181–85. Competing oil company interests in the Chaco region and Bolivia's desire for an outlet to the sea via river routes also have been proposed as reasons. See Bruce W. Farcau, *The Chaco War: Bolivia and Paraguay, 1832–1935* (Westport, Conn.: Praeger, 1996), 8–9, 138–39; and Roberto Querejazu Calvo, *Masamaclay: Historia política, diplomática, y militar de la Guerra del Chaco* (La Paz: Empresa Industrial Gráfica E. Burillo, 1965), 465–66.

7 René Danilo Arze Aguirre, *Guerra y conflictos sociales: El caso rural boliviano durante la campaña del Chaco* (La Paz: CERES, 1987).

8 In Bolivia the term *criollo* is generally used to refer to the white, or near-white, elite.

9 James Dunkerley, "The Origins of the Bolivian Revolution in the Twentieth Century: Some Reflections," *Proclaiming Revolution: Bolivia in Comparative Perspective*, ed. Merilee Grindle and Pilar Domingo (London: Institute of Latin American Studies, 2003), 144; Aurelio Melean, ed., *La sanidad boliviana en la campaña del Chaco (1933–1934)* (Cochabamba: Imprenta de la Universidad, 1938), 137–39; Ann Zulawski, *Unequal Cures: Public Health and Political Change in Bolivia, 1900–1950* (Durham: Duke University Press, 2007), 61–64.

10 Farcau, *The Chaco War*, 74; Querejazu Calvo, *Masamaclay*, 108–9.

11 James Dunkerley, *Rebellion in the Veins: Political Struggle in Bolivia, 1952–1982* (London: Verso, 1984), 6.

12 Ibid., 8–9.

13 Guillermo Lora, *Historia del movimiento obrero boliviano*, 5 vols. (Cochabamba: Los Amigos del Libro, 1967–80); June Nash, *We Eat the Mines and the Mines Eat Us: Dependency and Exploitation in Bolivian Tin Mines* (New York: Columbia University Press, 1979).

14 Federación Sindical de Trabajadores Mineros de Bolivia, *Tésis de Pulacayo* (La Paz: Ediciones Masas, 1988). The text is also available at http://pulacayo.blogcindario.com/2006/05/00004-la-tesis-de-pulacayo.html. See also Steven Sandor John, "Permanent Revolution on the Altiplano: Bolivian Trotskyism, 1928–2005" (PhD diss., City University of New York, 2006), 170–76. For a discussion of whether Bolivian Trotskyists thought there would be a separate bourgeois-democratic revolution, see John, "Permanent Revolution on the Altiplano," 173–74.

15 A *comunero* was a member of an indigenous community or *ayllu*.

16 Marie Danielle Demelas. "Darwinismo a la criolla: El darwinismo social en Bolivia, 1880–1910," *Historia Boliviana* 1:2 (1981), 55–82; Ramiro Condarco Morales, *Zarate, el "temible" willka: Historia de la rebelión indígena de 1899 en la república de Bolivia*, 2nd edn. (La Paz: Imprenta y Librería Renovación, 1982); Silvia Rivera Cusicanqui, "Oprimidos pero no vencidos": *Luchas del campesinado aymara y qhechwa de Bolivia, 1900–1980* (Geneva: United Nations Research Institute for Social Development, 1986).

17 Robert J. Alexander, *The Bolivian National Revolution* (New Brunswick, N.J.: Rutgers University Press, 1958), 17.

18 Rivera Cusicanqui, "Oprimidos pero no vencidos," 25–38.

19 *Colono* was the term used to refer to a person who lived on hacienda lands and in return for the right to farm a small piece of land had a rental or labor agreement with the hacendado. Many *colonos* were former *comuneros* who had lost their lands to large landowners in the privatization process, either because they could not prove they had proper titles or because they could not afford to buy the lands they worked.

20 Arze Aguirre, *Guerra y conflictos sociales*, 83–115; Carlos B. Mamani Condori, *Taraqu, 1866–1935: Masacre, guerra y "renovación" en la biografía de Eduardo L. Nina Qhispi* (La Paz: Ediciones Aruwiyiri, 1991), 134–39.

21 Laura Gotkowitz. "Revisiting the Rural Roots of Revolution," in Grindle and Domingo, *Proclaiming Revolution*, 164–82; and Laura Gotkowitz, *A Revolution for Our Rights: Indigenous Struggles for Land and Justice in Bolivia, 1880–1952* (Durham: Duke University Press, 2007), esp. chap. 7; Jorge Dandler and Juan Torrico A., "From the National Indigenous Congress to the Ayopaya Rebellion: Bolivia: 1945–1947," *Resistance, Rebellion, and Consciousness in the Andean Peasant World, 18th to 20th Centuries*, ed. Steve J. Stern (Madison: University of Wisconsin Press, 1987), 334–78.

22 Rivera Cusicanqui, *"Oprimidos pero no vencidos,"* 69.

23 Ken Lehman, "Braked But Not Broken: The United States and Revolutionaries in Mexico and Bolivia," in Grindle and Domingo, *Proclaiming Revolution*, 106.

24 James M. Malloy, *Bolivia: The Uncompleted Revolution* (Pittsburgh, Penn.: University of Pittsburgh Press, 1970), 149.

25 Ibid., 156–58.

26 Ibid., 175–78; Dunkerley, *Rebellion in the Veins*, 58.

27 Malloy, *Bolivia*, 179–82; Dunkerley, *Rebellion in the Veins*, 48–50.

28 Dunkerley, *Rebellion in the Veins*, 58; Malloy, *Bolivia*, 176–77.

29 Alan Knight, "The Domestic Dynamics of the Mexican and Bolivian Revolutions," in Grindle and Domingo, *Proclaiming Revolution*, 77.

30 Secretary of State to the Director of Foreign Operations Administration (Stassen), Washington, 2 September 1953, *Foreign Relations of the United States, 1952–1954*, vol. 4, *The American Republics*, ed. Warren Z. Slany (Washington: U.S. Government Printing Office, 1983), 535.

31 Ambassador in Bolivia (Sparks) to the Department of State, La Paz, 7 May 1953, ibid., 527–28.

32 The outline of the stabilization plan is available in *Foreign Relations of the United States, 1955–1957*, vol. 7, *The American Republics: Central and South America*, ed. John P. Glennon (Washington: U.S. Government Printing Office, 1987), 581–84.

33 Telegram from the Ambassador in Bolivia (Drew) to the Department of State, La Paz, 19 December 1956, ibid., 584.

34 Xavier Albó, "From MNRistas to Kataristas to Katari," in Stern, *Resistance, Rebellion, and Consciousness in the Andean Peasant World, 18th to 20th Centuries*, 383.

35 Ibid., 385.

36 Knight, "The Domestic Dynamics of the Mexican and Bolivian Revolutions," 88.

37 Albó, "From MNRistas to Kataristas to Katari," 386.

38 Ernesto Guevara, *The Motorcycle Diaries: A Journey through Latin America* (New York: Grove, 1995), 77.

39 First published in 1909, Alcides Arguedas's *Pueblo enfermo* was an exegesis on the difficulties of creating a modern nation in a country in which the majority of the population was made up of Indians and mestizos. It was the origin of many often repeated stereotypes about different population groups in the country: the Indian was isolated and removed from national life, the mestizo or cholo only thought about his personal benefit, and the tiny white population was the only group concerned with the progress of the nation. The book was popular for many years and was revised several times. See *Pueblo enfermo*. 3rd edn. (La Paz: Librería Editorial "Juventud," 1991).

40 Linke, *Viaje por una revolución*, 9.

41 Ricardo Rojo, *My Friend Ché*, trans. Julian Casart (New York: Dial Press, 1968). 28. See also Ferrer's account of this episode, *De Ernesto al Che*, 110.

42 Gotkowitz, *A Revolution for Our Rights*, 269–71.

43 Guevara, *Back on the Road*, 10.

44 The *autoridad indígena* was the leader of an indigenous community. Most likely, in this case, the community had lost its lands to a hacienda and was living on some of their former lands and working for the new landowner. However, they still retained their own leader and spokesman.

45 Linke, *Viaje por una revolución*, 216–22.

46 Ibid., 221.

47 Ibid., 209.

48 Guevara, *Back on the Road*, 7–8.

49 Linke, *Viaje por una revolución*, 145–46.

50 Ibid., 147.

51 Ibid., 148.

52 Ibid., 345–46. Jaime Mendoza, a Bolivian physician and writer, describes similar health conditions in the mines in the first decades of the twentieth century. See his "Una indicación (en favor de los niños de la clase obrera)," *Revista del Insituto "Sucre*," no. 38 (1920), 455–72; and Mendoza's famous novel of the mines: *En las tierras del Potosí* (1911; La Paz: Los Tiempos-Amigos del Libro, 1988).

53 Linke, *Viaje por una revolución*, 346–47.

54 Ibid., 348.

55 Ibid., 352–54.

56 Ibid., 356.

57 Ibid., 358.

58 Rojo, *My Friend Ché*, 32–33. It is worth noting that this account of events is denied by Ferrer, who claims that Rojo did not accompany them in this trip but met up with them later in Peru. See Ferrer, *De Ernesto al Che*, 113.

59 Panagra was the predecessor to Pan American Airlines.

60 Rojo, *My Friend Ché*, 33.

61 Alicia Ortiz, *Amanecer en Bolivia* (Buenos Aires: Editorial Hemisferio, 1953), 197.

62 Ibid., 94.

63 Ibid., 17.

64 Ibid., 25.

65 Ibid., 98–99.

66 Ibid., 103.

67 Ibid., 59.

68 Ibid., 68–69.

69 Ibid., 112.

70 Ibid., 107.

71 The *foco* theory argued that revolution could be sparked by the exemplary military actions of a guerrilla unit. That revolution would spread out from bases, or *focos*, as workers and peasants became aware that through armed struggle change was possible. It rejected the need for long-term organizing among workers or in various types of popular movements and questioned the necessity of a traditional vanguard party. One of the best-known leftist intellectuals supporting this strategy was Guevara's sometime comrade in Bolivia, Régis Debray. See his *Revolution in the Revolution? Armed Struggle and Political Struggle in Latin America*, trans. Bobbye Ortiz (New York: MR Press, 1967).

72 Dunkerley, *Rebellion in the Veins*, 140.

73 Ibid., 142.

74 Interview with Amy Goodman and Juan González on Democracy Now!, 26 September 2007, www.democracynow.org; my translation from online text.

75 Paul Dosal, "San Ernesto de La Higuera: The Resurrection of Che Guevara," in *Death, Dismemberment, and Memory: Body Politics in Latin America*, ed. Lymand L. Johnson (Albuquerque: University of New Mexico Press, 2004) 217–41.

Cindy Forster

"Not in All of America Can There Be
Found a Country as Democratic as This One"
Che and Revolution in Guatemala

Guatemala lay at the center of Che's thinking about revolution in Latin America. Ernesto Guevara was a young traveller recently graduated from medical school when his fascination with social justice drew him to Guatemala and held him there during the final year of that country's national revolution. Called the October Revolution, it followed a series of long dictatorships. The tyrant associated with the 1930s, Jorge Ubico, was driven out by a popular upheaval in 1944. Workers and peasants organized feverishly across the course of the next decade. They won a progressive labor code, social security, and broad popular representation in the electoral arena. In 1952, campesino pressure finally gave birth to the land reform signed into law by President Jacobo Arbenz. Guevara arrived in December 1953 and moved into the circles of the urban Left. The communist party (called the Partido Guatemalteco del Trabajo, or PGT) had been muzzled by President Juan José Arévalo who held office from 1945 to 1951. Under Arbenz, however, it entered an era of euphoria, winning new supporters, helping shape laws, and wielding influence in the highest halls of power. It was always one among a multitude of competing parties. Even so, it was viewed as a Cold War threat in the United States. President Eisenhower approved the plan for an invasion force. The era ended disastrously as Ernesto among others tried to defend the revolution from the Central Intelligence Agency's (CIA) coup. They were out-maneuvered. Widespread assassinations ensured the success of the CIA candidate at the head of a sort of Guatemalan Falange (the Movimiento de Liberación Nacional, or

MLN) that held the reins of state for a while. The overthrow of Arbenz unleashed nearly half a century of bitter struggles. Soon the Right fractured into an array of former colleagues, occasionally murdering each other, and developed in Byzantine relations with the generals. Across the 1960s, they escalated their terror against anyone who organized for the rights of the poor. As Che moved from Mexico City to Cuba's Sierra Maestra, many of his acquaintances in Guatemala moved into clandestine resistance. Many also drew the same moral about armed struggle, based on Guatemala's failure to mount a sustained defence when its revolution came under attack by imperial force in 1954.

In the early 1960s, various guerrilla groups were emerging in Guatemala. This first wave of insurgency began with junior officers protesting their superiors' decision to join the U.S. assault on Cuba at Playa Girón. Among the dissident army officers was Luís Turcios Lima, who received a hero's welcome in revolutionary Cuba. The charismatic Turcios Lima was soon assassinated. His co-conspirators suffered the same fate as that of Che in Bolivia, for reasons that pose interesting parallels. Two years of guerrilla warfare in eastern Guatemala against the U.S. Green Berets and the national military ended in a slaughter of several hundred rebels and many thousands of civilians.

Across half a century the popular movement has held fast to the memory of Che. After his death in Bolivia, three Guatemalan guerrilla armies built their strategies in response to the failed rebellions of the 1960s. They each claimed Che as their own. One of them, called the Ejército Guerrillero de los Pobres (EGP or Guerrilla Army of the Poor) took Alberto Korda's silhouette of Che as its emblem, and Che's theories as a foundation. They built links to a vast network of indigenous organizing in a country where the Ladino or non-Maya elite regularly employed terror to defend their dominance.[1] The EGP applied Guevara's thought in the most systematic and intriguing manner, while the other wings of the rebel forces took a more schematic approach to the *guevarista* legacy. This essay focuses on Ernesto Guevara's sojourn in Guatemala. It then turns briefly to a less well-known and possibly more critical history, the sojourn of Guatemalans with the thinking of Che ever since the time he left their soil.

Ernesto Guevara and the Guatemala Days

"The time of freedom" was the name that plantation workers gave Guatemala's short-lived democracy from 1944 to 1954. Urban revolutionaries coined the name October Revolution, after the date of the insurrection in Guatemala City that finally brought down the dictatorship of General Jorge Ubico. The dictator had been forced to leave office in June, but managed to install his henchmen in the national palace. Within weeks, by July of 1944, laborers in the coffee and banana groves went on strike, thereby changing the course of national history. They then joined forces with Mayan peasants in the highlands. Their agrarian radicalism pushed the state to more coherent definitions of equality across the six years of Juan José Arévalo's presidency, going far beyond the middle-class democracy most urban reformers had envisioned. The landed elite closed ranks to defend a labor regime akin to serfdom. It was a way of life that rural workers described as slavery. By the time Jacobo Arbenz Guzmán was elected on a platform of land reform, campesinos were the most powerful organized force in the country. In the year 1952 they finally achieved the law that gave land to the tiller. In the words of a banana worker, "I'll tell you this: the thing was good. The government under Arbenz wanted to help us, it wanted the poor to be free. They were giving out land, and money, all so that the campesinos could help themselves."[2] There was barely time to implement the partitioning of the land before the coup. Among the lands distributed to the poor were some of the uncultivated extensions of the United Fruit Company. At this point, the corporate giant and the Eisenhower administration were working hand in glove to remove Arbenz. Watching this as it unfolded, Guevara commented, "the U.S. State Department and the United Fruit Company—one never knows which is which."[3] From the time he arrived in late December 1953, the young Argentine was appalled by the tactics of the counter-revolutionaries. He called for stronger measures against them than his urban contemporaries were willing to employ. Neither did Guevara jump ship before the invasion, unlike many foreigners in Guatemala. He delayed his departure until September 1954 several months after the coup.

Che's physical state during his brief eight months in Guatemala was a far cry from the legendary man of action. He suffered constant and desperate asthma attacks (sometimes because he drank too much). His future wife Hilda Gadea commented, "What a shame it was that a man of such value who could do so much for society, so intelligent and so generous, had to suffer such an affliction; if I were in his place I would shoot myself."[4] He spent days in bed wrestling with his health, administering injections to himself, able only to read. When he was well, he knocked on doors seeking employment as a doctor. His intention was to place his medical skills at the service of the revolution. The conservative medical association did its best to deny him permission to practice on the argument that his Argentine medical degree would have to be enhanced with further training in Guatemala, an unusual logic given Argentina's superior educational system. There wasn't a pre-professional student in Guatemala who didn't wear a suit and tie when Ernesto Guevara appeared in 1953 wearing neither, which caused many to question whether he was in fact a doctor. In the meantime he worked without pay assisting physicians, and spent hours studying in public libraries. He persisted in his job quest and the weeks stretched into months. Though demoralized by his "collection of failures of every kind," he handled it well. He was always hungry. A well-paying physician's job in Venezuela awaited him, and at several points he could have compromised his principles to secure some income, but instead he seized whatever odd jobs he could find or invent such as selling images of the Black Christ of Esquipulas, deeply revered across Central America, not least because its site was sacred long before Europeans appeared. On "the Atlantic highway project" he unloaded "barrels of tar" all night "from 6:00 in the evening to 6:00 in the morning, and it is quite a killer even for guys in better shape than I am. By 5:30 we were complete robots." After countless rejections he secured a part-time medical post at the end of April in 1954, serving the College of Teachers. It was barely two months before the revolution fell.[5]

Most of Ernesto's closest friends were exiles from dictatorships in Venezuela, Honduras, Peru, and Cuba. Many Spanish republicans rfound their way to revolutionary Guatemala; the struggle against the fascists in Spain was one of the era's touchstones.[6] Guatemala was a magnet for people committed to social justice. Ernesto's first sustained introduction to Fidel's ideas took place not in Mexico, where the two developed what Bauer Paíz describes as "love at first sight," but in Costa Rica and then Guatemala where a number of the survivors of the attack on Moncada sought asylum. "The Cubans," Hilda Gadea wrote, "were different from the other exiles, very lively, practically without any schooling, and almost all of them workers." One among them who spent many hours talking about Fidel was Ñico (Antonio López was his full name). López "was convinced he would be in Guatemala only for a brief time before leaving to another country to join forces with Fidel working for the revolution; his faith was so enormous one felt compelled to believe in him." Said Che, "he left his heart and soul in the microphone and for that reason fired even a sceptic like myself with enthusiasm." It was Ñico who introduced Ernesto to Fidel in Mexico. López was among those who did not survive the battle when the Granma landed.[7]

Ernesto's most constant companion in Guatemala was Hilda Gadea, an aprista in exile from Peru, and eventually the mother of his first child. Gadea held a government position thanks to her degree in economics. She introduced Ernesto to a stream of revolutionaries. Though he moved in the circles of Communist Party youth, the Guatemalans sometimes kept him at arm's length. Many thought he was a Peronist agent because he freely came and went from the Argentine embassy to collect letters, occasional money wires from his relatives, and a steady supply of yerba mate.[8] In fact Ernesto despised Perón and one of his closest friends in Argentina was a communist, but his family ties to the creole elite, like his ties to the Left, opened doors wherever he wandered in Latin America and put him in the odd situation of hardly eating a meal a day for weeks on end and yet being able to converse through the afternoon with such people as the former minister of the economy and labor.

Ernesto sought out people who challenged him to clarify his thinking. Though Hilda Gadea was his closest friend, he never agreed with her politics and spent many hours sharpening his arguments against hers on the subject of Aprismo.[9] Together they tackled Marxist philosophy, a task made easier by Hilda's training as an economist. Ernesto spent many Sundays in the home of Helenita or Elena Leiva de Holst, conversing with other revolutionaries. Leiva de Holst was a well-known public figure in her role as leader of the Alianza de Mujeres or Women's Alliance. Some Guatemalans at these gatherings found the young Argentine arrogant. In his diary he dealt out his own dose of national and misogynist stereotypes.

Curiously, one of his closest friends in Guatemala was a "strange gringo who writes stuff about Marxism."[10] Ernesto often made Sunday trips to the countryside with Hilda and the gringo, a professor named Harold White who hardly spoke any Spanish at the time. Ernesto had little facility in spoken English but was able to read it, and thanks to Hilda's recommendation, was translating White's book on Marxism into Spanish to earn a little money. This translation was "probably Guevara's first methodical exposition of Marxism" in the judgment of Edelberto Torres Espinosa, one of Ernesto's acquaintances, who at the time was a "notable Nicaraguan exile" with an official position, and whose children were young adults at the center of leftist organizing in the capital.[11] When in doubt, Ernesto sought advice from Hilda whose English was more fluid.

Ernesto, Hilda, and Harold, an unusual trio, set about studying Marxism in depth on their Sunday retreats with Gadea translating as necessary. The three foreigners agreed that the poor needed to engage in serious and extensive study to seize hold of their revolution and guide it toward genuine social justice. It was not a common perception among their social peers at the time, excepting a few labor leaders who had thrown themselves into organizing, like Víctor Manuel Gutierrez, the tireless and widely respected leader of the national workers federation, who also helped build the Communist Party. At the very start of the revolution, Salvadoran and Honduran communists among others had felt the same urgency to engage the working class. They founded a workers school, called La Escuela Claridad, that trained campesino leaders from every corner of the land where people at that point were mobilized. This core of communists had worked to rebuild both a party and a trade union movement under the leadership of the Honduran Graciela García. Doctor Arévalo, the professor turned president, quickly shut down the school and deported all the non-Guatemalan labor leaders, bowing to pressure from the Right despite his declared commitment to freedom of expression. In other words, many who called themselves revolutionaries deeply distrusted the poor, especially the indigenous. Guevara was not among them. "With his talent for conversation," he talked to any revolutionary who would listen, expounding on the need to establish study circles.[12] It is worth noting that the obvious shortcomings of the October Revolution did not prevent people like Ernesto from holding it in high regard, probably because they knew dictatorship firsthand. "This is a country where one can breathe deeply and fill your lungs with democracy," Che wrote his family. "The way I see it, not in all of America can there be found a country as democratic as this one."[13]

Just as many in the urban Left were persuaded Guevara was a fascist agent, they thought White worked for the CIA and was trying to derail the revolution by pushing it to extremes.[14] White and Guevara didn't let the suspicions of their hosts stop them from doing everything in their power to accompany the revolution as the assault from the Right moved into high gear. Che later invited White to live in Cuba, where the professor died in 1968. "Owing to his powers of analysis," White wrote of their study sessions, "in six months [Che] was able to achieve a solid overview" of Marxist philosophy and political economy. This was done with perfect discretion. Guevara's closest associates, such as Alfonso Bauer Paíz who frequently visited Ernesto, Hilda, and their first-born when they were all in exile in Mexico, believed that Che was not at that point a systematic Marxist. Bauer Paíz characterizes himself and Ernesto during that era as "anti-imperialistas en la onda bolivariana," committed to Nuestra América on the model of José Martí.[15]

The study sessions did not preclude other models and probably these were the discussions Guevara permitted himself with Bauer Paíz. Ernesto believed that the genius of independence heroes José San Martín and Simón Bolívar lay in their call for solidarity among Latin American nations—their conviction that only an international struggle would safeguard any single country's liberty. José Martí's "lucidity" on the danger posed by U.S. hegemony was also a constant theme. The lessons were ever-present. Bauer Paíz was in Arévalo's cabinet during the United Fruit Company's declared maritime blockade, "when they had taken over Puerto Barrios and moreover owned the Great White Fleet of shipping fame. England had shamefully fallen in line." The fact that a private company had pursued such a policy did not trouble the U.S. government. The blockade was finally broken only because Perón sent Argentine vessels to enter Guatemalan waters. Such histories compelled alternatives. One of Ernesto's pet ideas at the time was the construction of a Bolivian tin refinery using Soviet capital; again one can see the seed of future decisions.[16]

The October Revolution grappled with inequalities of class, but was far more reticent on issues of race. Intellectuals of the era in the main understood ethnicity as a subset of class divides. Che reflects the slow coming to awareness among Latin Americans on the Left who were privileged as "white." He rejected his creole birthright and, in the process, began to see the racial character of economic injustice on a continent descended from African and indigenous roots.[17] On this score he was way out in the lead. Guevara was not free of the prejudices of his social milieu; alongside his racism, his attitudes toward women were often disrespectful, to put it mildly. Yet he stood apart from most of his class contemporaries in the belief that the indigenous present was a proud legacy of Latin America's ancient past. Two obsessions drove him toward Guatemala, one being the revolution, and the other, its Mayan roots. Ironically, the young man who travelled across formidable Andean mountain ranges and into the rainforest of the Amazon never made it to the Mayan ruins of the Petén during his nine-month stay in Guatemala. He constantly schemed about ways of doing so. Mayan campesinos often express the same obsession and the same inability to pay the costs of the trip. Che hardly even made it to the densely indigenous western highlands only hours from the capital. His travels were limited to the circle of *pueblos* accessible for Sunday outings and "the provinces" he visited as a vendor with his Cuban friends.[18] His asthma attacks and joblessness chained him to the city. In August he finally visited the mountain lake Atitlán, one of the hemisphere's most famous tourist attractions that is ringed by indigenous villages and volcanoes, and on that trip he was fascinated by the religious practices of the Mayan priests in the nearby town of Chichicastenango. Earlier, the need to renew his visa in El Salvador had allowed him, on the return journey, the opportunity to see the towering Mayan stelae of Quiriguá in a region with little contemporary Mayan presence. He went without eating in order to spend what money he had on having his picture taken beneath the sculpted stone.[19] The photos made their way into the underground publications of the guerrillas 30 years later, and after the war ended, even a Sunday newspaper featuring a special on Che in Guatemala. The edition was sold out, at nine in the morning, in the largest market in Guatemala's second city, Quetzaltenango, which is also one of the continent's indigenous capitals.[20] Guevara's passion for the pre-Columbian past was very much in the mold of his generation, mixing and matching all things ancient, devouring the dubious analyses of some of the contemporary scholarship, and at times disparaging the beliefs or the appearance of the indigenous. Yet that said, he also harbored a profound respect that has been repaid in kind by the Maya, a subject to which I'll return below.

The prevailing historical consensus suggests that the revolutionary leadership of the 1950s was "not prepared" to withstand U.S. backed invasion.[21] I would want to take this further and suggest that the urban political class was in fact fearful of the worker and campesino strength that the revolution had unleashed. Rather than permit the poor to fully occupy local power, and eventually take the helm of state, the leadership preferred to surrender.[22] The national press decried the deepening of the revolution as a descent into libertinage, an accusation of "the rule of libertines," to quote Guevara, "used to describe Guatemala" as a place overtaken by excessive freedoms (the word itself threatens sexual chaos). Since 1944, the fourth estate had spun a web of lies and half-truths that succeeded in deeply frightening many among newspaper reading citizens. Thousands more were reached through the tireless efforts of the rightwing church. The Catholic hierarchy turned to petty bourgeois women as a prime target of anti-government propaganda, and the strategy worked.[23] The residents of the capital were not to be trusted in Ernesto's view. He didn't know it, but two counter-revolutionary spies were present when he visited Gadea's boarding house where the dinner conversations invariably turned to defending the revolution. One of them was the indigenous cook, a deeply devout Catholic who believed she was serving the Antichrist; the other was the landlady, who was the niece of the wife of a leading revolutionary who at one point was foreign minister, Guillermo Toriello. The same Black Christ that Che had hawked was put to work by the priests, travelling in processions across the country to decry the "communist" government. In the face of these ideological divides Che wondered, "Does it mean that the resurrection of the dream of the Latin American people, embodied by this country and Bolivia, is condemned to go the way of its precursors?"[24] Ernesto was shocked by the daily barrage of invective and misinformation and his fears were warranted. To some degree, the defeat of the Guatemalan revolution shaped policies in Cuba that have received widespread criticism. In Guatemala, Ernesto did not tire of trying to convince revolutionaries that the press must be muzzled to protect the revolution. In Cuba, where others shared the analysis—so it is not entirely fair to pin it on Che—the lesson was put into practice.

Another lesson drawn from the debacle of the Guatemalan revolution's demise concerned hundreds of people who had sold out for money, many of them years before the government stood threatened. As in other histories of assault on an *ancien régime*, the Cuban and Guatemalan revolutions faced the problem of how to dismantle the old officialdom. Corruption during the October Revolution reached levels extraordinary for the era (if quite modest by today's standards). In Cuba, the party system was scrapped entirely, not least, one suspects, to avoid the fate of the Guatemalan Revolution overthrown just five years earlier.

Apart from the temptation of easy money, the question of class loyalties in Guatemala shattered the revolutionary project. The traditional landowning and commercial elites conspired to regain their privileges at any cost. They were assisted by a host of small-time fascists, primarily inspired by the Spanish model. Even so, they did not stand a chance of success without the crushing weight of the United States. The CIA chose an exiled colonel, Carlos Castillo Armas, for its invading army and established its base of operations in Honduras. Up and down the class ladder, Guatemalans understood that the old elites were willing to jettison national sovereignty to ensure their prerogatives, which had never really been abrogated though they did stand challenged.

In May of 1954 the counterrevolutionary attacks escalated. "Chiquimula was heavily bombed and bombs also fell on Guatemala City, injuring several people and killing a little girl of three," Ernesto wrote home.[25] Beginning in late May, poor neighborhoods were targeted in a pattern the United States has replicated across the decades, for example in San Salvador and Panama City.[26] Bauer Paíz recalled that progressive political parties recognized the danger and joined forces in the National Democratic Front (FDN) to defend the revolution. However, "It was very troubling to us that Arbenz didn't convoke the FDN, much less call for us to remain in permanent session." The revolution's supporters formed nightly patrols that kept vigil in the capital, instructing people to darken all windows to avoid attracting the enemy bombers. Ernesto joined the patrols and signed up for the medical brigades. "It was not only Ernesto but many of us who worked in the government who wanted to fight the invaders," said Bauer Paíz. "But we would only meet weekly or biweekly, and they denied us arms. In the incredible crisis we were facing, rather than turning to the strength of the organized workers federations, Arbenz closeted himself with a few confidantes."[27] Among them was the communist leader José Manuel Fortuny, who has since, with great bitterness, defended his advice to Arbenz to surrender the revolution without resistance.[28] Many on the Guatemalan Left believe the decision was among the most pernicious in their history. "Just think of it, Arbenz's secretary Fortuny was the one who prepared Arbenz's resignation. So how is it that he didn't even inform his comrades?" That fundamental question remains despite several recent books that rely mainly on interviews with Fortuny. "It was people like Ernesto who urged self-defence. He already carried within himself the seed of what he was going to do. It's only logical that such people were in favor of armed struggle."[29] Bauer Paíz tells Guevara's story as a tale of destiny, a strategy that works because Che became famous before his death, whereas in the example of equally worthy revolutionaries such as Ñico López, their commitment is usually subsumed in the heroic narratives of their leaders. The saints' lives, as it were, become a way of honoring something much more profound, the decision of vast numbers of unnamed people who gave their lives for justice.

Faced with the inertia of the government, "Guevara and other exiles designed plans to improve the nation's defences and reject the small invading force made up of 700 men, the greater part of them mercenaries." Ernesto believed that only the communist party was capable of organizing such a defence, and that once unleashed, campesinos and workers would rush to join. Moreover the country's thickly forested mountains would aid the resistance; the insurgents would be impossible to destroy. Even if the capital with its well-developed counter-revolutionary networks surrendered to the invaders, "they would continue the resistance in the interior." Guevara was foretelling the struggle of the 1980s with this scenario. In 1954, the frustration of like-minded revolutionaries was immense. Hilda Gadea wrote, "They gave no arms to the people, except in Puerto Barrios where a female leader, Haydee Godoy, of her own accord rallied a few workers who were able to beat back a small invading force. That was the sole attempt to turn to the people." All their efforts to mount a real defence failed. "We foresaw the destruction of the government, and it caused us great sorrow, especially for Ernesto, because he was convinced that by giving arms to the people they would repel any attack."[30] Those who felt this way were unable to derail the unfolding disaster.

During the October Revolution, "Che saw his dreams for the poor across Latin America as they were being turned into reality," said Jorge Ramírez, who was a guerrilla combatant in the Ixcán at the heart of the most heavily-fought terrain in Guatemala's recent war. He is also the son of Ricardo Ramírez, who was politicized as a young man by the October Revolution and then went on to found the Guerrilla Army of the Poor or EGP. For Che, said Jorge Ramírez, "Guatemala showed that such a revolution was not only necessary but possible among the widely different peoples of the continent." The country is at least half indigenous (the figure is higher depending on one's definition). "It was for exactly that reason that Che tried to defend the revolution. The communists were by that point a legal party, and they too saw the need to defend the revolution. If you remember, Che embraced the idea, although at the time he was neither a guerrilla nor a military man."[31]

Che has served as a lightning rod for the Right, who interpret him as a paragon of violence. It is not a subject that lends itself to coffee table conversation. Ernesto wrote his mother, "Treason seems to always be the patrimony of the army, yet again proving the adage that calls for the liquidation of the army, as the true basis of democracy (and if the adage doesn't exist, I'll invent it)."[32] Guevara argued that any army created by the old elites was inherently untrustworthy. It was a rephrasing of Lenin's call to smash the state and Marx's reading of the Paris Commune. Guevara's condemnation of Guatemala's only president of the people was both complete and passionate: "The raw truth is that Arbenz did not know how to rise to the challenge."[33] Where others might arrive at this conclusion through an analysis of the histories, in Che's thought, the sheer bitterness of having lived it deepened the perception.

But the lessons for political theory did not stop there. Not until later were urban revolutionaries like Hilda and Ernesto fully apprised of the blood that was shed by the invaders in the countryside. The number of campesinos who suffered summary execution ranges from hundreds to one thousand.[34] In Guatemala City it was known that "assailants had committed acts of real barbarity, killing members of the Fruit Company union" in cold blood. "One of the first towns the invaders occupied was owned by the Fruit Company and there the workers were on strike." Castillo Armas' men "announced the strike was over, seized the leaders, took them to the graveyard and killed them there by throwing a grenade at their chests."[35] Ernesto argued, "We must do away with softness; refuse to pardon treason. Let not the unshed blood of a traitor cost the lives of thousands of brave defenders of the people."[36] Herein lay the genesis of the decision, not his alone, to hold the people's trials that killed thousands of small-time Batista officials after the revolution's triumph in Cuba. In Guatemala, the civilian deaths in 1954 were followed by many thousands more across the decades, carried out by the CIA's military allies. This practice gave rise to the strategy of *ajusticiamientos* by the Guatemalan guerrillas, that is, executions of the rightwing death squad leaders and military commissioners who were committing the repression. It is a policy that the Guatemalan Left leadership has since deplored, and for which they have apologized. Their rightwing adversaries however have shown no similar change of heart. They continue to murder campesino organizers, over 300 just since the signing of the Peace Accords in 1996.[37]

Hilda was jailed after the coup, while Ernesto was not targeted by the invaders, so he spent his days escorting people to safe houses or the embassies. He was also possibly gathering weapons, which would explain his slowness in leaving the country if he thought there was still room to reverse events. He slept in the Argentine embassy. During the evenings he talked for hours to the asylees. Unbeknownst to them, he would then write up their psychological portraits as a sort of extension of his medical fascinations; given his interests, he always addressed their politics. He predicted Carlos Manuel Pellecer's turn to the far Right, though at the time Pellecer was a communist party luminary. Guevara used his mobility to safeguard others until finally he decided to leave in September. He made his closest Guatemalan friend at this time, Julio Cáceres, who was an organizer nicknamed Patojo ("Boy"). They met on the train headed north, leaving the ashes of the defeated revolution behind them. The two were inseparable in Mexico. They worked together as itinerant photographers while preparing with Fidel for the return to Cuba to wage war on Batista.[38]

Those forging Cuba's revolution have been careful students of history, though their adversaries of course dislike their analyses. Just about every decision that has earned Cuba the opprobrium of liberals and social democrats has its counter-argument in the unraveling of the Guatemalan revolution (the point is offered as an observation not a judgment, if such is possible on a subject so contentious). The Cuban triumph was won through prolonged guerrilla warfare and a popular insurrection that abjured partial victories. Following the ouster of the dictator in January 1959, they confronted many of the same challenges as had the Guatemalans, however the Cubans opted for utter eradication on every count. Thus in Guatemala, "former employees of the *ubiquista* dictatorship and those members of the bourgeoisie belonging to Congress and the judiciary sabotaged the revolution's reforms" according to Guatemalan scholar J. C. Cambranes, a leading historian of land as well as the author of the definitive work on Guevara's stay in his country. "They gave free rein to every legalistic recourse possible, to oppose the development of the revolutionary process and all the critical changes in land tenancy."[39] In Cuba during the 1940s, Ramón Grau San Martín's second presidency could be said to offer a similar lesson of unparalleled corruption among bureaucrats known for their egalitarian rhetoric. It was a pattern that the Cuban revolutionaries avoided by encouraging mass emigration of the elite, and more bloodily, the trials in the early 1960s that account for most of the executions committed by socialist Cuba. Moreover they imitated the Vietnamese in their preparations for U.S. attack.

The Left in Latin America and the Caribbean has always been intensely internationalist. Hence the tragedy that destroyed Chile's socialist experiment in 1973 added weight to the argument for armed struggle. United States strategists, for their part, did their best to block various armed revolutions from the 1960s to the present, often through wholesale slaughter. Today they face elected socialist regimes with various degrees of radical commitment across Latin America. As the United States continues to opt for force, for example on the model of its proxy occupation of Haiti using the United Nations, groups as dissimilar as the Zapatistas in Mexico and the Venezuelans who favour Hugo Chávez have vowed to fight to the death to defend their vision. Like-minded Bolivians and Ecuadorians have expressed their "anti-imperialist loyalties in the Bolivarian tradition," to borrow the phrasing of Bauer Paíz. He insists, "I am not saying this because I am Guatemalan, but the fact is, the experience that Ernesto Guevara had in Guatemala definitively shaped his thinking as a revolutionary. Here he saw what was possible in a small little country like Guatemala, a country that became an example to all Latin America."⁴⁰ Che's body of ideas continues to hold extraordinary power for Latin Americans on the Left. Returning to the 1950s, his association with Guatemala took on its most important contours after he crossed the border into Mexico.

Che's Metamorphoses for the Guatemalan Guerrilla

Che's activities in Guatemala gain their full historical meaning through the prism of his influence on later Guatemalan revolutionaries. His impact on generations of civilians as well as rebels is quite simply incalculable. The rage he inspires on the Right responds to this fact. While the young man's asthma-ridden days in the capital hold great interest for the icon-hunters, clearly the revolutionaries in Cuba's Sierra Maestra are the magnetic north of memory. One of Ernesto's aquaintances in the Argentine embassy in the days of the 1954 invasion was Ricardo Ramírez, who is better known by his nom de guerre, Comandante Rolando Morán. Ramírez grew up in a Ladino family in a town in the indigenous highlands outside the city of Xela. Like most Guatemalans, he has Mayan blood. His father was a military man loyal to Jorge Ubico, the dictator-general of 14 years who admired Hitler and Mussolini. While still a teenager, Ramírez had a falling out with his father. The son wandered across Central America picking strawberries in Honduras, contracting tuberculosis, losing a lung, and organizing a patients' strike in the TB sanatorium. Such behavior reminds us that Che was a type, and many fit the same mold before Guevara became its archetype. The revolution brought Ramírez back to his homeland where he worked in "Caminos" or the Roadworkers division that had built a strong union. He threw himself into organizing there and also with the communist youth wing. These ties allowed him entry to the Argentine embassy when the CIA invaded. Soon after arriving in Argentina he left for studies in the socialist bloc, in Czechoslovakia. His political loyalties also explain his lasting friendship with Raúl Castro, who was a declared communist before his more famous brother took the plunge. A few years before the Cuban revolution-aries ousted Batista, Ricardo Ramírez visited both Fidel and Raúl in Cuba and spent time as a prisoner with Raúl on the Isle of Pines.[41]

Che and Ramírez got reacquainted under different circumstances during the euphoric months following the rebel victory. As a young reporter, Ramírez was covering the triumph of the revolution. Mean-while in Guatemala, the barracks revolt of 1960 was sparked by the rage of junior officers over the training, on Guatemalan soil, of troops to invade Cuba, a sister Latin American republic. "One-third of the officer corps" in Guatemala sided with the rebels, but "the delay by some and errors in their conspiratorial strategy meant that the coup attempt was discovered and quickly neutralized."[42] The United States sent planes from their canal zone in Panama to aid in crushing the insurgent officers.[43] Many years later a Cuban news-paper noted that the Guatemalan revolt of junior officers was suffo-cated by "the same mercenary brigade that in April of 1961 landed in Playa Girón, and was wiped out."[44]

Luís Augusto Turcios Lima and a few others managed to escape the crackdown on the young officers. Hearing this news, Ramírez returned to Guatemala and threw himself into the struggle. In the dry season of 1962, they joined up with a "popular rebellion that was then taking place in the capital city, by staging armed actions." Then in 1963 they unleashed a revolutionary resistance, unlike the purely nationalist revolt of 1960. They formed a new front that took the name of Alaric Bennet to honor a martyr from the invasion of 1954, a Black leader murdered because he organized his fellow workers.[45] Ramírez was charged with educating and orienting combatants in the Sierra de Las Minas, and he often turned to Che for advice. They kept up a steady political correspondence. Ricardo's wife Aura Ma-rina Arriola served as a courier, hand-carrying their letters back and forth between the front and Havana.[46] At times Ramírez and Gue-vara were able to meet in Cuba and exchange ideas. Ricardo's baby, born at the time, was named after Ernesto, and Che became his godfather.[47]

Though the correspondence between Che and Ramírez is not known to have survived, other intriguing sources remain on Che's thinking about Guatemala. In 1963 he expressed his admiration for the Maya to a Guatemalan delegation visiting Cuba. He requested a special session with them and reserved his warmest greetings for those who identified as indigenous. The comandante had two main points he wanted to convey. First, "he explained to us the importance that the Maya had accorded Mother Earth, maize, and intensive agriculture" across the millennia. Regarding the present, he insisted that land and racial identity were closely joined in the Guatemalan struggle. It was an analysis that the Guatemalan communist party found misguided, and even dangerous, that is, when expressed by their own militants. Che spoke through the night into the early morning and left the delegation with his second main purpose: "Don't ever forget the situation of the campesinos," he said. "As soon as you can, decree an agrarian reform that will truly undermine the power of the landowning oligarchy that dominates the countryside."[48] Guevara's political sensibility about land and race had matured in Guatemala and in essence he was repaying the debt. By 1971, the EGP as well as ORPA (Organización del Pueblo en Armas or the Organization of the People in Arms) cited the political primacy of race as a central reason for breaking off from FAR, the original insurgent group called Fuerzas Armadas Rebeldes (Armed Rebel Forces). FAR had already broken off from the communist party for various reasons, however FAR shared the communist party's antipathy toward theorizing race.

When Che decided to unleash armed struggle in Latin America, he considered going to Guatemala but decided against it, said Jorge Ramírez, since he knew others were already engaged in that task.[49] Che and his circle of Cuban fighters left for the Congo in 1965 and Bolivia in 1966.[50] In the latter year, the first major guerrilla insurgency was ignited in Guatemala's eastern mountains. It was defeated by 1968. The expertise of the United States was critical to dismembering the rebel force in Guatemala as in Bolivia. In the Andean country the guerrillas formed a fledgling *foco*, while in Guatemala they were an insurgency with thousands upon thousands of civilian supporters. One might argue that Che's thinking was more attuned to the realities of Guatemala, not surprisingly since he had lived such a critical moment in their history.

In 1967, Ricardo Ramírez brought together the kernel of people that became the Guerrilla Army of the Poor (EGP). They turned to Che's ideas to guide them, since his body of thought "synthesizes an abundance of experience and condenses it down to premises that constitute a theory of waging revolution in Latin America, based on

Marxist-Leninist concepts insofar as they apply to our continent."[51] More importantly, "we believe that when Ladinos and indigenous join forces, the Revolution will advance and triumph." In another dramatic departure from their former associates in the FAR, they insisted that "The strength of our Revolution lies in the campesino struggle—precisely in the countryside—where we have found and will continue to find the Revolution's greatest force."[52] It was Ramírez's idea to select the image of Che as their emblem, taken from the photo when Che and Fidel were honoring the 81 dock workers who had been killed (many more were wounded) in a U.S.-backed attack.[53] The EGP expected to battle U.S. forces at some point in their struggle.[54] Across the decades Ramírez, now Comandante Rolando, continued his friendship with Raúl Castro. The EGP wove institutional ties with the Cuban state, even as the latter moved away from public declarations of the Latin American internationalism that Che embodied. The other guerrilla armies likewise benefited from Cuban training and medical care. FAR for its part paid extensive tribute to the Cuban model of socialism in its materials to educate combatants and reach out to the Guatemalan people.[55] ORPA by contrast rarely expressed its admiration in writing, yet its combatants hold the Cuban revolution in deep regard.

"In the main, Rolando was a guevarist," according to his son Jorge. "He identified to a great degree with Che who he had the opportunity to know personally. He knew from a very young age that the Guatemalan revolution would find its course only through the protagonism of the Mayan peoples." For Ricardo Ramírez, growing up in the indigenous highlands, Mayan culture trumped his father's loyalties to the Ladino state. "Maybe the most important point is that the figure of Rolando encompasses not only the leader, but also the development of an ideology that conceptualizes the role of the indigenous people."[56]

The Guerrilla Army of the Poor sprang from the same angers that generated the campesino organizing of the 1970s, demanding land and dignity. Across the course of that decade various peasant organizations theorized ethnicity in relation to their own revolutionary projects. Also in the seventies, the EGP incorporated Mayan elders and adolescents, women and men. Militants in the western highlands were termed "units of the indigenous in arms" referring to the geography of racial resistance that was always a physical space, but also a conceptual one.[57] To take the example of a Mam-speaking Maya community in the department of Huehuetenango, "when the national struggle in the form of the EGP came to Colotenango, practically the entire municipality joined up. But unfortunately where the people were a little isolated, it was the army that won more adherents."[58] The physical geography of most of the indigenous countryside consists of a Mayan majority in villages and scattered homesteads and a town center dominated by Ladinos (such as the father of Ricardo Ramírez). The Mam campesino speaking here, Arturo Méndez, matter-of-factly dismisses Ladino conceptions of their own centrality. He interprets as ignorant the state's influence that holds sway in the town center, "isolated" from the greater clarity of the outlying aldeas and small homesteads. The milpa and campesino hearth are the world axis of the indigenous geography. There, community is created free of state and planter abuses, and the EGP put down roots. By contrast, people in the Ladino orbit, although often themselves indigenous, gravitated to military doctrine, many volunteered with enthusiasm for the military project, and they received the dubious privileges of that relationship.

In 1982 the EGP summarized their thinking on race: "Regarding the national question in Guatemala, there does not yet exist a systematic or homogenous line on the part of the Revolutionary Movement." Moreover "it is one of our greatest deficiencies, given the self-evident importance of addressing and clarifying this problem in a multinational country of great complexity, with very fluid and relative situations of mestizaje." Among "the estimated 7,262,419 inhabitants of the country in 1980, approximately 50% are indigenous," according to a definition that requires the person to be wearing their indigenous clothing and speaking fluidly in an autochthonous language, which today would exclude many who identify themselves as Mayan. The sheer size of the Mayan population gave rise to "some nuclei of well-to-do indigenous sectors, above all in the western region," who fashioned "bourgeois indigenous institutions led by an intellectual elite." As one might predict, "they are often also colored by indigenist ideologies based in ethnicity to the exclusion of all else."[59] A world of difference separates these Mayan elites (many of them based in the city of Quetzaltenango) from the mass of indigenous who suffer the worst poverty in the country and whose conditions demand class strategies.

Taught by their own experience, the EGP recognized realities that many Ladinos preferred not to see in their majority Mayan country: "indigenous culture in all its vigor, with its deep roots everywhere—giving it due credit but at the same time, not idealizing its more backward elements—is a mother lode of human riches that the new society cannot ignore without denying its very self." For the EGP, their struggle was rooted in "the sense that the indigenous possess of the collective, their austerity, their bravery." They explained, "one of the primary tenets of our line and perhaps the least orthodox, locates the complexity of Guatemalan society and the problems posed by revolutionary transformation" squarely in the ethno-national reality. This thinking placed the EGP in a line of descent from Che and also at the forefront of those in Latin America conceptualizing the intersections of race and class. They proposed self-determination at the level of community, demanding "decisive and energetic respect of the legitimate rights of the different ethnic groups." Indigenous self-governance and "full participation at national levels of leadership," they said, "was decisive for victory."[60] By contrast, the FAR leadership showed a great unease with addressing race on a theoretical level. ORPA seized onto it at a more individual level as a matter of personal psychology. Yet each of the revolutionary armies agreed on the necessity of foregrounding racial equality in their platform when they finally joined forces in the URNG, the National Guatemalan Revolutionary Unity (Unidad Revolucionaria Nacional Guatemalteca).

The Maya and Che

"In the harshest of times, across this long struggle for respect for human rights and as indigenous peoples, the image of Che has embodied our conscience, and the determination to be faithful unto death to the ideas in which we believe." A Nobel laureate when she spoke these words that capture the profound sense of solidarity that is the subject of this last section, Rigoberta Menchú Tum had been a young organizer who lived through unspeakable injustices.[61] The Maya in struggles for justice have embraced Che as a champion of their dignity. Their path, which revealed new concepts and alliances in the emergence of the pan-Mayan movement, took them through the living hell of the war years. Their demands called on histories lost in time, but told as if they had happened yesterday. Organizers were not interested in splitting hairs over definitions of modernity. They painted the liberal elite of the nineteenth century with the same brush as its heirs in the twentieth. Indeed, their daily experience was hardly different than that of their great grandparents, some of whom had lived in caves to escape the labor drafts of the landowners. In 1954 the young man Ernesto had possessed the clarity to name the country's central dilemmas: its racism against a Mayan majority and its history of extreme land concentration. This analysis joins Che to millions of Maya.[62] Equally important, it separates him from that significant sector of Ladino Guatemala that blocked, by a slim majority in a 1999 referendum, the anti-racist measures promoted by the guerrillas and included in the peace accords.[63] The capital was heavily lobbied by the Right, and there, the proposal to incorporate the peace accords into the Constitution was crushed. Those who voted "no" feared being outnumbered, should institutional racism be dismantled.

At the heart of the associations with Che among the poor, one finds a commitment to the oppressed and to their participation in any genuine revolutionary process. Che was above all the symbol of the EGP when I started spending at least several months a year in Guatemala, beginning in 1982. The war was raging. At that time all reference to the revolutionary organizations and their *comandantes* was prohibited by the dictatorship. Mentioning their names could bring torture and death. Yet guerrilla slogans were painted everywhere. The audacity of it commanded attention. Even vaguely revolutionary words and places, or lyrics challenging the rule of the rich such as "Casas de Cartón,"[64] were signals met with repression. The deadly web of military intelligence covered the entire country from the smallest village to the streets of the capital. Everywhere Che's image or name would appear painted on walls, and then be white-washed.[65] Che has many avatars. In the early 1990s a friend, a Mayan campesina who was a refugee from El Quiché, gave birth to a son whose father was also indigenous, and though it wasn't the name on the infant's birth certificate, she called her baby Rolando. It took me years to understand why. Without ever saying so, she was honoring the comandante and founder of the EGP, constantly and in public.

Slowly Che started appearing on t-shirts in the shantytowns

where I lived with friends, while doing research in the national archives in Guatemala City. Che's image in working-class communities was not surprising since the urban land occupations were spearheaded by movements of largely indigenous refugees who were streaming into the city from the countryside, many of them with relatives fighting in the mountains. One also started hearing the revolutionary songs of Nicaragua in the shantytowns. On the buses, stickers of Che's face started appearing on the dashboards. All this was much more than an exercise in free expression: across the 1990s the leaders of the shantytowns suffered kidnappings and torture. One young woman living nearby, in a household of organizers, was gang-raped by paramilitaries, and after her denunciation, it happened again. A member of the extended household was disappeared. Government informers were thickly planted throughout those same sprawling tracts of cardboard and mud, with children splashing in the *aguas negras* alongside dead dogs and rats. People there did not read Che, they lived him, and with enormous tenderness.

For those who admire him, Che is shorthand for speaking of collective rights and the gains of the Cuban revolution. Guatemalan poverty became a far more sordid affair than what Ernesto Guevara saw after ten years of slow redistribution during the October Revolution. The proportion of people lacking the daily minimum caloric intake doubled between 1965 and 1980; when the war exploded across the landscape in the latter year, four of five people fell under this rubric. The price of the family food basket rose 30% between 1975 and 1982, a fact that made its way into the founding declaration of the united guerrilla forces. While the rich grew significantly wealthier after 1954, land became so scarce (and infertile as a result of chemical inputs) that 70 percent of the population employed in agriculture were forced to seek seasonal or permanent work on the plantations. In figures that do not disaggregate the well-to-do, an astounding one-fifth of all children died before they reached their fifth year of life; infant mortality averaged 100 deaths a day in 1975.[66] Neoliberalism was implemented in tandem with genocide, exceeding by far Augusto Pinochet's excesses in Chile with his embrace of the Milton Friedman model. The U.S. funded the forced resettlement of the Mayan population in areas of conflict, where production was redirected to export crops.[67] Because of the viciousness of the class divide, the anti-Cuban discourse of the Guatemalan right is worthy of Miami. Rural allies of the military insist that in Cuba, people eat out of the same bowl, their lands are stolen by the state, and they are forced to share their wives—exactly the same accusations that an earlier generation hurled at Arbenz's revolutionary project. Columnists allege that Cubans suffer far worse poverty than Guatemalans—an astonishing lie. Given the prominence of such assertions, Che's legacy takes on a certain Alice in Wonderland quality. In the telling of the Right, most of the more than 200,000 people murdered during La Violencia in Guatemala were carriers of the Cuban virus, hence killed by necessity. Ranged against this is "a profound if unadorned love for Che among the people," to borrow Jorge Ramírez's phrasing.

"Che gave the people of Latin America an example of how to struggle"[68]

Guatemalan campesinos on the Left express the central message of Che as one of dignity, or the meanings of sacrifice embodied by revolutionaries. In my judgment, this would be Che's most far-reaching legacy in Guatemalan history. The canvas is vast, and perhaps best understood in miniature. We can turn to one insurgent in particular, Arturo Méndez, of the township of Colotenango in the department of Huehuetenango that borders Mexico. A number of different Mayan languages are spoken in the region. Méndez consciously imitates Che in his advocacy of Mayan resistance to neoliberalism. The Maya and campesinos undoubtedly suffer most from free trade policies. In the 1980s, Méndez rose from the base to the national leadership of the farmworker organization CUC (the Comité de Unidad Campesina or Campesino Unity Committee). His journey is a story of decisions made collectively that led him to the electoral arena and a mayorship based on consensus. CUC, from the time it first emerged in the mid-1970s, made demands for racial justice. It drew its strength from land struggles and organizing in the progressive church. CUC members challenged "every form of discrimination." They demanded the right "to have and express ourselves in our own languages, to practice our customs, our ideas, and to speak them freely without fear of reprisal."[69] In short they upheld the rights to free expression, thought, and religious liberty. CUC understood its mission as inherently plural rather than individual. One might say that the way in which Che symbolizes the social gains of the Cuban Revolution, and Ricardo Ramírez represents the project of the EGP, finds a parallel in the role of Mayans like Méndez who joined thousands of campesinos organizing in groups like the CUC. In each instance, the individual pursued a much larger project that is profoundly anti-individualist, aiming to uproot classic liberal and now neoliberal economic agendas that have been imposed by national and transnational elites.

Méndez tells a history of struggle that seizes hold of theory and remakes it. Inescapably, Ladino power structures are challenged by consensus decision-making in the praxis of the indigenous. The rule of the collective is informed by principle and by centuries of experimentation. In Colotenango, "the people have come to realize that our objective is for the people themselves to be informed, not just the mayor. For the people to participate, to listen, to give their opinions. With all these changes, the ex-patrollers [paramilitaries organized by the dictatorship] didn't want to join the workshops on democratic practices since in their view, it was a very bad thing." By "bad," those in the Ladino orbit were viewing it as "un trabajito de indios"—another "scheme of the Indians." They had cast their lot with the army in order "to protect their possessions" according to Méndez. "Precisely because there has always been a great social divide, they live in fear of losing their property."[70] During the war, racial distrust burned white-hot, but even so it could always be reversed. When the poor formed a common front against their aggressors, the tide turned. In Colotenango, the sea change happened when the people decided in the late 1980s to get rid of the civilian patrols. In the full heat of war they organized to dismantle the paramilitary apparatus that presidents Romeo Lucas García and Efraín Ríos Montt had extended to all able-bodied males in indigenous Guatemala.

"It was a very hard task and it took a lot of work to persuade people to rejoin the struggle," Méndez explained, referring to the mid-80s right after the worst massacres. "We had a group of what we call internal compañeros, from the EGP, organizing clandestinely as members of the patrols." No work could be more dangerous. In short, Che's respect for the protagonism of the oppressed, and the EGP's belief in the centrality of the Maya, bore witness to the deeply rooted commitment of thousands of organizers like Méndez, whose participation bridged civilian and guerrilla networks. To do this, Méndez had to possess nerves of steel, though his own words disavow any special capacity. Méndez said, "I had been doing the same work a little more broadly because the army had named me to be the head of the civilian patrols. So I went along with the patrols but all the time I was talking to people one by one, educating them about the changing situation of the war. I would say,—It's not right, it's not just. Our constitution even says so.—Little by little we were making headway. But the people had tremendous fear knowing the things the army had done. Even so, by 1988 with all our organizing, people were coming around. Nobody wanted to go on patrol."[71] The world of which he speaks is the *aldeas*, the rural axis mundi, while the military continued to rule the town center.

"At this point there remained a small group opposing all the people in the surrounding hamlets who wanted to get out from under the patrollers' control," said Méndez. "Here in the town center, [those allied to the army] would openly say, 'The ones who aren't patrolling, they're guerrillas, over there is a thicket of guerrillas.' And they'd set out to uproot and destroy them. It was an incredibly hard time. People would go into town for market day and be met with threats. 'You're guerrillas,' the patrollers would say, along with many other insults." By this point in the narrative, the first person singular has given way to plural. "Through all this we never stopped working with the people: 'It's time to stop being so fearful,' we'd say, and they would risk taking a stand." Méndez celebrates the resistance of the collective. "When they finally kicked out the patrols in the villages, it was because the population could no longer stand all the outrages committed by the patrollers. The patrollers used their weapons to intimidate people, they verbally abused them, they stopped at nothing."[72]

Where Méndez speaks in overarching terms about the violence, human rights coverage is more explicit. The description of one journalist refers to people in Colotenango who had left the patrols: "Their bodies were found later that day. The old man's neck had been slashed by a machete, his mouth, nose and ears filled with fertilizer. His wife had much of her hair pulled out, and her head had been smashed with stones. . . . Three other peasants had been killed by the Xemal patrol in July 1993, and on February 10 of this year two former patrollers from Xemal were 'disappeared' according to . . . CUC."[73]

Like Che's story, the resistance of these campesinos is the stuff of legends. Méndez recounts, "And the people decided, 'Let's go ahead and hold a peaceful demonstration so the brothers [allied to the military] stop wreaking havoc.' On the day of the demonstration, the patrollers were waiting with firearms at the Naranjales bridge. I and the other compañeros were walking together with the people. We got to the bridge and they started shouting insults at us. When all the people reached the bridge, the patrollers opened fire on the demonstration." The Ladinos and their indigenous supporters turned deadly at every point they felt challenged. "In response, the people shouted, 'We're not trying to fight with you. What we're doing is working for a future that favors all of us.' And the people kept walking, they just kept coming. I was there." Flying in the face of eurocentric conventions, Méndez understates his leadership, instead giving voice to his admiration for the people when they confronted the paramilitaries. Moreover it is striking how the words *pueblo* and *gente*—both of which translate as people—always refer to the indigenous majority in his usage. "So that was the moment when Juan Chanay Pablo fell. It was five in the afternoon. We were just a little ways onto the bridge, moving slowly, and others in front of us, when Juan Chanay Pablo was killed and two others wounded."[74]

In those same years, the Mam-Maya of Colotenango elected a leftist mayor in a political party associated with the guerrilla. In the next election and following the signing of the peace accords, they gave their vote to a party in the ex-guerrilla (the URNG). By the year 2007 they had won four terms in a row, despite a steady string of murders committed by the rightwing. They have led their neighbors in struggles against trade agreements they believe will force them off their ancestral lands. In 2005, a campesino and gradeschool teacher named Juan López was killed in circumstances almost identical to the death of Juan Chanay Pablo, with the difference that it was police and army firing hundreds of bullets at the civilian protesters.[75] The aims of the majority mirror the longings expressed by a campesino in 1977 who said, "For a fatherland that serves all the campesinos and workers I would gladly give my life."[76] This temper of commitment continues to flourish. "We're not planning to wait for the national government to solve everything," said Arturo Méndez, at that point the mayor of Colotenango. "Here we can change things, we have the strength to win struggles. There's the example of how we got rid of the patrols, how we've built schools and clinics. In overwhelming struggles and ones that are more manageable, we've achieved our aims."[77] By seizing their place at the head of the struggles that affect them, the campesino and indigenous majority in this township has crafted alliances with their sworn enemies. In fact, many among the town's Ladinos have thrown their support to the leftists who they spent years attacking. The rightwing has had to find new allies. In 2008 they killed a well-respected organizer of the same generation as Arturo Méndez, just days before August 9, when the indigenous and popular movement closed down the international border for a day of peaceful protest to demand commercial treaties that respect the needs of the Maya. The victim's family lacks the funds to pursue justice. Guatemala's legal system requires the accuser to assume all the burdens of housing, transporting, and feeding the witnesses, which is a powerful deterrent, but even more so are the ongoing threats. In the preceding month, another victim in Colotenango had his face and his genitals mutilated before being assassinated. The year before, a relative of a municipal officer was shot to death by the same aggressors, a manner of killing that never enters the national or international press as a political crime, although everyone in Colotenango understands it to be such.[78]

The people of Colotenango offer an example of the indigenous dignity that Che recognized fifty years ago. For his part, Méndez consciously embodies Che's commitment to radical democracy. "In Colotenango we follow in Che's footsteps. Like him, we are going to have to struggle our entire lifetime," he said. "We also admire his bravery in confronting the large corporations." (His point had an immediate reference—in July 2006, Colotenango and four nearby Mam-Maya municipalities called a special congress to denounce the latest arrival of foreign mining companies that are strip mining in the neighboring province of San Marcos.)[79] "Che never turned traitor to his way of thinking," said Méndez. "There are many stories, many books about Che and I have read some of them. Recently when I was in Cuba I saw the film about his motorcycle journeys. He served lepers and treated them with great dignity, using the human warmth of his bare hands rather than accepting surgical gloves. For me, I was especially taken by his example of how to lead, that one has to walk with the people."[80] Contemporary conversations about Che are refracted in a multiplicity of ways, in the foregoing example by campesino readers of Che's writings, by the mature Cuban revolution, and by the Latin American film industry (which sparked the conference that led to this volume of essays). Scholars are trained to parse, while organizers build an inclusivity that decenters what might be called the oppositional instinct of the academy. In this spirit Méndez argues that "Che was one of the best guides on how to end the discrimination suffered by the oppressed. He left a vision of the future for all people, and especially for the marginalized."[81]

It hardly needs saying that Latin America has been powerfully influenced by the Cuban Revolution. Cuba's political meanings, its varied economic practice and experiments in social change, have been felt from the most destitute corners of the continent to every national palace, while becoming a driving obsession of the world's great powers. Che's contributions to the theories of that revolution took form in intimate conversation with Fidel, and the praxis of both men unfolded in dialogue with a wide array of social actors, but that said, the body of ideas we attribute to Ernesto Guevara was shaped during his long, involuntary unemployment in Guatemala. In the realm of intellectual history, the maturation of Che's analyses takes us to his understanding of the October Revolution. After it was crushed, the unfolding political histories of Guatemala take us to the decisions of people like Ricardo Ramírez to wage war on the dictatorship. The most important questions concerning Guevara in Guatemala involve the meanings of Che for the vast insurgency of the 1980s. The Mam-Maya campesino Arturo Méndez made a journey across various organizing terrains that allows us to widen the story beyond political elites and national leaders on the Left. Theirs was a struggle in which many hundreds of thousands of Mayan farmworkers understood their decision to join the revolution not only as the righting of ancestral wrongs, but also as the imitation of Che.

Notes

Many thanks to Tanalís Padilla for her close reading of this article (any errors of fact or interpretation are of course my own). The discussion of the 1960s below is based on documents produced by the various revolutionary organizations, the secondary literature, and a number of interviews, largely addressing the October Revolution. From the 1970s forward it also draws on dozens of oral histories, mostly with Mayan campesinos who chose to join the resistance, either armed or unarmed. These form part of two manuscripts I am close to completing.

1 José González and Antonio Campos, Guatemala: Un pueblo en lucha (Madrid: Editorial Revolución, 1983), 159, 157. Yet the EGP was not really foquista. In the group's own words, "the participation of the masses was always at the forefront of our minds." Guatemala News and Information Bureau Archive (hereafter GNIB), now housed at Princeton University, RO 2.5, EGP, Compañero, No. 7, November 1983, 24–25.

2 Interview 38, anonymous Ladino banana worker during the revolutionary period; Interview 39, another worker. The author's interviews occurred on three separate occasions in May 1990 and were published in Cindy Forster, The Time of Freedom: Campesino Workers in Guatemala's October Revolution (Pittsburgh, Penn.: University of Pittsburgh Press, 2001). This rural history in relation to the politicians is laid out in Jim Handy, Revolution in the Countryside: Rural Conflict and Agrarian Reform in Guatemala, 1944–1954 (Chapel Hill: University of North Carolina Press, 1994). The classic account of U.S. intervention is Stephen Schlesinger and Stephen Kinzer, Bitter Fruit: The Untold Story of the American Coup in Guatemala (Garden City, N.Y.: Anchor Press, 1983).

3 Víctor Casaus, ed., Self Portrait, Che Guevara (Melbourne: Ocean Press, 2004), 77.

4 Hilda Gadea, Ernesto: A Memoir of Che Guevara, trans. Carmen Molina and Walter I. Bradbury (Garden City, N.Y.: Doubleday, 1972), 29.

5 Ernesto "Che" Guevara, Back on the Road: A Journey through Latin America, trans. Patrick Camiller, (New York: Grove, 2000), 38–42, 44, 46, 55, 58. Alfonso Bauer Paíz, interview, Guatemala City, June 2006. Julio Castellanos Cambranes, La presencia viva de Che Guevara en Guatemala (San José, Costa Rica: Editora Cultural de Centroamérica, 2004), 205. This book by a Guatemalan historian offers an encyclopedic treatment, as well as the most reliable chronology; my large debt to the work is evident in the notes. The source for Guevara's attire is Bauer Paíz. See also Ernesto Guevara Lynch, Aquí va un soldado de América (Buenos Aires: Sudamericana/Planeta, 1987), 49; and Gadea, Ernesto, 45.

6 Cambranes, La presencia viva de Che Guevara, 214. When the revolution fell, Guevara wrote a poem to ease his grief, and its frame of reference was republican Spain.

7 Ibid., 84, 86; Bauer Paíz, interview; Guevara, Back on the Road, 45.

8 Guevara, Back on the Road, 60.

9 Cambranes, La presencia viva de Che Guevara, 170. Gadea writes of

Guevara, "He asked: 'How can a woman who thinks like a Communist belong to APRA?'" (*Ernesto*, 32).

10 Guevara, *Back on the Road*, 38.

11 Cambranes, *La presencia viva de Che Guevara*, 94, 79–80.

12 Alfonso Bauer Paíz, "Testimonio sobre Ernesto," *Casa de Las Américas*, 18:104 (1977), 13.

13 Guevara Lynch, *Aquí va un soldado de América*, 36, 34; translation mine—I omitted a phrase referring to a Guevara family joke. On the Escuela Claridad and the deportation of Central Americans who had sought refuge from neighboring dictatorships, see Graciela Garcia L., *Las luchas revolucionarias de la nueva Guatemala* (Mexico City: n.p., 1952), 62–66, 79–95, 136, 145; and by the same author *Páginas de lucha* (Tegucigalpa: Editorial Guaymuras, 1981), 53–55.

14 Cambranes, *La presencia viva de Che Guevara*, 151. In Mexico several years later, many Guatemalan exiles were convinced that Castro was a U.S. agent. While other exiles were denied work at every turn as alleged communists, Castro came and went at will in the United States, returning with his pockets full "not of hundreds but rather thousands of dollars from the Cubans living there." Bauer Paíz, interview.

15 The Bauer Paíz family maintained a safe house for the *Granma* expedition because Guevara ended up there, without his family at that point, and decided to tell his hosts that he was collecting medicines rather than arms, which arrived one day when the Guatemalans were meeting to plot politics, as was their custom: "And would you believe it, that box was so heavy we could barely lift it between five men." The next day their house guest vanished. Bauer Paíz, interview; and Bauer Paíz, "Testimonio sobre Ernesto," 17–18. The official Cuban chronology dates Che's political maturation to the Mexico years; see Departamento de Consulta y Referencia de la Biblioteca Nacional José Martí de La Habana, *Tiempo de Che: Primer ensayo de cronología* (Barcelona: Editorial Anagrama, 1976), 25.

16 Bauer Paíz, interview; Cambranes, *La presencia viva de Che Guevara*, 170, 100; Gadea, *Ernesto*, 11.

17 Guevara's mother counted the first Spanish viceroy of Peru among her forbears, while his father's maternal surname is Irish. Cambranes, *La presencia viva de Che Guevara*, 55.

18 Guevara Lynch, *Aquí va un soldado de América*, 46; Gadea, *Ernesto*, 42.

19 Guevara, *Back on the Road*, 54–55. Both Gadea and Cambranes elaborate on Guevara's Guatemalan travels. See Cambranes, *La presencia viva de Che Guevara*, 187, 57, 245, 200, 233. Guevara's first real acquaintance with indigenous communities took place on his bicycle trip to northern Argentina (before the famous motorcycle treks). In El Salvador his en-

thusiasm for the revolution landed him in jail for exercising his rights of free speech, the same reason for which he found himself deported from the United States, though in the north he was criticizing imperialism rather than praising Guatemala. Cambranes, *La presencia viva de Che Guevara*, 203. Guevara, *Back on the Road*, 83.

20 Most residents call it Xela, a Mam-Maya name, but it appears on maps as Quetzaltenango, which is the Náhuatl name given it by Toltec-Maya conquerors.

21 See, for example, Cambranes, *La presencia viva de Che Guevara*, 223.

22 For the fullest explication, see Tomás Herrera, *Guatemala: Revolución de Octubre* (San José, Costa Rica: Editorial Universitaria Centroamericana, 1986). Cambranes, *La presencia viva de Che Guevara*, 148.

23 Cambranes, *La presencia viva de Che Guevara*, 229, 213, 225. In 1989, when reading the same press coverage from the 1950s in the archives, I was struck by its similarities to the war of words then being waged in Nicaragua during a presidential campaign that most people were absolutely convinced would be won by the Sandinistas.

24 Cambranes, *La presencia viva de Che Guevara*, 79, 148, 213, 229; and Casaus, *Self Portrait, Che Guevara*, 77.

25 Casaus, *Self Portrait, Che Guevara*, 94; see also Guevara, *Back on the Road*, 62–63.

26 Gadea, *Ernesto*, 46; Guevara Lynch, *Aquí va un soldado de América*, 55–56. On this and other details, Paul Dosal's *Comandante Che: Guerrilla Soldier, Commander, and Strategist, 1956–1967* (University Park: Pennsylvania State University Press, 2004), is often odd: "Rebel planes bombed storage dumps and other targets in Guatemala City, causing little material damage" (41).

27 Bauer Paíz, interview.

28 José Manuel Fortuny, leading member of the Communist Party in Guatemala during the revolution, editor of the communist newspaper, and advisor to President Arbenz, interview, Mexico City, February 6, 1990.

29 Bauer Paíz, interview.

30 Cambranes, *La presencia viva de Che Guevara*, 211, 102, 218–22, includes quotes from Gadea.

31 Jorge Ramírez, interview, Guatemala City, August 2006.

32 Guevara Lynch, *Aquí va un soldado de América*, 57.

33 Cambranes, *La presencia viva de Che Guevara*, 226. Or "the harsh truth is that Arbenz did not know how to rise to the challenge" (Guevara, *Back on the Road*, 67).

34 The first estimate comes from Jim Handy, *Revolution in the Countryside: Rural Conflict and Agrarian Reform in Guatemala, 1944–1954* (Chapel

Hill: University of North Carolina Press, 1994), 194, while the higher estimate is taken from campesino organizers who lived near the United Fruit Company plantation that became an execution camp for some six months.

35 Cambranes, *La presencia viva de Che Guevara*, 210, 227; Guevara, *Back on the Road*, 62–63, 65. The little girl is said to be two in a letter to his mother.

36 Casaus, *Self Portrait, Che Guevara*, 77.

37 Moisés Guzmán Grijalba and Santos Natalio Chic Uz of the Coordinadora Nacional de Organizaciones Campesinas (CNOC), interview, Guatemala City, 18 August 2008.

38 Guevara, *Back on the Road*, 69–73; Bauer Paíz, interview; Cambranes, *La presencia viva de Che Guevara*, 227–30, 234–38, 242. When they sailed for Cuba, Guevara left behind both his new baby and his wife.

39 Cambranes, *La presencia viva de Che Guevara*, 250; see also 169.

40 Bauer Paíz, interview. The point is critical, though others might underscore the influence of other "small little countries" and other moments in Guevara's intellectual journey. Bauer Paíz served as Arévalo's minister of the economy and labor and then gained fame as a revolutionary politician and lawyer. He filed suit against the United Fruit Company (and won many years after the coup, in U.S. courts). Forced into exile, he became an author, and at the end of the war back in Guatemala, a leftist congressperson. Bauer Paíz explained, "Not even Mexico or Argentina was willing to stand up to the U.S. assault on Guatemala when the Organization of American States voted that the Arbenz regime posed a grave danger to the security of the continent. Che was deeply impressed having seen the revolution in Guatemala resist such attacks for ten years."

41 Ramírez, interview.

42 GNIB RO 4.5, ORPA, El Militante, 3:5, November 1995, 14.

43 GNIB RO 1.1, EGP, *Compañero*, July 1975, No. 1, International Bulletin, "A Genocide That Has Lasted Twenty Years: Guatemala," 2.

44 GNIB RO General, "Turcios Lima: La Revolución, Su Razón para Vivir y para Morir," *Granma*, 10 March 1970, no page and 55.

45 GNIB RO 1.1, EGP, *Compañero*, July 1975, No. 1, International Bulletin, "A Genocide That Has Lasted Twenty Years: Guatemala," 6.

46 The family is searching for that correspondence, as well as for other writings and photos. A video of Comandante Rolando discussing his friendship with Che will be released by the Ramírez family in the future.

47 Ramírez, interview.

48 Cambranes, *La presencia viva de Che Guevara*, 15, 25.

49 Ramírez, interview. In this interview Ramírez said, "According to a Cuban in the audience of a recent event in Cuba, Che had decided against going to Guatemala because 'en Guatemala estaba Rolando.'" Another of Guevara's obsessions was winning the revolution in Argentina, and he arranged funding for an armed *foco* there that was quickly crushed. The admirers of the objective—if not the strategy—are as numerous as those who decry its terrible costs.

50 Michael Ratner and Michael Steven Smith, eds., *Che Guevara and the FBI: The U.S. Political Police Dossier on the Latin American Revolutionary* (Brooklyn, N.Y.: Ocean Press, 1997), xix.

51 GNIB RO 2.5, EGP, *Compañero*, No. 7, November 1983, 24–25. GNIB RO 1.1, Combate, Marta Harnecker, "Guatemala, El camino de las armas hacía la victoria," extractos en *Le Monde Diplomatique en Español*, no date, p. xx; handwritten "septiembre 1982" on same document in archive at CIRMA, Antigua Guatemala Col. Infostelle, Signatura 137, Represión, 12.01.01. Rolando Morán joined forces with Régis Debray to write about the theory of revolution in Latin America.

52 Guevara of course promoted this strategy of turning to campesinos. Centro de Investigaciones Regionales de Meso América Archive (CIRMA), Antigua, Guatemala, Colección Mario Payeras, Caja No. 1, 29.1, "Carta abierta del Comandante Luís Augusto Turcios Lima a la dirección nacional del movimiento revolucionario 13 de noviembre," Guatemala, Centroamérica, 6 de marzo de 1965, 2–13. Regarding the FAR, see also GNIB PD 6.1, Héctor Díaz-Polanco, *Etnia, nación y política* (México City: Juan Pablos Editor, 1987), "Anexo 4, Entrevista al comandante Nicolás Sis (FAR), La cuestión étnico-nacional y la revolución guatemalteca," 175.

53 *KordaVision, A Cuban Revelation*, documentary on Alberto Díaz Gutiérrez "Korda," A Héctor Cruz Sandoval film. Christophe Loviny, ed., *Cuba by Korda* (Melbourne: Ocean Press, 2006), 76.

54 González and Campos, *Guatemala*, 166.

55 In the 1960s the Left fractured badly, and in the following decade feelings were so heated between the different rebel groups that "it almost got to the point of a fratricidal war." GNIB, RO 2, General, Marta Harnecker, "Entrevista al . . . Rolando Morán, un trabajo de masas para la guerra," *Punto Final*, March–April 1982, 30.

56 Ramírez, interview.

57 CIRMA, Colección Inforpress, no document number, EGP, Antigua, Guatemala, "La guerra de guerrillas revolucionarias se desarrolla . . . ," 17 February 1980.

58 Arturo Méndez, interviews, Colotenango and Huehuetenango, July 2001, June 2005, August 2006, and July 2007. Méndez was a long-time leader of the Campesino Unity Committee (CUC) and a clandestine member of the EGP. At the time of my first interview, Méndez served as mayor, a post to which he was later reelected.

59 GNIB RO 2.5, EGP, *Compañero*, No. 5, 1982, 11–14.

60 Ibid., 17–19.

61 Menchú was a spokesperson for the CUC at the time she was quoted in "Acerca del Che," *Casa de Las Américas* 37:206 (1997), 55. Born to a Mayan campesino family, she won the Nobel Peace Prize on the quincentennial of Columbus's invasion for her work defending indigenous rights in the face of genocide in Guatemala. She has since attracted controversies not unrelated to those that surround the figure of Che.

62 The United Nations Development Program and the World Bank have repeatedly found that Guatemala outpaces other Western Hemisphere countries in the gap between rich and poor, with the exception of the infinitely poorer Haiti. See, for example, United Nations Development Program (UNDP), *Human Development Reports* (New York: UNDP, 1996, 1993).

63 These were signed with the state in 1996. My analysis is based on my oral history interviews, personal conversations, and David Carey Jr., "Maya Perspectives on the 1999 Referendum in Guatemala: Ethnic Equality Rejected?" *Latin American Perspectives*, no. 31 (2004), 65–95. The propaganda blitzkrieg of the elite claimed that the "Indians" were scheming to take over the country. In rural Mayan areas, the "yes" vote won, thanks to tireless organizing through campesino networks. Unlike their opponents, they had no money.

64 The famous song by the Venezuelan group Los Guaraguao.

65 Today, political murals across Guatemala City, painted with permission, are destroyed by night.

66 GNIB PD 6.2.2, Comité Nacional de Unidad Sindical, "El Fascismo en Guatemala, Un Vasto Plan Represivo, Antipopular y Antisindical," June 1977, 1; RO 1.1, "Proclama Unitaria de las organizaciones Revolucionarias EGP, FAR, ORPA y PGT al Pueblo de Guatemala," February 1982, 4; GNIB, no numbered archive, *Maya News Informationen*, No. 4, June 1982, clipping, *Excelsior*, 9 February 1982, 127–28, and No. 3, June 1981, clipping, "Opposition," 94; RO 2.5, EGP, *Compañero*, No. 4, no date, 2, 23. See further detail in GNIB PD 1, Campesinos, Alberto Hintermeister, "Modernización agrícola y pobreza rural en Guatemala" in *Polémica* (1985), 28, 26, 32, 31, 29, 37–39, 43.

67 See, for example, GNIB RO 2.5, EGP, Informador Guerrillero 3:34 (1984), 14, 3:36 (1984), 4–7, and 3:32 (1984), 12. GNIB PG 3.3, Lexis-Nexis . . . MLN, UPI, "AID gives $1 million . . . ," 13 December 1984.

68 Méndez, interview, 24 August 2006, Colotenango.

69 GNIB PD 5.2.2, Comité de Unidad Campesina, "Voz del Comité de Unidad Campesina, Periódico Informativo," 1:4 (1979), 7.

70 Méndez, interview, 15 July 2001, Colotenango.

71 Ibid.

72 Ibid.

73 Minor Sinclair, "Patrols in Guatemala's Highlands: A Death Grip in Indigenous Communities," *Christian Century*, 4 May 1994, 466. Xemal is an *aldea* or village in the municipality of Colotenango.

74 Méndez, interview, 24 August 2006, Colotenango.

75 Personal conversations and observations, 15 March 2005 and following (written up as human rights bulletins).

76 GNIB PD 5.2.1, Comité de Unidad Campesina, "De Sol A Sol, Periódico Campesino," No. 18, September 1977, numbered page 7 but it is the sixth.

77 Méndez, interview, 15 July 2001, Colotenango.

78 Ibid. Conversations in Colotenango in 2007 and 2008.

79 Méndez, interview, 24 August 2006, Colotenango. The municipalities of Colotenango, Todos Santos, Huistla, San Juan Atitán, and Santiago Chimaltenango held their congress on the mining companies on 25 July and presented their demands in the capital on 17 August 2006. The national protest in 2007 was held on 9 August; the information here is based on various personal conversations.

80 Méndez, interview, 24 August 2006, Colotenango.

81 Ibid.

Eric Zolov

Between Bohemianism
and a Revolutionary Rebirth
Che Guevara in Mexico

The Mexico Ernesto Guevara de la Serna encountered when he became, as he put it, a "voluntary exile" from Guatemala in September
1954,[1] was a country entering the throes of a rapid capitalist expansion. For many U.S. observers, still conditioned to think of Mexico
in terms of *banditos*, radical politics, and cultural lethargy, this was a
different Mexico, one "waking up after a long siesta."[2] As one travel
writer gushed in an article from 1953, "Politically, the country has
never been more stable. The intense activity all around, the big
building program and flourishing private enterprise point up a new
era coming."[3] Indeed, by the end of the Second World War, as
Stephen Niblo emphasizes, the rules of the game that had governed
Mexico since the early 1930s had fundamentally changed: the socialist coalition mobilized behind the leadership of President Lázaro
Cárdenas (1934–40) had been eclipsed by a new coalition within
the ruling party centered around the figure of President Miguel Alemán (1946–52), avowedly committed to capitalist development and
closer ties with the United States.[4] Under the pressures created by
this reorientation, in 1958–59—precisely at the moment of the unfolding of the Cuban Revolution—the intricate ideological balancing act pursued by the ruling Partido Revolucionario Institucional
(PRI) came close to collapsing. Already by the time of Guevara's
border crossing, fissures indicative of a pending split in the "revolutionary family" coalition were in fact present, despite glowing assertions of political stability from tourists and investors. It was an
interesting time to be in Mexico for a would-be revolutionary, or so
one would expect.

Although initially regarded by Guevara as but a way station for his future travels to Europe and beyond, Mexico eventually became the context in which Guevara's revolutionary consciousness crystallized and his continental meanderings took on concrete purpose: to join the revolutionary struggle in Cuba. Yet prior to his encounter with Fidel Castro in Mexico City in July 1955, Guevara seemed more concerned with escape from the trappings of married life with his new wife, the Peruvian Hilda Gadea, and the sudden advent of fatherhood, both of which he appeared to have stumbled into somewhat haphazardly, than with any engagement with Mexican left-wing politics per se. As Jorge Castañeda writes in his biography of Guevara, he was "at that time essentially a tramp, a wandering photographer, an underpaid medical researcher, a permanent exile, and an insignificant husband—a weekend adventurer."[5] Indeed, Guevara's first year in Mexico—the country that for him stood at the end of the "American continent"[6]—was largely consumed with leisure travel and idle contemplation, interspersed with the halfhearted pursuit of a medical career. Alternately bored and depleted by the challenges of domesticity, on the one hand, and the struggle to make ends meet, on the other, in his writings Guevara seemed largely oblivious to the caldron of political activity in Mexico that, by the mid-1950s, pointed to a widening schism in the nation's body politic centered around the future direction of the nation's own revolutionary project.

Coincidentally though not insignificantly, Guevara's travels directly overlapped with those of two other great bohemians of the era —Jack Kerouac and Allen Ginsberg—who likewise viewed Mexico, in Kerouac's later immortalized phrasing, as "the end of America."[7] The fact that Mexico became an unbeknownst meeting ground for these two very different (yet parallel) sets of middle-class wanderers spoke to Mexico's place in the hemispheric imaginary: as a crossroads of the Americas, where Latin America ended (or began) and the Anglo, yanqui America loomed menacingly (or enticingly). Kerouac's On the Road (published in 1957) soon provided a literary roadmap that located Mexico along the axis of countercultural self-discovery and thus helped steer succeeding generations of U.S. youth south of the border. For Mexican youth, in contrast, pride in the fact that Mexico had served as the final staging ground for the Cuban revolutionary movement and was the place where the mythic duo of "Fidel and Che" joined forces helped forge a special connection with Guevara as a revolutionary icon, one whose feats seemed equally heroic—if not more so—and held greater resonance than the feats of Mexico's earlier, long-buried revolutionary heroes.

In an era in which, for Mexico's urban student population especially, figures such as "Pancho" Villa and Emiliano Zapata had become little more than static signifiers of an official nationalism grown increasingly authoritarian, Guevara quickly became lionized by the Mexican Left as a relevant, modern revolutionary hero. The Right repudiated him with equal vehemence as a foreign interloper into the nation's revolutionary pantheon. Conservatives rightly feared the ideological pull of Guevara's revolutionary spirit on a generation of youth restless for dramatic social and political change. In the context of the student movement of 1968, however, Mexican youth came to reembrace the country's own revolutionary figures, in particular Zapata, as a means for contesting the ruling party (PRI) on its own terms, while upholding the image of a now martyred Che as a defender against U.S. imperialism more generally. The legacy of this dual embrace still manifests in the present, with numerous Leftist movements in Mexico claiming Zapata as the standard-bearer of a *nationalist* resistance to the impact of economic neoliberalism and state repression, while Che lives on as a symbol of *internationalist* solidarity with revolutionary, progressive movements everywhere.

Miguel Alemán's Counterrevolution

The consolidation of a new political economy in Mexico after the Second World War gave clearer guarantees to domestic and foreign (especially U.S.) capital. Politically, this conservative realignment was rendered possible by the monopolization of the electoral process by the PRI and the accompanying deification of the position of the presidency. The Mexican historian Daniel Cosio Villegas later described the country's political system as one headed by a "president who is actually a king"; politics was "not made at the public plaza, at the parliament or by newspapers, at sensational debates or controversies," Cosio Villegas lamented, but rather via "courtier intrigue."[8] Guevara himself wryly marveled in his journal at the "complete absence of checks" in acquiring registry for participation in local elections. "You just show up, give a name and address, and that's it. That's what the elections will be like."[9]

The onset of the Cold War, moreover, introduced the rhetoric of anticommunism as an additional organizing principle of political discourse. On the one hand, the official dissemination of anticommunist sentiment helped ensure an adequate flow of U.S. capital investment and diplomatic support for the *alemanista* faction within the PRI. On the other, anticommunism served as domestic cover for the repression and marginalization from political decision making of the left-wing forces associated with the ex-president Cárdenas, alongside other vocal critics of the PRI's increasing authoritarianism.[10] As Elisa Servín writes: "As part of this process, between 1947 and 1948 the trend begun during the previous regime [Ávila Camacho] was consolidated, resulting in the definitive exclusion of the official Left in those areas in which the Left had been politically active: Congress, the official party [PRI], and the unions. Far from the conciliatory approach taken by Ávila Camacho [1940–46], the confrontation with the Left was now fully legitimized through the new governmental discourse of anticommunism."[11] By combining pro-business policies with an assault on independent union organizing and a generalized attack on left-wing political actors, Alemán thus implemented what Niblo has termed a "counterrevolution" against the political forces identified with *cardenismo*.[12]

"The Mexican Revolution is dead—and has been for a while, without us realizing," Guevara commented after observing the rote genuflection of workers during a May Day march in the capital in 1955, nearly a year after his arrival. "The parade of organized workers looks like a funeral procession," he summarized dryly.[13] Whether or not the Mexican Revolution had indeed "died" was in fact the central question debated by the country's left-wing intelligentsia at the time, a discussion later invigorated by the triumph in 1959 of the Cuban Revolution and the ensuing radicalism of Castro's revolutionary project. By the early 1960s this debate had formed the core of an impassioned "New Left" movement led by student groups and a younger generation of intellectuals determined to push the Mexican Revolution back to its founding principles of land redistribution, social welfare, and economic nationalism.[14]

For Mexico's expanding middle-class population, who largely benefited from the stability ushered in by the presidentialist system and a political economy that subsidized urban growth at the expense of the peasantry, this counterrevolution spurred the dynamic growth that became known internationally as the "Mexican Miracle." In turn, the new political economy introduced new opportunities for upward social mobility and pride of place, as thousands of tourists and investors flocked to Mexico during the 1950s and 1960s to take advantage of the country's vaunted progress.[15] In exchange for relative political stability and upward economic mobility, however, the middle classes sacrificed not only democratic checks and balances— virtually nonexistent under the monopoly control of the ruling party—but also the transparency of government authority itself, epitomized by widespread corruption and a political culture of nepotism. Less obvious was a deepening web of domestic spying aimed at the containment of domestic critics of the regime.

The epicenter of this domestic surveillance was the Departamento Federal de Seguridad (DFS), Mexico's counterpart to the FBI.[16] As Sergio Aguayo notes, the range of political activities that came under the purview of the DFS was expansive and, given the limited real threats to the regime, agents learned to justify their role by "exaggerating the importance and danger" of political opposition.[17] "The subjects of this vigilance were leftists, unionized workers (oil workers, railway workers), some foreigners, critical journalists, *políticos* who upset those in power, and members of the PRI who decided to join the opposition in pursuit of their own political self-interest," writes Aguayo.[18] During the 1950s this surveillance included keeping tabs on U.S. communists and communist sympathizers fleeing the political repression of McCarthyism in the United States. And in the summer of 1955, either in collaboration with or under pressure from the Cuban dictator Fulgencio Batista, the DFS successfully disrupted Castro's revolutionary training, capturing Guevara, among others, and subsequently subjecting the men to physical and psychological torture.[19]

Since the 1920s Mexico had developed a favorable reputation as a safe haven for political exiles, a reputation nurtured by the pro-republican stance of President Cárdenas during the Spanish Civil War. During the 1950s political exiles from all over Latin America (including Guatemala) also found refuge in Mexico, especially in the capital. For those escaping political witch hunts in the United States, Mexico similarly beckoned. But in the context of the Cold

War, concern with getting "thirty-threed out of the country,"[20] a reference to the Mexican constitutional Article 33 proscribing political activity by foreigners, kept American expatriates and other exiles in line. The U.S. embassy, working closely with the DFS, was also proactive. "Well, there were informers all over the place," one American living in Mexico recalled. "You could pick up $10 or $25 by giving somebody's name to the Embassy. . . . That's how they got these huge lists of . . . people who really had nothing to do with anything, but found themselves blacklisted and in trouble."[21] In short, by the time Guevara crossed over from Guatemala, the political climate in Mexico had changed dramatically. Once regarded as an incubator of vanguard revolutionary ideas and a bulwark against further U.S. expansionism, Mexico had become a vital outlet for U.S. capital and a reliable ally in the global Cold War then underway.

The Mobilization of Mexico's "Old Left"

To grasp the shifting politics in Mexico during Guevara's stay, we need to go back two years to the presidential elections of 1952 when, for the first time since 1940, the ruling party faced a significant political challenge to its authority from a coalition on the Left, led by the ex-general Henrique Guzmán. Positioning themselves as inheritors of the *cardenista* mandate, the *henriquistas* freely appropriated the image of Cárdenas in their political propaganda while Guzmán "assured followers that the ex-president supported Henríquez's candidacy," a position Cárdenas himself did little to contradict.[22] While the elder Cárdenas remained officially neutral during the campaign, his son, Cuaúhtemoc, publicly supported Guzmán. The government-dominated press, in turn, published numerous accusations by the elder Cárdenas's detractors denouncing his supposed intervention into politics in support of a Guzmán candidacy. In any event, Guzmán's supporters overwhelmingly identified with Cárdenas's policies, and the campaign used that identification to bolster its credibility.[23] As the outsider populist, Guzmán not only represented the promise of a return to the Cárdenas era and thus to "the recuperation of worker and peasant conquests";[24] he also garnered support across the political spectrum (including among disaffected conservatives) as a credible "no vote" to the official PRI party designate, Adolfo Ruiz Cortines.[25]

Nostalgia for the populism of the former president Cárdenas loomed large and was used by another charismatic figure who ran in the elections of 1952, Vicente Lombardo Toledano. Toledano, who flirted with joining forces with Guzmán before ultimately deciding to make an attempt on his own, ran as the presidential candidate for the Partido Popular (PP), an agglomeration of labor, peasants, intellectuals, and student groups hostile to the new direction of the ruling party. Toledano could also claim a close affiliation with Lázaro Cárdenas, as he was central to the creation of the official labor movement (Confederation of Mexican Workers, CTM) during the Cárdenas era and had led the CTM until he was marginalized from power during the conservative reorientation of the PRI after the Second World War. As a result of losing his stature in the PRI, Toledano formed the PP in 1948 and in 1949 helped found and became the leader of a left-wing continental trade movement, the Confederation of Latin American Workers (CTAL). Toledano used both platforms to project himself as the person best positioned to recapture the socialist mandate formerly advocated by the PRI under Cárdenas.

The defeat of the opposition and the triumph of the official candidate, Ruiz Cortines, was a foregone conclusion in the elections, given the strength of the PRI's political machinery. Yet following the elections and peaking in the period during which Guevara sojourned in Mexico, Toledano constituted for many on the Left the emblematic heroic personality capable of reorienting Mexico toward the realization of the nation's revolutionary ideals. Under Toledano's leadership, the PP not only embraced those economically impacted by the new conservatism; it also resonated with intellectuals and students disaffected by the coziness between the PRI and the United States in the Cold War and the vitriolic anticommunism of the Alemán and Ruiz Cortines administrations. Indeed, a U.S. State Department document from the time of Guevara's arrest in Mexico asserted that he belonged to the PP and had found work in Mexico through Toledano connections, a series of associations that certainly would have made sense given Toledano's prominence in left-wing politics at the time. But the State Department vastly overestimated Guevara's engagement with the Mexican political scene, while also misjudging his political inclinations: prior to connecting with Castro, Guevara was likely oblivious to the politics of the PP, disdainful of Toledano's populism, and simply too caught up with the vicissitudes of daily life to pay much attention to the transformations taking place in Mexico's political landscape.[26]

If Toledano was an active presence in the nation's politicized landscape, the former president Cárdenas served as the silent consciousness of the country's revolutionary ideals. Reviled by the Right and lionized by the Left, Cárdenas was a lightning rod for political attack. Interpreting the political motives behind his every gesture and utterance became a parlor game for political observers and the media, earning him the nickname "Sphinx of Jiquilpan" (a reference to the town of his birth in Michoacán). Yet the overthrow of the Guatemalan president Jacobo Arbenz in 1954 marked the beginning of the return of Cárdenas to prominence in the domestic and international political scene. From the start of the democratic reform process in Guatemala, Cárdenas had defended the Guatemalan revolution, in a private letter calling the Guatemalan president Juan José Arévalo (1944–50) an "example for the oppressed nations."[27] When Arévalo's successor, Arbenz, came under assault in the Organization of American States (OAS) and faced the threat of an imminent invasion by U.S.-directed forces, Cárdenas underscored to Guatemala's foreign minister his "personal friendship and sympathy" for the country's revolutionary goals and his defense of the besieged nation's sovereignty:[28] "In this difficult hour for your nation, which sees its sovereignty threatened, one must hope that the intrigue being spread under the pretext of fighting international communism must not succeed, and what must be established are the principles of continental solidarity and feelings of patriotism that all citizens of our America must express in cases such as that presented by the Republic of Guatemala."[29] While offering a rhetorical defense of Guatemala's sovereignty in the OAS, President Ruiz Cortines in fact "felt a relief" at the fall of the Arbenz government.[30] "In the end," writes Jürgen Buchenau, "only the necessity of demonstrating a certain degree of independence from the policies of the United States to appease the political faction associated with Cárdenas—by casting a 'no' vote in favor of Guatemala at the Caracas Conference—had distanced the regime from a complete approval of the U.S. anticommunist campaign."[31] Within Mexico the overthrow of Arbenz reverberated throughout the political establishment and laid the basis for a continued polarization of politics along the Cárdenas-Alemán axis, which shortly found expression in popular mobilization and an intensification of anti-U.S. (and, more obliquely, anti-P RI) rhetoric.

For Guevara the overthrow of Arbenz proved decisive on at least two accounts. For one, it was the factor that prematurely forced him to cross the border into Mexico, since it is likely he would have stayed longer in Guatemala and, therefore, never have met Castro in Mexico as he eventually did. Second, it was an event that made explicit for him the connection between U.S. imperialism and reactionary politics in the region. Although it would be many years before historians unearthed the elaborate covert operation (Operation Zapata) that the CIA concocted to overthrow Arbenz, the assumption that the United Fruit Company and other U.S. interests were behind the revolt against Arbenz was widespread on the Left, and certainly more so from the ground-level view in Guatemala. "The Yankees have finally dropped the good-guy mask that Roosevelt gave them and are now committing outrages in these parts,"[32] Guevara wrote in his journal days before Arbenz unexpectedly resigned fearing the threat of a full-scale U.S. invasion of his country. In a bitter, unpublished essay written in late 1954 from Mexico and titled "The Dilemma of Guatemala," Guevara saw Arbenz's overthrow as "another dream of the Americas to be destroyed."[33] For the Mexican press, however, Guatemala's mistaken course had been corrected; communists alone paid the price. A political cartoon by the popular caricaturist Rafael Freyre that originally appeared in Excélsior in the days following the overthrow of Arbenz aptly captured this perspective. Under the caption "Libertad y paz," a Ladina woman, seated and labeled "Guatemala," has her blindfold removed by a dashing mestizo man, standing behind her and labeled "Castillo Armas" (leader of the coup that overthrew Arbenz), to reveal the nation's "new era"—that of "liberty and peace." The editorial cartoon was one of various reproduced later that year in a collected volume featuring the seven leading caricaturists of the day. Titled Siete dibujantes con una idea, the collection focused on a common "idea," namely, that of anticommunism. The volume's editor, Víctor Velarde, celebrated Freyre along with his cohort as a "truth soldier . . . [doing] combat against the monstrous lies of tyrants, destroying with a pen stroke fetishes and false symbols."[34] Armas would in fact soon usher in a bloody backlash against the Arbenz

1. Newly imposed President Castillo Armas "unmasks"
Guatemala after ousting Jacobo Arbenz. Rafael Freyre,
"Libertad y paz," *Excélsior*, 15 July 1954; republished in Víctor
Velarde, *Siete dibujantes con una idea* (Mexico City: Libros y
Revistas, 1954).

reformist movement, a response little noted in the mainstream media, which closely kowtowed to the official (pro-U.S.) line.

But outside of conservative discourse, the impact of the overthrow of Arbenz was profound in Mexico and beyond. Despite the
disavowal of any role in the army rebellion that ousted Arbenz, the
presumption (ultimately proven correct) of direct U.S. involvement
was widely invoked by the Left to question the sincerity of the
decades-old "Good Neighbor" pledge of nonintervention in Latin
America's domestic affairs. Defense of Guatemala's sovereignty and

the socialist goals of the Arbenz regime were now used to rekindle a discourse of anti-imperialism that had been put aside during the era of the Popular Front.[35] In an action meant to highlight the symbolic death of the Good Neighbor, Cuauhtémoc Cárdenas, accompanied by students of the recently formed group Consejo Nacional Estudiantil de Solidaridad con el Pueblo de Guatemala (National Student Council in Solidarity with the People of Guatemala) laid a wreath in front of the U.S. embassy in Mexico City, "in memory of the Good Neighbor Policy."[36] Within moments, police swept in to confiscate the wreath and dissolve the protesters. It was one of many such protests by student groups and prominent intellectuals and artists in Mexico, acts repeated elsewhere in the hemisphere.

United States Policy toward Mexico

The Eisenhower administration, on the other hand, saw the overthrow of Arbenz as a Guatemalan success story. "We in the United States have watched the people of Guatemala record an episode in their history deeply significant to all peoples," Vice President Richard Nixon remarked the following autumn during a dinner to honor Castillo Armas, the handpicked leader of the CIA-led coup against Arbenz. Maintaining a facade of U.S. nonintervention in Guatemalan internal affairs, Nixon hailed "the Guatemalan people [who] revolted against Communist rule, which in collapsing, bore graphic witness to its inherent shallowness, falsity and corruption."[37] The reception for Castillo Armas during his trip to the United States was ostentatious in its celebration of the military leader's alleged Cold War triumph over communism: "He received a twenty-one gun salute in Washington, a ticker-tape parade in New York City, and honorary degrees from Fordham and Columbia universities,"[38] writes the historian Richard Immerman. Indeed, U.S. policy toward Latin America in the early 1950s was premised on the assumption that the Good Neighbor sentiment had carried over from the Second World War alliance. Any short-term crisis generated by the radical reformist regime of Arbenz in Guatemala had seemingly been "resolved" with his overthrow, at least from the U.S. perspective. Secure in the belief that Latin Americans widely supported United States leadership in the region and beyond, the Eisenhower administration implemented a policy of the "Cheap Backyard," a strategic approach of low-cost intervention coupled with a decentralized policing of communist inroads.[39]

A little more than six months after the coup against Arbenz, Nixon arrived in Mexico City on the second leg of his first goodwill tour of Latin America. Guevara, whose interest in the Mexican political scene could aptly be described as lackadaisical, had nothing explicit to say about the visit. Still, Nixon's arrival did not pass completely unnoticed. In a letter to his father on the second day of Nixon's tour, Guevara wrote dejectedly, if not without a considerable dose of hyperbole: "Mexico is entirely given over to the Yankees. . . . There is no independent industry, much less any free trade."[40] Since arriving Guevara had stayed economically afloat through a series of odd jobs, including working at a book fair and, especially, playing his hand as a wandering portrait photographer in Mexico City's numerous parks. Around the time of Nixon's visit he had begun work as a freelance photographer for the Argentine news agency Agencia Latina de Noticias, a position that he noted was "a nicer job, though just as insecure."[41] Yet despite Guevara's evident photographic abilities and the media attention surrounding Nixon's visit, he did not seek to document the vice president's arrival nor the accompanying political attacks launched against the United States by the Left. In fact, around the time of Nixon's visit Guevara noted in his journal, "I haven't met anyone interesting these days, and it seems that I never will if I keep this life up."[42] Seemingly relieved to avoid any engagement with the local political scene, shortly after Nixon's trip Guevara found himself busily preparing for the pending Pan-American Games, which took place in Mexico City at the beginning of March, a job that proved "exhausting in every sense of the word."[43]

Historians have likewise overlooked Nixon's visit, although the apparent success of his trip underscored for the U.S. State Department the continued utility of "Good Neighbor diplomacy" in the aftermath of Guatemala.[44] Indeed, one of the tour's central goals was to sound out Latin American sentiment toward the United States, while demonstrating U.S. commitment to the hemisphere despite Cold War distractions in Europe and Asia. This balancing act came with challenges. Nixon's visit occurred in the context of a shift in U.S. policy toward Latin America encompassed by the Eisenhower policy of "trade, not aid" and captured by the semantic shift that the

United States desired to be a "Good Partner" in business with Latin America—there would be no Marshall Plan for the region, despite expectations in various quarters that Latin American support for the Allied cause during the Second World War would be appropriately compensated.[45]

Mexico's conservative press quickly baptized the notion of a new "partnership" rooted in capitalist investment and trade as the "Good Business Partner policy" (política del Buen Socio) and effusively embraced it as a signal of Mexico's own political and economic maturity.[46] A caricature by Arias Bernal, who along with Freyre was one of the era's most important political caricaturists and an ardent anticommunist, graphically depicted the new era: "Confianza" ("Trust"). Here Bernal shows the positive effect of the PRI's control over unionized labor—now, full of "workers without illegal strikes" and "without arbitrary or demagogic actions"—which had allowed a partition of the curtain (in the metaphor of the cartoon) to "North American investors."[47] Bernal's caption plays on the word confianza, which in Spanish breaks down as con and fianza, literally, "with (financial) guarantee." Thus a new era of business partnership is premised on the "guarantee" of access to U.S. capital, which in turn solidifies a relationship of Good Neighborly trust.

In the end both sides regarded the vice president's trip, which included a visit to the Basilica of the Virgin of Guadalupe (Mexico's most famous shrine), as a diplomatic triumph. The public animosity that infamously confronted Nixon on his follow-up tour of Latin America three years later was almost completely absent, as evidenced during a wreath-laying ceremony at Mexico's Monument of Independence when, "breaking restrictions of protocol," the vice president "crossed the police barricades and approached the crowd, which immediately surrounded him."[48] Two days later, a lead editorial in the newspaper El Universal lauded Nixon as a "young champion of anticommunist liberalism."[49]

Nixon returned to the United States with a declaration that the region was politically and economically sound, set to embark on a "new era" of peace and prosperity.[50] Oblivious to a mounting backlash against U.S. economic and diplomatic policies, earlier on this same goodwill trip Nixon had publicly embraced the dictatorial strongmen Batista of Cuba, whom he compared with Abraham Lincoln, and Rafael Trujillo of the Dominican Republic, whom he

2. Arias Bernal, "Confianza" and "Pase Usted," *Excélsior*, 14 February 1955.

praised for his efficiency, thus creating a set of images that would come to haunt the United States in succeeding years.[51] As for the twenty-year-old Good Neighbor alliance that sustained U.S. relations with the region, which the trip had meant to "reaffirm and strengthen,"[52] Nixon boasted that the association was indeed strong. "These countries are our friends. . . . We must not take good friends for granted. We have not and will not in the future."[53] The impression was not Nixon's alone. The Mexican mainstream press shared it, as reflected in an editorial published in the newspaper Excélsior: "What is important for both nations is to support fundamental common ideals, such as desire for liberty and belief in God, as Mr. Nixon stated. . . . Being established on such comprehension and mutual respect is an authentic and long-lasting friendship between Mexico and the United States."[54]

Nixon's trip and subsequent diplomatic exchanges formed part of a broader strategy of restoring confidence in U.S. intentions toward Mexico, thus paving the way for the accomplishment of U.S. objectives, namely, the containment of Mexican left-wing nationalism and the transformation of the country into a reliable investment and strategic partner in the Cold War. Paradoxically, however, as Mexico's ruling class became more conservative—and thereby more reliable as a strategic ally—the PRI also became more outwardly nationalistic, which can be explained as a direct reflection of the party's strategy of channeling left-wing mobilization to demobilize and contain opposition politics. This strategy in turn generated various impediments to the full realization of U.S. goals—economic, diplomatic, and military—in the country and regionally. This held particularly true in the wake of the Cuban Revolution when, as Arthur Schmidt argues, the "nationalist 'solution' " to the governing crisis provoked by the Cuban Revolution "created a 'formula' of expanded government, authoritarian politics, and debt-reliant industrialization."[55] Not until the mid-1960s, once the initial impact of the Cuban Revolution had passed, would State Department officials and the U.S. media alike grasp a basic paradox underlying the logic of Mexican politics: officially sanctioned nationalism was a unifying and stabilizing force that needed to be tolerated and even encouraged.[56] In the 1950s, however, nationalism emanating from the ruling party appeared petty and antagonistic to U.S. interests.

Moreover, despite Nixon's earlier sanguine remarks about the continuation of Good Neighbor politics, a very different set of discourses concerning U.S.-Latin American relations and the Cold War was in fact transpiring. This was reflected in the Asamblea Nacional por la Paz y la Seguridad (National Assembly for Peace and Security), a three-day gathering at the end of March 1955 of "elementos izquierdistas" (leftist elements)[57] held in Mexico City. The conference was directly linked to the international World Peace Conference movement, itself an outgrowth of the World Peace Council, a broad communist front movement that promoted humanitarian ideals while presenting the USSR as the champion of world peace.[58] Guevara's absence from the conference—and the complete lack of mention of these events anywhere in his writings—seems remarkable, especially given that many of Mexico's most prominent leftist intellectuals attended.[59]

For Mexico's conservative press, the conference was nothing short of a showcase for "homegrown reds" (criollos rojos) whose atavistic revolutionary ideology represented an immature Mexican past, while the participants' celebratory evocation of the Soviet Union readily branded them as "outside" the Mexican (and thus Pan-American) imaginary.[60] Still, the conference provided an opportunity for disaffected leftists and especially followers of Toledano to take pride in numbers and assert that history, indeed, was on their side. Over the next year several additional regional conferences linked to the World Peace Council were held in the Mexican states of Sonora, Nayarit, and "other provincial cities of Mexico."[61] In a noteworthy response to one of these meetings, the Bishop of Nayarit denounced the conference in a pastoral letter to be read in every church throughout the diocese. Exhorting Catholics in the state "not to listen to the voice of these rojillos criollos," the bishop excoriated the conference for its communist links, calling the attendees "traitors to Mexico."[62] The groundwork for a vitriolic politics with no room for compromise that would explode during the 1960s was becoming increasingly evident.

The Twin Faces of Bohemianism

Oddly Guevara's time in Mexico was spent completely disengaged from the radicalization of politics underway. Whereas elsewhere during his travels in Latin America he sought out and was introduced to political luminaries such as the Dominican Republic's Juan Bosch and Venezuela's Rómulo Betancourt, about whom he wrote extensively in his journal, in Mexico Guevara neither met with nor reflected on any of the significant intellectual or political figures of the time. He did not seek an interview with Lázaro Cárdenas (or his son, Cuauhtémoc, who was close in age to Guevara), Toledano, or any number of prominent intellectuals who would surely have been accessible to him. At one point in his journal he noted an attempt to meet "the Gonzales [sic] Casanova couple,"[63] presumably a reference to Pablo González Casanova (part of the younger generation of public intellectuals and a rising sociologist at the national university, UNAM), but his interest appears halfhearted and no follow-up seems to have occurred. Guevara must have had some interaction with students at the UNAM, where he briefly audited classes taught by the economist Jesús Silva Herzog (who helped to engineer the oil expropriation of 1938), but any outward involvement with university life occurred without great passion.[64] Although he had "the unmistakable appearance of a university student on vacation,"[65] as his Argentine friend Ricardo Rojo later noted, he had limited interest or ability to establish relationships with Mexican youth. "I haven't made any really worthwhile friendship, either intellectual or sexual,"[66] he wrote in his diary in late 1954, despite having been in the country for several months.

Instead of mapping out Mexico's political factions—as they would for other countries through which Guevara passed—Guevara's early letters and journal writings from Mexico focus on his lack of steady employment, the melodrama in his relationship with Gadea, and his on-again, off-again attempts to engage in the practice of medicine. Castañeda, in his biography of Guevara, similarly observed how "the skillful, affectionate descriptions [Guevara] devoted to the rest of Latin America are missing in the case of Mexico— a country that has enthralled far less sophisticated travelers than Che, and that should have fascinated him much more than the other stops in his Latin American wanderings." In seeking an answer to this apparent riddle, Castañeda asks, "Was this curious omission a sign of his ongoing Mexican depression, or of his concentration on the struggle ahead?"[67] Guevara's journal throughout the period leading up to his meeting with Castro is scattered with commentary reflective of a persistent, and perhaps guilt-ridden, ennui. Thus he notes "days of feverish inefficiency,"[68] "days [that] have passed blankly,"[69] and simply, "there is nothing new to report."[70]

In fact, Guevara passed the time with activities that many other foreign tourists might similarly take part in while in Mexico. For instance, he took time to visit the "ruins of Teotihuacán, or something like that,"[71] where he noted "huge pyramids without artistic value, and others that are of value,"[72] to view the famed murals of the "great quartet," as he put it ("I was especially keen on Siqueiros, but they all seemed very fine"[73]), and tried, without success and on more than one occasion, to reach the summit of Mexico's famed snowcapped volcano, Popocatepetl, "El Popo" ("It is wonderful and I would like to do it again fairly often"[74]), here continuing a tradition of attempted foreigner conquest of the volcano that extended at least to the time of the Porfiriato (1880–1910).[75] More fundamentally, he regarded Mexico as a launching pad for his "great leap to Europe and, if possible, China,"[76] rather than as some final training ground of his revolutionary experience. By the time he reached Mexico he appeared practically fed up with politics, noting in a letter to his mother that his "objective is Europe, where I intend to go come what may."[77]

Guevara's meanderings while in Mexico must be understood not simply in terms of the pleasure he clearly experienced in leisure travel but also more fundamentally in terms of his natural bohemianism and his struggle for self-discipline. "[I] don't wash my clothes much and I still don't have enough money for a laundry,"[78] he wrote at one point, noting that between the whims of his landlady and his lack of finances, "some of my paunch has been disappearing."[79] A year after his arrival in Mexico he nonchalantly mentions in a letter to his mother his marriage to Gadea, the Peruvian activist he had met while in Guatemala, and the pending birth of their child. From the start, his relationship with Gadea was full of drama (owing in large part to Guevara's philandering and indecisiveness) and their reunion in Mexico, following the coup against Arbenz, continued to be rocky. "As always, Hilda got angry because I didn't want to go with her to a party,"[80] Guevara remarked in his journal. Not long after and following a melodramatic breakup, he wrote: "I've started to fancy a girl who's a chemist: she's not very intelligent and doesn't know a lot, but she has a very appealing freshness and fantastic eyes."[81]

Restless, bored with the potential trappings of domesticity, and in an increasingly untenable living arrangement, he writes: "I have to get out of the house and don't know where to go. . . . I'm practically living on air in every sense."[82] He anticipated a final paycheck from the Agencia Latina de Noticias and once it arrived he was ready simply "to pay off some debts, travel around Mexico and then clear the hell out."[83] Tellingly, in a letter to his mother shortly before his encounter with Castro, Guevara writes: "I think [the communists] deserve respect, and sooner or later I will join the Party myself. What most prevents me from doing it right now is that I have a huge desire to travel in Europe, and I would not be able to do that if I was subject to rigid discipline."[84]

Mexico, in short, provided Guevara with the freedom to roam—just as it did for a parallel set of foreign travelers who entered the country from the opposite border in the north. Political stability, a growing infrastructure oriented toward tourism, and a favorable exchange rate (the peso was devalued in 1953) proved a boon for foreign visitors, and what began as a trickle in the years right after the Second World War had become a steady flow of tourism by the 1950s.[85] Students and would-be students also crossed the border, many under the pretext of a GI bill that generously funded higher education for returning veterans from the Second World War. One of the central destinations for these students was Mexico City College (MCC), which offered undergraduate degrees for American youth. The college attracted a range of students, some of whom (such as James Wilkie) went on to become noted Mexican scholars.[86] Among the MCC's most famous students (despite their infrequent classroom attendance) were the Beat writers Allen Ginsberg and Jack Kerouac. In an era in which Protestant morality and expectations of upward social mobility, on the one hand, and a rigid, racial divide, on the other, defined life in the United States, Mexico seemingly offered an "other world": exotic, slightly dangerous, and full of adventure. "Danger and the possibility of death were in the air at all times," writes Richard Wilkie, James Wilkie's brother, in a memoir of the period, adding somewhat ominously: "A number of my friends and acquaintances died or nearly died in Mexico at that time."[87]

This was an era in which Mexico City was rapidly becoming a vibrant metropolis, and many of these youth, imbibed with the

Beats' sensibility of the avant-garde, embraced the vibrant art, music, and cultural scenes the capital had to offer. "For many of the intellectually oriented veterans and students at MCC," Wilkie reflects, "this was potentially the new Paris where ideas, art, literature, and revolution could be discussed in cafes, taverns, and at numerous and risqué parties where inexpensive liquor and 'Acapulco gold' could be found."[88] The recently finished Pan-American Highway featured as a central component of this bohemianism, for it linked the possibility of crossing the border with that particularly American pursuit of freedom via the automobile. Hence the Wilkie brothers unsurprisingly traveled to—and throughout—Mexico by car, as do the characters in Kerouac's On the Road.

In short, Mexico had quickly become not only a fabled destination for the new bohemians but also a place where a new sensibility was to be forged. The coincidence of close proximity between these U.S. adventurers and the young bohemian from Argentina is uncanny for, although unaware of one another, two blocks from where the Wilkies rented a room, "Che Guevara was living with his Peruvian-born wife. . . . Their apartment was at 40 Calle Napoles . . . near the corner of the block with Calle Hamburgo in the Zona Rosa."[89] As it turns out, Kerouac also lived in the same neighborhood.

Of all the Beats, Kerouac had the most experience living and traveling in Mexico, and, despite his "ambivalent feeling" about the country, as one critic has written,[90] his immersion was significant. He first arrived in 1950, at the height of President Alemán's conservative reorientation, and would enter and leave the country on several occasions over the next six years. In the midst of Mexico City's new capitalist boom, Kerouac sought out the capital's underside, "sewage-strewn spaces, grime, social filth,"[91] and thus in his own way sought, like Guevara, to commune with the Other. Each empathized, via the transcendence of his own class and ethnic and national identity, with those viewed as the racial and social underdogs. Jorge García-Robles seeks to push the comparison still further, creating a vivid reconstruction of how the two bohemians may have indeed conceivably crossed paths: "Walking along the street, San Juan de Letrán, Jack [Kerouac] heard the sounds of cha cha cha that streamed out of the last bars, where it was played without end. It was raining and Jack ran toward the Roma neighborhood. He arrived at Cuahutemoc [sic] Avenue, three blocks away from Napoles

Street, number 40, where at that same moment another amazing personality, surely auto-destructive and still unknown, E[rnesto] C[he] G[uevara], lived with his wife, who just like Jack was devoured by an undesireable reality—it was the street right in front of the Mexican Cinema."[92] Still, Kerouac's experiences in Mexico were circumscribed by language and cultural codes, barriers that Guevara would have had little difficulty navigating. As Rachel Adams suggests in writing about the Beats in Mexico, "While passage into Mexico could appear to be one more version of lighting out for the territory, these travelers escape into another national space governed by laws and conventions of its own. Instead of uninhibited freedom, their arrival on the other side of the border requires them to negotiate language barriers, the dynamics of citizenship, and cultural difference. Instead of a conflict between wilderness and civilization, they find competing versions of modernity."[93]

No wonder Mexico had profoundly different meanings for these two sets of parallel travelers. For Guevara, who could assimilate the country's cultural and political logic into a framework of Latin American experience, Mexico eventually became a training ground in which he finally came to terms with his struggle with indiscipline. In contrast, for Kerouac (and others) Mexico remained a screen on which to project and act out fantasies of an escape from the staid, rigid modernity of the "American way of life." Mexico remained fixed in the imaginary of the Beat writers and countercultural tourists who followed in their wake as an "Other"—inscrutable, exotic, transgressive. Thus, with Guevara, one can sense in his multiple attempts to climb Popocatépetl a foreshadowing of the rigid discipline he would impose on himself, and later on others, in seeking to launch a continental-wide revolution from Bolivia. By contrast, in describing his effort to ascend the pyramids at Teotihuacán, Kerouac writes: "When we arrived at the summit of the pyramid, I lit a marijuana cigarette, so that we could all get in touch with our feelings for the place."[94]

Finding Discipline: Che Discovers His Calling

Guevara's meeting with Castro in July 1955 changed everything. "He is a young, intelligent guy," he notes in his diary about Castro, "very sure of himself and extraordinarily audacious; I think we hit it off

3. In a Mexico City park, November 1956 (rear, left to right) Jack
Kerouac, Allen Ginsberg, Peter Orlovsky; (front, left to right): Gregory
Corso and Orlovsky's brother Lafcadio. Copyright Allen Ginsberg
Estate. Used with permission.

well."[95] Guevara, who associated more with the hodgepodge Latin American exile community than with Mexicans, had met Castro through the latter's younger brother, Raúl, with whom Guevara had socialized on several occasions. Although not entirely random, given the relatively close-knit interchanges among the exile community, the meeting was certainly fortuitous, for it provided Guevara with the sense of mission and purpose that he had clearly been seeking. Equally important, through Castro Guevara discovered the method by which he would impose the self-discipline he had earlier bemoaned as lacking. It is the discipline of revolutionary preparedness but, more fundamentally, a repudiation of the bohemian expression of antidiscipline that he had embraced up to that point. In a letter sent to his mother after joining forces with Castro and several months before he embarked on the overloaded yacht, the *Granma*, leading to Cuba and his revolutionary struggle, he insisted adamantly and yet somewhat defensively: "I must tell you that I have done a lot to wipe him out—I mean, not exactly that unfamiliar spineless type, but the other bohemian type, unconcerned about his neighbour and imbued with a sense of self-sufficiency deriving from an awareness (mistaken or not) of my own strength."[96] Affirming his new identity as one with a sense of missionary purpose, he signs this letter for the first time simply, "el Che."[97]

In the weeks and months that followed, "Che" dedicated himself wholeheartedly to the Cuban revolutionary cause. Determined to reach the summit of El Popo, he now set out each weekend to climb the volcano, finally accomplishing the feat symbolically on Columbus Day, in Latin America known as Día de la Raza (Day of the Race).[98] A couple of weeks later, Che was introduced via Raúl Castro to a young Soviet diplomat, Nikolai Leonov—like Guevara, he was only twenty-seven at the time—who served as an attaché at the Soviet embassy and was an acquaintance of Raúl's. In a fateful exchange, Leonov gave Guevara his card—"the plain business card he carried"[99]—and over the next several months Guevara became a frequent visitor to the Mexican-Soviet Cultural Institute, where he studied Russian and read books on Russian literature, Marxism, and economics.[100]

Later that fall Guevara began more formal training and, along with the other Cuban recruits, submitted to the physical discipline imposed by the Mexican wrestler, Arsacio Vanegas, who had been hired by Fidel Castro to whip the would-be revolutionaries into shape. Vanegas led Guevara and the others on long marches across the sprawling capital, took them on day hikes in the mountains surrounding Mexico City, and rented out a gymnasium downtown where he provided training in some of the methods of his trade: "All-in wrestling, some karate, fall techniques, kicks, how to climb walls."[101] The revolutionaries also worked on their marksmanship, practicing at a gun club on the outskirts of the city where they shot at turkeys using rifles equipped with telescopic sights.[102]

The following June, at the peak of their training, a series of raids by the Mexico City police cracked the revolutionaries' safe houses.[103] Although possible collaboration between the Mexican secret police and Batista's police should not be discounted, according to a U.S. embassy document, the crackdown followed the "chance arrest of a group of armed Cubans in an automobile. After the initial arrests were made and it became apparent that the Cuban exiles formed an armed group with aggressive intentions, President Ruiz Cortines gave his approval to further roundups."[104] Fidel Castro and others were arrested and turned over to Mexico's secret police, the DFS, where several were subject to waterboarding—the so-called wishing-well technique—and other forms of physical and psychological torture.[105] Guevara, who was at the group's training center, a ranch rented from a former Pancho Villa supporter in Chalco, about an hour's drive from the city, escaped this first roundup, though in his place the police arrested his wife. Recognizing the impossibility of his predicament, Fidel Castro led the DFS to the ranch and encouraged the others to surrender. (Guevara, who was on guard duty up a tree, nearly escaped; Raúl Castro was luckier and did slip away.)[106] Transported to a detention center in Mexico City, the new detainees faced interrogations that "ranged from friendly to brutal."[107] Guevara was still carrying the business card from the Soviet attaché, Leonov, which became the smoking gun that linked the revolutionaries, and Guevara in particular, to the Soviet Union and the cause of international communism.[108] The U.S. embassy report, quite erroneously, identified Guevara as a "well known Argentine Communist who had been active in Guatemala."[109] Determined to find a Soviet connection, the DFS threatened to torture Gadea and the new baby if Guevara did not confess to a greater communist conspiracy, a threat to which the Argentine reportedly responded by

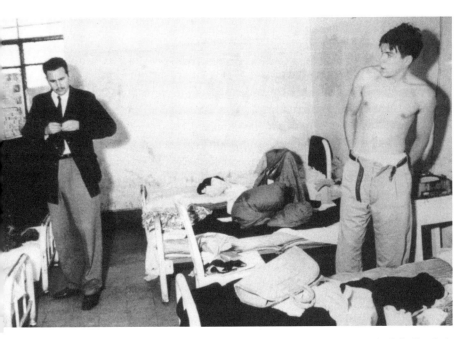

4. Fidel Castro (left) and Che Guevara (right) in a Mexico City jail after their arrest by the DFS, Mexico's security police. Source: Oficina de Asuntos Históricos del Consejo de Estado de Cuba.

clamming up.[110] Three days later the majority of the prisoners were freed with the understanding that they were to desist in their political activities and leave the country immediately. Fidel and Che, along with a handful of others, remained in the hands of the DFS.

A photograph (figure 4) taken of Fidel Castro and Guevara at some point during their time in jail tellingly captured the transformation of Guevara from "bohemian" to "revolutionary." Here, Guevara—tousled hair, pants unbuckled, and shirtless—stands juxtaposed with a buttoned-down and quite serious-looking Castro. Though perhaps inadvertently, the photographer captured the precise moment of Guevara's sidewise glance back at Castro, a gesture reflective of Guevara's determination to "find discipline" and the evident role Castro would play as a mentor in that disciplinary process.

Although a bribe may have helped grease the wheels for their release, credit is historically given foremost to the behind-the-scenes intervention of Lázaro Cárdenas. Having evaded capture by the DFS, Raúl Castro tracked down Cárdenas "through his old nanny in Jiquilpan [Michoacán]" and impressed on him the importance of gaining the release of Fidel, if not the others as well.[111] In this way the two revolutionaries came to meet one another—the elder Cárdenas, celebrated across Latin America for his defense of Mexican sovereignty, and the young Fidel Castro, still obscure to all but his Cuban compatriots. Writing in his personal diary, Cárdenas described Castro as "a young intellectual with a vehement temperament and the blood of a fighter."[112] The ex-president could not have anticipated the historical consequences of his intervention, but it was a gesture of revolutionary solidarity that Castro never forgot. Within a short time after their release from jail, and fearing the repercussions of a Batista-paid spy in their midst, Castro gave the order for the group to disembark from Veracruz. The revolutionary adventure was about to begin in earnest.

Two years later, in a letter sent to Cárdenas from the Sierra Madre mountain range, Castro wrote to express his "eternal gratitude for the incredibly noble support you provided when we were persecuted in Mexico, thanks to which we are now fulfilling our duty in Cuba." After predicting the revolutionaries' imminent triumph over Batista, he ended by calling Cárdenas a "great revolutionary," signing the letter with a heartfelt "your sincere admirer."[113]

Conclusions

Several months after Guevara left Mexico for the start of the Cuban armed insurrection, Cárdenas received the Stalin Peace Prize in a ceremony organized by the Movimiento Mexicano por la Paz, the national branch of the World Peace Council. Numbering in the thousands, the assembled crowd crammed into every available space to see and hear from Mexico's greatest living revolutionary. An article in Excélsior described the chaotic scene: "The multitude surpassed by several times the occupancy limit; each seat contained up to three people; dozens of men and women hung from the curtains and walls of the amphitheater. And stretching from the doors to the street to the main hall, a compact mass—expectant, enthusiastic— continued to struggle to get in."[114] Cárdenas gave a brief acceptance speech. Remarking that "at the present hour there is not a single nation that does not desire peace and work toward its consolidation," the former president denounced the Cold War while praising the noninterventionist traditions of the Mexican nation.[115] When he finished, the audience's ovation lasted nearly five minutes, yet Cárdenas, faithful to his moniker, "Sphinx of Jiquilpan," maintained a presence of absolute inscrutability: "Not a single muscle on his face moved, his lips were immobile, he never smiled."[116] Outside the theater, it would take Cárdenas nearly twenty minutes to reach his car through the density of the adulatory throng.

The timing of the prize, however, proved historically ironic, for it came in the wake of the Soviet premier Nikita Khrushchev's denunciation of Stalin's excesses at the Twentieth Party Congress of the Communist Party, a connection openly mocked in some quarters of the Mexican press. In a cartoon by Bernal, for example, a figure shown reading a newspaper with a photograph of Cárdenas alongside a headline about Khrushchev's revelations notes to his friend that the prize is "a little 'devalued' " (un poco "devaluado").[117] But the timing was also symbolic politically, for it transpired at the moment of a shift taking place within Mexico—and across Latin America—away from an Old Left politics, characterized by admiration for the socialist leadership of the Soviet Union, toward a New Left politics—irreverent, decentralized, and ultimately shaped by the youthful radicalism unleashed by the Cuban Revolution.[118]

By the start of the 1960s Cárdenas was in fact newly at the forefront of a broad leftist coalition, the Movimiento de Liberación Nacional (MLN), an outgrowth of the World Peace Council. For a brief moment in the early 1960s the MLN seemed capable of bridging an Old Left worker-peasant front with an emergent New Left sensibility and thus revitalizing—and revising—the democratic socialist principles of Mexico's own revolutionary heritage. But Cárdenas's willingness to serve as spokesperson for this new movement was hampered by other political considerations and, following his vigorous defense of Cuban sovereignty in the wake of the Bay of Pigs invasion in 1961, his leadership role waned; the coherency of the MLN as a reformist project that seemed capable of unifying the Left quickly unraveled.[119] As the 1964 presidential elections approached, Cárdenas threw his political prestige behind the PRI's official candidate, Gustavo Díaz Ordaz, a man reviled on the Left for his role as minister of the interior under President López Mateos (1958–64).

With this act Cárdenas signaled to supporters that his primary allegiance resided with the ruling political party he had helped establish, not with an upstart political movement (the MLN) that aimed to reform the PRI, if not contest the ruling party for real political power. The popularity of Cárdenas among a younger generation who had admired his stance in the face of the Cuban Revolution would soon be overshadowed by the militant heroics of an emergent cohort of Latin American revolutionaries. A new era of radicalized political action was already underway.

As the conservative press railed against Cuban socialism and warned about the danger of political tendencies "outside the nation's revolutionary traditions," many on the Left grew increasingly detached from their own country's revolutionary symbols. In turn, Guevara came to be embraced (by left-wing, urban youth especially) as Latin America's true, authentic revolutionary; the Cuban revolutionary experience became a model to defend and emulate. That Guevara competed with the popularity of the nation's own "true revolutionary," Zapata, pointed to a profound cynicism and lack of connectedness that many urban youth felt toward their national icons and revolutionary history.

By the 1950s Mexico's own heroic narrative had become so overly played by the ruling government for propaganda purposes that revolutionary figures such as Zapata and Villa had become emptied of their revolutionary valence. This disconnect became clear during the student movement of 1968, a political and cultural struggle whose goals were to make the PRI more accountable and democratic. As Taibo writes: "We didn't know why, but for us the past was an international realm that produced novels and revolution, not a local realm belonging to the people. . . . We felt absolutely no connection to Morelos, Zapata, Villa, to Vicente Guerrero, Hidalgo, Leandro Valle, to Guillermo Prieto, or to Mina. They were characters from a foreign history that bored preparatory teachers, really just bureaucrats, strove to misteach us; or, at best, more street names."[120] Che, on the other hand, embodied the passion of revolutionary commitment that the students pursued, and even more so in martyrdom (after 1967). He was untainted, pure, heroic. What Taibo left unstated was that Che was young and male, with strong European features; unlike Zapata (a dark-skinned mestizo with a characteristic Mexican peasant mustache), Che looked like many Mexican middle-class youth, certainly many of those who assumed leadership positions during the student protests in 1968. In letting their hair grow long and exchanging a mustache for a scruffy beard, these protesting males could mimic their new hero of international struggle. "We lived in thrall to the magic of the Cuban revolution and the Vietnamese resistance," Taibo reflects. "[Che] was our number one ghost [in 1968]. He was no more, yet he was with us still—the voice, the personality, the rousing injunction to throw everything aside and go on the road, the mocking dialogue, the project, the photograph looking down at you from every corner, the ever-growing and seemingly endless stream of fact and anecdote, the only context in which corny expressions like 'total commitment' no longer seemed laughable. But above all, Che was the guy who was everywhere even though he was dead. He was dead—but he belonged to us."[121] Che's mystical power—encapsulated in the image made famous by Alberto Díaz Gutiérrez (Alberto Korda) and disseminated within months of Guevara's assassination in Bolivia—was palpable among Mexico's urban youth, as it was elsewhere in Latin America at the time.[122] In the heat of the protests in 1968, striking students at the Faculty of Philosophy and Letters at the national university (UNAM) voted to change the name of the school's auditorium from Justo Sierra (after the famed nineteenth-century Liberal intellectual and politician) to Ernesto Che Guevara, whose goals of social justice and anti-imperialist struggle were held up as similar to those of the students. Inside the auditorium—the epicenter of protest politics during the student movement—Guevara's memorable slogan, "Hasta la victoria siempre!" was (and remains) prominently displayed.[123] This deification of Che became further manifest during the long protest marches, where Che's face and slogans were splashed across banners. As one student demonstrator commented, "I never thought of Zapata as a student symbol, an emblem. Zapata has become part of the bourgeois ideology; the PRI has appropriated him. Maybe that's why we chose Che as our symbol at demonstrations from the very first. Che was our link with student movements all over the world!"[124]

The obsession with Che, however, had its costs. Namely, it enabled the state-influenced press to denounce the students as manipulated by foreign symbols and ideologies. Accusations by the media against the students for being "unpatriotic" threatened to undermine popular support for the movement, support already made tenuous because of the students' political disruptiveness, vandalism, and general challenges to parental authority.[125] In response to these accusations, an important shift occurred that led Mexican youth to turn inward, toward a reembrace of their own revolutionary icons in a way that had not occurred in a generation. "Let's have no more vituperative slogans, no more insults, no more violence," student leadership in the movement proclaimed. "Don't carry red flags. Don't carry placards of Che or Mao! From now on we're going to carry placards with the portraits of Hidalgo, Morelos, Zapata, to shut them up. They're our Heroes. Viva Zapata! Viva!"[126]

The 1968 movement thus marked an important transformation, a renationalizing of youth consciousness that ultimately proved more threatening to the political hegemony of the ruling party than the open celebration of foreign revolutionary figures. For in reclaiming the country's own heroic iconography, youth in turn wrested control from the PRI over the symbolic meanings of those figures, in particular, of Zapata, whose own martyrdom in the cause of social justice provided an historical analogy with Guevara's death. One of the more interesting ways in which Zapata was reappropriated and came to have new meanings for urban youth was through the early 1970s rock band, La Revolución de Emiliano Zapata. Although the band performed its music in English (a particular attribute of Mexico's rock counterculture) and the lyrics had little to do with social revolution, simply naming themselves after the "nation's most revered peasant revolutionary . . . had proved that via rock the state could be mocked while national identity was reinvented on new terms."[127]

Today in Mexico Guevara is enjoying renewed vitality as a symbol of defiance to neoliberalism and the U.S. war in Iraq and of solidarity with movements of resistance globally. This holds true no doubt across the Americas, and perhaps it derives as much from the commodification of Che as from his continued resonance as a figure of Latin American "purity."[128] But if asked which of the two figures best represents the struggles Mexicans wage against the forces of capitalism and authoritarian politics, most people would undoubtedly point to Zapata. Zapata's reevaluation among urban youth began in the late 1960s, but his stature as a contemporary hero was sealed with the advent of the Ejército Zapatista de Liberación Nacional, EZLN, better known simply as "the Zapatistas." The public face of the EZLN is Subcomandante Marcos, a figure who himself has come to be seen as an incarnation of Guevara. And while the EZLN has elevated Zapata to a symbol of antiglobalization, nationally and internationally, Che remains for many Mexican youth, as well as for those of the generation of 1968, a symbol of international solidarity and anti-imperialist struggle—an irreverent revolutionary who overcame his bohemianism while never repudiating his wanderlust spirit.

Notes

I thank the Provost's Office at Franklin and Marshall College for research and travel support. Earlier versions of this essay benefited tremendously from the critical feedback of two outside reviewers and the close readings by Terri Gordon-Zolov. Certain portions were previously published in "Expanding Our Conceptual Horizons: The Shift from an Old to a New Left in Latin America," A Contracorriente 5:2 (2008): 47–73. I am appreciative of the editors of the journal for permission to reproduce those portions here.
1 Ernesto "Che" Guevara, Back on the Road: A Journey through Latin America, trans. Patrick Camiller (New York: Grove, 2000), 82. The Guatemalan president Jacobo Arbenz resigned on 27 June 1954 after confronting a CIA-directed coup d'état against him.
2 "Mexico: Waking Up after a Long Siesta," Scholastic, 5 April 1956, 9–11; Eric Zolov, "Discovering a Land 'Mysterious and Obvious': The Renarrativizing of Postrevolutionary Mexico," Fragments of a Golden Age: The Politics of Culture in Mexico since 1940, ed. Gilbert M. Joseph, Anne Rubenstein, and Zolov (Durham: Duke University Press, 2001), 234–72.
3 Robert Scott Burns, "Simpatico, Senor!" [sic], Travel, May 1953, 15.
4 Stephen R. Niblo, Mexico in the 1940s: Modernity, Politics, and Corruption (Wilmington, Del.: Scholarly Resources, 1999).
5 Jorge G. Castañeda, Compañero: The Life and Death of Che Guevara, trans. Marina Castañeda (New York: Alfred Knopf, 1997), 76.
6 Guevara, Back on the Road, 3.
7 Jack Kerouac, On the Road (New York: Viking, 1957), 224. These were not the only Beat writers who traveled to Mexico during this period (William Burroughs, who infamously shot his wife while living in Mexico City, was another), but they emblematize an era.
8 Daniel Cosio Villegas, "Politics and Mexican Intellectuals," The Intellectual in Politics, ed. H. Malcolm MacDonald (Austin: University of Texas Press, 1966), 34; Eric Zolov, "The Graphic Satire of Mexico's Jorge Carreño and the Politics of Presidentialism during the 1960s," Estudios Interdisciplinarios de América Latina 17:1 (2006): 13–38. Ironically, the presi-

dentialist regime was institutionalized under Lázaro Cárdenas who established the basis not only for the undisputed authority of the president but also, more important, the monopoly of power by the ruling party. In anointing his political successor and suppressing the opposition vote in the 1940 election, Cárdenas established the precedent of presidential politics as political theater in which the outcome of campaigns was predetermined.

9 Guevara, *Back on the Road*, 98.

10 Jürgen Buchenau, "Por una Guerra fría más templada," *Espejos de la Guerra fría: México, América Central y el Caribe*, ed. Daniela Spenser (Mexico City: CIESAS, 2004), 132–33; Elisa Servín, "Propaganda y Guerra fría: La campaña anticomunista en la prensa mexicana del medio siglo," *Signos Históricos*, no. 11 (2004), 9–39.

11 Elisa Servín, *Ruptura y oposición: El movimiento henriquista, 1945–1954* (Mexico City: Cal y Arena, 2001), 101. All translations from Spanish are mine, unless otherwise indicated.

12 Niblo, *Mexico in the 1940s*, chap. 4.

13 Quoted in Paco Ignacio Taibo 11, *Guevara, Also Known as Che*, trans. Martin Michael Roberts (New York: St. Martin's Press, 1997), 52.

14 For a detailed discussion of the rise of a Mexican New Left, see Jaime Pensado, "Student Resistance, Political Violence, and Youth Culture in Mexico City, c.1867–1965: A History of the Antecedents of Porrismo" (PhD diss., University of Chicago, 2008), chap. 5. For a theoretical discussion of the New Left in Latin America, see Eric Zolov, "Expanding our Conceptual Horizons: The Shift from an Old to a New Left in Latin America," *A Contracorriente* 5:2 (2008), 47–73.

15 Eric Zolov, "Showcasing the 'Mexico of Tomorrow': Mexico and the 1968 Olympics," *The Americas* 61:2 (2004), 159–88.

16 Sergio Aguayo notes that the exact origins and date of the creation of the DFS are not known. See Sergio Aguayo Quesada, *La charola: Una historia de los servicios de inteligencia en México* (Mexico City: Grijalbo, 2001), 62; W. Dirk Raat, "U.S. Intelligence Operations and Covert Action in Mexico, 1900–1947," *Journal of Contemporary History* 22:4 (1987), 615–38.

17 Aguayo Quesada, *La charola*, 72.

18 Ibid., 71.

19 Taibo, *Guevara*, 68–69.

20 Diana Anhalt, *A Gathering of Fugitives: American Political Expatriates in Mexico, 1948–1965* (Santa Maria, Calif.: Archer Books, 2001), 117.

21 Ibid., 118.

22 Servín, *Ruptura y oposición*, 267.

23 Ibid., 263–67.

24 Ibid., 294.

25 Ibid., 175.

26 Castañeda, who located the State Department document, writes: "Everything indicates that this was not the case: Che was not a member of the People's Party, was not a friend of Vicente Lombardo Toledano, and did not find employment thanks to him" (Castañeda, *Compañero*, 91).

27 Buchenau, "Por una Guerra fría mas templada," 129.

28 Ibid., 134.

29 "Breve Reseña de un Crimen," *Problemas de Latinoamerica* 1:2 (1954), 24.

30 Buchenau, "Por una Guerra fría más templada," 135. See also the cartoons collected in Victor Velarde, *Siete dibujantes con una idea* (Mexico City: Libros y Revistas, 1954).

31 Buchenau, "Por una Guerra fría más templada," 137.

32 Guevara, *Back on the Road*, 64.

33 Ibid., 134. The best treatment on the progressive regime in Guatemala is Piero Gleijesis, *Shattered Hope: The Guatemalan Revolution and the United States, 1944–1954* (Princeton: Princeton University Press, 1991). For a history of the U.S. role, see Nick Cullather, *Secret History: The CIA's Classified Account of Its Operations in Guatemala, 1952–54* (Stanford: Stanford University Press, 1999).

34 Velarde, *Siete dibujantes con una idea*, n.p. That the succeeding era was anything but a time of "liberty and peace" has been amply documented. See, for example, Greg Grandin, *The Last Colonial Massacre: Latin America in the Cold War* (Chicago: University of Chicago Press, 2004).

35 The era of the Popular Front refers to the period leading up to and continuing through the Second World War, when Communist Parties internationally responded to the Soviet Union's directive to forge a common electoral alliance with non-communist parties, including Socialists and members of the "progressive bourgeoisie," with the shared goal of defeating fascism. For a discussion of the Popular Front in Mexico see Barry Carr, "The Fate of the Vanguard under a Revolutionary State: Marxism's Contribution to the Construction of the Great Arch" in *Everyday Forms of State Formation: Revolution and the Negotiation of Rule in Modern Mexico*, Gilbert M. Joseph and Daniel Nugent, eds. (Durham: Duke University Press, 1994), 326–52.

36 "Breve Reseña de un Crimen," 27.

37 Quoted in Richard Immerman, *The CIA in Guatemala: The Foreign Policy of Intervention* (Austin: University of Texas Press, 1982), 180.

38 Ibid.

39 Stephen Rabe, *Eisenhower and Latin America: The Foreign Policy of Anticommunism* (Chapel Hill: University of North Carolina Press, 1988);

"Cheap Backyard" is from John Coatsworth, *Central America and the United States: The Clients and the Colossus* (New York: Twayne, 1994), 89.

40 Quoted in Castañeda, *Compañero*, 76.

41 Guevara, *Back on the Road*, 89.

42 Ibid.

43 Quoted in Taibo, *Guevara*, 49. For a useful discussion of the significance of the Pan-American Games in Mexico, see Kevin B. Witherspoon, *Before the Eyes of the World: Mexico and the 1968 Olympic Games* (DeKalb: Northern Illinois University Press, 2008). A recent review of an exhibit of Guevara's surviving photographs from the period praises his work as "well executed and sensitive." See Bill Kouwenhoven, "Che Guevara, the Photographer," review of the photography exhibit at Hamburg: Museum für Kunst und Gewerbe, http://www.contemporary-magazines.com/reviews54&53_1.htm, (accessed 11 November 2007). Guevara also pursued his study of medicine, working three days a week at various hospitals; he thus participated in a medical conference and published a short article on allergy.

44 Rabe's book, *Eisenhower and Latin America*, for instance, does not mention the Mexico leg of Nixon's trip in 1955.

45 Ibid., chap. 4.

46 "El Sr. Nixon y la 'Buena Vecindad,' " *Excélsior*, 11 February 1955.

47 Arias Bernal, "Confianza" (cartoon), *Excélsior*, 14 February 1955. For a discussion of political caricature during this period, see Zolov, "The Graphic Satire of Mexico's Jorge Carreño and the Politics of Presidentialism during the 1960s."

48 "Gráficas de la llegada del Señor Nixon a México," *Excélsior*, 10 February 1955. For an excellent discussion of Nixon's tour in Latin America in 1958 and the backlash he encountered, especially in Caracas, see Alan McPherson, *Yankee No! Anti-Americanism in U.S.-Latin American Relations* (Cambridge: Harvard University Press, 2003), chap. 1.

49 "El Vicepresidente Nixon," *El Universal*, 12 February 1955.

50 "Nixon Sees Gains in Caribbean Area," *New York Times*, 6 March 1955.

51 Rabe, *Eisenhower and Latin America*, 87–88.

52 "Nixon Goes Today on Goodwill Tour," *New York Times*, 5 February 1955.

53 "Nixon Sees Gains in Caribbean Area"; Rabe, *Eisenhower and Latin America*, 87–88.

54 "No sólo de pan vive el hombre," *Excélsior*, 12 February 1955.

55 Arthur Schmidt, "The Political and Economic Reverberations of the Cuban Revolution in Mexico, 1959–1970," *History Compass* 6, no. 4 (July 2008), 1140–63.

56 Ibid.; Eric Zolov, "Toward an Analytical Framework for Assessing the Impact of the 1968 Student Movement on U.S.-Mexican Relations," *Journal of Iberian and Latin American Studies* 9:2 (2003), 41–68.

57 "Funcionarios e izquierdistas en la junta de la paz," *Excélsior*, 29 March 1955.

58 The World Peace Council had its origins in a meeting of the World Congress of Intellectuals for Peace in Wroclaw, Poland, in August 1948. At this meeting a committee was created that led to the calling of a First World Peace Congress held in Paris in 1949. From this meeting, a World Committee of Partisans of Peace was launched. By the mid-1950s the conference had undergone another name change to World Peace Council.

59 The list included Vicente Lombardo Toledano as well as the renowned muralists David Alfaro Siquieros and Diego Rivera. While Cárdenas was not present, his role as vice chairman of the international committee of the World Peace Council nonetheless directly linked him to the event.

60 "El extraño pacifismo soviético," *Excélsior*, 31 March 1955.

61 American Consulate (Guadalajara) to Department of State, "Communist 'Peace' Assembly in Tepic, Nayarit, Mexico," 21 October 1955, 712.001/10–2155, National Archives and Records Administration (NARA), College Park, Maryland.

62 "Es comunista la Asamblea pro Paz, dice la iglesia," *El Nayar*, 26 September 1955; enclosure located in 712.001/10–2155 NARA.

63 Guevara, *Back on the Road*, 86.

64 Taibo, *Guevara*, 47.

65 Ibid., 51.

66 Guevara, *Back on the Road*, 95.

67 Castañeda, *Compañero*, 87.

68 Guevara, *Back on the Road*, 84.

69 Ibid., 84.

70 Ibid., 88.

71 Ibid., 84.

72 Ibid.

73 Ibid., 85.

74 Ibid., 99.

75 The Porfiriato refers to the era of the dictator, Porfirio Díaz, who ruled in the period leading up to the Mexican Revolution. For conquests of Popocatepetl during the Porfiriato, see William H. Beezley, *Judas at the Jockey Club and Other Episodes of Porfirian Mexico* (Lincoln: University of Nebraska Press, 1987).

76 Guevara, *Back on the Road*, 82.

77 Ibid., 87.

78 Ibid.

79 Ibid., 88.

80 Ibid., 95.

81 Ibid., 97.

82 Ibid., 96.

83 Ibid., 97.

84 Ibid., 88.

85 See Zolov, "Discovering a Land 'Mysterious and Obvious' "; Dina Berger, *The Development of Mexico's Tourism Industry: Pyramids by Day, Martinis by Night* (New York: Palgrave Macmillan, 2006).

86 The best history of the college is found in Richard W. Wilkie, "Dangerous Journeys: Mexico City College Students and the Mexican Landscape, 1954–1962," *Adventures into Mexico: American Tourism beyond the Border*, ed. Nicholas Dagen Bloom (Lanham, Md.: Rowman and Littlefield, 2006), 88–115.

87 Ibid., 91.

88 Ibid., 92.

89 Ibid., 90.

90 Drewey Wayne Gunn, "The Beat Trail to Mexico," in Bloom, *Adventures into Mexico*, 80.

91 Jorge García-Robles, *El disfraz de la inocencia: La historia de Jack Kerouac en México* (Mexico City: Ediciones del Milenio, 2000), 89.

92 Ibid., 90.

93 Rachel Adams, "Hipsters and Jipitecas: Literary Countercultures on Both Sides of the Border," *American Literary History* 16:1 (2004), 59–60.

94 Quoted in García-Robles, *El disfraz de la inocencia*, 105; translation mine.

95 Guevara, *Back on the Road*, 99. For discussion of this meeting, see Castañeda, *Compañero*, 83–87; Taibo, *Guevara*, 53–54.

96 Guevara, *Back on the Road*, 109.

97 Castañeda writes that the moniker "Che" was acquired by Guevara in Guatemala, given to him by his Cuban exile friends "because of his Argentine nationality and his countrymen's habit of endlessly repeating this expression" (Castañeda, *Compañero*, 75). Taibo, on the other hand, notes that it was during the Mexican days of training that the nickname came into being: "He interspersed his conversation with *che*, used as the Mexicans used 'hombre,' and addressed everybody as *Che*. The Cubans found this very funny and nicknamed him Che" (Taibo, *Guevara*, 67). *Che* in Argentine Spanish is roughly the equivalent of "dude" or "man," said at the beginning and/or end of a sentence in American English.

98 Castañeda, *Compañero*, 87; Taibo, *Guevara*, 58.

99   Castañeda, *Compañero*, 92.

100   Ibid., 91–92; Taibo, *Guevara*, 58, 62.

101   Taibo, *Guevara*, 62–63.

102   Ibid., 63.

103   Ibid., 68.

104   Andrew Donavan, 29 June 1956, 712.00(w)/6–2956, NARA. For a different interpretation, see Taibo, *Guevara*, 68.

105   Taibo, *Guevara*, 68.

106   Ibid., 69.

107   Ibid.

108   The U.S. embassy mistakenly wrote in its reports that Fidel Castro was carrying this card, but both Castañeda and Taibo state that the card was on Guevara, and it is unlikely that Castro would have made such an error.

109   Donavan, 29 June 1956.

110   Taibo, *Guevara*, 69.

111   Ibid., 70.

112   Quoted in Enrique Krauze, *Biography of Power: A History of Modern Mexico, 1810–1996*, trans. Hank Heifetz (New York: HarperCollins, 1997), 622.

113   Fidel Castro, "Carta de Fidel Castro al General Lázaro Cárdenas desde Sierra Maestra," 17 March 1958, *México y Cuba: Dos pueblos unidos en la historia*, vol. 2, ed. Martha López Portillo de Tamayo and Boris Rosen Jélomer (Mexico City: Centro de Investigación Científica Jorge L. Tamayo, 1982), 495–96.

114   Manuel Becerra Acosta Jr., " 'No hay país que no busque la paz,' declara Cárdenas," *Excélsior*, 27 February 1956.

115   Ibid.

116   Ibid.

117   Arias Bernal, "Tardío," *Excélsior*, 27 February 1956. The twentieth party congress was held 14–26 February 1956; Van Gosse, *Where the Boys Are: Cuba, Cold War America and the Making of a New Left* (London: Verso, 1993).

118   See Pensado, "Student Resistance, Political Violence, and Youth Culture in Mexico City, c.1867–1965"; Zolov, "Expanding Our Conceptual Horizons."

119   Eric Zolov, "¡Cuba Sí, Yanquis No!: The Sacking of the Instituto Cultural México-Norteamericano in Morelia, Michoacán, 1961," *In from the Cold: Latin America's New Encounter with the Cold War*, ed. Gilbert M. Joseph and Daniela Spenser (Durham: Duke University Press, 2008), 214–52.

120 Paco Ignacio Taibo II, '68, trans. Donald Nicholson-Smith (New York: Seven Stories Press, 2004), 22.

121 Ibid., 16–17. For a critique, see the important article by Lessie Jo Frazier and Deborah Cohen, "Mexico '68: Defining the Space of the Movement, Heroic Masculinity in the Prison, and 'Women' in the Streets," *Hispanic American Historical Review* 83:4 (2003), 617–60.

122 Diana Sorensen, *A Turbulent Decade Remembered: Scenes from the Latin American Sixties* (Stanford: Stanford University Press, 2007); Michael Casey, *Che's Afterlife: The Legacy of an Image* (New York: Vintage Books, 2009).

123 Luis Hernández Navarro, "Che," *La Jornada Semanal*, 13 July 2008, http://www.jornada.unam.mx. See also *El grito* (dir. Leobardo López, 1968).

124 Quoted in Elena Poniatowska, *Massacre in Mexico*, trans. Helen R. Lane (New York: Viking, 1975), 32.

125 Elaine Carey, *Plaza of Sacrifices: Gender, Power, and Terror in 1968 Mexico* (Albuquerque: University of New Mexico Press, 2005). Carey's work tends to emphasize the widespread popularity of the student movement, despite the obvious disruptions to the middle-class social order caused by the students.

126 Poniatowska, *Massacre in Mexico*, 41. See the discussion in Eric Zolov, *Refried Elvis: The Rise of the Mexican Counterculture* (Berkeley: University of California Press, 1999), 126–27.

127 Zolov, *Refried Elvis*, 179.

128 Sorensen, *A Turbulent Decade Remembered*, chap. 1.

List of Contributors

MALCOLM DEAS was one of the founders of the University of Oxford's Latin American Centre at St. Antony's College in the early 1960s. He is now an Emeritus Fellow of the college.

PAULO DRINOT is a lecturer in economic history at the University of Manchester. He is the coeditor of *Más allá de la dominación y la resistencia: Estudios de historia peruana, siglos XVI–XX* (2005), the author of several articles on the economic, social, and cultural history of twentieth-century Peru, and has a book forthcoming from Duke University Press, *The Allure of Labor: Workers, Race, and the Makings of the Peruvian State.*

EDUARDO ELENA is an assistant professor of history at the University of Miami. He is currently completing a book project titled *A "Dignified Life": Peronist Politics and Consumption in Mid-Twentieth-Century Argentina.*

JUDITH EWELL, a Newton Professor of History emerita at the College of William and Mary, has published books and articles on twentieth-century Venezuela. She has held Fulbright professorships in Venezuela and Ecuador and is a past editor of *The Americas.*

CINDY FORSTER teaches history and Latin American studies at Scripps College.

PATIENCE A. SCHELL teaches Latin American history at the University of Manchester. She is the author of *Church and State Education in Revolutionary Mexico City* (2003), as well as of essays on both Mexico and Chile. She is currently working on a manuscript about science and friendship in nineteenth-century Chile.

ERIC ZOLOV is an associate professor in the Department of History at Franklin and Marshall College and the author of *Refried Elvis: The Rise of the Mexican Counterculture* (1999), among other works. His current research examines the impact of the Cuban Revolution on Mexican political culture and U.S.-Mexican relations during the 1960s.

ANN ZULAWSKI is a professor of history and Latin American studies at Smith College. She is the author of *Unequal Cures: Public Health and Political Change in Bolivia, 1900–1950* (2007).

Index

Page numbers in italics indicate illustrations

Acción Argentina, 35

Achury Valenzuela, Dario, 140 n. 3

AD (Acción Democrática) (Venezuela), 1, 148, 153–55, 160, 162; after the Cuban Revolution, 166–68, 171, 173; Che's meetings with AD exiles, 14, 148, 161, 164; Che's opinion of, 122 n. 48, 162; and Pérez Jiménez's ouster, 165–66. *See also* Betancourt, Romulo

Adams, Rachel, 265

Agencia Latina de Noticias, 256, 263

agrarian reform. *See* land distribution and reform

agriculture: in Chile, 74–75, 77

Aguas bajan turbias, Las (film), 41–42

Aguayo, Sergio, 249

Albania, 137–38

Albó, Xavier, 191–92

Alegría, Ciro, 99–101

Alemán, Miguel, 16, 247–50, 251

Alessandri, Jorge, 82

Alexander, Robert J., 100

Alfaro, Hipólito, 98

Allende, Salvador, 81–82

Alliance for Progress, 82, 133, 136

Almaraz, Sergio, 201

Altamirano, Carlos, 52 n. 38

Amazon region: Che in, 113–15

American Federation of Labor, 92

Anaconda Copper Company, 70

Andahuaylas (Peru), 107

Andean Peru. *See* Peruvian Indians; *specific locations*

Anderson, Jon Lee, 5, 35–36, 95, 99, 140 n. 2

Andrade, Víctor, 190

anti-Americanism, 51 n. 34; Castro brothers and, 164–65; Chávez and, 174; of Che, 14, 36, 45–46, 90, 148, 161–62, 164; in Mexico, 253–55. *See also* anti-imperialism

anticommunism: Betancourt and, 149, 154–55, 161, 163; in Bolivia, 190, 201; in Mexico, 248, 249, 251–52, 260. *See also* cold war

antiglobalism, 274–75

anti-imperialism, 12, 46–47, 90, 223–24; Bolivian mine workers and, 198; Che as symbol of, 204, 247, 275; Che's views of political reformers and, 97–98, 122 n. 48; Otero Silva and, 151; Peronism and, 36, 45–47, 51 n. 34, 162. *See also* anti-Americanism; nationalism

ANUC (Asociación Nacional de Usuarios Campesinos), 145–46 n. 26

APRA (American Popular Revolutionary Alliance) (Peru), 13, 93, 94–95, 109, 153; attempts to undermine, 93, 121 n. 26; Che and, 95, 96–98, 122 n. 48, 214; Che's impact on, 116; outlawing of, 92; radicalization of younger members of, 95, 116

Araucanian people, 42–43, 55, 56–57, 64

Chile, Che in, 53–55, 74, 77–78, 80–81; encounters with Chileans by, 57–61, 70–71

Chile, o una loca geografía (Subercaseaux), 55, 64–65, 74–76, 78

Chilean women, 53, 57–61; beauty discourse of, 12, 61–66; Che's interactions and descriptions of, 57–61; foreign travelers on, 55–56, 61–63, 68–69; linked with national progress, 61, 64–66; opportunities available to, 61, 66–67; political participation of, 68–71; sports and exercise and, 65–66

China: Che's intention to visit, 262; Mao's revolution and influence in, 117, 137–38, 203

Chispas, 132

cholos. See mixed-race people

Christian Democratic Party (Peru), 94, 95

Chuquicamata mine, 70–71

CIA (Central Intelligence Agency): Guatemalan coup and, 210, 253; Harold White and, 216. See also Guatemalan coup

Cisneros, Cristobal, 108

Cita en la trinchera de la muerte (Achury Valenzuela), 140 n. 3

cities: Che's lack of interest in, 14, 28, 43, 148–49, 159, 168. See also rural-urban migration; slums; urbanization; urban poor

COB (Confederación Obrera Boliviana), 189, 190

Cold War, 3, 82. See also anticommunism; U.S.-Latin American relations

Colombia, 13–14, 127–47; Che's legacy in, 13–14, 137–39; guerrilla movements in, 13–14, 128, 131–39, 141 n. 9, 142 n. 13; Haya de la Torre and, 121 n. 38; land reform in, 136–37, 145 nn. 25–26; political context, 13–14,

128–32, 134–35, 141 n. 9; politics after the Cuban Revolution in, 132–39

Colombia, Che in, 13, 127, 130, 156

colonialism: Lima as postcolonial city, 110–13; in Peru, 103–7

Coloteneango (Guatemala), indigenous activism in, 228, 232–36

Comentarios reales de los Incas (Garcilaso de la Vega), 100

COMIBOL (Compañia Minera Boliviana), 190

communist parties, 137; in Argentina, 164; in Bolivia, 201, 203; Che's intention to join, 263; in Chile, 60; in Colombia, 131–33; in Costa Rica, 154, 162; in Guatemala, 210, 214, 215, 220, 221, 224, 226; Otero Silva and, 151; in Peru, 92, 95, 109, 116, 121 n. 26; in Venezuela, 153–55, 160, 165– 68. See also anticommunism; Cold War

Compañero: The Life and Death of Che Guevara (Castañeda), 5, 44, 246, 261, 277 n. 26, 280 n. 97

Congo, 202, 226

Consejo Nacional Estudiantil de Solidaridad con el Pueblo de Guatemala (Mexico), 255

Conservative Party (Colombia), 128–30, 131, 136

Contreras, Antonio, 108

Conversation in the Cathedral (Vargas Llosa), 89–90, 110

Cooke, John William, 46

COPEI (Comité de Organización Política Electoral Independiente) (Venezuela), 153–55, 166, 168, 173

Córdoba, Argentina, 37, 42, 77–78, 112; as Guevara family home, 24, 26, 28–29

Corso, Gregory, 266

Cortázar, Julio, 6

Cortéz, Julia, 25, 49 n. 5

Cosio Villegas, Daniel, 247

Costa Rica: Betancourt in, 154, 161; Che's meetings in, 14, 148, 161, 163–64

CP–ML (Partido Comunista–Marxista Leninista) (Bolivia), 203

Cristo de Vallegrande, Che as, 204

Cruz, Cupertino de la, 108

Cruz, María de la, 69

Cruz Varela, Juan de la, 132, 136

CTAL (Confederation of Latin American Workers), 251

CTM (Confederation of Mexican Workers), 251

Cuba: Betancourt in, 154, 160; Che in, 225–26; Che's ignorance of culture in, 146 n. 27; Colombian guerrillas and, 132, 142 n. 11; counterrevolutionary efforts against, 211, 225; political parties outlawed in, 219; postrevolutionary, 218–19, 227. See also Castro, Fidel; Cuban Revolution

Cuban exiles: Che's contacts with, 164–65, 213–14. See also specific individuals

Cuban Revolution, 16, 44, 82, 135, 165, 223; Che as emblem of, 45; Che's activities and contributions to, 142 n. 13, 237; Che's exposure to ideas of, 213–14; impact in Colombia of, 128, 131–33; impact in Guatemala of, 227, 231–32, 237; impact in Mexico of, 259, 271, 272; impact in Peru of, 116–17; impact in Venezuela of, 167–68; impact on Peronists of, 46; Mexico as staging ground for, 16, 246, 265, 267–70; U.S. responses to, 82, 211, 225

Cuban revolutionaries in Mexico, 265, 267–70; arrests and imprisonment of, 249, 251, 268–70, 269; release and departure of, 269–70; training of, 267–68. See also Castro, Fidel

CUC (Campesino Unity Committee) (Guatemala), 232–35, 242 n. 58, 243 n. 61. See also Méndez, Arturo

Cuzco, Peru, 106, 112–13, 116

Dager, Jorge, 168

Daily Journal (Caracas newspaper), 159

Darío, Rubén, 99

Debray, Régis, 6, 133, 142 n. 12, 209 n. 71

Delgado Chalbaud, Carlos, 153–55

Demare, Lucas, 41

Desquite, 132

DFS (Departamento Federal de Seguridad) (Mexico), 249, 250, 276 n. 16; arrests of Cuban revolutionaries by, 249, 251, 268–70, 281 n. 108

Diaz, Porfirio, 279 n. 75

Díaz Gutiérrez, Alberto (Alberto Korda), 211, 273

Díaz Ordaz, Gustavo, 271

Di buen día a papá (Vargas), 205

Dickinson, Stirling, 110

discipline: Che as disciplined revolutionary, 133, 142 n. 13; Che's new sense of purpose through Fidel's revolutionary training and, 267, 269; in FARC's operations, 132, 142 n. 13; young Che as lacking, 48, 262, 265, 267

Discovery of India, The (Nehru), 36

Dodds, James Leishman, 92–93, 98

domestic violence: in Chile, 59

Dominican Republic, 154. See also Trujillo, Rafael

Dosal, Paul, 90

Dulles, John Foster, 190–91

Duncan, James S., quoted, 8

Easter Island, 58–59

economic inequalities. See poverty; socioeconomic inequalities economic policies and programs: in Argentina, 29, 36; in Bolivia, 181, 189–91, 194, 197–98; in Peru, 92–93, 98, 121 n. 26; in Venezuela during 1940s, 153, 174. *See also* land distribution and reform; neoliberalism

Ecuador, 91, 223–24

education: of Guatemalan workers by communists, 215; opportunities for Chilean women, 67; reforms of, 93–94, 153, 187

EGP (Ejército Guerrillero de los Pobres) (Guatemala), 16, 211, 221, 226–30, 233

Eisenhower administration: Bolivian revolution and, 190–91; Mexico and Latin American policy of, 255–56. *See also* Guatemalan coup

Ejército Revolucionario del Pueblo (Argentina), 45

elites, 233; in Bolivia, 181, 183, 187, 193–95; in Chile, 56, 81; in Cuba, 223; in Guatemala, 211, 212, 214, 219, 221, 228, 230, 243 n. 63; in Peru, 90, 113; in Venezuela, 153–54, 165, 171, 173. *See also* Chilean women

ELN (Ejército de Liberación Nacional) (Colombia), 128, 131, 133, 138, 142 n. 11, 142 n. 13; mistakes of, 134–36

ELN (Ejército de Liberación Nacional) (Peru), 116

El Salvador, 217, 219, 239 n. 19

El Teniente mine, 59, 65–66, 68

employment opportunities: for Chilean women, 61, 67–68

Enver Hoxha Front, 138

EPL (Popular Liberation Army) (Colombia), 137–38

Ernesto de La Higuera, San, 204

"Ernesto Guevara: The Last Reader" (Piglia), 19 n. 14, 25, 48 n. 1

Escobar, Pablo, 146 n. 30

La Escuela Claridad, 215

Eskelund, Karl, 96–97, 105–6, 111–12, 123 n. 84

ethnicity. *See* indigenous peoples; race

eugenics, 105–6

Europe, Che's intention to visit, 262

European influence: in Chile, 55, 75; in Venezuela, 151, 152, 157–58

Eva (magazine), 63–64, 66

Eva Perón Foundation, 30, 31, 38

Excélsior (newspaper), 253, 270

executions: in Colombia, 133, 138; in Guatemala, 221, 222, 240 n. 34; in postrevolutionary Cuba, 223. *See also* violence

EZLN (Ejército Zapatista de Liberación Nacional), 223, 274–75

Facundo (Sarmiento), 25

FAR (Fuerzas Armadas Rebeldes) (Guatemala), 226–27, 229

Faraday, Margaret, quoted, 55, 62

FARC (Fuerzas Armadas Revolucionarias de Colombia), 132–33, 135, 138, 142 n. 13; rural base, 133, 145 n. 26; UP founding, 138, 146 n. 30

Farinas, William, 175

fascism, 35, 50 n. 23, 219, 277 n. 35

FDN (National Democratic Front), 219

FEI (Frente Electoral Independiente) (Venezuela), 155

female beauty, 12, 61–67

Ferrer, Carlos "Calica": in Bolivia, 51 n. 34, 181, 184, 193–95, 198–99; in Peru, 88–89, 121 n. 43, 123 n. 79; truck trip with Indians by, 102, 198–99

Ferreyra, María del Carmen "Chichina," 31, 33, 54, 150

Figueres, José, 14, 122 n. 48, 161, 163
film: Che on 3D, 98; in Peronist Argentina, 41–42, 52 n. 41. See also *Motorcycle Diaries* (Salles)
focos and *foquismo*, 47, 133, 167, 209 n. 71; alternatives to, 176, 186, 204; Bolivian guerrilla and, 204; Colombian guerrilla movements and, 133, 135; Cuban Revolution and, 135, 169; as flawed, 135, 169, 176; Venezuelan guerrilla movements and, 167–69
folk culture: Che's attraction to, 34; nationalism and, 39, 41–43. *See also* indigenous peoples; rural areas and peoples
Fondo Unico Social (Venezuela), 175
Fortuny, José Manuel, 220
Franco, Francisco, 35
Frei, Eduardo, 82
Frente Nacional (Colombia), 131–32, 134–35, 138
Freyre, Rafael, 253, 254
Frondizi, Arturo, 44
FSTMB (Federación Sindical de Trabajadores Mineros de Bolivia), 186, 188, 190
Fuenmayor, Bautista, 162

Gadea, Hilda, 15, 57, 95–96, 116, 163; arrest in Guatemala of, 222; arrest in Mexico of, 268–69; Che and, 214–15, 246, 261–62; on Cuban exiles in Guatemala, 214; on defense of the Guatemalan revolution, 220; observations about Che by, 97–98, 101, 122 n. 48, 159, 213
Gaitán, Jorge Eliécer, 129–30, 132, 141 n. 6
Gallegos, Rómulo, 154, 163
Galván, Lucio Edilberto, 116
Galvarino (Chile), 71–72
García, Graciela, 215

García Bernal, Gael, 33
García Márquez, Gabriel, 141 n. 6
García Peláez, Francisco de Paula, 105
García Ponce, Guillermo, 155
García-Robles, Jorge, 264–65
Garcilaso de la Vega, Inca, 100
Ginsberg, Allen, 16, 246, 263, 266
globalization, 47, 139, 275
Godoy, Haydee, 220
Goldberg, David Theo, 106
Gómez, Álvaro, 133
Gómez, Juan Vicente, 151
Gómez, Laureano, 129–30, 156
González, Efraín, 132
González, Roberto, 72
González Casanova, Pablo, 261
González Videla, Gabriel, 60
Good Neighbor policy, 254–56, 259–60
Gorriti, Juana Manuela, 26
Granado, Alberto, 7, 23, 27, 49 n. 6, 150; in Chile, 58–59, 70, 74, 77–78; in Colombia, 140 n. 2; in Peru, 88, 100–102, 107, 114, 123 n. 77; political views of, 35, 37–38, 164; in Venezuela, 156–57
Grau San Martín, Ramón, 223
Gregory, Derek, quoted, 8
Guatemala, 44, 210–44; barracks revolt in (1960), 211, 225; Che's legacy in, 7, 16, 211, 224–26, 229–32, 236–37; guerrilla movements during 1960s–1980s in, 16, 211, 220–21, 226–29, 242 n. 55; indigenous activism in, 228–30, 232–37, 243 n. 61; land reform in, 210, 212, 226; political context, 210, 212; political exiles in, 15–16, 98, 213–15; socioeconomic inequalities in, 212, 231, 243 n. 62. *See also* EGP
Guatemala, Che in, 4, 15–16, 210, 212; arms collecting by, 222, 239 n. 15; departure by, 222, 253; encounters with Mayan people and

past by, 217–18; friends and associates of, 15–16, 213–15, 222; Gadea and, 214–15; Leftist suspicions of, 214, 216; Marxist studies of, 214–16; physical health of, 212–13, 217; pro-revolution efforts of, 219–21; search for employment by, 213

Guatemalan coup (1954), 210–11, 219–22, 241 n. 40; Betancourt's response to, 163; Che and, 16, 164, 222, 253; Mexican views of, 252–55; Nixon on, 255; U.S. role in, 210, 212, 253–54

Guatemalan revolution (October Revolution), 15–16, 210, 212, 216–17; Che's interest and opinion of, 160–61, 215–16; counter-revolutionary efforts in, 160, 212, 218–19; defense efforts in, 219–21; impact in Mexico of, 252–55; Organization of American States response to, 241 n. 40. See also Arbenz Guzmán, Jacobo; Guatemalan coup

La guerra de guerrillas (Guevara), 45, 82, 95

Guerrero, Vicente, 272

Guerrilla Army of the Poor (EGP) (Guatemala), 16, 211, 221, 226–30, 233

La guerrilla del Che y la narrativa boliviana (Siles del Valle), 20 n. 15

guerrilla movements, guerrilla warfare, 46–47; appropriate ground for, 46, 136, 144 n. 23; Che as inspiration to, 6, 14; Che's efforts toward, in Bolivia (1966), 45, 116–17, 137, 182, 202–4, 226; urban operations of, 168. See also focus and foquismo; specific countries and groups

La guerrilla por dentro (Arenas), 134, 142–43 n. 13

Guerrilla Warfare (Guevara), 45, 82, 95

Guevara, Aleida, 175

Guevara, Ernesto Che, 269; childhood and youth of, 24–25, 42, 161; death of, 15, 25, 45, 49 n. 5, 133, 169, 204–5; Debray on, 142 n. 12; Gadea and, 214–15, 246, 261–62; health of, 25, 212–13, 217; marriage and fatherhood of, 215, 246, 262; personality of, 4, 163–64; as reader, 25, 36, 96, 99, 150–51, 267; as revolutionary disciplinarian, 133, 142 n. 13; scholarship on, 4–7; ship's medic job of, 26–27, 150. See also Guevara legacy

Guevara, Moisés, 203

Guevara, Also Known as Che (Taibo), 5, 165, 280 n. 97

Guevara family, 24–25, 28, 34–35

Guevara legacy, 2, 6–7, 17, 142 n. 12; in Argentina, 7, 44–48; in Bolivia, 15, 204–5; in Chile, 81–82; in Colombia, 13–14, 137–39; in Guatemala, 7, 16, 211, 224–26, 229–32, 236–37; in Mexico, 7, 17, 247, 272–75; in Peru, 115–18; in Venezuela, 6–7, 14, 149, 169–71, 173–77. See also Guevara mythology and iconography

Guevara Lynch, Ernesto, 24, 25, 27, 32; political sympathies of, 35, 36, 40

Guevara mythology and iconography, 1, 5, 6–7, 47, 220, 272–73; in Argentina, 47–48; in Bolivia, 15, 204–5; Che as religious spirit or symbol, 7, 14–15, 114–15, 170, 173, 204; El Che nickname and persona in, 21, 23, 32, 44, 48, 267, 280 n. 97; in Chile, 81; in Guatemala, 211, 230–31; in Mexico, 247, 272–74; in Peru, 117; political uses of Che's image and, 149, 174–77, 227, 230; in Venezuela, 7, 169–70, 173–77. See also Guevara legacy

indigenous activism, 7; in Bolivia, 191; in Guatemala, 228–30, 232–37, 243 n. 61; in Peru, 108–9. *See also* rural politics and organizing

indigenous peoples: in Argentina, 42–43; Che's interest in and empathy for, 12–13, 55, 101, 217–18, 239–40 n. 19; Che's stereotyped views of, 42–43, 99, 101–2, 192, 197; in Chile, 12, 55–57; in Guatemala, 16, 105, 217–18, 225–32; paternalist views of, 107, 197; photographs of, 56–57. *See also* Bolivian Indians; indigenous activism; Peruvian Indians; race; rural areas and peoples; rural politics and organizing; rural-urban migration; *specific peoples*

Infante, Tita, 98, 182

insurgent citizenship, 124 n. 99; among Peruvian peasants, 108, 118

internal migration. *See* rural-urban migration

internationalism: Che as symbol of, 247, 273, 275. *See also* pan-Americanism

International Petroleum Company, 89

Los isleros (Demare), 41

Jamaica, 27

Jankus, Alfred P., 157

Johnson administration, 82

Kelly, Dot, 115

Kelly, Hank, 115

Kennedy, John F., 143 n. 18

Kennedy administration, 82

Kerouac, Jack, 16, 246, 263–65, 266

Khrushchev, Nikita, 271

Klubock, Thomas Miller, 59, 68; quoted, 65–66

Korda, Alberto, 211, 273

Labarca, Amanda, 67

labor movements and unions. *See* organized labor; workers' movements

Lake District (Chile), 75–76

land distribution and reform, 145 n. 25; in Bolivia, 181, 186–87, 191, 194–95, 200–201; in Chile, 12, 77, 137; in Colombia, 136–37, 145 n. 25, 145 n. 26; in Guatemala, 210, 212, 226, 230; in Mexico, 136; in Peru, 108

landscape: Chile's natural beauty and bounty, 12, 53, 73–77

La Paz, 15, 110, 181–82, 199–201

La Rioja province (Argentina), 40

Larrazábal, Wolfgang, 165–66

Lechín Oquendo, Juan, 182, 188–91, 201

Leguía, Augusto B., 93

leisure time, and tourism in Peronist Argentina, 29–30

Leiva de Holst, Elena, 214

Lenin, Vladimir, 221

Leoni, Raúl, 149

Leonov, Nikolai, 267–68, 281 n. 108

leprosarium, in San Pablo (Peru), 27, 43–44, 88, 114–15

Liberal Party (Colombia), 128–32

Lima, 89–90, 98, 108–13; Che's visits and descriptions of, 43–44, 88, 95–96, 98, 112–13, 149

Lincoln, Abraham, Batista compared to, 257

Linke, Lilo, 15, 194–98

Lionza, María, 14, 170–71, 173, 175

literature: rural life and peoples in, 99–101. *See also* books; *specific authors and titles*

Lleras Restrepo, Carlos, 145 nn. 25–26

Llovera Páez, Luís Felipe, 154

López, Antonio "Ñico," 214, 220

López, Juan, 235

López Contreras, Eleazar, 162

demographics in Santiago, 78–79; Guatemalan revolution and, 219; Peronism and, 34–35, 35–36, 40, 183; and race in Guatemalan revolutionary politics, 227–30. *See also* elites; middle class; working class

socialism, socialist parties: in Argentina, 35, 36, 40; in Bolivia, 204; in Chile, 12, 80; in Mexico, 245, 251; in Peru, 88, 95; in Venezuela, 169, 172–76. *See also* Cuba; Cuban exiles; Cuban Revolution; Cuban revolutionaries; *specific parties and politicians*

social policies and programs: in Bolivia, 189, 194–95; in Peru, 92–94, 98, 104, 121 n. 26; in Venezuela, 153, 173–74

socioeconomic inequalities: in Bolivia, 184, 194–95; Che's interest in, 44, 118; in Guatemala, 212, 231, 243 n. 62; in Peru, 113, 118; in Venezuela, 157–58. *See also* poverty; social class

Soderbergh, Steven, dir.: *Che Part I* and *Che Part II*, 17 n. 1

solidarity: Che as symbol of, 274. *See also* internationalism; pan-Americanism

Somoza, Anastasio, 154

Soviet Union: Che's studies at Mexican-Soviet Cultural Institute of, 267; efforts to connect Cuban revolutionaries to, 268–69; Khrushchev's denunciation of Stalin and, 271; Popular Front and, 255, 277 n. 35; World Peace Conference movement and, 260

Spanish Civil War, 35, 151, 213, 249

Spanish conquistadores, 100, 103–4; colonialism in Peru, 103–7

sports: women's athletics in Chile, 66

Stalin, Joseph, 271

Stalin Peace Prize, 270–71

Standard Oil, 89, 153

students and student movements: in Chile, 81–82; in Colombia, 137, 146 n. 28; in Mexico, 17, 246–47, 255, 261, 272–74; U.S. students in Mexico and, 263; in Venezuela, 155, 156

Suazo, Siles, 182

Subercaseaux, Benjamín, 55, 64–65, 74–76, 78

Sumapaz, 132, 136

Szulc, Tad, 91, 97

Taibo, Paco Ignacio, II, 5, 165, 272–73, 280 n. 97

Talara (Peru), 89

Tarata (Peru), 103

Taylor, Lewis, 100

Temoche, Ricardo, 98

Tesis de Pulacayo, 186, 197

Thorp, Rosemary, 93

Time (magazine), 91–92

Tintay (Peru), 108

Tlatelolco massacre, 17

Toledano, Vicente Lombardo, 251–52, 260–61, 277 n. 26, 279 n. 59

Tor, Frances, 110–13

Toriello, Guillermo, 218

Torre, Juan Carlos, 30

Torres, Camilo, 128, 133, 136, 143 n. 15

Torres Espinosa, Edelberto, 215

torture, of Cuban revolutionaries arrested in Mexico, 249, 268

tourism: in Argentina, 9, 22–23, 29–33, 50 n. 13; Che's visits to destinations of, 31–32, 262; Che's rejection of conventional, 29, 30–33, 99; in Mexico, 249, 263; in Peru, 50 n. 18, 99; Santiago as destination of, 78; vs. travel, 29–32

Townsend, Andrés, 98

travel: Che as vagabond wanderer, 22, 24–27, 29, 48, 61, 71, 262–

Paulo Drinot is a lecturer in economic history
at the University of Manchester.

Library of Congress Cataloging-in-Publication Data
Che's travels : the making of a revolutionary in 1950s
Latin America / edited by Paulo Drinot.
p. cm.
Includes bibliographical references and index.
ISBN 978-0-8223-4748-4 (cloth : alk. paper)
ISBN 978-0-8223-4767-5 (pbk. : alk. paper)
1. Guevara, Ernesto, 1928-1967—Travel—Latin America.
2. Latin America—Description and travel.
3. Latin America—History—20th century.
I. Drinot, Paulo.
F2849.22.G85C2817 2010
980.03′5092—dc22
2010005178